Connections

Technologies of Communication

Connections

Technologies of Communication

Jarice Hanson

University of Massachusetts

▦ HarperCollins*CollegePublishers*

Dedication

This book is fondly dedicated to two teachers who changed the way I look at the world:

Bette Strassman and Norman (Doc) Senski

Thank you.

Acquisitions Editor: Daniel F. Pipp
Project Coordination and Text Design: Proof Positive/Farrowlyne Associates, Inc.
Cover Design: Kay Petronio
Production Manager: Kewal Sharma
Compositor: Proof Positive/Farrowlyne Associates, Inc.
Printer and Binder: R. R. Donnelley & Sons Company
Cover Printer: The Lehigh Press, Inc.

Connections: Technologies of Communication, *First Edition*
Copyright © 1994 by HarperCollins College Publishers

Library of Congress Cataloging-in-Publication Data

Hanson, Jarice
   Connections: technologies of communication / Jarice Hanson.
     p.   cm.
   Includes bibliographical references and index.
   ISBN 0-06-500700-X
   1. Telecommunication.   I. Title.
TK5101.A3H36   1993
303.48'33—dc20   93-6169
93 94 95 96 9 8 7 6 5 4 3 2 1   CIP

Contents

vi

Chapter 6

Improvements in Video Technology   155

Chapter 7

Cable Distribution and Interactive Services   175

Chapter 11

Changes in the Workplace   267

Chapter 12

Rights, Regulations, and Content   293

Chapter 13

The Internationalization of Information   327

C h a p t e r 14

The Information Society   361

Preface

Today's technologies of communication do not all fit the definition of mass communication. New technologies and systems deliver messages to smaller segments of the audience, and provide a variety of alternatives to mass distribution of messages. While many of the technologies available today maintain a connection to the industries that control mass media, changes in the regulatory environment and economy, as well as a proliferation of innovations, have created a variety of contexts in which individuals use communication technologies.

Mass media like radio and television now compete with satellite, cable, and other distribution systems that, when connected to other communication technologies like telephones, computers, videocassette recorders, compact discs, and laser discs, present a multitude of different communication experiences. The ways in which these technologies are connected are also important. They are linked physically, through additional technologies, and figuratively, through a history of innovations, a network of industries, and the myriad ways people use communication technology.

Connections: Technologies of Communication is intended to clarify the ways in which communication technology both challenges and reinforces assumptions about what happens to messages in the communication process. A key premise of the book is that individuals are responding to changes by using communication technologies in new ways. The speed of change in our world is partly a result of advances in communication systems. For students to become critical users and consumers of communication technology, they need to be able to make connections between the use of technologies and the social consequences of that use.

The organizing principle of *Connections: Technologies of Communication* is a review of traditional media uses in the light of new ideas and purposes to encourage students to think about the consequences of change. Discussions focus on values and ethical practices that influence how communication technologies operate and how they are perceived. Discussion questions challenge students to draw from their own experiences, question how their values have been formed, and consider what values are important in an increasingly technologized world.

Each chapter includes:
1. explanations of how different technologies work
2. discussions of the effect of technological change on systems and institutions
3. considerations of the impact these changes have on the quality of life
4. explorations of the ethical dimensions of social change introduced by communication technologies

A number of features are intended to make the material more accessible:
1. opening remarks on the connections that will be made in the chapter
2. boxes and figures that explain related concepts
3. "Connecting with . . ." boxes that present perspectives from individuals in the business and regulatory environments
4. summary sections that reinforce key points
5. discussion questions for use inside or outside of the classroom

Following is a summary of the contents of each chapter:

Chapter 1: "Living in an Electronic Age" addresses the characteristics of electronic communication technology and discusses how the history of communication technology has created expectations for living in an increasingly technologized world.

Chapter 2: "Understanding Communication Technologies" focuses on the impact of visual forms of communication and the individual's ability to understand messages. The unique characteristics of each communication form and the way it affects its users are described to provide conceptual issues as background for other chapters.

Chapter 3: "Wired Systems of Communication: Telegraph and Telephone" presents background information on the first electronic communication technologies and addresses the role of wired systems of communication. The development of the telephone industry as a monopoly and the impact of deregulation on the industry provide a foundation for issues of regulation and deregulation discussed in later chapters. The impact of the telephone on social interaction is also considered.

Chapter 4: "Broadcast Systems: Radio" charts the development of wireless communication. The formation of the radio industry and the radio networks, as well as the importance of radio communication, are central themes of the chapter.

Chapter 5: "Broadcast Systems: Television" looks at the television industry; its growth and unique contribution to information and entertainment in the home; and the way audiences relate to televised content.

Chapter 6: "Improvements in Video Technology" addresses video distribution systems and the process of video communication. The invention of videotape and video recording devices and their impact on the television industry are connected to changes in audience perceptions of content. Future video technologies like HDTV and three-dimensional television are discussed.

Chapter 7: "Cable Distribution and Interactive Services" focuses on how connections between wired and broadcast forms of communication provide new alternatives for entertainment and information.

Chapter 8: "Technologies and Services: From Mass Audience to the Individual" addresses alternative distribution forms like LPTV, SMATV, MMDS, telco, and satellite, and the changes created by different reception technologies. Issues considered include the number of communication forms that enable the individual to choose content and avoid mass distribution forms, and the impact of these forms on the relationship between communication industries and audiences.

Chapter 9: "Computers and Peripherals" discusses the impact of the computer as a means of connecting other technologies, but also as a unique communication tool in its own right.

Chapter 10: "Technology in the Home: Our Changing Lifestyles" includes information on the changing work force and alternatives to traditional home use of communication technologies, such as electronic shopping, banking, telecommuting, and leisure activities.

Chapter 11: "Changes in the Workplace" looks at the role of computers in the workplace and the variety of services available to business and industry today. Social changes caused by new technologies are contrasted to social changes created by the growth of an information and service economy.

Chapter 12: "Rights, Regulation, and Content" gives the background of the deregulatory climate in the United States and describes the effect of deregulation on the communications industries and media content.

Chapter 13: "The Internationalization of Information" broadens the scope of this book's consideration of the impact of communication technologies on the world today. It addresses issues of incompatible technical standards, inequities in services and resources, and the role of global communication in defining international power relations.

Chapter 14: "The Information Society" explores the various connections discussed in other chapters and relates today's communication technologies to communication needs in the future.

A list of abbreviations and a glossary are included.

Connections: Technologies of Communication is intended for undergraduate college students in Communication, American studies, sociology, and related fields. In institutions where a telecommunications sequence is offered, this text could serve as an introduction. In departments that rely on more traditional approaches to mass media, this text would best serve in courses about the social impact of media.

Acknowledgments

There are many people who have contributed to the preparation of this book, and I sincerely thank every one of them. The project was initiated and sustained by the interest of Susan Mraz, Anne Smith, and especially, Melissa Rosati at HarperCollins.

Dan Pipp of HarperCollins provided excellent editorial guidance. He and Colleen Quinn orchestrated the details, from the minuscule to the most important. Anne Boynton-Trigg, Development Editor par excellence, kept me inspired with her insight, skill, and encouragement. It's a pleasure to have worked with these professionals, and to now be able to call them friends.

Throughout the writing of the book several reviewers gave careful attention to details and sometimes offered very candid comments. The book's successful completion is due in large part to their valuable input. Special thanks to Barry Litman, Michigan State University; Paul Prince, Kansas State University; John Doolittle, American University; Robert West, Kent State University; Vernone Sparkes, Syracuse University; Joseph Turow, University of Pennsylvania; George Mastroianni, California State University at Fullerton; Fred Owens, Youngstown State University; L.A. Caskey, Ferris State University; James Schwoch, Northwestern University; Norma Pecora, Emerson College; Mark Tolstedt, University of Wisconsin; and Juliet Dee, University of Delaware.

In the course of tracking down information, searching for pictures, and seeking out connections, I met many wonderful people who helped me with research and related information. Dr. Sheldon Hochheiser and Mrs. Norma McCormick at AT&T Archives were wonderful hosts and guides. Elliot Sivowitch of the National Museum of American History at the Smithsonian Institution was an excellent advisor and a great help. Debbie Goodsite at the Bettmann Archive provided invaluable assistance in locating historically important photographs. To these people and the many others who went out of their way to help me, I extend my deepest appreciation.

At the University of Massachusetts I had research assistance from a number of graduate students who have since gone their own ways and are probably writing their own books. Over the years David Donnelly, Tom Conroy, and David Easter contributed background research to several parts of the book. In the final days of preparation Ziv Neeman became very adept at finding obscure references, tracking down the owners of copywritten material, and proofreading manuscript. Karen Schoenberger's "poster child" talents were put to use on much of the artwork.

A person who worked as hard as I did to make this book a reality is Debra Madigan, whose attention to detail, superior efficiency, and constant support made it possible to meet publishing deadlines and manage an academic department at the same time. Debbie, you're great!

Finally, my thanks go to David Maxcy, who shared the ups and downs of preparing the manuscript, the pressure of deadlines, a computer, and a very messy study. Thank you everyone!

Jarice Hanson

One

Living in an Electronic Age

Making Connections

In today's complex society we find that much of what we know and what we think about comes to us through electronic communication technologies. When we investigate the relationship between electronic media and society we learn more about the phenomenon of communication. Why do some messages survive the communication process undistorted, while others change completely? What are our communication technologies capable of doing, and how can they be used to their fullest potential? How does communication technology affect our lives? How is media use connected to human beliefs and values, and how does it contribute to a sense of community?

Many of the basic ideas behind the way in which communication technology operates are changing. Mass media for consumption by mass audiences is no longer the dominant way of thinking about media. New technologies and services that are connected to mass distribution forms offer new contexts for use by audiences and individuals. As communication

Chapter

1

technologies are used for an increasing variety of purposes and in a number of new contexts, the inter-relationships among technical innovation, established industries, program content, and new patterns of use present new ways of thinking about the impact of communication technology on society.

This chapter examines the concepts that influence contemporary use of communication technology. It introduces the types of connections made throughout this book:

- how people use knowledge of past communication processes to understand the present and shape a vision of the future

- how technological invention often precedes an understanding of how a technology may be used, and for what purposes

- how use of technology influences behaviors, attitudes, and values

- how industry ethics influence technological use

- how personal ethics influence the way people use media content

- how communication technology and content introduce and reinforce social change

---

The digital clock flashed 6:00 A.M. when Joe was awakened by his favorite audiotape, programmed to start at his favorite tune. Though he really didn't think of himself as a "morning person," he wanted to get to work early to make final preparations for a presentation to his boss later that morning. He had ingeniously set the timer on the coffeemaker so he could have a cup in hand while his scrambled eggs puffed up in the microwave. As he ate, he tuned the television set to the weather channel to see if rain was in the forecast for that day.

While driving to work Joe listened to a favorite compact disc and used his car phone to leave a message on the answering machine at work. He asked the receptionist to check the fax machine for any late-breaking information he might need for his presentation. Before returning the videocassette he had rented the night before, he made a quick stop at the bank to use the automated teller machine. Once in the office, Joe logged onto his computer to see if any messages had been sent by his co-workers around the country. By 9:00 A.M., he was standing in front of a video camera waiting for a signal to begin his presentation, which would be carried live, by satellite, to his boss in her office three hundred miles away.

There is nothing remarkable about Joe's morning except that he accomplished a good deal without ever having face-to-face contact with another person. He was able to interact with others, gather information he needed, and orchestrate the quick and effective completion of several tasks because **technology** allowed him to control his activities. Even though he woke to an audiotape, watched a program on cable television, listened to a compact disc in his car, communicated with others by car phone and answering machine, received information over fax and computer, and even used a satellite link to make his presentation, Joe never engaged in mass communication that morning. He did, however, use many communication technologies.

Today people have many ways of communicating electronically. Some of these technologies have long histories as forms of mass media. The distinction between "mass" media like radio or television and more personal communication tools like telephones or answering machines is becoming blurred. A number of new technologies and services have provided opportunities for a convergence of technologies. Convergence suggests two or more technologies connected to each other to provide a new pathway for communication. People use new technologies and configurations based on their experiences with earlier forms. As a result, communication technology today presents a situation in which some "connections" are made to other forms of technology as well as to preconceived ideas about the art of communication.

Connecting Concepts

Connections can be thought of as both literal and figurative. Literally, communication technology uses physical connections such as wires and switching systems that convert some types of signals (like broadcast) to others (such as wired communication). These types of connections link different pieces of hardware for use in a variety of contexts. For example, telephones make connections to other phones through systems of wires, but may also use satellite distribution (a broadcast form) for long-distance service. Similarly, cable television relays both broadcast and closed circuit programs to subscribers. In each case, two types of distribution media must be connected to make communication possible.

Figuratively, people make connections to earlier forms of media to describe expectations and patterns of use, as well as to understand the effect of communication technology on society. It is difficult to describe the impact of videocassette recorders (VCRs) without also explaining the history of the relationship between film and television. Likewise, cable television has challenged the prominence of the broadcast networks and has also moved into many new formats for programming. The relationship suggests a number of connections between different entities, including the two industries, the economy, and regulatory bodies.

The literal and figurative connections discussed throughout this book examine the following relationships:

- between senders and receivers of messages
- between industries and regulatory bodies
- between the economy and technological innovation
- between mass audiences and the beliefs and values of individuals
- between ideas and social actions
- between nations and cultures

Patterns of communication are changing as new technologies present more options than people have had in the past. When content is transferred from one form to another the message changes. When a panoramic shot that was effective on film is shown on a small television screen, the impact of the visual image changes. The audience's perception of the intended message is distorted by the change in the medium displaying the image. When a computer is used to play games, the user's attitude toward the computer may be different from that of someone who uses it for work.

The way in which industries produce messages for public consumption has also changed, due to a number of different distribution forms and industry practices. These include changes in patterns of ownership. The recording industry markets compact discs (CDs) that contain more music than traditional records, but also recognizes the impact of a successful music video as a marketing tool. Radio has responded to the variety of audio entertainment technologies, such as audiotape players and CDs, by targeting different types of audiences and examining the viability of improved radio broadcasting to make radio sound as good as the digitally recorded music available in other forms. In these examples, connections among different elements help us understand the dynamics involved in communication today.

One of the most significant factors in technological communication today is the changing size of the audience. Not long ago, the most influential communication technologies were those used for mass communication. These technologies were (and still are) used to relay messages that had been created at considerable expense by large organizations for distribution to large, heterogeneous audiences. Today however, the power of the mass media industries has been weakened and the nature of electronic communication has been changed by new technologies that challenge the concepts of mass media and mass audiences. While we still use mass media like print, radio, film and television, other technologies have provided opportunities to use electronic communication in more personal environments. As we saw in the story of Joe, who actively chose the audiotape he woke up to, the television program that told him the weather, and the CD he listened to in the car, today's communication technologies allow individuals to use media in more personal environments, and exercise more options for using different media.

Communicating over Distances

New distribution technologies influence **telecommunications,** the sum of the technologies and processes used to communicate over great distances. Today's telecommunications include global communication, which may require a whole new dimension of connections that are more difficult to determine. Not all regions of the world share common histories, social relationships, or equal access to communication technology.

Satellites, microwave links, digital information processing and optical fiber are all newer distribution forms that have changed national and international telecommunications. Other technologies that are smaller and less expensive than telecommunications technologies also have the power to influence what audiences know about. These forms, including personal computers, VCRs, CDs, answering machines, fax machines, and cellular radio, increase the possibilities for communication, and can be used to distribute messages over short or long distances. When the capabilities of these "smaller" technologies are considered with regard to their global impact, a number of questions arise. Who has access to these technologies? How do people in one culture use media and content developed in another culture? Can traditional beliefs and practices survive in environments where communication technology offers new ideas and values?

Ethical Issues

Ethics have to do with conduct. Often it is easier to explain ethics by giving examples in which ethical behavior is not practiced. When a journalist makes up information for a factual story, or willingly distorts a story, most people agree that the journalist's conduct is unethical. If an advertisement conveys false information and thereby violates truth in advertising guidelines, most people agree that the advertiser has not produced an ethical message.

Ethics provide standards that make it easier for us to understand what's right and what's wrong. They influence our individual values and the value system supported by society. We confront ethical questions whenever we make judgments about how we use the media, or consider the role communication technologies play in our society or in the global arena. Looking at both the traditional mass media and the newer communication technologies, we can learn something about the way our society develops, practices, and changes its ethical ideas.

Ethics and communication technology are connected in some special ways. First, the individuals who create messages for public consumption are assumed to act ethically. Underpinning many laws governing censorship and questionable content in the media is a sense of responsibility for reflecting ethical values that society endorses.

Society assumes that industries will conduct their business in an ethical manner. Sometimes the economic motives that drive commercial media industries will create tension when brought face-to-face with an ethical issue. Should television and cable companies refuse to sell advertising time to companies that want to advertise war toys, or to those that encourage children to ask their parents for expensive products they may not be able to afford? Should sexually explicit lyrics in popular music be censored? Should commercial enterprises exercise social responsibility, and if so, should codes of ethics be developed to guide their actions? These questions all involve connections between actions and values. Some values influence the regulation of industries and of communication content; others influence the way members of a society think about the role communication technology plays in defining the world.

The second area where ethics connect with communication technology is in the way the technology is used. Most people will probably agree that societal values say stealing is wrong, and that a person who steals is not engaging in ethical behavior. Does a person in effect "steal" a program that has been created for broadcast television when he or she records it? Is it "stealing" when someone makes an audiocassette copy of a recording to give it to a friend? The television and recording industries are aware that people do this, but does that awareness make it right? Does a person break a law when they photocopy a book rather than buy it?

One of the challenges of new communication technologies is that they make it so easy to duplicate original content that it is easy to rationalize the fact that the artists who sold their labor to make a program or a record will receive no remuneration for their work. Because copying programs, recordings, software, and print material is so easy, the communications industries raise the cost of their products to make up for losses caused by unauthorized duplication. This is why the music industry and Congress hesitated to make digital audio tape (DAT) technology available to the general market. When they did, the cost of the tape was set higher than it needed to be to compensate for lost sales in records and discs once people could duplicate high quality sound on their own DAT machines. These examples show how behavior influences what values will be socially sanctioned, and how the ease of using technology today is connected to legal and economic issues. The role of ethics in communication goes beyond just determining whether something is right or wrong. New communication technologies present many questions involving the complex interconnections among media, society, regulation, and values.

Drawing from the Past to Predict the Future

If communication technologies present ethical questions today, how might increased use of technology shape the values and images of the future? With the many technologies available today it is easy to believe the future will be even more technology-rich. It is comforting to think of the future as a place in which technology changes but people remain the same, but it is not unreasonable to ask whether the technologies might contribute to different behaviors, attitudes, and values.

All of us have expectations for the future, but how many of those expectations are borne out in reality? As a college student, is college what you thought it would be when you were in high school? Probably some of your expectations have been realized, while others have been entirely unfulfilled. No one can predict the future completely and correctly, but we can attempt to make some predictions based on the knowledge we have about how social institutions operate.

Certainly the year 2000 represents a milestone that encourages speculations about what the future may bring, and futurists have not been shy about predicting how we will lead our lives after that momentous change in the calendar. All of the following predictions are influenced by communication technologies. Consider some of the more popular futurist predictions for life after the year 2000, and judge whether more and better use of communication technology increases the likelihood that each prediction will come true:

1. *Prediction:* In the future there will be almost no street robbery, because most people will carry little cash (Martin 1981, 6).
   Fact: In industrialized nations alternative payment methods such as checks and credit cards have already reduced the need for individuals to carry cash. Currently communication technologies are creating alternative systems of purchasing things, such as "point-of-purchase" cards. The growing mail-order industry, using televised shopping networks or direct mail campaigns, is revolutionizing the way people purchase. Computer software is now available that allows consumers to access bank balances, investigate the charges they owe, and even transfer money electronically. The associated technologies needed for this are telephones, home computers, or specially adapted services through cable lines. Whether street crime will be lessened by these developments still remains to be seen.
2. *Prediction:* People will experience a trend toward greater affluence and . . . leisure (Kahn and Wiener 1967, 64).

Fact: Since the mid-1980s Americans have had to work longer hours for less pay. In addition, vacation time offered by companies in the United States is some of the shortest in the world (Schor 1991, 25). Americans have tended to spend a disproportionately high amount of their income on such consumer electronics as televisions, VCRs, audio systems, and portable video systems. Though we have less leisure time, we have more communication technology to fill that time. But does having more technology reflect greater affluence and create more leisure time?

3. *Prediction:* The control of information systems will someday surpass the role of the military and the police in maintaining social order (Deutsch 1963, 3).

   Fact: The Persian Gulf War provided an excellent example of how information can be controlled by limiting visual images and giving access to only "official" statements. The videotape recording of the Rodney King beating, combined with a court judgment that appeared to refute what people could see, caused violence that spread across the country. The power of the visual images transmitted by television did much to influence people's behavior, and therefore created a shift in people's ideas about what is socially accepted.

4. *Prediction:* The traditional nuclear family (a working husband, a housekeeping wife, and two children) will no longer be the "typical" family in our society (Toffler 1980, 211).

   Fact: In the same book Toffler refutes the prediction, stating that in 1980 only seven percent of the population fit the classic definition of a nuclear family (211). Now that there are more single parent families, questions arise over how to balance family life and work. Some alternatives include **telecommuting,** in which the employee works at home and communicates with the office by telephone lines, fax machines, or computers; **flextime,** in which the hours, and often the pay, of workers are altered; and **job sharing**, where two or more people are splitting the duties (and the pay) of a job traditionally done by one person.

5. *Prediction:* Someday electronic communication technologies will unite the world as "one big gossiping family" (Clarke 1981, 185).

   Fact: Though the potential for connecting various nations through telecommunications technology already exists, there are great inequities in the distribution of technologies within less developed countries (LDCs). Until economic and political issues are addressed, communication links will provide the opportunity for very few to engage in global communication.

What all these predictions share is a reliance on technology to fulfill their possibilities. Parts of each of them have already come true. The predictions highlight the fact that the relationship between technology and society remains one of the most critical questions for understanding the present and making judgments about the future.

What sometimes complicates our ability to prepare adequately for the future is that we tend to remember only incomplete parts of the past. We often believe that technological innovations come about to meet a particular need. Sometimes this happens, but the history of inventions in the field of communications generally disproves this idea.

When there is an assumption that a particular technology will be used for a certain purpose, but it later acquires a different use in society, the assumption is called a **technological fallacy**. Thomas Edison thought his phonograph would be used as a telephone answering device, or to record the voices of loved ones so that they could be heard after they died. In 1877, a year after Alexander Graham Bell patented the device that made the telephone work, a Massachusetts newspaper predicted it would be used to carry music and news reports (Barnouw 1966, 7). When the radio was invented, some people thought it would be used for personal conversation, much like CB radio today.

Jacques Ellul (1985) has written that we often have "preconceived ideas about mediated information" that are shaped by sociological, political, and economic studies that appear to express scientific evidence, even

---

Box 1.1   Technological Apprehension

The introduction of almost all new technologies is met with excitement on the part of some people and skepticism on the part of others. When new ways of doing things threaten traditional ways, some people become uneasy. Each new form of communications media elicits some seemingly irrational responses.

When radio was introduced as an experimental medium, reports of people frightened by "disembodied voices" began to appear in newspapers. Some people thought this unique form of communication had the potential to brainwash listeners.

When television came along, some people feared that radiation from the screen would be harmful. Still others feared that television in the home would prevent family members from talking to each other (some researchers feel this concern has come true.)

Though these examples are amusing now, their equivalent today is the anxiety many people still feel about using computers, automatic teller machines (ATMs), and answering machines. In each of these cases technology elicits fear or at least a hesitancy to work with it. In many cases this apprehensiveness is caused more by fear of change than by fear of the technology itself.

9

though their real messages distort the original ideas. Opinions that have been formed as a result of scientific research tend to simplify reality (Ellul 1985, 95–96). People distort the way in which technology is used by focusing on the good effects, while ignoring the possible negative effects.

If you were told that there was a technology that could virtually eliminate problems caused by space and time, it might sound pretty good. If this technology promised to allow you to see things you had never seen before or meet people who you couldn't normally meet, wouldn't that be intriguing? But what if you were told that this technology would result in over thirty thousand deaths a year? Would you still think the positive benefits outweigh the negative?

The previous example clearly illustrates how one technological invention, the automobile, offered great promise to society when it was created; but after

Figure 1.1 *Thomas Edison, Henry Ford, John Burroughs, and Harvey Firestone.*
In the above picture, inventor Thomas Edison, naturalist John Burroughs, automotive assembly giant Henry Ford, and tire magnate Harvey Firestone can be seen on one of their outings. Though each of these men was a major figure of the industrial era, their inventions and ideas did not always complement each other. This picture was taken on a camping trip to the Old Evans Mill in Lead Mine, West Virginia on August 21, 1918.
Source: From the collections of Henry Ford Museum & Greenfield Village.

many years we know that automobiles can be dangerous and have a negative effect on the environment. Would we stop production now though? Probably not. The point is that technology becomes a force before people have a full understanding of its impact or effect.

 ## Attitudes Toward Technology

The literature on the history and influence of communications media is extensive, but does not always support the same conclusions. Many of the theories and methods developed to study media and society have subtly reflected the attitudes of the researchers. Preconceived ideas about technology often reflect peoples' biases. It will be helpful to explore some of the general attitudes most often associated with technology.

Perhaps the most common attitude is that of the **technological determinist** who sees all social effects as inevitably related to the processes and techniques of technological domination. Determinism seeks to find one cause for all effects in a generalized activity. According to this point of view, all the ills of society can be blamed on the increasing use of technology. For example, a determinist might see the breakdown of the family unit as a result of television changing interpersonal relationships within the home. Most thoughtful people today, however, acknowledge that adaptation to technology is influenced by phenomena far more complex than the determinist would acknowledge.

In contrast to the technological determinist stands the **technological liberal**, who feels that technology is not inherently wrong or problematic, but that it must be used responsibly. This position says that technologies should not be adopted unthinkingly, but that the positive and negative effects should be considered before making the decision to use them. Environmentalists and anti-nuclear activists object to the establishment of nuclear power plants not on the basis of an opposition to nuclear technology, but on the grounds that the potential hazards of nuclear power outweigh its advantages as an efficient source of electricity. Likewise, some people feel that television is not inherently bad, but that many people don't use it responsibly. These "technological liberals" are particularly concerned that children are being exposed to too much sex and violence on television.

Perhaps the most strident opponent of technology is the person sometimes called a **Luddite.** The term itself became current in England after a group of workers led by Ned Ludd in Lancashire, fearing loss of their jobs, rioted and destroyed farm equipment in 1811 (Hobsbawm 1959). During the early days of the industrial revolution, many new machines were destroyed by individuals who feared that technology would usurp traditional ways of living. Historians have generally ascribed the name "Luddite" to anyone who favors the destruction of technologies, but as Slack points out, "Luddism is really a spirit—a spirit that is suspicious of the very structure of certain technologies" (Slack 1984).

11

What all these positions indicate is the human ability to see that innovation in technology is related to social practices—a theme that will emerge throughout this book.

All these biases help explain why there is seldom unanimity of attitudes toward communication technology. Each helps explain why technology can be applauded, feared, embraced, or marginalized.

The Relationship Between Technology and Media

Marshall McLuhan was a futurist who is often seen as a technological determinist. In his book Understanding Media: The Extensions of Man (1964) he provided a perspective from which to evaluate the relationship of media, society, and peoples' uses of communication technologies. His work suggests that:

1. All media are developed before a need has been created, and
2. All media are overburdened by our expectations.

McLuhan believed that predictions about what technologies can do and how they will be used are often ill conceived, but technological innovation nonetheless changes the way we do things. Many of the communications media available today were originally developed for purposes vastly different from their current use. Their impact on society can only be viewed in retrospect, and even then, their histories are continually developing. People don't yet understand the full impact of television in the home. We don't know the long-term effects of low-level radiation from computers, televisions, or microwave ovens. Nevertheless, it is already obvious that each of these technologies changes traditional ways of doing things. These types of connections shed light on our present world and the way people begin to think about the future.

Relating Technological Development to Social Use

Throughout history, technology has helped people meet their basic needs. At the same time, human behaviors, attitudes, and values all influence the activities of meeting those needs. In his book *The Third Wave* (1980), Alvin Toffler[1] investigates relationships among these factors by suggesting a metaphor that explains how traditions, practices, and beliefs are interrelated. He divides

---

[1]*Alvin Toffler's trilogy includes* Future Shock *(1970), focusing on the process of change;* The Third Wave *(1980), exploring changes in society from a historical perspective; and* Powershift *(1990), addressing the changes we experience today and prophesying changes that will occur tomorrow.*

human history into three periods and likens them to waves on a shore; each wave may overlap others, or may make a different impression on the sand. In each of these eras; the first dominated by agriculture, the second by industry, and the third by electronics; dominant technologies have influenced attitudes, values, and behaviors.

The agricultural age   Toffler describes the period from about 800 B.C. to sometime between 1650 and 1750 as the era when people engaged in agriculture to meet their basic needs. During that period such simple technologies as wheels, levers, pulleys, and winches facilitated people's work. In order to survive, people grew their own crops and livestock or engaged in trade to meet their basic needs.

At the same time a particular value system supported the ability of the family to meet its needs through agriculture. In many societies arranged marriages were a common practice because they featured a courtship or dowry system that ensured that families would be able to produce more or better because of the union. Larger families were approved because they increased the potential labor force that would allow the continued meeting of basic needs. When agriculture was overtaken by the industrial revolution as the dominant mode of production in the western world, the custom of marrying to increase one's wealth and family size began to be seen differently. As the first "wave" of civilization gave way to the next, some traditional beliefs and practices began to change.

The industrial age   From around 1700 to 1955 (Toffler's second wave), western civilization shifted from an agricultural to an industrial economy. The factory assembly line provided a powerful model for a host of behaviors that contributed to the production of goods. Technology was primarily mechanical, which reinforced the importance of sequential movement and efficiency. Fewer people engaged in agriculture to meet their basic needs, and more people engaged in activities that produced consumer items that made life more comfortable (see box 1.2).

Box 1.2   The Industrial Lifestyle

The industrial revolution created new lifestyles and a new social order. One of the first cities in the United States to be planned as an industrial area was Lowell, Massachusetts. From 1826 to 1836, the population of Lowell expanded from 6,540 to 16,000 as jobs in mills lured employees from other New England states and Canada. By 1850 Lowell had become the largest cotton textile center in the country. The factory owners built special housing for workers which was sometimes poorly designed and inappropriate for harsh

New England winters. Workers could purchase necessities at the company store, located conveniently to the mills and homes, but sometimes offering goods at higher prices than other stores farther away.

In many households both parents worked. Accommodations for children posed a problem, if the the children were not old enough to work in the mills and there was no one available to watch them. Institutionalized education began to be seen as a way to keep children occupied while their parents were at work.

From 1850 to 1920 Lowell was a center for immigrant laborers, who brought their own customs, traditions, and attitudes to the mills. The social life that emerged in the mill communities reflected different cultures. Social life was sometimes influenced by tensions between people of different ethnic and racial backgrounds.

As the mill communities grew, the maintenance of housing and other amenities was often turned over to private entrepreneurs who managed housing, made groceries and other products available, and even structured social activities. These managers often treated laborers with less consideration than the factory owners had. The new managers sometimes exploited the tensions between different ethnic and racial groups. The low-cost housing was left to deteriorate while workers were forced to work longer shifts, and in the interest of producing more goods at the expense of the labor force, the amount of leisure time available to workers diminished.

The textile industry began to collapse in 1920 which led to massive unemployment and a legacy of abandoned buildings and displaced workers. Today, the city of Lowell is home to a state park that serves as a monument to the industrial revolution, but is also a reminder of the disruption that results when old modes of production give way to new ones.

All across the country today one can find communities that have experienced the same fate as Lowell. Flint, Michigan, reflects the changes in the auto industry; Gary, Indiana, mirrors upheaval in the steel industry. As the high-technology and information industries become dominant, the United States will be left with more monuments to earlier ways of doing things. These poignant reminders illustrate vividly the connections between the organization of production and the nature of social life.

In the new economy, the old custom of arranged marriage no longer fit the social pattern. Marriage in the industrial revolution validated a "sexual split" which deemed some work "men's work," and some, "women's work." Marriages that were arranged on economic grounds gave way to relationships that were fostered by mutual attraction. Men were employed outside the house

14

while women handled the non-paid chores of home and family. Smaller families were considered those that could be best cared for in a family unit, and the nuclear family (a father working, mother at home, and two children) became the ideal in a country like the United States.

Similarly, the industrial revolution reinforced the idea that bigger means better. Success could be measured by the size of one's house or car. Massive industrial complexes produced massive environmental waste. The realization that the primary energy resource, fossil fuel, was non-renewable encouraged research to find alternative sources of energy.

The electronic age   Toffler's 1980 book, *The Third Wave*, summed up the era between 1955 and 1980 as one dominated by electricity and the computer. It also proposed that the efficiency afforded by microcircuitry led to a sense that smaller might also be better.

The energy necessary to fuel large scale production in the industrial age was more effectively channeled by solid state microcircuitry and more efficient means of electrical conductivity created by new developments in metals and other resources. Silicon, used to make circuit boards, fiber optics, and other "pathways" for electrical connections, was a renewable resource that was plentiful and cheap. Characterized as an age in which the dominant mode of production shifted from goods to services, the electronic era was envisioned as a harbinger of what might ultimately be called "the information society." The ultimate technology was the computer.

Many social questions emerged during the electronic age. The division of work by gender was questioned. Telecommunications sometimes made it possible to work over long distances. Available jobs sometimes made it necessary for married couples to live apart and commute to see each other. Single parent and non-traditional families became more prevalent. Divorce and the rise of living-together relationships threatened the sanctity of the traditional home. The impressions in the sand left by the first two waves were fading as the third wave began to recede and a new, fourth wave was rushing to the shore. This one would bring new ideas, sometimes changing practices from the earlier waves, sometimes reinforcing their impressions.

The Information Society

In 1990, Toffler published the last book in his trilogy chronicling historical change. *Powershift* (1990), unlike *The Third Wave*, deals with the "corporate takeovers and restructurings . . . [that signal] the first salvos in far larger, quite novel business battles to come" (xviii). Has the third wave peaked and begun to recede as another one rushes in to shore, or have we embraced the new modes of production so thoroughly that the fourth wave will be a continuation of the third?

Clearly, the computer remains the dominant technology today, and silicon remains an abundant resource for research and development. The institution of marriage has continued to erode as more people embrace alternative lifestyles. But what Toffler had not fully prophesied in *The Third Wave* becomes the main theme in *Powershift*. Throughout the 1980s industries in our own country and around the world began to experience rapid change as new business practices came into being. We in the United States experienced a radical change in government supervision of communication technologies as a result of *deregulation,* which lifted restrictions on business operations to encourage greater activity. A greater reliance on market principles revolutionized traditional practices that had been originally intended to protect some of our basic rights. Deregulation opened competition in media industries at the same time as new communication technologies were being introduced at a faster rate than ever before. New distribution systems and services began to flourish. But the efforts to open competition began to backslide as traditional ownership restrictions in the media industries were altered. Corporate mergers and **vertical integration**, the practice by which media industries specializing in different areas are all owned by the same company or corporation, began to change the diversity of information, ideas, or voices heard in the media. For example, Rupert Murdoch's vertically integrated holdings might influence the way in which a program on the Fox television network might be prominently featured on the cover of TV Guide, and distributed in a series on Fox Home Video cassettes. Murdoch's business interests in all three areas increase the likelihood of publicity for similarly held product.

Toffler's wave metaphor suggests why it is critical now to build an understanding of the uses of communication technologies. Critics are divided on whether we are currently in an information society or headed toward one. We know that we live in an era when several of the "waves" have left an impression in the sand. The result is that the image of an information society is now being formed—and that image will undoubtedly affect and shape what really constitutes the new way of life.

 ## Preparing for the Future

Today's college students should consider whether they are preparing for a job that will be obsolete in the near future. Most schools still reward the qualities that make a good factory worker—punctuality, obedience, and specialization. Conformity to the requirements of an already established system is often a measure of success. The overwhelming pressure to choose a major in college and define one's special area of interest is a hold-over from the industrial wave, when specialization was viewed as a key to career success.

The possibility that workers will need to relocate based on job availability is accepted in our society today, and it has led to increased reliance on new technologies. Because families don't always stay in the same geographic area, communication among family members has become increasingly dependent on telephone service. Local communications media have become increasingly useful in helping people to acclimate to a new surrounding—whether they are searching for a home using videocassette or television, searching for a job through computer listings, or locating potential partners and friends through electronic dating services.

Living in an information society requires individuals to take more control over their lives by increasing their self-motivation. Factory assembly-line work offered few opportunities for job mobility, and those who showed excellence in perfecting their contribution to the entire assembly line's end product were rewarded. The once-inviolate assumption that a job in a major company or corporation would provide long-term stability is no longer true. Today union workers in manufacturing industries constitute much of the unemployed work force. It is necessary to rely on self-motivation when choosing an education, when changing jobs, and when deciding how to use technologies. The following paragraphs examine how these choices are required by today's business practices and government mandates in one industry.

Prior to 1983 American Telephone & Telegraph Company (AT&T) had a monopoly over telephone service in the United States. The only choice a consumer needed to make was whether to have a telephone or not. Today, in most geographic areas, you need to choose among competing long distance telephone services. If you want to purchase the most cost-effective service, you must consider your local calling needs, your long distance service needs, and the times of day you usually use the phone. Prior to the deregulation of the telephone industry you had the option to rent your telephones. Today, you need to buy a telephone and make a decision about what type you want. Can you be satisfied with a ten-dollar basic telephone, or must you have the more expensive cordless model?

In addition to increasing the number of decisions a consumer must make, the government's decision to open competition in the telephone industry combines with today's new technologies to affect our personal lives. In earlier days, the names of telephone customers were automatically listed in the telephone book. When more people chose not to have their names listed, the telephone company realized they could make money by charging a fee for an unlisted telephone number. Are you willing to pay an extra fee to delete your name so you will not be hounded by telemarketers who use the telephone book as a source for their sales calls?

If you decide to buy a telephone answering machine what type of message will you create? Will it be funny or serious? Will your recorded answer impress

Box 1.3   Connecting with Arthur C. Clarke

Arthur C. Clarke is familiar to millions of readers as the author of numerous science fiction works, including *2001: A Space Odyssey*. Also an accomplished scientist, Clarke first conceived of using satellites for communications in 1945. Twenty-five years later, the first satellite for communications purposes was launched into outer space.

From his youth in a small English village where he worked as a switchboard operator who was fascinated with the power of communications and once overloaded the circuits as an experiment, to his research in space and oceanography, Clarke has remained actively interested in long-distance communications. In a collection of his thoughts on changes in telecommunications (1991) Clarke reminisced:

> Back in 1945, while a radar officer in the Royal Air Force, I had the only original idea of my life. Twelve years before the first Sputnik started beeping, it occurred to me that an artificial satellite would be a wonderful place for a television transmitter, since a station several thousand miles high could broadcast to half the globe. I wrote up the idea the week after Hiroshima, proposing a network of relay satellites twenty-two thousand miles above the Equator; at this height, they'd take exactly one day to complete a revolution, and so would remain fixed over the same spot on the Earth.
>
> The piece appeared in the October 1945 issue of *Wireless World*; not expecting that celestial mechanics would be commercialized in my lifetime, I made no attempt to patent the idea, and doubt if I could have done so anyway. (If I'm wrong, I'd prefer not to know.) But I kept plugging it in my books, and today the idea of communications satellites is so commonplace that no one knows its origin.*

As Clarke indicates, new ideas that propel us toward the future are sometimes surprises, even to the people who envision their use. The best ideas are not always those that are most effectively marketed; they are born when people break from their traditional ways of thinking about how communication takes place, and they grow over a period of time.

*Source: Arthur C. Clarke, How the World Was One (New York: Bantam Books, 1991) 182.

your friends or possibly offend an employer? Does it leave you wondering when someone calls but never leaves a message? The services we pay for and the ways we use them often reveal more about ourselves than was possible with telephone service in the days of monopoly operations and before answering machines. The ways we use the telephone today would probably surprise Alexander Graham Bell!

 # Characteristics of Today's Communication Technologies

We can investigate communication technology and its relationship to society by looking at the connections between the characteristics of today's technologies and their social uses. As discussed earlier, today's communication technologies can be used to extend our ability to communicate over long distances through **telecommunications.** At the same time there are smaller new technologies that also influence our ability to communicate. These smaller, more personal technologies are increasingly being referred to as **ethnotronic** technologies, meaning they have "interactive 'cultural' characteristics, shared with people and/or other systems" (Joseph and Harkins 1980, 308). But before we address the differences between telecommunications and ethnotronic technologies, some of their similarities should be considered.

The Importance of the Visual Image

One important similarity is the feature of visual display in many telecommunications and ethnotronic technologies. One of the most profound consequences of our shift to an electronic era is our increasing reliance on visual images as a substitute for words. This phenomenon has been blamed on high illiteracy rates and inadequate access to education, and there are indeed major problems in the United States. The Department of Education estimates that the number of "functionally illiterate" adults in the United States is 27 million. Functional illiteracy occurs when a person cannot understand material written at the fifth-grade level or above. The same department classifies another 45 million adults as only marginally literate (Kozol 1985). These facts help explain the growing importance of the visual image in modern communications.

As authority Jonathan Kozol warns, the inability to read often translates into greater costs for taxpayers:

> Six billion dollars a year [in the mid-1970s] go to child welfare costs and unemployment compensation caused directly by the numbers of illiterate adults unable to perform at standards necessary for available employment.
>
> Thirty percent of naval recruits were recently termed "a danger to themselves and to costly naval equipment" because of inability to read and understand instructions. (Kozol 1985, 18)

Does this create a problem for communication? The connection between these social and economic factors affects the way people communicate.

Print was the dominant mode of communication during the industrial age. But the shift to an information society appears to involve a shift toward sound and visual images and away from the written word. Today's dominant technologies, such as satellites, relay visual images from around the globe. Both network and special cable communications services translate news and information into visual images. Even the "sound bite," an artifact of the electronic age that uses words to communicate memorable images, exemplifies the way our society is becoming inundated with images. Many children learn not to fear computers because their first interaction with them is through a visual context, such as videogames. These attitudes, then, reinforce the use of images to communicate at a level different than traditional print.

Altering Time and Space

Both telecommunications and ethnotronic technologies have the capacity to alter people's concepts of time and/or space. Communication technologies mediate messages, and electronic communication technologies allow us to communicate over long distances with little regard for different time zones or even the amount of time it takes to complete transmission of the message. Through **mediation,** the message is altered from one form to another; it may take on a new meaning, or be influenced by the characteristics inherent in the mediation process.

Telecommunications obviously extend our ability to communicate over distances through broadcast forms such as satellites, microwaves, or radio waves. The latter includes the portions of the electromagnetic spectrum that also make television broadcasts possible. When personal technologies like the telephone are linked to a telecommunications system, many of the same principles that influence mediation dynamics influence the message communicated over distances. Messages may be transferred through systems of cable as well as satellite distribution services. Today it is possible to make telephone calls or see satellite-transmitted television pictures from virtually any place in the world within a matter of seconds. The capacity of the VCR to alter time by recording a broadcast for later viewing is an excellent example of shifting a message from one format to another.

Ethnotronics also change our concept of time and space. Telephones can "erase" the space separating families, friends, or business colleagues. The answering machine can give you privacy without adding walls or doors. Cordless phones allow you to move far beyond the range of the phone's traditional cord.

The new trend in personal communications systems (PCSs) shows other ways in which ethnotronics can alter time and space. Some of the PCSs include portable telephones (in addition to the cellular kind used in cars) and radios with headsets. Photocopiers that fit in the palm of a hand, message "beepers," and language translators all fit into this category.

Personal use of ethnotronic technologies seldom requires the individual to be aware of these time- or space-shifting characteristics, but these technologies create conditions that reinforce certain behaviors. No longer do we have to do certain tasks when the machines are available or are placed in particular locations. The technologies themselves have freed us from being restricted to specific areas. We use them in our own time, unburdened by the schedules of others.

Miniaturization

The idea that smaller technologies might be more efficient than larger ones first arose in the 1950s when scientists at Bell Labs in New Jersey developed the transistor. Soon, solid state technologies decreased the size of this device by allowing electrical energy to flow more efficiently. Miniaturization has affected the development of many forms of media by making them smaller and more portable. Televisions, radios, and computers are only a few examples.

Precision and control

The qualities of precision and control are closely related. Technologies that use solid state circuitry, integrated circuits, and materials that conduct electricity more efficiently than earlier forms tend to operate more quickly. When we turn on a television set or radio, we don't have to wait for any tubes to warm up before an image or sound appears. As a result, newer communication technologies are more responsive to our use, but they sometimes make us wonder whether we exert control over our technologies, or they exert control over us.

An example of a technology that has become more precise and that has the potential to be either controlled or a controlling agent is the digital watch. Have you ever asked someone with an analog watch what time it was? The answer might have been, "Oh, about quarter to three." Now, if you ask someone with a digital watch what time it is, they may respond, "It's two-forty-three and twenty seconds." The precision of the technology allows for a *technique* or presentation that is far more accurate. The old-fashioned analog watch requires that the owner and the person who asked for the time have a common understanding of an hour containing 60 minutes divided into four quarters. The expression "about quarter to three" requires the knowledge that within those sixty units, some time within the hour had passed, while some remained before the next cycle began. The digital watch owner has no need for a sixty-unit or four-quarter concept. The time is precise; the owner gives the literal answer to the other person. Figuratively speaking, the digital watch suspended the need to think of clock time measured in 60 seconds. The digital watch gives the impression of time as a more precise measurement. Similarly, the user of a digital watch can be controlled more by the time-piece by not thinking in time expired—time left—but by thinking numerically rather than associatively. The digital watch may appear to control time as well as the user's concept and attitude toward time.

This example can be extrapolated to other technologies. When a person has easy access to electronic calculators, is knowledge of mathematics necessary? When computers are available, do people really have to exercise their memories? When television presents images from around the world and packages the most salient events of the day into a 30 or 60 minute time frame, do people need to read a newspaper to know what's happening in the world? Your answers to these questions can indicate your predilection for technological determinism, technological liberalism, or Luddism.

 ## Social Uses of Communication Technologies

Technologies, and in particular, communication technologies are often compelling subjects for study because they have the potential to do so many things. They can entertain us, make our lives easier, make us feel better about our lifestyles, facilitate interactions, or even protect us from face-to-face conversations we would prefer not to experience. What often makes us think about these issues is the startling realization that we take so many of these technologies for granted. Most of them are easily available, and the idea of life without them is difficult for us to comprehend. Like Joe, whom we met in the introduction to this chapter, we use communication technologies easily and without much concern for doing things other ways.

Communication Technologies and Ethics

Our social uses of communication technologies are sometimes subtly and sometimes overtly tied to our media consumption. All human beings make sense of their immediate positions and surroundings by juxtaposing the images in their minds with the images they see. Many of these powerful images come to us through media. Do you measure the happiness or success of your family by the images of happy or successful families on television or film? Do you learn the current fashions in clothes or speech from the media? Do you think our expectations of appropriate behavior are influenced by the behavior of celebrities, politicians, or sports heroes, whom we see and hear primarily through communications media?

There are no simple "yes" or "no" answers to these questions. After many years of communications research, it is possible to say that sometimes, under certain circumstances, the media may affect some individuals more than others. Researchers have a long history of examining the impact of media content on the behavior of both individuals and groups, but only recently have they begun to understand the uses, access, and economic imperatives that influence relationships among some of the newer forms of media. The connections made among these issues help us understand the role of the context for use as a determinant in interpreting the power and impact of communications technology. One way to better understand these connections is to investigate how technology use changes in different settings or contexts.

Communication technologies in the home   We might expect that most of the changes associated with telecommunication technologies are taking place in the business world because these technologies are expensive, but the real impact of both telecommunications and ethnotronics technologies is most clearly felt in the home.

While U.S. Census figures now show that the television set is on in the average home for 7 hours and 45 minutes a day, this does not automatically mean that people are sitting in their living rooms glued to the television set during that whole time. People use television for a variety of purposes, including background noise. There are conflicting theories about how much of an impact television has in the home when people are doing other things, like talking to each other, cleaning the room, or having the television on while thinking about something else. The actual use patterns of different forms of media are examined throughout the chapters of this book.

Between 1985 and 1990 the amount of money the average American family spent on home entertainment technologies grew by 10.2 percent (Veronis, Suhler and Associates 1991, 13). Much of the increase can be attributed to changing media habits including greater use of cable television, recorded music and home video. The increase indicates a change from traditional entertainment patterns such as going out to a movie, a play, or using the library for entertainment reading, but it also indicates that people are staying home more; perhaps not engaging in the types of interaction they used to have outside the home.

Other shifts in behavior indicate that home technologies such as the telephone and television are expanding their functions to facilitate both entertainment and information—sometimes called "infotainment." As more people link home computers via telephone to data bases to do shopping, banking, or bill paying, or link television sets to VCRs, videodiscs, or electronic games, the separation of "entertainment" and "information" becomes harder to discern.

When a greater number of communication technologies are brought into the home, particularly if they connect with other technologies for special services, more information is recorded by companies about the household, and consumers become a target for salespersons who want to sell something new. Why do credit card companies offer so many special incentives ranging from home shopping services to travel plans and insurance? The answer is that most people are more vulnerable to sales pitches when they are in the comfort of their own homes. Telephone and direct mail sales have become lucrative businesses, especially when demographic information about potential customers can predict the spending habits of the household and the effectiveness of targeting that consumer.

Are these sales practices ethical? Do you mind when a company releases information about you that may result in more telephone sales calls and direct mailings to your home? Many individuals have strong feelings about these issues. These practices underscore how intertwined communications technologies have become with behaviors and values.

Issues in International Communications Industries

As previously discussed, the nature of telecommunications is international in scope. Telecommunications bring to the communication experience several characteristics contributed by technology. In addition, because the scale of communication is so large, it has far-reaching implications involving political, social, and economic issues. The easy availability and heavy use of telecommunications technologies that require transmission of messages in the electromagnetic spectrum (airwaves) has caused "governments and commercial interests . . . [to divide up and commodify] spheres within spheres, reducing the entire planet to a market complex made up of exploitable resources" (Rifkin 1991, 62). Because the airwaves are now regarded as an important pathway for telecommunications, their effective management is more important than ever before. The political consequences of access to telecommunications is beginning to influence international politics and attitudes as well as business practices.

Industrialized societies have an advantage in using telecommunications because they have greater access to new technology, greater financial backing for new products, and a greater understanding of how technology influences social change within their own societies. Sixty percent of the world still lives in areas that are agriculturally based. In some of these areas people are using new technologies that speed their ability to communicate or radically alter their lifestyles without ever having experienced the long, slow evolution of the industrial age. People in nations where communication technologies are changing traditional behaviors tied to agricultural production are said to be **leapfrogging** from one era of history to another. Perhaps literacy will be less important in these societies and they will be unburdened by adjusting beliefs, traditions, and behaviors as we have had to do in our shift from an industrial society to an electronic one.

Some industrialized nations such as the United States, Canada, Great Britain, France, Germany, Japan, and Sweden are considered high-technology countries, while many nations traditionally considered less developed countries (LDCs) have rapidly accumulated technological know-how and industry. Korea, Singapore, Brazil, and China may be among the information technology leaders of the future, but what will be the future of the nations that haven't the resources available to produce technologies for internal use or for export?

Many individual nations are experiencing change at various rates of speed and with differing social implications. Countries such as India, Saudi Arabia, and Nigeria have each targeted specific types of communications technologies that they wish to use, but the inequities in their economic and social systems are even more easily upset than in those industrialized nations that are far more adaptable to change. One of the most important questions for LDCs involves who will benefit from advanced technology and at what cost to other segments in society? Will only the educated elite benefit? Will the poor become further marginalized as money from social programs is diverted to cities to fund telecommunications projects? In the LDCs, the importance of traditional practices and social values are extremely embedded in every aspect of daily life. These nations may find that the changes brought by electronic technology tax all economic, religious, cultural, and social institutions, potentially creating wider divisions between the "haves" and the "have nots."

CONCLUSION

New technology leads to changes in the way we do things. Communication technology has the potential to change not only the way we relate to our world through mass communication, but also the way we adapt to the characteristics of technologies that emphasize visual images, time and space alteration, and ideas of precision and control.

Many people go through the day like Joe, who never gave a thought to how many technologies or services he used in one morning, or how these eliminated the need for face-to-face interaction to complete his tasks. But if our society is to prepare for a future that will inevitably involve more communication technology and a greater array of technological services, we must reflect on the broader social consequences of using these technologies.

As the world changes through the use of new communication technologies, people need to be aware of the ethical dimensions of change. How are our lives changing, and with what effect? Should people be forced to change, or should they be allowed to cling to some of the principles and traditions that they have grown comfortable with? How do individuals and nations maintain social stability when change is introduced at an ever-increasing speed?

SUMMARY

Technological development does not always occur by plan or design. By studying how technology is invented, used, and the social changes it brings to us, we gain a better understanding of the dynamics of the world in which we live. This chapter has outlined the connections between communications technology and other areas of living. It has addressed:

- the relationship between communication technology and society
- how the use of technology in the past has conditioned us to have certain expectations of technology in the present and future
- how beliefs about technology sometimes distort the original intention for which a technology was developed
- how our uses of technologies within specific contexts influence our attitudes, beliefs, and behaviors
- the ways in which the unique characteristics of various technologies influence the way we think
- whether ethics and responsibility should be a part of the way individuals and industries use communication technologies
- how values, influenced by the competing forces of business practices and basic needs, both create and respond to social change

DISCUSSION QUESTIONS

1. Can you estimate the amount of time you spend with communication technologies in an average day? How conscious are you of using them? Do you see any ways in which your own behaviors have been influenced by interaction with these technologies? For example, many people who use computers for word processing find that their system of writing changes. Often they cite the ease of editing, making changes, or storing things in computer files as elements that influence the writing process.
2. Think about and discuss what images of the future you had as a child. How many of them have come true?
3. Discuss ethical issues raised by photocopying print materials, making copies on tape from CDs or records, and taping material from television or radio. Are there fine lines that separate these various uses, or are they all similar? In each case, does anyone suffer from the loss of the

sale of their labor? How might adequate compensation be guaranteed, if at all?

4. Almost everyone knows someone who has "Luddite" tendencies. Who do you know who refuses to interact with a specific communication technology, and what reasons do they give? How rational are their stated objections to that technology? If you share these tendencies, why? If you don't, why?

5. Are you now thinking of pursuing a specific career in any of the media industries? How certain are you that those jobs will exist by the time you finish school, or within ten or twenty years thereafter? How might some of the industries change? What jobs will probably remain, and what new ones might open up? What skills will be necessary for jobs in the future?

6. Conduct a content analysis of articles dealing with social change. A Sunday newspaper or a combination of news magazines will provide interesting materials to study. What scenarios of the future do these materials present? Are they realistic?

7. Discuss what life for your children might be like in the next twenty years. How great a reliance will they have on technology? What skills and values do you hope they will have? Will those skills and values be appropriate for a more technology-driven society?

REFERENCES

Barnouw, Erik. 1966. *A tower in babel: A history of broadcasting in the United States.* Vol. 1, To 1933. New York: Oxford University Press.

Clarke, Arthur C. 1991. *How the world was one.* New York: Bantam Books.
———. 1981. *Media Asia,* 8 (4): 185–90.

Deutsch, Karl. 1963. Some problems in the study of nation-building. In *Nation-building,* ed. K. W. Deutsch & W. J. Foltz. New York: Prentice-Hall.

Ellul, Jacques. 1985. Preconceived ideas about mediated information. In *The media revolution in America & Western Europe,* ed. E.M. Rogers and F. Balle, 95–107. Norwood, NJ: Ablex Publishing Corp.

Hanson, Jarice and Narula, Uma. 1990. *New communication technologies and the developing world.* Hillsdale, NJ: Lawrence Erlbaum Associates.

Hobsbawm, Eric J. 1959. *Primitive rebels: Studies in archaic forms of social movement in the 19th and 20th centuries.* Manchester: Manchester University Press.

Joseph, Earl C. and Harkins, Arthur M. 1980. The emergence of ethnotronic systems in the 1980s. In *Through the '80s,* ed. F. Feather, 308–11. Washington, D.C.: World Future Society.

Kahn, Herman and Wiener, Anthony J. 1967. The next thirty-three years: A framework for speculation. In *Toward the year 2000: Work in progress,* ed. D. Bell, 73–100. Boston: Beacon Press.

Kozol, Jonathan. 1985. *Illiterate America.* New York: New American Library.

Martin, John. 1981. *Telematic society: A challenge for tomorrow.* Englewood Cliffs, NJ: Prentice-Hall, Inc.

McLuhan, Marshall. 1964. *Understanding media: The extensions of man.* New York: McGraw-Hill.

Rifkin, Jeremy. 1991. *Biosphere politics.* New York: HarperCollins.

Schor, Juliet B. 1991. *The overworked American.* New York: Basic Books.

Slack, Jennifer Daryl. 1984. *Communication technology and society: Conceptions of causality and the politics of technological intervention.* Norwood, NJ: Ablex.

Toffler, Alvin. 1970. *Future shock.* New York: Random House.

———. 1990. *Powershift.* New York: Bantam Books.

———. 1980. *The third wave.* New York: Bantam Books.

U.S. Bureau of the Census. 1989. *Statistical abstract of the United States,* 109th ed. Washington, D.C.: Government Printing Office.

Veronis, Suhler & Associates. June 1991. *Communications industry forecast.* New York: Veronis, Suhler & Associates, Inc.

Understanding Communication Technologies

Making Connections

As indicated in Chapter 1, the way in which new communication technology is evaluated requires a different approach than that traditionally taken in evaluations of mass media. Harold Lasswell's classic explanation of communication as examining "Who, says what, in which channel, to whom, with what effect?" (1948) was an adequate model from which to understand the process of mass communication. Today the senders of messages (who) may involve a number of individuals or corporations; their messages (what) may be received in more than one context; the technologies involved (channels) could be several; and the audiences (to whom) may bring a number of perspectives to the message exchange that influence the outcome of the communication process (the effect).

This chapter discusses ways to understand communication technology and how connections are made among different elements of the technology, and it provides tools for interpretation. The chapter discusses:

Chapter

- the importance of developing critical standards to evaluate communication technology and content

- the ways in which both form and content influence the meaning of a message and how it communicates to an individual or audience

- how the context of use contributes to the user's interaction with the technology

- the process by which people perceive and understand messages

- the ways in which technology requires a new form of "media literacy"

When motorist Rodney King was beaten by Los Angeles police officers in 1992, a bystander with a portable video camera recorded approximately nine

Figure 2.1 *The Rodney King Beating. This photograph was made from the videotape recording by George Holliday.*
Photo source: AP/Wide World Photos

minutes of the action. When allegations of police brutality were brought to court, jurors watched the full nine minutes of the videotape and, at the end of the trial, found the officers not guilty of using excessive force in restraining King (see figure 2.1).

The verdict shocked people around the world. How could such a verdict have been reached when such powerful visual images, broadcast on television news reports and printed in newspapers, apparently contradicted the findings? The apparent injustice sparked riots in major cities around the country, and the world's media seized the opportunity to affirm the violent nature of people in the United States. Even though the news media showed only a few seconds of the beating, the powerful image was hard to deny. People who saw the actions with their own eyes found it hard to believe the verdict they heard. Perhaps nowhere has the power of the visual image been put to such a test as in this celebrated trial.

The Rodney King videotape and the impact it had on audiences suggests some basic questions to ask when exploring the impact of communication technology. If people had no knowledge of how videotape is used, or the portable nature of video technology, would they have reacted so strongly to the images presented? If people were not aware of widespread violence in our society, would they have understood how to "read" the images of the officers beating King? Nowadays people in the United States are sophisticated about video technology. While years ago images on home video might not have been judged an effective means of documenting a real event, audiences today are aware of the capability of home video recording equipment, and no longer question how the images were recorded—just what they meant!

Media Literacy

A metaphor for understanding the ways in which people respond to the messages presented in different forms of communication technology is the phrase **media literacy**. This phrase describes how people make sense of the content of communication technology. The word *literacy* reflects the fact that people "read" or interpret the messages of various forms of media. These readings influence how people perceive messages and the ways they comprehend messages (how they understand the content and relate its meaning to the larger social sphere).

Every technology has the capability to communicate some things better than others. These unique characteristics are usually defined as the medium's **form.** Understanding forms helps us determine how and what the technology is capable of communicating.

Analysis of content has provided a variety of critical tools because generalizations can often be made more easily about types of media content than about forms of media. The study of *genres* investigates how content is classified.

Westerns, soap-operas, sit-coms, action-adventure shows, and romance stories represent genres that are often the focus of critiques. In each case, content from one example of a genre can be compared to other examples from the same genre. By comparing books, programs, or films that are already known to be similar in some ways, the critic's task becomes easier.

Media literacy combines understanding of both form and content. Acquiring media literacy is sometimes a difficult task because it relies on our ability to distinguish among forms that have apparent similarities, but may in reality be distinctly different. The content of cable television is similar to that of broadcast television, but the two forms function differently, have separate structures, and are regulated in different ways. Thus we see that media literacy requires that we consider issues of both form and content, and attempt not to collapse the two together.

One way of keeping the two separate is to consider the **context** in which the messages are received. Audiences may have different expectations of a film they see in a movie theater than of one they see on television. In a movie theater the audience would probably not tolerate commercial interruptions. Similarly, using a home computer in the context of playing a video game is experienced differently than using a home computer to telecommute (work at home and communicate with the office by computer).

An understanding of form, content, and context are all necessary to achieve media literacy. Sometimes cultural features influence how these terms are used. The word *culture* has many connotations and is therefore difficult to define in simple terms. Throughout this book the term *culture* is used to describe the attitudes, biases, and values that people hold in a particular society, but also the artifacts produced by the society that express these same characteristics. By looking at some of the critical standards that reflect culture, we can understand why form, content, and context have often been subject to multiple explanations, theories, and interpretations (see box 2.1).

Box 2.1 Media Research

Since researchers first became interested in the relationship between communications media and society, there have been several phases of attention to different aspects of the communication experience. In retrospect the influence of emerging types of communication media can be seen to have reflected the research agenda.

Some of the earliest research (1920–30) focused on the impact of the mass media in shaping public opinion. The dominant forms of media available in those years were print, radio, and film; and none of them was used in exactly the same way they are used today! As we look back at media research prior to 1930, it is possible to see the public's fascination with what were then the new technologies of film and radio, and efforts to use them to persuade audiences to take certain actions or think in certain ways. Not surprisingly, the influence of the new communications media on people's ideas about World War I strongly shaped the government's approach to regulation of radio. The new advertising industry also made use of the ability of the media to influence and persuade. In short, direct effects of media were recognized and exploited for purposes of influencing the public's behavior.

The Payne Fund Studies were the first serious attempt to understand how film could influence the attitudes and beliefs of audiences. The data provided by these studies suggested that all sorts of variables could affect the communication process, including personal contacts, social environment, and motives for paying attention to a medium. Media began to be considered not as the central component of understanding how people interpret messages, but as only one of many social and cultural factors that influenced the process.

From 1930 to 1950 attention was given to the media's ability to persuade or inform audiences on a more subtle level. Most of the studies during this era concentrated on the psychological effects of media.

From 1950 to 1960 media research was strongly affected by the presence of television in society. The increasing amount of media available to people in 1950 also influenced theorists who began to reconceptualize ways of thinking about media that ascribed greater but not total importance to the role of communication technology in the home. Researchers also focused on the power of mass communications media to shape messages.

Between 1960 and the present the quantity of technology available to people in the United States has skyrocketed, and attention has turned to other ways of understanding media and society. Altheide and Snow (1991) have written that recent research in media analysis has focused on different formats and their ability to shape messages through "rhetoric, frames, and formats of all content, including power, ideology, and influence. In this period, significant social analysis is inseparable from media analysis" (x).

It has taken nearly a century of theorizing about media to reach the place where both form and content are examined to understand the impact of messages. Moreover, form and content are no longer seen as isolated factors, and the individual attending to the message is no longer seen as a passive sponge waiting to absorb the message. Today the audience is considered an active agent, as are the industry that produces the message and the culture in which the message is transmitted. All these factors help us understand the impact of communications media on society.

Critical Standards

Not too many years ago the products of popular culture were considered less worthy of study or analysis than the products of "high" culture, which were viewed as artistic creations. Popular cultural artifacts were regarded as less legitimate parts of culture, and many critics turned up their noses at performers and media that were directed toward a mass audience. Some went so far as to classify these performers and their materials as examples of culture with a small "c." Many of the same critics viewed painting, classical music, the "legitimate" theater, and art films as "high" culture. These were often regarded as the only true culture, and distinguished with a capital "C."

Today, performers like Madonna, Michael Jackson, and Prince, and the music, videos, and performances they produce, are considered by many to be just as worthy of study as the most highly praised artists in traditionally more respected areas of endeavor. One reason for the legitimation of popular culture today is the changing nature of the **critical standards** that are applied to different forms of media. These standards provide ways of criticizing and understanding the messages of media.

It sometimes seems that everyone has an opinion about media content. Often the reasons why something is regarded favorably by one person and dismissed by another have to do with the very different criteria used by each. Many people tend to blur the differences between personal taste, review, and criticism. Personal taste has to do with whether a person likes something, even though he or she may not be able to articulate why. Taste is largely an emotional reaction to something, but as Fenster (1991) has written, taste is partly determined by range of material available within the culture.

Reviews tend to focus on a synopsis of the contents of a given work of art so that consumers may judge whether they want to see or hear what is being reviewed. Reviews will usually offer an opinion as well. Many of our discussions about whether something is worthy of our time come from our attention to reviews from people with whom we usually agree.

Detailed analysis of a program or a form of media is found in criticism, and a good critic understands the program or medium so well that he or she has an intimate knowledge of the limits or boundaries within which the artists have worked. A good critic understands the communication potential of both media form and content.

The difference between a film that is a "critical success" and one that is a "popular success" may have to do with whether the film elicits an intellectual (critical) or an emotional (taste) reaction. In the world of media where so many products are promoted for profit, producers hope to generate as much publicity for their products as possible. The distinctions between new products and those with successful histories form one basis for comparison. Similarly, as content is adapted for different forms, another comparative dimension is added. Media criticism has traditionally included an element of comparison, largely because the critical standards used to evaluate one form of media are often applied to other media (Nye 1971). As a result, TV may be compared to film, a radio newscast to a news story in print, or any dramatic portrayal to theater.

The distinctions between mass and popular culture have also become blurred over recent years. Traditionally, the term "popular" referred to the traits that represent a specific group in society. Folk cultures, ethnic traditions, and styles adopted by certain age groups were often called "popular," while messages produced by industry for economic reasons were described as "mass" phenomena.

An example of the difference between pop culture and mass culture can be seen by comparing two styles of music. Rap music mirrors the interests of a particular segment of society. The content of rap music tends to deal with issues and values confronting urban African Americans and other minorities in society. An example of "mass" music would be what is commonly called "elevator" music, which is a version of a more popular form that has been sanitized and packaged for use as background sound. Other analogies could include the independent cult films which would be labeled popular (such as *The Rocky Horror Picture Show*) compared to Hollywood's mass-audience films like *Die Hard* or *Pretty Woman,* and comic strips that become big business, like *Peanuts* (popular) which Charles Shultz created to serve as a microcosm of adult concerns (Short 1978) compared to Strawberry Shortcake (mass), a character created to sell products as well as an image in the comics.

The ability to mass-produce both communications technology and media content is a by-product of the industrial revolution. Like the factory assembly line, the channels of communication open opportunities for producing products for sale and consumption. Once communication technologies exist, content must be created so that there is a reason to use the technology. We live in a society that has experienced several generations of both popular and mass culture, but because our technologies of communication are hungry for content, they often use more mass-oriented content than that which specifically deals with popular values. Once a program, film, or character is successful, we can expect to see the formula followed by others. This creates a cycle of popular content followed by clones that are geared more to mass outlets. The mass distribution of toys and games following a popular movie like *Jurassic Park* is one example. The performer Madonna has had great success since adapting the look and manner of Marilyn Monroe. As the cycle continues, the distinctions between popular and mass become further blurred.

The economic imperatives behind the creation of content for these technologies has generally required that much of the content appeal to the largest number of consumers for maximum profit. The success of a form of media or a type of content is often measured by how much money it makes, or by how many people want to own it. The economic imperative often drives the communications industries to shape their business practices so that mass production of messages remains profitable for those who distribute them.

Does this mean that industry's desire to create mass messages rather than popular ones will necessarily drive popular values out of existence in media? Though some critics have warned that this could occur (Benjamin 1969, Schiller 1969) and can cite evidence that this practice is the norm, later critics have maintained that popular values—those that express the values and ideas of a smaller representative audience, can survive quite well in a marketplace that has a variety of channels of information (Gabriel 1990; Meyerle 1991).

Messages and Ideas

When applying critical standards it is useful to understand the ways in which the technology, or form, influences the communication process. Some of these factors include the size of the screen, how the image is constructed—electronically or in some other way—and the range of colors available to that form. The context in which technology is used influences our ability to understand or respond to its messages. A television image in the home is perceived differently than a large screen image above a crowd in Times Square or at a rock concert. For these reasons, both the unique characteristics of the medium and the context in which it is used are important for understanding the effect of any communication experience. What often confuses people, however, is their tendency to think of all media as having similar qualities or effects. This can easily be seen in the way people like to think about newer technologies or services as simply extensions of similar earlier media, so that VCRs may be seen as merely an accessory to television, or word processing on a computer as an extension of print technology. In reality, each new form or use of communication technology presents a new experience, and each may require special critical standards.

Languages of Media

A way of conceptualizing these special qualities is to think of each medium as communicating through its own unique language. This metaphor is related to the role of literacy; we "read" forms of media and understand their meanings only if we are fluent in that medium's language. The idea that each medium has its own language has been documented by many influential critics of communications. Arnheim (1967) describes language as a set of perceptual shapes that may be auditory, visual, or kinesthetic (capable of movement) (229). Communication scholars have also used these ideas to express the communicative power of specific forms of media. Communication technologies have a profound ability to express meaning by the language they use.

Fiske and Hartley (1978) also draw on the metaphor of language to explain how television in particular, is read using skills traditionally in the domain of literary criticism. They state: " . . . the codes which structure the 'language' of television are much more like those of speech than of writing" (15). As in learning any language, experience helps us understand the subtle nuances expressed in the language.

Postman (1988) adds yet another dimension to the metaphor of technologies communicating through language. In his explanation of the impact of the theorist Alfred Korzybski's work on language, he writes:

> . . . we may conclude that humans live in two worlds—the world of events and things, and the world of *words* about events and things. In considering the relationship between these two worlds, we must keep in mind that language does much more than construct concepts about the events and things in the world; it tells us what sorts of concepts we ought to construct. . . . Each language, as Edward Sapir observed, constructs reality differently from all the others (141).

Media technology comes between images of events and things, and often uses words or pictures about events and things. Therefore, media packages and expresses messages in a special way and serves to construct reality in its own way. Each time content is transferred from one medium to another, its message is shaped further by the characteristics of the new medium.

Oral language and media that work primarily through the sense of hearing (like radio) present information by juxtaposing images or presenting spontaneous thought. The "images," or sets of impressions, must be put into a pattern that allows the listener to remember what is being said. Stories that relate a long set of numbers or statistics are harder to remember than those that present the audience with more memorable images, such as "a half," or "a country about the size of Rhode Island." This, of course, is the key to the success of the "sound bite," a phrase that communicates a powerful message and stays in the memory.

Carpenter and McLuhan (1960) described important effects of the invention of the printing press beyond allowing the mass production of books. This remarkable technology permitted the use of pictures, colors, and space, and made the chronological arrangement of events the accepted norm for presenting information. This last element has often been cited as evidence that some media (like print) lead audiences to believe that events are also arranged causally (Boorstin 1961; Kraft, Cantor & Gottdiener 1991; Lewis 1991).

The structure of news in traditional print media uses the inverted pyramid; at the top of the story the headline summarizes the event. Most of the key information is given in the first few paragraphs, after which the article moves to details of lesser importance. The consumer of print news never has to read the entire story to get the gist of it.

In broadcast news the same format is often followed, but because the details are not supportive of the initial information, the story is less memorable. Television viewers are presented only with transitory fragments of information and have no way to return to the "headline" or story lead to check their perceptions. Instead, broadcasters rely on visual images to reinforce the meaning of the story.

Unique characteristics   Every medium communicates in its own way, depending on the characteristics inherent in its design. The way each medium presents the content, through projection on a screen (like television), through reflection on a screen (like film), or through the stimulation of the eye, ear, or both simultaneously, influences how much the audience must consciously involve themselves in the process of perceiving the message.

Formats are the organizational structure by which content is adapted to a medium's form. The format of television is made up of longer segments of programming interrupted by shorter segments of commercials called commercial breaks. Once audiences are familiar with formats they use them as short-cuts to thinking about what the medium can express, and they are likely to accept the characteristics of the form. Commercial breaks don't disrupt most people's understanding of a program, and allow natural breaks for conversation, going to the kitchen, or engaging in other activities.

Context of use   Everyone uses several different styles of spoken language. A person will speak one way to authority figures, a different way to acquaintances, and a third way to friends. Formality of speech usually varies depending on who is being addressed, and the social context of the dialogue. Communication technology also allows for various styles of language, also often dictated by the context of the experience. An "art" film will have a different style of language than a popular movie. Some people regard playing a video game as a very different form of computer interaction from using the computer for word processing or analyzing data.

The Relationship of Form and Content

Genres are formats that relate content to form. The word *genre* means order. Different media such as print, film, radio, and television each rely on certain structures of order, or genres, that become synonymous with that form of technology. Soap opera is a genre that is closely identified with television. Even though they may not be able to list the characteristics of a soap opera, most people can summon an image of what a soap opera is and does, just by thinking about it as representative of a genre of programming. Tight close-ups, the relationship of plot to actual calendar events, and the repetition of story lines have become well known as the elements of the soap opera genre.

The format of a newscast is also familiar. At the beginning of the program the headlines are given. Following a commercial break the lead story is presented, and the features are ordered according to importance, with sports and weather usually concluding the show.

Often genres have characteristics that become indicators of the format: laugh tracks identify comedies; music suggesting mood or pace identifies action-adventure programs. These signals can be thought of as the punctuation of the technology's language, and they are often tied to the target audience for the medium's content. The use of the laugh track is a significant example of how television producers try to punctuate their work in such a way as to influence audience perception of the content. Because people watch TV comedies in the privacy of their own homes, a laugh track may give them the impression of enjoying the program with a larger audience. Viewers become so familiar with the punctuation that they may not even be consciously aware of the laugh track. Even if the material is not funny, the viewer is left with an impression that it was, and the audience participates in a communal experience, even though they may be home alone.

Genres become associated with audience expectations of what the message of the medium will be, and it is at this level that most academic attempts at analyzing media have been focused. The emphasis placed on how a medium communicates has to do with the message in relation to culture, and the most common way of exploring this relationship is through sociological or anthropological analysis. Ethnic, racial, or gender images often present examples of these forms of relating content to reality, and do so obviously. Think, for example, of the powerful way advertising communicates. Advertisers know that audiences rarely absorb their messages the first time, and therefore mount campaigns to strengthen and reinforce images and product identification. The target audiences are attracted by personalities and images that exemplify desire, creating the wish for fulfillment through purchasing the product.

Understanding how the audience reads or decodes messages can be approached through semiotic analysis. Semiotics is the study of signs and the way they communicate. The following section discusses the nature and use of semiotics.

Semiotics as a Tool for Understanding Images

The study of semiotics is usually traced to two individuals, Ferdinand de Saussure (1857–1913) and Charles Saunders Pierce (1839–1914). Each had his own concept of a sign. Saussure divided signs into two categories: the **signifier,** or image, and the **signified,** which expressed the larger conceptual dimension of the message. Pierce broke signs down into three components: icon, index, and symbol. The **icon** is the simplest representation of a sign, the **index** refers to its meaning, and the **symbol** is the final concept of the sign's meaning.

The two differing conceptions of semiotics are better understood through examples. An image of a burning American flag might attract the attention of someone who lives in the United States more than someone who lives in France. The meaning one would infer from the experience would be slightly different depending on which "reading" one used. According to Saussure's interpretation, the flag would be a signifier and the fire would signify a change from the traditional image of the flag waving in the wind. Perhaps the meaning of the signifier could be interpreted as anti-Americanism, revolution, a political statement, or an accident—depending on the viewer's attitudes, values, and knowledge of the flag-burning issue in the United States.

If Pierce's logic were followed, the flag would be the smallest unit of analysis, the icon; the fire would be the index that helps interpret meaning; and finally, the symbol created by the two would embody attitudes, behaviors, and knowledge of flag-burning and its meaning in our society today.

In the case of the Rodney King videotape, the image of an African-American man and a number of white police officers in the same scene suggests another complex set of relationships that incorporates sociological knowledge and personal attitude. In the Saussurian view, the images of black/white, powerless/powerful, dominated/dominators, all signify such complex conditions as racism and police brutality. In the Piercian view, each individual is an icon, the positions of the participants and the visibility of the police uniforms are indexes, and these elements symbolize racism, domination, and brutality.

Signs are always read or interpreted, within a system of relationships. The conditions surrounding those relationships are arbitrary. Whoever reads the signs uses his or her own history, education, and cultural experience to interpret meaning.

Even though the reading of signs can vary from individual to individual, many signs can elicit uniform readings within a culture. Systems of signs that are socially structured and culturally learned become grouped into **codes.** Codes are rules understood by all people who speak the same language, even though there may not be strict guidelines to indicate what value people place on the codes. Two people might agree that a red, octagonal sign saying STOP means that a driver should stop before proceeding, but one person might come to a full stop while the other only makes a short hesitation while the car is still rolling. The literal translation of the rule of the stop sign is interpreted differently, while both drivers believe they are in compliance with the law.

Technology creates codes similar to those found in languages. These codes transmit meaning through the use of the technology's form. Creators of media content are well aware of their technological capability to influence viewers through camera angles, sound effects, or staging of actors and events. A zoom-in to a close-up shot is a technological code that implies the viewer will receive more important information by focusing on the close-up image instead of the background. Cutting from one scene to another may suggest either simultaneous time or discontinuous time—depending on how the images are established in relationship to each other. A fade-in or a fade-out could suggest the passage of time. These technological codes are culturally learned and highly dependent on the technology's ability to introduce and integrate new technical variations to media content. Special effects are the most obvious means of experimenting with technologically induced codes, and many of the effects we see in television commercials or introductions to programs are products of new technology that we quickly learn to respond to.

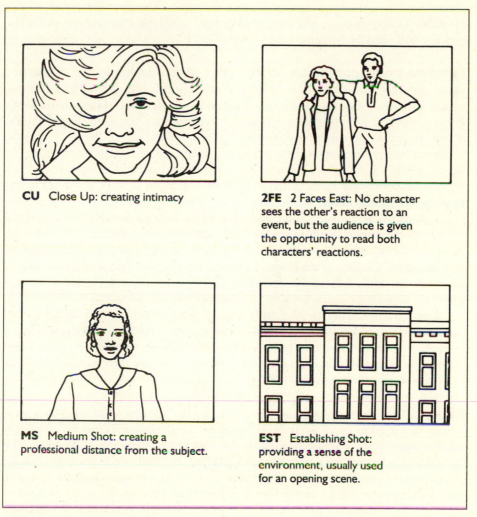

CU Close Up: creating intimacy

2FE 2 Faces East: No character sees the other's reaction to an event, but the audience is given the opportunity to read both characters' reactions.

MS Medium Shot: creating a professional distance from the subject.

EST Establishing Shot: providing a sense of the environment, usually used for an opening scene.

Figure 2.2   Implied Codes

Languages and Technologies

Each medium's language is influenced by elements of form, content, and the use of technology. While different forms of media will be discussed at greater length in the following chapters, a brief discussion at this time will help explain the communicative power of today's dominant media technologies.

It is important to know that when different technologies are connected to provide new services or to create new forms, aspects of the languages of the original technologies may still be apparent, but a new language is created. Most of the communication technologies we regard as "the media" today have capitalized on their ability to speak to large groups of people (mass audiences). Modifications to mass media require attention to whether or not the technologies are still used in the same way.

Point-to-point communication
Though the technologies of printing made messages available for individual consumption, the necessity to communicate quickly over long distances could not be accommodated in this way. Point-to-point communication was an attempt to communicate long-distance. Many attempts to create point-to-point communication led to the development of several other languages. Semaphore is a language of flag positions that can signal across a wide space. Many cultures developed systems of smoke or drum signals for communication across long distances. Each is an example of point-to-point communication.

Telegraph, telephone, and radio were all inventions intended to speed the distribution of special messages, and all shared similar patterns of discovery and innovation. Once knowledge of electrical energy was applied to specific technologies, additional methods of communication became available, such as Morse code. Still, only those skilled in deciphering these languages had the privilege of, and the responsibility for, interpreting the messages for others.

The earliest forms of telegraph messages were transmitted using special pens that recorded a system of notations only a trained telegrapher could interpret. Morse code translated short and long sounds into a series of dots and dashes that required interpretation by a trained operator, but it made the communication process far more efficient.

Radio
The language of radio appears to be the spoken word, and to a great extent this is true. But if we focus on form as the defining feature of language, we then see radio as a medium highly dependent on the sense of hearing. The "disembodied voice" of radio requires that we mentally construct the images suggested by words, sound effects, and music. As a result, audiences think about things that they cannot see. The ability of people to create images in their minds is a major component in the power of radio as a tool for communication. Of course, radio is often used as background sound that does not

require conscious attention, and this is why the widespread early fear that radio would be used for brainwashing has been largely unrealized.

The only things that seriously impede the ability of radio to communicate are external interference, such as signal jamming, and internal interference, such as poor reception. These are both characteristics that relate to the medium's form.

In order to be listened to, radio must fill every minute of the broadcast time period, so its format evolved in such a way as to present nonstop, never-ending sound. The need to fill time saw several styles of programming emerge, including "all records" formats, re-broadcasts, "all news," and even "all ads" radio.

The radio industry changed drastically after the introduction of television, and countered the dominance of television by targeting smaller, more distinct audiences. As a result, the number of national radio services has dwindled and more locally-oriented programming has become standard radio fare. Radio transmission also encompasses other types of formats like CB (Citizens Band) and cellular (mobile) telephone. The feature of portability so associated with radio technologies today contributes to radio's use as a personal medium. The average household in the United States reports having access to over five radio receivers, making radio the most pervasive of all electronic media technologies (United States Bureau of the Census 1991, 556).

Television

Television   Television's ability to transmit news immediately, or with the appearance of immediacy, has given the medium an edge over both print and radio. This is because the form of television allows on-the-spot reporting with words and visual images that reinforce the notion that the viewer is at the scene of the event. The style of language used by television news is often translated to other programs that want to create a news-broadcast-like impression. Even though "60 Minutes" is considered a "magazine" program, the stories are presented in a news-like format. The famous tight close-ups used on the program "60 Minutes" are an excellent example of the intrusiveness of the camera and the extreme intimacy created by television's form. This can be contrasted with film's powerful use of panoramic views and special effects that often have a much bigger impact on the large screen than on the smaller television screen.

Television's power of communication lies in the small, intimate surroundings in which it is viewed. We watch TV at home in our living rooms, our bedrooms, and our kitchens. The size of the screen makes the medium appropriate for close-ups and intimate content that is perceived quite differently than it is in other media. Close-ups in a movie theater would not be as important as on the small screen, found in situations in which audiences sit only a few feet from the image. Audio and visual signals received in the home have tremendous communicative power. In addition, the typical weekly schedule allows television to present much of its material in serialized fashion. This weekly format permits continuity in programming. The audience can watch the same families grow and change on such shows as the "Cosby Show," or "Roseanne," or the seemingly endless ironies of the legal system in a show like "LA Law."

Television has often been judged for its ability to reflect reality. This is in large measure because the images on television appear to be taking place in "real time." In view of the fact that audiences are accustomed to an appearance of reality, it is surprising how willingly they will overlook some of the discrepancies found in the construction of images.

The *establishing shot* (see figure 2.2), which is often used as an opening for television programs, particularly comedies, often bears no resemblance to the interior scenes where most of the activity takes place. If audiences viewed critically the establishing shot of "Murphy Brown," and compared it to the living room set, they would quickly realize that the exterior and interior images of the house do not match. The spatial dimensions of the living room are not compatible with the view of the front of the building. Producers know that establishing shots suggest an environment that the audience will accept, even if later shots show images that do not match.

Television has become noted for its emphasis on domestic or situation comedies that take place in one room or in a very few locations. Television comedy must create a rapport with the audience, and it does so in part by using small interior spaces. Television comedy also relies on television's form—that of a relatively small piece of technology that is viewed in the intimate environment of the home and can convey the subtleties of humor, both visual and auditory.

Television is, then, an intimate medium. We view it in our home, and we relate to the content in intimate terms.

Computers   The number of computers, both in the home and in the public domain, is growing rapidly. In addition, computer technology is used in a number of everyday applications. Video games are dependent on the computer chip; maps in malls use computerized information to draw pictures for users; bills and mail are processed through the use of computer data; and automatic teller machines (ATMs) use computer programming to help individuals conduct their banking business. Because so many of these uses are relatively new, it is easier to see how the language of the computer differs from the other communication technologies discussed so far.

Anyone who has learned how to use a word processor knows that a personal computer can radically change the way a person relates to ideas and the writing process. The ability to move blocks of text or save fragmented thoughts in an **exosomatic memory** (memory located outside of the body) can change the way a person thinks about his or her work. Many people who use word processors claim that they lose their ability to envision the whole project in their mind, and instead, work on fragmented thoughts that represent more sponta-

Box 2.2   The Nanosecond Culture

The computer introduces a new time perspective and with it a new vision of the future. We are so used to telling time by means of the clock that our minds rebel at the prospect of adopting an entirely different form of timekeeping. While at this emergent state it is difficult to grasp, or even to imagine, the full impact of a shift in time reckoning from clock to computer, an examination of the distinguishing features of this new timepiece provides a clue to the changes in time consciousness that lie ahead.

To begin with, the clock measures time in relationship to human perceptibility. It is possible to experience an hour, a minute, a second, even a tenth of a second. The computer, however, works in a time frame in which the nanosecond is the primary temporal measurement. The nanosecond is a billionth of a second, and though it is possible to conceive theoretically of a nanosecond, and even to manipulate time at that speed of duration, *it is not possible to experience it*. This marks a radical turning point in the way human beings relate to time. Never before has time been organized at a speed beyond the realm of consciousness.

Source: Jeremy Rifkin, *Time Wars,* (New York: Simon & Schuster, Inc., 1989) 23.

neous mental imagery. Another common complaint of serious word processor users is that they rely on the computer's ability to proofread the work for spelling mistakes, and tend to be more sloppy in their own spelling and punctuation.

Computer language is fascinating but sometimes difficult to comprehend because computers process information much faster than the human brain can. While humans tend to think in seconds or, as an athlete might, in tenths of seconds, computers "think" in nanoseconds—a billionth of a second (see box 2.2). As a result, the processing of information by a computer speeds by too quickly for most people to comprehend. The means of message distribution appears to separate the beginning and the end of the message, and the user has no knowledge or understanding of what happens in the middle. As a result computer language seems fragmented, discontinuous, and transitory.

Connecting technologies   When one technology is linked to another technology, there are certain remnants of the original languages to contend with, but a new and unique language usually results. Ironically, the ability of people to use different technological languages gives the impression that there is more dialog among users of the technology. It could be said that television gives us something to discuss, and to a certain extent it does, but when television is used as an escape from conversation, the medium limits any meaningful interaction with others. Even more importantly, technologies like the computer may mislead us into thinking that we have greater capacities for connecting with others through electronic mail or interactive data services, but, in fact, the use of the computer limits spontaneous interaction and substitutes communication that is tied to times when the computer is available.

 Perception and Cognition

An audience's ability to interpret the meaning of messages has to do with **perception** and **cognition.** These are the tools that help the individual connect the discrete images he or she sees and hears with his or her own personal experiences, education, and belief system. Perception is the act of seeing, hearing, or otherwise taking in the message. Perception is not always a conscious act. We can perceive attitudes and emotions on a subconscious or unconscious level. Even though we may find a film to be thoroughly engaging, we may not be consciously aware of the subtle use of sound effects or editing that helps achieve that effect. We've learned over decades of communications research that different audiences perceive messages differently.

The act of cognition helps the media user make sense of a message. Cognitive processes allow receivers of messages to relate the images they perceive to their former experiences and education, and to the culture, and society in which they live. In many ways, cognition helps people store images and retrieve them from their memories to add history to their understanding of images.

In a culture that has a number of channels of information using visual images, the individual is constantly presented with messages that have the potential to leave an impression on his or her mind. This visual **information overload** causes the individual to unconsciously screen out unwanted or unnecessary information. This perceptual act also helps the individual negotiate the meaning of messages.

Advertisers tend to present their messages in longer time frames (a 30-second or a 60-second spot) in the earliest stages of an ad campaign. As audiences become familiar with the message, the amount of time spent on the ad can be reduced. The effectiveness of the ad is maintained by mentioning or showing a product, rather than explaining the message in a longer narrative commercial. The shorter message reinforces the idea that the product is a good one and is available to the audience. It reinforces earlier cognitive processes.

Environment as Context

External factors also influence a viewer's perception of a message. These factors include the environment in which the viewer receives the message. People may be accustomed to watching television in the home for entertainment and therefore may bring the idea that television is an entertainment medium to the possible pedagogical use of television or a videotape in the classroom. While students often learn how to recognize the important features of a lecture by the instructor's voice, style, or choice of information to put on the blackboard, it is more difficult for them to determine what information shown in a videotape should be recorded in their notes. The language of television and video has come to be seen as primarily a purveyor of entertainment largely because it is observed in the home for this purpose.

Likewise, whether the viewer attends to media individually or in a group can significantly influence the meaning he or she takes from it. A person might be more inclined to laugh out loud in a public setting where other people laugh than he or she would at home watching television alone. A sad story might coax tears from someone alone at home, while social expectations in public would elicit greater restraint.

Internal Factors

Internal factors are those specific to the individual attempting to make sense of the content he or she sees. Some internal factors are the products of genetics, such as **physiological factors,** and some are the result of experiences, social relationships, and interpersonal practices that influence the *psychological make-up* of an individual.

Physiology   People's physiological capabilities influence their ability to understand messages. Biological "equipment" for perceiving messages is different from person to person. Some people are born with perfect eyesight, while others have visual irregularities that require corrective lenses. Some people have heightened senses of hearing, taste, smell, or touch.

One out of every five males is born with red-green color-blindness. These men may never know it because they learn to perceive different shades of color as red or green. Their ability to perceive colors is different from others—not wrong, just different.

Cognitive scientists estimate that 75 percent of the information that reaches our brain comes from the eyes, which may help explain why the visual media are regarded as the most powerful in our society. Because the eyes have over 100 million sensors in the retina and only five million channels to the brain from the retina, much information is screened out before it registers in the conscious mind (Hunt 1982, 38). The eye-brain connection filters information, though much of what we don't consciously see may nonetheless be stored in our memories. While cognitive scientists don't have all the answers about the brain's functions, it is likely that the "extra" information may be stored elsewhere in the brain. These impressions may be expressed to us in dreams or through feelings of "deja vu."

When we move our eyes around when searching for a static object, they move differently than when they are following a moving object. When searching, the eyes move in rapid jerks called **saccades** (the term comes from Old French and means "the flick of a sail") (Gregory 1974, 42–43). When following a moving image the eyes seem to move smoothly, but when focusing on a still object the eyes have to work harder to focus, making the saccadic motion more rapid. The combination of saccadic eye movements with the perception of real movement is the result of **persistence of vision** (Monaco 1981, 125), an important concept in understanding why moving pictures appear to be moving, and why images on television appear to move in real-time motion. When one looks at a strip of processed film it is possible to see a number of still images. When those still pictures are projected at twenty-four frames per second and the eye and brain perceive the images, it is persistence of vision and the speed of projection that makes the pictures appear to be moving in real time. Similarly, the timing of the projection of electronic information and persistence of vision makes the appearance of the television image seem as realistic as possible.

Psychology   There are many theories that attempt to explain psychological factors involved in interpreting media messages, and a large body of research on media effects takes a psychological approach to understanding how messages are processed by different individuals. Some of the most significant studies on the effects of violence and pornography on behavior have focused on the interaction between audiences and the images they process. (See, for example, Haskell 1973, Chesler 1978, and Faludi 1991.)

Freudian psychology, with its concepts of id, ego, and superego, focuses on the individual's ability to create a balance among these competing internal forces. The id is the component of the self that seeks pleasure. The ego is the rational part of the self, and often takes control of the irrational strivings of the id. The ego channels needs and desires into more productive actions that are tempered by social appropriateness. The superego acts as the internal conscience, and controls the moral sense of the individual. Freud used these three concepts to explain why individuals often experience conflicting senses of self. When people read or view media, their psychological states may well mesh with the content for fulfillment.

There have been many psychoanalytic studies of media content. A simple example of an analysis might find that the typical hero, or main character of a story, represents the highly personified ego—the rational character in control or attempting to take control of the situation. Detective stories in particular usually personify a character with a detached sense of super-heightened ego that allows him or her to see reality more fully than others. Through association with these characters in media, a part of the viewer's personal psychological needs or desires may be either fulfilled or sublimated through transference.

Many of these attempts to understand why it is so easy to relate to some of the strongest images we see recurring in various forms of media content can be attributed to Jungian analysis. According to Jung, conflict takes place between the self and the ego. Jung defined the self as an entity that is constituted by the person within a society. The self always relates to the person in relationship to others, whether they are family, community, peer group, or nation. Jung's concept of ego is the expression of one's uniqueness within the larger environment. Through mediated images we have the opportunity to relate to character traits that might not be apparent in ourselves or people we know.

Jung further separated different types of beings through the suggestion of **archetypes,** or symbols that constituted a portion of the whole individual. Many Jungian analysts of media content focus on how representations of these various archetypes are manifested in the media, leading audiences to relate to the sense of wholeness.

Psychological investigation offers other ways to understand media content. Small issues, such as the colors displayed on a screen or the relationship of a character's name to a role could be psychological triggers that resonate with the individual's construction of meaning. For example, the names of characters in television can represent certain characteristics. "Norm" on the television program "Cheers" may represent the common man, or someone who exhibits "normal" behavior. Matt Groening, creator of "The Simpsons," has claimed that the name of the character "Bart" is an anagram for "brat." These subtleties may influence our psychological relationship to content.

Other psychological factors involve how and why media consumers pay attention to a particular media message at a given time. The concept of selective attention, selective retention, and selective memory help explain this process. Selectivity is operating when an individual chooses what is useful or important to him or her within a given context. When people fall in love they often experience a heightened sense of awareness. They may retain an especially vivid memory of music or smells they experienced at the time. Similarly, people who have recently experienced a great loss or disappointment might consciously seek out material that will distract them from their feelings or confirm that others feel the same way they do. Either of these experiences would be termed **selective attention,** because the individual has chosen, consciously or subconsciously, to attend to certain materials. **Selective retention** occurs when we choose, sometimes unconsciously, to remember certain things depending on whether our experiences were wonderful, terrible, or memorable for some other reason. And finally, **selective memory** causes us to distort our memories of certain events. Have you ever shared an experience with someone only to realize later that each of you interpreted the experience very differently? When you discuss the matter, the reasons why one person remembered events one way and you remembered them another way often illuminate what your own personal investment in the experience was.

Preconceived ideas   People also have preconceived ideas about what the message in any communication experience is going to be. Audience expectations about the behavior of others at a rock concert is different than expectations of behavior at the symphony. Often people remember images from films they saw when they were younger, but when they watch the film again, the actual images seem far removed from their memories.

Carpenter and McLuhan (1960) have compared the perceptual act to looking at a mosaic. If viewers look at a mosaic closely, they see isolated bits of color and shape. When they stand back, the colors and shapes blend into each other to form a much larger picture. Mosaics suggest ways to explain how people perceive messages. The messages exchanged between two people in a face-to-face interaction are enhanced by body language and the physical proximity of the parties. On the telephone, gestures and body language are missing. These subtle indicators influence the meaning of the message in real life, as they do in media content when participants act in certain ways to communicate beyond the words they speak.

Our level of activity also influences our perceptions. The television producer Garry Marshall, who produced four programs with viewer ratings in the top ten in the 1970s, has remarked that most people usually do something else while the television set is on. Adults may be noticing that the drapes need cleaning, or the kids may be playing with their toys—so it is the task of the producer to get the audience's attention. Marshall always seeks to create strong visual images that people will remember and perhaps copy. The image of Mork, in the 1970s sitcom "Mork and Mindy," drinking orange juice through his finger is just such an example. When parents saw their children sticking their fingers into their orange juice, they wanted to find out what the show was all about!

Memory   Everyone has had the experience of trying to study, but allowing their mind to drift. Eyes scan several pages before the reader realizes that he or she hasn't really absorbed anything. The same thing is true about listening to the lyrics of music. Some people remember some of the words, but in all likelihood they can't repeat the entire song unless there are some particularly catchy phrases.

Everyone has the experience of seeing a commercial on television that drives them crazy, but when they try to describe the commercial they can't remember the name of the product. Conversely, some people are able to go to the grocery story and hum the jingles of several products—but do they buy them?

People take in so much information in their daily lives that they use a **perceptual screen** to filter out unnecessary images. In fact, it has been estimated that if we were truly conscious of all of the ads we see each day, including product logos and trademark designs, we would be seeing in excess of 1500 of them!

One of the more intriguing questions studied by cognitive scientists involves assessing whether the brain processes information, or whether the mind constructs messages. The two possibilities reflect the knowledge that the brain and mind are related in a number of ways. This is usually approached as a study of the bicameral mind in which the left side of the brain is assumed to process detail work and the right side of the brain is assumed to perform surveillance functions. The problem, however, is that the left brain tends to tire quickly, and when it does, it passes the job of perception over to the right side of the brain, which makes it harder to concentrate. When this happens, a type of **narcotization** takes place. An individual may be seeing or hearing something, but not be totally aware of what is taking place. Watching television often turns from a left brain to a right brain activity, unless something calls our attention back to the program and we jolt the left brain into action. When the faculty of attention, or the left brain, is stimulated, it is easier to remember what took place.

The Relationship Between Media Literacy and Society

Though most people would like to believe that there are only a few "right" ways to think or theorize about media, the technologies and the conditions under which media are used create many exceptions to what people believe is fact. Because so many would like to think that understanding media is a simple process, many approaches toward understanding the real power and impact of communication technology are oversimplified or dismissed.

Common sense efforts to understand the impact of media show how absence of theory can create a misunderstanding of reality. As recently as 1985, rock music lyrics and album covers were examined by a congressional committee to assess whether or not they encouraged sexual promiscuity, drug use, violence, and Satanism. The Parents Music Resource Committee (PMRC) assumed that rock music naturally elicits a certain effect. Despite congressional testimony providing evidence that there are seldom direct effects of music lyrics on children, the PMRC echoed the fears of concerned parents over several decades. Lack of evidence shifted the issue from material that might be inappropriate to the issue of freedom of speech.

Like the fears associated with the introduction of radio and television, only understanding of the larger picture can adequately address the range of thoughts suggested by media content and the way in which certain audiences may use the messages. Most people can view film, listen to the radio or records, or watch television without turning into antisocial monsters. These attempts to see direct effects from media content usually reflect a projection of fear, rather than an understanding of how technology mediates messages between senders and receivers. Simple reactions often overlook the complex nature of media content and its relationship to social practices. These areas are far more difficult to understand, and require that researchers investigate a variety of connections to better understand how media presents images that audiences then twist to fit their own biases.

A study of audience reactions to "The Cosby Show" (Jhally and Lewis 1992) uncovered some major differences in minority and majority viewers' ideas about African Americans in our society today. While African-American and Hispanic viewers felt that "The Cosby Show" presented strong, positive images of family life but an idealized version of African-American culture in the United States, a predominant number of white viewers felt that the images in the show proved that affirmative action had worked in the United States, and that the socio-economic status for African-Americans was now equal to that of the white population. Many of these viewers used the presence of an upper-class African-American television family as evidence that there is no problem with racial inequality in our country today. This is a clear example of how one communications technology, television, alters viewers' perceptions of reality.

Media industries have extraordinary power to influence the meanings people find in facts and events through the use of unique forms of communication and the choice and formatting of media content. When the intentions of the producers and the expectations of the audiences match, there is usually no major problem in setting the context for the communication experience. If entertainment is the purpose of the producers, and that is what the audience is seeking, the thickets of languages, codes, and expectations are reasonably negotiated. But sometimes the boundaries between information and entertainment purposes become crossed.

Ethical Actions

The issues discussed so far suggest that the messages in a communication process are subject to individual interpretations, but that the individual will use his or her knowledge of social norms to make sense of a message within the social context. Knowing how people are likely to interpret messages is part of the media industries' approach toward developing certain types of content for public consumption.

Such industries as advertising, that try to sell products, and public relations, that tries to create positive images, know how the public responds to certain types of images, and will spend extraordinary amounts of money to make sure that the desired audience response is created. Are they operating ethically? Perhaps if everyone could read the media and had the ability to understand the messages, the question of ethics would not have to be asked. But since many people are not media literate, are they subjects for exploitation by the people who know how to manipulate and influence through message design?

While most journalists (print and broadcast) believe they act ethically and attempt to remain objective in constructing their stories, the increasing importance of visual images in our culture makes this more difficult. These visual images often eclipse the spoken word, and are an important aspect of understanding the media's relationship to society. Understanding how messages are transmitted through various communication technologies is an important aspect of understanding how each of the actors in a communication message contribute to the meaning of the message.

If audiences expect communication industries to act ethically, it is only reasonable to expect those audiences to exercise their own critical faculties to evaluate the messages they encounter. Becoming media literate is a first step in accepting this responsibility.

Conclusion

Aspects of form control the ability of a medium to be used for communication. Because forms are limited by the unique characteristics inherent in technological design, the content must be suited to the form's ability to communicate. Still, producers may not always get the desired response from their audience, because subjective experience and external factors influence how the message will be received.

Over the years there have been a number of attempts to understand how media communicates, and how generalizable those messages may be. We've learned that there are several factors that influence the audience's perception of the message, but that the reason the individual seeks to use or make sense of the message is of great importance. The context for the use of any form of communication technology helps provide an understanding of the audience's relationship to the content.

As traditional "mass" media are enhanced by adding various components or adapting technologies for different purposes, the idea of context becomes even more important to our understanding of the technological/human interface. The development of new technologies brings with it a need to understand how people use them in their daily lives.

SUMMARY

This chapter has outlined several issues relating to the way individuals use communication technologies and content to create meaning from the messages transmitted. The key elements to remember include:

- people use critical standards to make sense of messages; the more highly developed the critical standards, the more thoroughly the message can be understood
- each communication technology has unique characteristics that influence its ability to transmit messages
- considering form and content together are crucial to understanding the communicative power of the media
- context helps bridge the theoretical gap between the content of a message sent, and the way it is used by the individual or audience
- media users' subjective experiences affect their ability to perceive messages and make sense of them at the cognitive level
- ethics extend to understanding the potential for use and the actual use of communication technology and content

DISCUSSION QUESTIONS

1. Can you explain the differences between taste, review, and criticism? Find examples from the media for each category and explain why easy classification is sometimes difficult.
2. Watch a television program with no sound. Do the technological codes give you an idea of what the action is? How easy is it to construct a plausible story, based only on visuals, with no sound? Try this with a news program.
3. Discuss some of the media you remember from your childhood, such as stories, television programs, or films. Do members of the class have similar recollections of the same content? Can you determine what subjective experiences you had that influenced your memory of the content?
4. Get several news stories about the same issue and read them out loud to the class. What images are presented? How are they constructed?
5. Have one member of the class read a news story from a newspaper, another from a news magazine, and have others listen to television or radio newscasts. Ask each to write down what he or she remembers. Discuss any differences, and try to understand whether the individual's perceptions played a role in interpreting the story, or if the medium communicated the story in a different way.

54

6. Examine the television listings for usual children's programming hours, like Saturday morning or after school. Are the characters "popular" or "mass" creations? How much marketing of goods accompanies the "mass" produced messages?
7. Discuss the ethics behind advertising and public relations. Can you give examples in which these two industries seem to have gone "too far?"

REFERENCES

Altheide, David L. and Snow, Robert P. 1991. *Media worlds in the postjournalism era.* New York: Aldine de Gruyter.

Arnheim, Rudolf. 1967. *Visual thinking.* Berkeley, Calif.: University of California Press.

Benjamin, Walter. 1969. The work of art in the age of mechanical reason. In *Illuminations.* Trans. by Harry Zohn. New York: Schocken Books.

Boorstin, Daniel J. 1961. *The image.* New York: Harper & Row.

Carpenter, Edmund and McLuhan, Marshall, eds. 1960. *Explorations in communication.* Boston: Beacon Press.

Chesler, Phyllis. 1978. *About men.* New York: Simon & Schuster.

Faludi, Susan. 1991. *Backlash: The undeclared war against American women.* New York: Crown Publishers.

Fenster, Mark. 1991. The problem of taste within the problematic of culture. *Communication Theory* 1 (2): 87–105.

Fiske, John and Hartley, John. 1978. *Reading television.* London and New York: Methuen.

Gabriel, Michael R. 1990. The astonishing growth of small publishers 1958–1988. *Journal of Popular Culture* 24 (3): 61–68.

Gregory, Richard L. 1974. *Eye and brain: The psychology of seeing.* 2nd ed. New York: McGraw-Hill.

Haskell, Molly. 1973. *From reverence to rape: The treatment of women in the movies.* New York: Holt, Rinehart, and Winston.

Hunt, Morton. 1982. *The universe within.* New York: Simon & Schuster.

Jhally, Sut and Lewis, Justin. 1992. *Enlightened racism.* Boulder, Colo.: Westview.

Kaminsky, Stuart M. with Mahan, Jeffrey H. 1985. *American television genres.* Chicago: Nelson-Hall.

Kraft, Robert N., Cantor, Phillip, and Gottdiener, Charles. 1991. The coherence of visual narratives. *Communication Research* 18: 599.

Lasswell, Harold D. 1948. The structure and function of communication in society. In *The communication of ideas,* ed. Lyman Bryson. New York: Harper & Row.

Lewis, Justin. 1991. *The ideological octopus.* New York: Routledge.

Meyerle, Judine. 1991. *Roseanne*—How did you get inside my house? A case study of a hit blue-collar situation comedy. *Journal of Popular Culture* 24 (4): 71–88.

Monaco, James. 1981. *How to read a film.* Rev. ed. New York: Oxford University Press.

Nye, Russell B. 1971. Notes for an introduction to a discussion of popular culture. *Journal of Popular Culture* 5 (Spring): 1032–38.

Postman, Neil. 1988. *Conscientious objections.* New York: Vintage Books.

Real, Michael R. 1989. *Super media, a cultural studies approach.* Newbury Park, Calif.: Sage.

Rifkin, Jeremy. 1989. *Time wars.* New York: Simon & Schuster.

Schiller, Herbert I. 1969. *Mass communications and the American empire.* Boston: Beacon Press.

Short, Robert L. 1978. *The parables of peanuts.* Westminster, U.K.: John Knox.

United States Bureau of the Census. 1991. *Statistical abstract of the United States, 1991.* 111th Ed. Washington, D.C.

Three

Wired Systems of Communication
Telegraph and Telephone

Making Connections

The advent of wired communication technology presented a new opportunity for communication. At first, many people didn't understand how it worked, or the potential for telegraph or telephone to radically alter the way in which people communicated. As the history of wired communication indicates, telegraph and telephone were just the first in a long series of wired technologies that now include cable, closed circuit systems, and other technologies that connect through wire, cable, or optical fiber.

Some of the basic principles that underlie all forms of electronic communication technologies came from attempts to understand electrical phenomena and to channel electricity. The knowledge gained about controlling electricity in experiments with the electric light bulb became the basis for the development of other distribution forms, such as radio, telegraph, and telephone.

Telephone technology, in particular, grew because of the efforts of the industry to create "universal service"—a

Chapter

euphemism for what resulted in monopoly control over telephony in the United States. This chapter will examine the telephone industry, social practices that resulted from the new communication opportunities, and the efforts of the federal government to act responsibly toward the development of telephony. A knowledge of these areas will create a basis for understanding regulation and industrial actions in other communication industries.

This chapter explains:

- how telegraph and telephone were the first electronic communication technologies to facilitate point-to-point communication

- the basic principles behind wired communication

- how the telephone industry in the United States got its start and how its evolution progressed

- how the concept of universal access influenced the development of the telephone industry

- how the power of a monopoly influenced telecommunications business practices and regulation

- how the manufacture, structure, and use of telephony is connected to social patterns in our society

- the influence of telephony in providing precedents for other telecommunications industries

---

Can you imagine what would happen if telephone systems required one wire from your home to be connected directly to every other phone you wished to call? The spiderwebs of wires would be so complex, you'd have difficulty seeing across the street! Business offices would look like cocoons, wrapped in layers of wire extending in every direction, and undersea cables would be so thick the level of the oceans might rise! The cost of wiring one place to another would make most calls too expensive for most people. Obviously, the systems that make some of our most basic communication technologies work, like the telephone, include sophisticated hardware connections we seldom see.

From the earliest days of the development of wired communication systems the public's understanding of how the technology worked has taken second place to the industry's efforts to get people to use the services. Also important to the development of the telephone was a national economy that could support the expansion and use of these new technologies.

Both the telegraph and telephone were improvements over earlier systems for communicating over distances. Their development was enabled not only by the inventors, but also the business leaders who learned how to market and distribute the technologies in such a way as to ensure their success.

Communication Technologies in the Nineteenth-Century United States

In many ways the "communication revolution" began when it became possible to communicate over wires. There have been two bursts of activity in the development of wired communication. The first period lasted from 1844 to 1900 and involved the inventions of the telephone and the telegraph. A resurgence occurred after 1970 when cable television, enhanced telephone services, and closed-circuit systems became available. These are all discussed in subsequent chapters. Today wired and wireless technologies can be connected by new hardware patterned on the systems previously used in telephony. The resulting systems result in integration on a large scale. Integration means making physical connections among various forms of technology.

New technologies allowed people living in the United States between 1844 and 1900 to witness unprecedented growth and change. In the early 1800s most people lived and died within a 50–mile radius of where they were born. By the end of the century telegraph, telephone, and railroads had united the country and challenged traditional notions of near or far. At the same time radio and automobiles were in the experimental stages. Women were beginning to enter the workforce, and the development of the electric light extended the working day into the night. The increasing number of modes of transportation and communication allowed people to move from the country to city and later to the suburbs. Between 1870 and 1914 over 25 million immigrants came to America, bringing their own traditions, customs, and cultures to the society. America was experiencing change so quickly that any technology that would facilitate development had remarkable potential.

As with all inventions, so many people contributed to the development of the telegraph and the telephone that it is hard to identify only one inventor. Today Italians celebrate the invention of the electrical telephone by Antonio Meucci (1807–1889) who lived on Staten Island, and in Germany there is a permanent display of a telephone developed in 1860 by a schoolmaster named Philipp Reis. In the United States several amateurs were working on telephone technology, including a young immigrant salesclerk in Washington, DC, who fashioned a telephone transmitter from a child's drum, a needle, a steel dress button, and a guitar string. This young man, Emile Berliner, would someday become chief electrician for the Bell Telephone Company. He went on to develop the disc phonograph record and a method of mass-producing phonograph records (Boettinger 1977, 96).

The telegraph and telephone were not considered unique technologies when they were first being developed. Each evolved through improvements to earlier forms of wired communication. Each found uses different than those originally intended. While the telegraph was originally a means of sending business communications over distances, its success was tied to the growth of the railroads as the most viable means of coordinating time schedules and shipments of goods.

The Development of the Telegraph

Even though most people in the United States regard Samuel F. B. Morse as the father of the telegraph, many other inventors contributed to the development of this device. Morse's greatest contribution to the technology involved a system of dots and dashes (a very distinctive language) that used sound rather than writing to transmit information. Morse's contribution was to improve on the technology being developed by two British scientists, William F. Cooke and Charles Wheatstone, who had been experimenting with what they called **electrical telegraphy** (meaning distant writing) in the early 1820s.

Wheatstone and Cooke had developed a simple system using five lines with corresponding needles that could record electrical energy and cause the needles to point to a letter of the alphabet on a grid. Though their system was patented in Britain in 1837, many other inventors continued to improve on the basic technology, and liberally borrowed from the methods Cooke and Wheatstone had used.

Samuel Morse did not intend to be an inventor, but rather a painter of landscapes. In 1832 he took a sea voyage from England to the United States, and while en route had a fateful discussion with Dr. Charles Jackson about the possibility of some form of ship-to-shore communication using the Wheatstone-Cooke technology. When they arrived in the United States, Morse set out to make improvements in electrical transmission, but he did not have a final product to patent until 1840. For three years, Morse and his partner, Alfred Vail, continued to tinker with the telegraph, and in 1843 they received a $30,000 appropriation from Congress to build an experimental telegraph line between Washington, DC, and Baltimore. The Morse telegraph was patented in 1844, and the first message of Morse's improved transmitter relayed the now famous

Figure 3.1 *How the Telegraph Works.*
Morse's early telegraph (1835-1837) had a comb (a "port rule" transmitter) with "teeth" spaced at intervals that would conform to Morse's code of dots and dashes. When the comb passed beneath a contact lever (activated at one end by an operator), an electric circuit was either connected or broken, depending on the position of the lever. As pulses passed through the receiver's electromagnet, an armature deflected horizontally and, with attached pencil, scribed zig-zag marks on a moving paper tape. A later version put dots and dashes on the tape. By 1844 the port rule was replaced by a key that could be manually operated and by a receiver or register designed to emboss dots and dashes with a twin-coil magnetic armature system. Over the next decade operators learned that the armature clicks, detected by ear, provided a more practical code reading technique for longhand, or later, typing transcription. The recording mechanism was relegated to a secondary role.
Picture Source: National Museum of American History, The Smithsonian Institution.

message, "What hath God wrought."

    The speed with which the telegraph could transmit information became widely recognized when, in 1848, James Gordon Bennett of the *New York Herald* amazed readers by arranging to have Henry Clay's keynote address to the Whig

Party Convention relayed from Lexington, Kentucky to Cincinnati by riders on horseback, and then telegraphed from Cincinnati to New York. The telegraph's ability to transmit news was further extended when the Associated Press (AP) laid a transatlantic cable between England and France in 1851. During the same year, a businessman established a line from Buffalo, New York, to St. Louis, Missouri, and with other investors, formed the New York & Mississippi Valley Printing Telegraph Company, which in 1856 changed its name to the Western Union Telegraph Company.

Western Union arranged for a variety of lease options to speed the development and use of the telegraph throughout the West. By acquiring smaller telegraph companies and affiliating with the railroad companies expanding westward, Western Union became as important as the Pony Express in transmitting information across the country. It was also very important to the effective running of the railway, since railroad personnel could alert stations along the line about delays, types of shipments, or other relevant information. When the spikes were driven into the last tie completing the first transcontinental railroad in 1861, the news was telegraphed all over the country.

Though it seems odd to think of the United States 150 years ago as a country with no standardized time zones, the reality was that local communities could set up their own systems of time. In 1870 a passenger traveling from Washington to San Francisco would need to reset his or her watch over two hundred times to reflect the various times established by local communities along the way. Until the railroads developed some means of communicating with depots along the route, it was difficult for the railroads to coordinate their schedules. The standardization of time zones in the United States did not occur until 1884, and when it did, the telegraph did much to help coordinate the zones and train traffic.

The first industries to use the telegraph were railroads, newspapers, and big business interests like banks and financial institutions. Some of the news and information in newspapers was transmitted by telegraph, a fact of which the average reader was generally unaware, but aside from this most people remained relatively unaffected by the technology's communicative power until Western Union began offering personal services. Then operators in rail stations could transmit important personal messages for any paying customer.

The Telephone

Several of the inventors who contributed to the development of the telephone started out with the intention of improving the telegraph so that it could transmit several signals simultaneously. In 1876 a young teacher of the deaf, Alexander Graham Bell, was working with this goal in mind, but in the course of his experiments he began to think about whether the human voice could also be transmitted over wires. Bell was the third generation in his family to

One of the most versatile inventors in history, Alexander Graham Bell, is known best for his role in developing the telephone. But he made many other valuable contributions to technology. In his later years he experimented with airplanes, helicopters, submarines, and hydrofoils. He developed the iron lung, and developed the prototype for optical fiber used in surgery. Despite his many accomplishments, he always introduced himself as "a teacher of the deaf."

Bell's interest in teaching deaf children seemed natural. His family came from Scotland, where his grandfather had been an actor who developed an intense interest in the study of elocution. Bell's father followed his own father's interests and began to study the organs of speech. When he married a deaf woman who later became Alexander Bell's mother ("Graham" was added when the child was eleven), Alexander's father developed a system of "visible speech" to help the deaf learn how to make speech sounds. Years later, George Bernard Shaw modeled Professor Henry Higgins of *Pygmalion* on Melville Bell, Alexander's father.

At the age of 17 "Alec" began to work as a teacher at a boys' school in his native Scotland. It was there he began studying the phenomenon of sound.

In 1870 the Bell family moved to Newfoundland, and a year later, Alec presented a number of lectures for his father at Boston's School for the Deaf. His theatrical manner and impressive performance gained him other speaking engagements throughout New England.

At the age of 25 he set up a "School of Vocal Physiology" in Boston, where his students included the son of George Sanders and the daughter of Gardiner Hubbard. Both men would later play a role in the development of telephony. Gardiner Hubbard's daughter Mabel would eventually become Mrs. Bell.

Bell engaged in the study of the physiology of the ear and became interested in Elisha Gray's experiments with what was called the "harmonic telegraph,"— a technology that used sound waves to transmit telegraph messages. In the process Bell realized he was too limited in his understanding of electricity to fully grasp the finer points of electrical energy. His encounter with electrician Thomas A. Watson led to one of the most fortuitous collaborations in the history of science.

Bell's interest in the telephone lasted until the new technology began to become popular; at which point he turned his business interests over to Hubbard and Watson. Despite litigation over the telephone patents and other legal problems with his inventions, Bell earned $3,000 a year from his interests in the Bell Company until 1880. As the company began to grow, his stock in the company rose and he and his family became wealthy.

Box 3.1

Alexander Graham Bell (1847–1922)

Though he was discreet in public, he was occasionally given to grandiose claims about his inventions. He also was a person who fought passionately for his beliefs. When his black assistant of 35 years, Charles Thompson, was refused rooms at a hotel in Nova Scotia, Bell organized a public protest and later gave a public interview in the United States to protest racial injustice.

Bell's desire to bring the handicapped into mainstream society remained one of his chief ambitions, but he had other interests as well. In 1912 he started the first Montessori Schools in Canada (during the summer) and in the United States (in the fall), both at his homes. When he became a regent of the Smithsonian Institution he organized and subsidized the scholarly journal *Science*. After becoming president of the nearly defunct National Geographic Society in 1897 he started the *National Geographic Magazine*.

When he died from complications of diabetes at the age of 75, all telephone service in the United States was stopped for one minute in his honor. His wife Mabel died five months later.

Source: H.M. Boettinger. *The Telephone Book* (Croton-on-Hudson, New York: The Riverwood Publishers, 1977).

become a professor of speech, specializing in the problems of the deaf. His mother was deaf, and his father had been very successful in devising a written language that could help teach deaf people to speak.

The 24-year-old Alexander Graham Bell reasoned that if the telegraph worked by making and breaking a continuous electrical current, perhaps sound waves could be used to break the continuous ebb and flow in the strength of the current. If successful, the new device would be able to transmit speech over distances through the same type of wire the telegraph used.

Bell's "harmonic telegraph," as he called it, intrigued Gardiner Hubbard and Thomas Sanders, who attempted to get financing for the invention. The two entrepreneurs were unsure of their investment, but Bell was so confident in his invention that he applied for a patent before completing it. His patent for the "Improvement in Transmitters and Receivers of Electrical Energy" was granted on February 27, 1875. Another inventor, Elisha Gray, arrived at the patent office three hours later, only to find that the application for **variable resistance** (the alteration of energy by means of a transducer) had been claimed.

Still, because Gray's patent differed slightly, he was able to file a caveat with the patent office, meaning that he could continue to improve his invention because the final result promised to be significantly different from Bell's device. (See box on Elisha Gray.) Bell then filed for another patent,

Figure 3.2 *A Simulation of Bell Speaking into the Centennial Phone, 1876.*
The person in the picture is actually an actor made up to look like Bell for a Hollywood movie on the invention of the telephone.
Picture Source: AT&T Archives

"Improvements in Telegraphy" (granted March 7, 1876), and later, on June 6, a patent for "Telephonic Telegraph Receivers." The three patents gave Bell the edge on a telephone that could modulate energy, control vocal tone, and boost the sound enough for the signal to be heard by the human ear. All three of these patents improved the telephone to the point where the sound was strong and relatively stable.

On August 1, 1877, Hubbard, Sanders, and Bell formed the Bell Telephone Company, with one employee, Thomas A. Watson. At the time only 778 telephones were actually in use (Brown 1991, 66).

When Bell's telephone debuted at the Centennial Exposition in Philadelphia in 1876 (see figure 3.2), it attracted little attention. Many people were still laughing at the claim made by some that the telegraph was responsible for spreading a recent cholera epidemic. Despite the lack of interest by investors and society's failure to accept the telephone, Gardiner Hubbard was undaunted. With little prospect of finding new investors, Hubbard approached the railroad magnate Chauncey M. Depew, asking that he invest $10,000 in the telephone business. But Depew followed the advice of a friend associated with Western Union and declined the offer, convinced that if there were to be a better means of communication, it would be developed by Western Union. Hubbard's offer to sell Bell's telephone to Western Union for the sum of $100,000 was laughingly dismissed.

One problem to overcome was the high price of the telephone. Many people, not yet realizing the potential of the telephone to make life easier, or lacking confidence in the reliability of service, were not enthusiastic about purchasing a telephone. Hubbard came up with the idea of renting telephone receivers, and by spring of 1878, the Bell Company established the New England Telephone Company and started leasing telephone receivers for $20 a pair.[1] The first customers were banks and businesses in the Boston area. Soon Hubbard and other promoters began to advertise and market the telephone as a status symbol and a sign of American technological advancement, and Bell, an excellent and flamboyant speaker, often gave demonstrations for the public with the help of his assistant, Thomas A. Watson (see box 3.3).

In the summer of the same year, Bell married Mabel Hubbard. While the two were on their honeymoon in London, the Bells were guests of Sir William Thomson, who would some day head the Thomson Electronics empire. Thomson introduced them to Queen Victoria and arranged for a demonstration of the telephone. Soon thereafter a wire was strung through Windsor Castle connecting the Princess of Wales' private apartments with her children's nurseries, and the utility of the telephone began to be recognized by visiting royalty from other countries as well as other wealthy individuals.

Back in the United States, Western Union became increasingly interested in the attention the telephone was receiving. In the fall of 1877, it acquired a company called The Gold and Stock Telegraph Company, which had the rights to another inventor's telephone patents and the pending patent of Elisha Gray. By the following spring Western Union had purchased a telephone transmitter developed by Thomas Edison which was superior to any Bell had developed. It then started building the components to offer its own telephone system in competition with Bell's. But since Western Union gained control of telephone technologies that were in some ways superior to Bell's, why did Western Union's bid to become a telephone company fail?

The answer lies in large part with the business acumen of Theodore Vail, who was hired by Gardiner Hubbard to provide professional management and form a company that would extend the use of Bell's telephone. Vail had been

---

[1]*The New England Telephone Company, established in 1878 by the Bell Telephone Company, is not now, and has never been, associated with the New England Telephone and Telegraph Company now providing local service to the Northeastern part of the United States.*

Box 3.2

Elisha Gray

(1835–1901)

When Alexander Graham Bell filed his first patent for the telephone, Elisha Gray was considered the foremost electrician in America; a considerable achievement, since Gray's life had not been an easy one. Before Gray completed his early education, his father, a man of modest means, died, and he attempted to become a blacksmith. He soon learned that he was not strong enough for the work, and turned his energies toward carpentry and boat-building. A professor at Oberlin College encouraged him to attend school, and Elisha entered Oberlin at the age of 22, working as a carpenter to pay his way. He worked so hard that by the time he completed his studies in electrical engineering, his health was too poor for him to go back to work for another five years.

After he began working again he quickly invented several devices to improve and enhance the telegraph. In 1872 he moved to Chicago and, along with a colleague, E. M. Barton, organized the firm of Gray & Barton, which would later become the Western Electric company.

In 1875 Gray obtained two patents to improve the transmission of musical tones over telegraph wires, and he began to develop an idea for transmitting vocal sounds. When he arrived at the United States Patent Office on February 14, 1876, to file a caveat (a confidential report of an invention not fully perfected), he found that Bell had filed a patent for a speaking telephone hours earlier.

A long and bitter patent infringement battle ensued, involving accusations of malpractice within the Patent Office and outside. In the end, Bell's patent was sustained, and Gray never fully recovered from the disappointment. He made considerable sums of money from some of his other inventions, but invested most of it in his own research.

One of Gray's most notable inventions was the telautograph, patented in 1888, and improved in 1891. This machine transferred handwritten messages by telegraph lines over distances as long as 250 miles. It could be argued that Elisha Gray was the grandfather of the fax machine.

Source: A. Johnson and D. Malone, eds. *Dictionary of American Biography* (New York: Charles Scribner's & Sons, 1931) 514.

superintendent of the Post Office's Railway Mail Service, earning the impressive sum of $4,500 a year. Thomas A. Watson, Bell's assistant, had heard about Vail's work and recommended that Hubbard hire him as a general manager. Seeing the opportunity ahead of him, Vail accepted Hubbard's offer of a salary of $2,500 a year, with a $1,000 bonus if he performed well (Boettinger 1977, 96).

Known as one of the great assistants of all time, Thomas A. Watson was an electrical genius in his own right, and a man hungry for education and new experiences. In 1872 he was working in the electrical shop of Charles Williams, Jr., in Boston, where many inventors had their models constructed. In 1874, Watson performed some work for Alexander Graham Bell, and soon he was working full-time as Bell's assistant. He brought his technical ability to enhance Bell's imagination, and served as both the speaker and the listener during various experiments.

During the many demonstrations of the telephone, Watson sang into a telephone receiver for reception by listeners in another room. His voice was continually hoarse from all of the shouting he had done during experiments with the telephone, but he still received requests for encores. Complaints from Watson and Bell's landlady about noise prodded Watson to develop the first telephone booth.

After Bell left on his honeymoon, Watson helped Hubbard establish the Bell Telephone Company, and he applied himself to procuring the components necessary to manufacture telephones and searching for talented electricians to do research for Bell Labs.

In 1881, Watson resigned from the company, married, and started a machine shop to build engines and ships. He became interested in the lives of shipbuilders, and became involved in politics and public education, where he worked for better social conditions for laborers and their families.

When he was 40, both he and his wife entered the Massachusetts Institute of Technology (MIT) to study geology and literature. Watson became well known among scientific and literary circles, spent a season acting at the Stratford-on-Avon Shakespeare Festival in Canada, and in later life became a student of music and painting.

Source: Boettinger, *The Telephone Book,* and Johnson and Malone, *Dictionary of American Biography,* 548–49.

Box 3.3

Thomas A.

Watson

(1854–1934)

Between 1878 and 1879 the Bell Company began to grow. Emile Berliner was hired as an electrician, and he brought a transmitter he had developed that was equal or superior to Western Union's Edison model. Additionally, Berliner, Watson, and a growing cadre of young electricians developed the first switchboard, which eliminated the necessity for the single wire that had been necessary to connect each telephone. Exchanges were established. These were locations where telephone switches could be manually plugged into larger systems, thereby reducing the number of wires permanently connected. Switchboard operators were hired to make the physical connections. By 1879 Theodore Vail had mapped out a strategy to expand telephone service throughout the United States, and had embarked on a plan to create "universal service"—guaranteeing access to all. This plan involved hiring people knowledgeable about running complex organizations. Hubbard and Sanders stepped down, and the National Bell Telephone Company was established to consolidate the New England Telephone Company and the Bell Company. Vail became the Chief Operating Officer.

In November 1880 National Bell sued Western Union for infringement of its patents, claiming that Edison's transmitter (patented after Bell's) had really been modeled on the same principle and had infringed on Bell's patent. Before a court decision was reached, Western Union decided to settle and agreed to sell all of its emerging telephone systems, totaling about 56,000 phones in 55 cities, to National Bell. In return, National Bell agreed to stay away from the telegraph business, and to pay Western Union 20 percent of its royalties due under former licensing agreements which it had been holding. The most significant result of the decision was that telegraph was relegated to long-distance communication while telephone had a monopoly on local service. The new name for the service was the American Bell Telephone Company. It was chartered for operation in the Commonwealth of Massachusetts.

By 1881 only nine cities in the United States with more than 10,000 inhabitants lacked the facilities to connect with other telephones. It took many more years to extend service to homes and businesses within certain localities, but most communities had an exchange that allowed telephone connections to other localities. The Bell Company also introduced pay phones for public convenience. By the end of 1892 the Bell Company had about 10,000 employees working to service approximately 240,000 telephones in various exchanges.

As average citizens became more familiar with the telephone they found more uses for it. Telephones were installed in mines so that miners could communicate problems and progress. Neighbors in communities used their party lines to facilitate group discussions among households. Some regions and towns filled telephone lines with phonograph recordings or live music, oblivious of the need or desire someone might have to make a call elsewhere. Violin music was favored for this purpose, being well-suited to the frequencies used in telephony. People began talking about the possible uses of the telephone and the demand for service grew so rapidly that several independent companies began to set up their own telephone systems in an effort to compete with the Bell Company's services, but all remained too small to challenge the giant that was emerging.

Under Theodore Vail's guidance, the Bell Company grew steadily from 1880 until 1883. In 1885 the company again changed names; it became the

---

Box 3.4   Instructions for Telephone Use from
The New York Telephone Company

After speaking, transfer the telephone from the mouth to the ear very promptly. When replying to a communication from another, do not speak too promptly, give your correspondent time to transfer, as much trouble ensues from both parties speaking at the same time. When you are not speaking, you should be listening.

Subscribers should bear in mind that on a telephone line they are within the possible hearing of a number of ladies and gentlemen. We ask all to be courteous.

Source: Marion May Dilts, *The Telephone in a Changing World* (New York: Longmans, Green, and Co., 1941), 15.

American Telephone and Telegraph Company (AT&T). Under the new name the company was chartered for the purpose of providing long distance service in the United States, coordinating the operations of local telephone services affiliated with what had been called the American Bell Company, and coordinating services with the independent phone companies. The company's charter was in the state of New York, where rules about corporate operations were far less restrictive than in Massachusetts.

The new charter allowed the Bell Companies to buy as many independent telephone services as possible, but competition continued into the early 1900s. In an effort to spread service quickly, AT&T franchised regional operating companies who were given exclusive rights to the use of Bell patents. By this time the company had obtained control of Western Electric and a number of subsidiary telephone companies that became known as the Bell Operating Companies.

In 1909 Theodore Vail bought 30 percent of Western Union. This gave AT&T tremendous power to regulate service and pricing all over the country.

The independent telephone companies were understandably worried about the power of AT&T. Through their national association, they approached the United States Department of Justice, who, in turn, filed an anti-trust suit against AT&T for acting in a manner that would restrict interstate trade. AT&T agreed to divest its Western Union holdings and acquire no more independent companies. The result then, was the first divestiture of AT&T in 1913.

Figure 3.3   *Dr. Jekyll and Mr. Hyde.*

When the United States entered World War I in 1917, the need for national and international communication increased. AT&T had purchased the Audion, a successful energy booster which gave AT&T telephones supremacy in long distance services by improving the sound quality of long distance calls. The Audion proved to be essential for stabilizing the level of energy for effective transmission. By an act of Congress in 1918, AT&T and the independent telephone companies were put under government control to ensure that communication channels would not be seized by the enemy. The companies were returned to their owners a year later. During the period of government control, however, telephone service grew enough to require the development of sophisticated switching systems that could handle the increased telephone traffic.

AT&T eventually grew to become the largest company in the world, employing more people than any other firm. It is sometimes said that if we had never moved beyond the system that required an operator to make a connection by pushing a plug into a switchboard, every person in the United States could be working for the telephone company switching the phone calls of the world. Instead, computers now do most of the work.

Telephone's Early Effects on Society

The telephone changed more than just the way people communicate. It facilitated new jobs and changes in social status. Perhaps one of its most significant effects was to increase the role of women in the work force.

Though the first telephone operators were boys who had been telegraph operators (usually no older than 13), their youth often impeded their ability to speak in the professional manner that was encouraged by telephone promoters. The idea of trying young women as operators dawned on the managers of the New England Bell Telephone Company and the New York Telephone Company almost simultaneously. Thus, New England Bell claimed that Emma Nutt held the distinction of the first female operator, while New York Bell claimed that honor for Margaret Kennedy. It was decided that the female voice and style of communication would be well-suited to the new technology and to the new style of doing business brought about by the telephone. It was difficult at first to get young women to be telephone operators because it was considered improper for women to work outside the home, and particularly in an office where they could come into contact with men. The story goes that office managers went to the homes of soft-voiced young women to persuade them and their parents that it was alright for them to work. Women and their parents were promised protection by the managers, who also assured that the women would be given directions in manner and appropriate style. Carolyn Marvin (1988) has written:

> The telephone girl was generally not so fragile, and more often depicted as a woman of ambiguous social status. Though frequently in need of protection from predatory males, she was also bound to be at their mercy by the service nature of her work. On the other hand, she was independently employed, saucy in her pursuit of the slightly racy recreations of the young and unobligated, and possessor of a free-floating social identity that was particularly suspicious in women.

These new working women held an ambiguous status in the office, but the social hierarchy was undisturbed because they did not contribute to the running of the business but merely facilitated the men's talk. Although the telephone increased women's presence in the workplace, it also relegated their type of work to that of low pay and relatively little status.

Telephones in the home also changed the lives of women by replacing the need to seek interpersonal contact outside of the house. Instead of conversing at the market or paying a social call, women could stay home and speak with friends on the telephone. Often the presence of the telephone tied women to the home, exacerbating their loneliness and isolation (Rakow, 1988). Social discourse by means of the telephone did not fit the male principles of brevity and efficiency in the workplace, and has since given rise to many negative stereotypes about women's use of the telephone for long conversations.

How the Telephone Works

The principle behind telephony is the notion that when people speak, the sound that emerges resembles analog waves (see figure 3.4). When you inhale, you push a muscle in your abdomen, called the diaphragm, down. As you begin to speak the diaphragm starts to return to its normal curved shape, while energy in the form of flowing air moves over your vocal chords and comes out in sound waves.

Vocal chords are like transducers in that they vibrate, breaking the stream of energy. A transducer regulates and breaks the speed of sound waves so that they can be modulated into different sounds. The air energized by your breathing apparatus is modulated by the tongue, lips, and teeth into recognizable sounds.

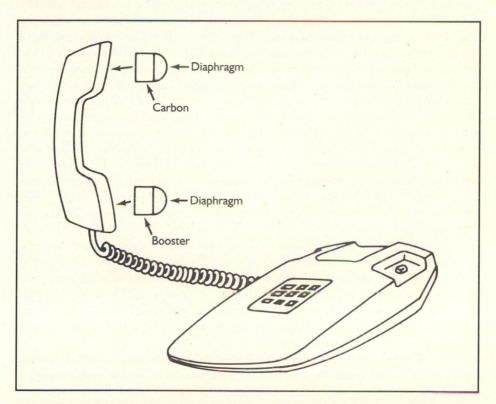

Figure 3.4 *How the Telephone Works. When someone speaks into the mouthpiece of the telephone, a diaphragm passes the energy to carbon elements, which convert the speech to electrical energy. The signal is carried through the telephone to a **multiplexer** (a system that allows several calls to be transmitted over the same wire). Various switching points route the signal to its destination, where the sound is boosted in the telephone earpiece and reconverted to sound energy through another diaphragm.*

Bell's three patents improved a system of carbon elements and a diaphragm that could successfully translate the analog waves of speech into electricity, and boosted the sound to a level that could be heard. Carbon translates analog speech waves into electrical energy. As an efficient conductor of electricity; carbon mediates the electrical energy so the sound of a voice is captured and transmitted reliably. By transferring electricity from one form (speech) to electrical energy, the entire system operates more efficiently. The diaphragm acts as the coder of electronic information in the mouthpiece and the decoder at the receiving end in the earpiece.

Connecting Telephones

The very simplest form of sending a signal from one place to another via telephone wires can be likened to the game we all played as children in which we would take two paper cups and attach them with a string. The simple bottom of a cup reverberated like a diaphragm as you spoke into it, and the energy in the form of analog waves traveled down the vibrating string and was then boosted by the other diaphragm, or bottom of the second cup. This makes a simple "dedicated wire" system, meaning one wire connects only two receivers, but cannot facilitate calls to any additional receiver. Dedicated wires are used today for very important purposes like governmental hot lines or when there is no need for excess outside dialing of a telephone. A dedicated wire has only one place to go. Obviously, having a system composed entirely of dedicated wires would not be very cost efficient nor would it be very successful. The cables that are commonly used for telephone service contain 1,200 pairs of copper wires and have the capacity to transmit 14,400 phone conversations at once (Geller 1991, 10).

The simple switching systems that developed as telephones spread throughout the United States can be seen in old films. A switchboard operator sitting at a big board plugging one call into another call is physically making a connection between one set of wires and another. Soon phone service between different areas was linked mechanically by a **trunkline** that could make connections mechanically rather than by the operator's hand. The trunk system could process several different calls simultaneously.

The next invention was called the Public Branch Exchange (PBX). It took phone calls and boosted their energy to a higher level so that one exchange could interact with another mechanically. When the Public Branch Exchange system was introduced in the 1960s in the United States calls began to be routed by area codes. If you wanted to go outside your local trunk line you would dial an area code, which would send the signal immediately on to the PBX where it could be sorted and routed from one exchange to another. While PBX was a wonderful technology, the rapidly growing number of phones in the United States was taxing the capability of even this work-horse switching system.

Soon it was necessary to come up with yet a faster operation. The result was the **Extra Public Branch Exchange (EPBX)**, which is the system most in use today. The key to this technology was a shift from the old mechanical form of processing information to a new electronic one, which was faster, more precise, and less costly.

The cost of making a telephone call is tied to the number of **access points** necessary to complete a call. Every time a message transfers from one switching system to another the cost of the call goes up because it passes another access point. When you dial outside your own area code, you have to access another area code. When doing this you go from one exchange to another, which raises the cost because you must access another exchange.

Telephone rates paid by businesses subsidize home consumer charges. But the cost of home telephone service goes up as people use it for a greater variety of purposes, such as sending faxes and accessing computer data bases through

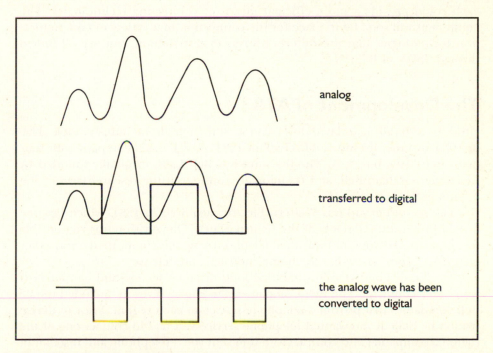

Figure 3.5 *Analog to Digital.*
When an analog wave is converted to a digital wave, the wave itself is converted to a numeral equivalent; when the digital information is "packaged" each "top" and "bottom" of the signal is given equal size, but the mathematical information stored in each wave—now called a bit—*has a range that can be mathematically decoded.*

a modem. These services increase the number of access points that must be passed. Competing long-distance companies provide some alleviation of rising costs when they offer discounts when calls are made at certain times of the day or night. These are offered as enticements to use services at times when business demand is low.

The most sophisticated form of switching is through Integrated Services Digital Networks (ISDN). This system is likely to be in use by the mid-1990s, and will create global networks capable of sending and receiving all kinds of different signals, such as telephone, telex, computer, fax, videotex, and full motion video (Singh 1991, 3). ISDN will have the capability to convert analog waves to digital codes so that signals can be sent through cables, optical fibers, or satellites. Its effectiveness will be measured by the number of simultaneous messages transmitted and the speed of the signal completion.

A variation of ISDN is Broadband ISDN (B-ISDN), which uses optical fibers bundled into larger systems to transmit information, and promises to be effective in non-broadcast communication systems. With ISDN and B-ISDN, history repeats itself. Both switching systems are being developed simultaneously, and each could provide a more efficient means of connecting technologies. The equipment will soon be in place for the connection of a variety of communication technologies that use different forms of distribution, but are all linked through ISDN or B-ISDN.

The Development of AT&T

Until the federally mandated deregulation of the telephone industry took place in 1983 and the divestiture of AT&T in 1984, AT&T was a company with four main units (see box 3.5). The first unit was Bell Labs, originally founded by Alexander Graham Bell, and traditionally considered the research arm of the organization.

The second group was Western Electric, acquired in 1881, which became one of the industrial giants of the United States. This division was responsible for the manufacturing of individual telephones, system components, and other electronic products used in the home, industry, and defense.

The Long Lines Division handled long distance service and connections with other countries. The Bell Companies, the largest division, included the 22 Bell companies that provided telephone service to each region. Prior to **deregulation** in 1983, if you wanted telephone service you had to contact one of the regional companies and contract with it to rent you a telephone and install it in your home. The regional company would take care of billing and the integrated components of completing your calls.

Each one of these 22 companies had intrastate facilities, interstate facilities, international components, and certain exchange services.

Box 3.5   AT&T Divisions Before and After Deregulation and Divestiture

Two Structures of AT&T

BEFORE 1983 DEREGULATION

AT&T Headquarters
Bell Labs
Long Lines
Western Electric
22 Bell Companies

AFTER 1984 DEREGULATION

AT&T Headquarters
AT&T Bell Labs
AT&T Communications
AT&T Western Electric
AT&T Information Systems
AT&T Share Owner Services
AT&T International

AFTER 1984 DIVESTITURE

Divested Regional Operating Companies:
NYNEX - New England, New York
US West

AMERITECH
Bell Atlantic

PACTEL
Southwestern Bell
Bell South

AT&T had been allowed to grow as a monopoly because the U.S. government, coming out of the Great Depression, felt that any competition to the emerging system would be detrimental to the consuming public.

Inventions at Bell Labs

Before the establishment of AT&T, Alexander Graham Bell was considered the company's primary electrician and earned a salary of $300 a month. Though

Bell had a financial interest in the new Bell Company, he spent much of his time experimenting with other technologies such as deep sea diving helmets, submarines, and flying machines. For the most part, he had little to do with technologies that directly affected the development of the telephone.

Thomas Watson was primarily responsible for the development of the telephone into a public convenience. For a salary of three dollars per day, (and later, a share in the profits of the Bell Telephone Company) Watson initiated the developments necessary to market and improve the telephone and its related systems, such as long distance service.

Earlier, while Alexander Graham Bell was studying how to use the telephone for sound transmission, he developed the Induction Balance, an optical probe that improved the ability of surgeons to explore the human body. The probe was effectively demonstrated in 1881 when President James A. Garfield was shot. Bell was immediately contacted and rushed to Washington D.C., where he used the probe to locate the bullet in Garfield's body. Unfortunately, it took so long for Bell to reach Washington that the President died before the bullet could be located and surgically removed. Bell was awarded an honorary M.D. degree from Heidelberg University for his development of this important medical tool.

Figure 3.6 *Bell's Picture Sent by Phototelegraphy, 1925.*
Picture Source: AT&T Archives

The photophone, a predecessor of light wave communication, was patented in 1880, but there was little use for it then. It did, however, give later engineers at Bell Labs the opportunity to experiment with **phototelegraphy,** and by 1925 it was possible to send a picture image through a telephone line (see figure 3.6). The costs associated with using phototelegraphy were far too great for the average consumer, but the technology was displayed at fairs and expositions around the world, and it suggested the future direction of Bell Labs inventions. It also provided the promise of television.

As previously described, Bell's photophone used light energy to register movement. The study of basic principles of light energy as a means of communication provided the groundwork for the optical fiber technology that would be one of AT&T's primary developments in the 1980s. AT&T was seeking a replacement for copper—a finite, expensive resource used to make telephone cable. Copper cable lasts a little more than thirty years before it begins to wear and break, and must be repaired or replaced.

To create optical fibers, silicon is heated to a very high intensity, stretched as though it were taffy, and spun at the same time to the width of a strand of hair. Gravitational pull on the silicon and the force of the spinning results in a strand very much like a tiny glass tube. Digital information can be passed through the tube as quickly as the speed of light, far faster than by any mechanical or electronic means. In fact, the speed at which digital information is transmitted generates light as it passes through the optical fiber. Optical fibers have the potential for eventually eliminating the telephone wires we see outside our homes, and that mar the landscape, because they can easily be buried underground. Optical fibers, made of silicon, are flexible and more durable than copper cable, and far more reliable as conduits of electricity.

Though there are some optical fibers in use in the United States now, there have been drawbacks to their widespread use. When AT&T attempted to lay a transatlantic optical fiber cable, it found that the vibrations emitted by the optical fiber attracted sharks. Now, in addition to the difficulty of laying the optical fiber cable, the cable must be wrapped in a web of mesh so sharks do not bite through the cables.

In addition, the cost of manufacturing and installing optical fiber was not as low as originally expected. Since 1982, however, the costs have steadily declined. With the cost of material expected to decrease about five percent each year from 1990 to 1998, optical fiber is likely to provide a key transmission system before the year 2000. Since each half-inch thick optical fiber bundle will have 72 pairs of fibers, and will be capable of transmitting 3.5 million conversations (either voice or data), the eventual savings could be enormous (Geller 1991, 10).

Another powerful invention from Bell Labs was the transistor, which debuted in 1957. It utilized semi-conductors of electricity and thereby reduced the size of several components in electronic communication technologies today. The transistor became the key technology in making some types of media equipment, like radio, portable. Transistors are also key components in computers because they switch electrical energy extremely rapidly and efficiently.

A Changing Business Environment

Even though AT&T had a virtual monopoly on telephone service until 1983, different companies had tried to challenge the monopoly, and eventually won the battle for competition in telephony.

These entrepreneurs benefited by the federal government's desire for **deregulation,** or the lifting of government restrictions and regulations surrounding industries to allow for greater competition. Deregulation restricted government's involvement in the communications industry, and called for *marketplace rules* to guide industry actions.[2] These rules were thought to benefit the industries themselves by creating an environment that would encourage business cooperation, which would ultimately benefit the public through more efficient business practices.

The Carterfone Decision
The first successful challenge to the AT&T system came in the late 1960s from Thomas Carter, a businessman working in the oil fields of Texas. Because workers were constantly on the move, the only way calls could be completed was through radio contact to a central operator who would then plug the call into the phone system. The process was time consuming and created poor sound quality. Carter developed and proposed to the FCC a simple switching system that bypassed the central operator. Hand-carried portable telephones using radio waves could be connected directly with the AT&T system through Carter's device, which modulated the signal from airwaves to electrical circuits.

When the Federal Communications Commission (FCC) (the agency responsible for reviewing technical issues and recommending policies concerning communication technologies) approved Carter's invention in 1968, it set a precedent, allowing telephone units other than those manufactured by Western Electric to be joined to AT&T systems. The Carterfone Decision, as it became known, challenged the monopoly of Western Electric on the manufacturing of all telephones in the United States and introduced competition into the industry. Before the Carterfone Decision, Western Electric made only two major models of telephones; the wall phone and the desk phone. With the

---

[2]*An especially vivid description of the communications field as a marketplace can be seen in the writings of Mark S. Fowler, Chair of the FCC from 1981 to 1987. Envisioning an "open" market, where more competition was likely to occur if government stayed out of the way, Fowler used the marketplace metaphor to explain how greater competition would result from an unregulated business environment.*

advent of competition from other manufacturers, consumers soon had a choice of several models including French-style phones, Mickey Mouse phones, and other novelty phones that could be connected to AT&T lines. As might be expected, this action reduced demand on the manufacturing arm of Western Electric and AT&T began to feel the challenge to its monopoly in the telephone industry.

Deregulation   It is important to understand why the FCC, after many years of permitting AT&T to have a monopoly over telephone service, suddenly became more accommodating to greater competition in the industry. By 1970 the demand for telephone service in the United States had reached crisis proportions. People who wished to have telephone service, especially in big cities, had to wait for weeks or sometimes months to have service installed. Inflation in the 1960s had driven AT&T's costs up and reduced its profits. Rather than step up supply and take on more workers, AT&T made the decision to cut costs and stop investing in upkeep so that its profits would remain high. The quality of service declined. This business decision angered people who wanted or needed service, and public attention began to focus on AT&T's business practices.

During the early 1970s, other major industries in the United States were reeling from earlier inflation, and President Jimmy Carter advocated the deregulatory business practices that had been initiated by former Presidents Richard M. Nixon and Gerald R. Ford. Deregulation was an attempt to make conditions more hospitable to greater competition in business; it was also an acknowledgment that government should reduce its own costs as an industry "watchdog," and allow businesses to do more self-regulation. AT&T joined the airline and trucking industries in facing the challenge brought by deregulation.

The next big threat to AT&T's dominance in the telephone industry came in 1969 and was resolved in 1970 with the FCC's **MCI Decision.** Microwave Communication International (MCI) received FCC approval for an experiment that involved selling private long-distance lines to business customers in Chicago and St. Louis for communications only among those businesses that subscribed for service. MCI was originally not allowed to sell long distance services to residential customers.

By 1972 MCI was up and running as a business, and in 1973 the new MCI chairman, William McGowan, made MCI a public company. McGowan's plan was to bypass AT&T's long distance system by using a satellite for distribution of the telephone signal. When satellite transmission was shown to be as effective as the wired system, McGowan persuaded the Justice Department to allow the use of alternative carriers for telephone service.

In 1974 the United States brought an antitrust suit against AT&T, and the suit was eventually assigned to U.S. District Court Judge Harold H. Greene, who would make his place in history by ruling on the break-up of the largest company in the world. The hearings in the case of the deregulation of AT&T

lasted from 1978 to 1981 and involved a small army of attorneys. Even after the final decision was reached full compliance with the rules took several years.

Divestiture

Attorneys from the United States government and AT&T negotiated for years, proposing what could be kept or lost. At the same time they attempted to keep the largest company in the world from crumbling so quickly that it would adversely affect the economy of the United States and the quality of telephone service at home and abroad. The Consent Decree, terminating the seven-year antitrust suit, was signed on January 8, 1982. Even then, AT&T attorneys filed motions and petitions for the next 18 months in an attempt to protect the organization.

When the official date of deregulation arrived January 1, 1983, few consumers noticed any changes, but the FCC received a flurry of applications to license telephone systems. Among them were requests from such well-known companies as Sprint and GTE.

The final decision required that AT&T divest itself of its 22 local operating companies on January 1, 1984, which is referred to as the date of divestiture. The 22 operating companies would be consolidated into seven regional companies, commonly referred to as Baby Bells. These included 75 percent of AT&T's employees, and about half its revenues. The new regional companies would be allowed to provide—but not manufacture—new telephone equipment, and they would be given five years to become profit-making organizations themselves. If, after five years, they were not profitable, they would be forced to close and their business made available to other alternative companies. To help preserve their place in the field, the seven new **Regional Operating Companies** (ROCs) were allowed to keep the Yellow Pages services, which brought in about $2 billion in annual revenue. All of the ROCs have succeeded beyond original hope. Though the ROCs are restricted from manufacturing telephones, they are allowed to enter into other business fields, and many of them manufacture office products, develop new software systems, or engage in other fields of communication, like radio and television.

AT&T was allowed to maintain its research and manufacturing facilities. It could offer consumers equipment—rented or purchased—for use with other telephone systems. Though it might seem that AT&T was headed for financial ruin, it was allowed to keep any equipment or services that it had installed up until the 1983 deregulation date, and at that time, 60 percent of the homes and businesses in the United States still had AT&T equipment—the other 40 percent having changed equipment after the Carterfone Decision.

Though AT&T had to relinquish the Bell name and company logo (except for the Bell Labs division), it was allowed to enter the lucrative field of developing advanced information systems, and this area has become the largest profit component of AT&T since deregulation.

Judge Greene realized that a major change in organization for a business as complex as the telephone system would have to be carefully monitored and periodically reviewed. Every five years the deregulation of AT&T is reviewed, new evaluations of the system and services made, and **Modified Final Judgments** (MFJs) to the Consent Decree are considered.

At first, AT&T lost few subscribers to the new companies. One reason was that the other phone companies operated digitally and required push-button phones. At the time of deregulation, 70 percent of the telephones used in the United States were Western Electric rotary phones.

AT&T had EPBX switching systems to convert rotary/analog phone messages to digital modes for satellite distribution, but other providers lacked the large infrastructure needed. A cooperative system between the alternative phone company and the Bell Regional Operating Company (ROC) had to be arranged to organize billing. In the first few years after the deregulation and divestiture, individuals using alternative companies for long-distance service had to dial several numbers just to access the alternative company. AT&T long-distance service could be accessed by simply dialing "1." Therefore, AT&T maintained a strong competitive advantage over the other companies, at least in residential service.

Changes Since Deregulation

The changes for home telephone consumers since deregulation are obvious when you establish phone service in a new location. Purchasing a telephone, deciding which long-distance carrier to subscribe to, and what "package" of caller options to buy are all new decisions to be made since deregulation.

For residents in many communities, arranging for service when something goes wrong can be a time consuming and costly project. In many communities local telephone companies no longer service wired systems from the point of the outside **multiplexer** to the home unit, as they once did when local companies assumed responsibility for home service. As the companies streamline their activities, they leave the least profitable areas to independent vendors.

On the other hand, buildings now are often outfitted with plug-in receptacles so that a resident may establish service before moving in, rather than having to wait for a telephone installer to make the physical connection.

The major effects of deregulation have to do with the number of services the telephone companies can legally operate. Many of these are the results of further advancements in technology and services, some of which may soon affect the home consumer.

Personal choices and privacy issues
Today we have to decide what kind of telephone service we really want, and how much privacy we are willing to risk

when considering our telephone needs. Do we want a certain type of long distance carrier? Do we want certain features such as call forwarding, call waiting, or voice mail? While we can attach our own telephone answering machines to most telephones, there are now combination telephone/voice mail instruments.

There has been a rapid rise in deregulation, not only in the United States but increasingly throughout the world. Added-on technologies such as telefacsimile (fax) and telex machines, which combine telegraph-like messages with teletype services, use traditional telephone wires or the increasingly more common optical fibers. All can use a system of billing that records minutes and seconds.

New technology and services
One of the most important recent changes in the telephone distribution system has been brought about by the use of optical fibers instead of copper cables. Because fiber has a much greater capacity, the newer transmission system may be capable of bringing much more than telephone service to a home or business.

In 1992, Judge Greene's Modified Final Judgment raised the possibility of the seven Bell Regional operating companies competing in the area of video distribution. Instead of having a special cable laid for television, customers could have both television and telephone service delivered through the same optical fiber (regular telephone cable does not have the capacity for video signals). The diversified ROCs and alternative telephone companies (all called **telcos**) allowed to compete in different information services welcome the opportunity to engage in additional information services such as value-added services, which may include picturephone. On February 9, 1993, Southwestern Bell was the first telco to purchase a cable company to enter the information delivery market (see discussion in chapter 7).

Video dial tone
On July 16, 1992, the FCC approved the option for telephone companies to transmit television programming through a service called **video dial tone.** While the procedure will not be practical until more optical fiber links are installed, the FCC decision paved the way for telephone companies to deliver a broad array of video services, such as movie channels, home shopping, and interactive educational services. The phone companies will be allowed to package their programs and own up to five percent of the programming service, but they may not yet engage in producing their own programs for distribution (Andrews 1992, D5).

Under the new system, all telephone companies (telcos), including the Regional Operating Companies, MCI, Sprint, and others, will act as **common carriers**—distributors of programming created by other companies. The telcos themselves may institute systems called video gateways. These act as on-screen menus, and may also be able to aid the companies in billing and collection of fees paid for video services distributed.

The controversial video dial tone approval has worried cable companies and broadcasters who fear greater erosion of their audience by yet another form of competition for viewers. As the controversy develops and the FCC continues to work toward lifting earlier regulations on all communication companies, it is likely that video dial tone will be further defined before it is available on a wide scale.

Value-added services   Other types of service telephone companies may now provide are sometimes called *value-added services*. In most regions there are 1–900–XXX–XXXX or 1–976–XXX–XXXX numbers you can call to find out about a wide variety of information and entertainment programs. Some of these can provide you with a wake up call in your home, job listings, or apartment listings. Other information like horoscopes, weather, jokes, or traffic conditions can be located by dialing a special number. Phone companies charge a rate higher than a local or long distance call for these services.

One of the most controversial new services is "caller ID," which allows telephone customers to identify the telephone numbers and sometimes the names of incoming callers. Various forms of caller ID have been available in some regions since 1987. These often allow customers to choose from a number of different services, including the blocking of calls from certain numbers, special ringing sounds that identify certain calls, or the tracing of incoming calls.

While the benefits of the service are obvious, the service also permits several negative possibilities, such as privacy invasion and abuses of the system. Despite benefits of seeing the calling number of a harassing caller or someone in need of help, the service publicizes the use of phones so that the presence of a caller in the home can be detected. One of the most obvious problems occurs when companies record the phone numbers of incoming calls and then use those numbers to develop client lists. Sometimes these lists are sold to other firms and the home customer is then inundated with telemarketing pitches (Sponseller 1990, 56). So far, the uses and abuses of caller ID have preceded the establishment of laws or regulations to govern its use.

Telephones and People

Today, 93.3 percent of the homes in the United States have access to at least one telephone (United States Bureau of the Census 1991, 556). Though most people still think of the telephone as a way of extending oral communication, the telephone now also provides a means for connecting other forms of technology and adding new services for both the home and the workplace.

By attaching a simple **modem,** a device that can transfer analog signals to digital signals and vice versa, the telephone line can perform a variety of tasks, including transferring computer data, accessing various information banks, or hooking households and businesses to security systems. As optical fibers replace copper cables, we may find ourselves using the familiar telephone jack as the source for an impressive amount of information, including video signals and other specialized services. When this happens, the telephone system will become an even more important part of how we communicate and how we locate information. These changes show how far telephony has developed since deregulation, but they also suggest changes in the telephone company's business practices.

From the early days of telephone service until the 1970s, most people had their telephone numbers listed in the phone book, or with Directory Assistance. The Bell companies themselves took care of listing everyone in the telephone book. If you didn't want your name listed for personal reasons it was very simple—the phone company would just delete your name. As more people decided not to list their names and addresses in the telephone book for reasons of privacy, the phone companies realized that it would be more lucrative to charge people for having *unlisted* numbers.

The right to service   When telephones first became popular in the United States, most people regarded them as a luxury. Soon, however, they were classified as a necessity. Theodore Vail's program for creating "universal service" has survived the marketing and distribution phases, and has now been taken over by Congress and the FCC, which have mandated that telecommunications services should be made available to as many people as possible.

In recent years, the United States Congress has attempted to determine whether telephone service should be considered a necessity or a luxury in today's world. Though they have yet to resolve the issue, the outcome of their deliberations may affect the cost of service for residential customers. The desire for universal service is also related to the idea of access. A dominant value in U.S. society is that everyone should be able to make use of technological improvements. If Congress decides that telephone service is a necessity, there may be federal or local programs to determine whether those with special needs, such as low-income individuals or the elderly who are on fixed incomes, would get cost reductions in service. The cost of these calls might be underwritten by higher charges to businesses or other residential customers.

The problems of universal service may be easily solved if the number of technologies and services continues to multiply, but only if the costs are kept low enough so that people who cannot afford premium rates still have access to them. This could either foster a multi-tiered payment scale, or could result in capping the profits any company attempts to create through higher charges to consumers. The regulatory problems in bringing about universal service are inseparable from the social issues and the economic ones.

CONCLUSION

Perhaps nowhere in this book can the significance of the word "connections" be more clearly seen than in our examination of the telephone industry. Not only do telephones rely on the physical connections necessary to complete calls, but the growth of the telephone industry has been connected to social conditions and changes, and to the advent of ever-more-complex new technologies.

The unrestricted growth of the telephone business as a monopoly in the United States allowed telephone technology to reach both business and residential customers with virtually the same services. Key decisions by the Congress, the FCC, and the communications industry were always made with the assumption that service would be extended to as many people as possible. In the early phase of telephone history this argument was used as a rationale for creating a monopoly, but more recently it has been used to break up the monopoly and create greater competition.

The telephone industry provides examples of a monopoly and a deregulated business at different times in its history, and thus, provides an interesting case study for evaluating the benefits and drawbacks of each system of operation. Certainly, deregulation has given consumers many different options to consider when choosing service for their homes. At the same time costs have risen to the point where legislators are considering what legal rights individuals have to telephone service. The attempt to act in a socially responsible manner has created many concerns for regulators who try to balance economic and social issues.

As new communication technologies rely on telephone wires or optical fibers to transmit more than just live voice messages, the regulation of wired communications will become even more important. Technologies on the horizon, such as ISDN, B-ISDN, and more effective use of optical fibers, have the capacity to change the ways communication technologies are connected on a global scale.

The issues discussed in this chapter on telephony provide a framework for evaluating the development of other communication technologies. Radio, television, and alternative distribution forms, all discussed in subsequent chapters, are bringing further changes to the social environment and are challenging users' perceptions regarding the role of communication technology.

SUMMARY

The early development of telegraphy and telephony show the close connections between technology and social change. The growth of the telephone industry in particular suggests the following connections:

- the growth of wired communication technology industries and social change
- business practices and the national economy
- "universal service" and its political, social, economic, and global consequences
- how the social environment responded to new communications technologies by developing a value system and hierarchy of responsibilities that affected home and the workplace, creating a place in the public sphere for women, while also changing their activities traditionally based in the home
- how the deregulation and divestiture of the telephone monopoly in the United States has radically altered telephone service and the number of information technologies services available to us
- how new services in a deregulated environment present possibilities for using technology in different contexts

DISCUSSION QUESTIONS

1. Discuss what you think life was like in the late 1800s, when many of the technologies available today did not yet exist. How would your view of the world be different?
2. In what ways has the deregulation of the telephone industry affected the growth and development of other communications industries?
3. What jobs are emerging today in response to new communications technologies and services? Are these jobs influenced by the gender of their users?
4. How might privacy be threatened or controlled by using a greater number of wired technologies?
5. What does it mean for our economy if messages in more traditional formats, like television broadcasting, find their way to video dial tone services? What will happen to advertising as a means of underwriting broadcast costs?
6. How might our personal communication patterns and activities be dif-

ferent if the picturephone were available to everyone now?

7. How does greater choice over the number of communication technologies challenge you to make decisions about how you spend your time and money?

References

Andrews, Edmund L. 1992. F.C.C. approves tv on phone lines. *New York Times,* (July 17): D:5.

Boettinger, H.M. 1977. *The telephone book.* Croton-on-Hudson, New York: Riverwood Press.

Brown, Charles L. 1991. The Bell system. In *Encyclopedia of telecommunications, Vol. 2,* ed. F.E. Froelich and A. Kent. New York: Marcel Dekker, Inc.

Bruce, Robert V. 1973. *Bell.* Boston: Little, Brown & Co.

Coll, Steve. 1986. *The deal of the century: The break up of AT&T.* New York: Athenaeum.

Dilts, Marion May. 1941. *The telephone in a changing world.* New York: Longmans, Green & Co.

Federal Communications Commission. September 17, 1992. Rules and regulations implementing the telephone consumer protection act of 1991. CC Docket No. 92–90. Washington, D.C.

Geller, Henry. 1991. *Fiber optics: An opportunity for a new policy?* The Annenberg Washington Program in Communications Policy Studies of Northwestern University. Washington, D.C.

Hochheiser, Sheldon H. 1991. The american telephone and telegraph company. In *Encyclopedia of telecommunications. Vol. 1.* ed. Fritz E. Froehlich, Allen Kent, and Carolyn M. Hall. New York: Marcel Dekker, Inc.

Johnson, A. and Malone, D. eds. 1931. *Dictionary of American biography.* New York: Charles Scribner's & Sons.

Malone, D., ed. 1936. *Dictionary of American biography.* New York: Charles Scribner's & Sons.

Marvin, Carolyn. 1988. *When old technologies were new.* New York: Oxford University Press.

McLuhan, Marshall. 1964. *Understanding media.* New York: Signet.

Rakow, Lana F. 1988. Women and the gendering of a communications technology. In *Technology and women's voices,* ed. C. Kramarae. London: Routledge & Kegan Paul.

Singh, Indu B. 1991. ISDN and the developing world. In *Advances in telematics,* vol. 1. ed. Indu B. Singh and Jarice Hanson. Norwood, New Jersey: Ablex Publications.

Sponseller, Diane. 1990. Who's got your number? Regulators confront the new caller ID service. *Public Utilities Fortnightly* 61: 55–58.

United States of America v. Western Electric Company Incorporated and American Telephone and Telegraph Company. Civil Action No. 82–0192. August 24, 1982. *Modification of Final Judgment.*

United States Bureau of the Census. 1991. *Statistical abstract of the United States, 1991* (111th Ed.). Washington, D.C.

Four

BROADCAST SYSTEMS
RADIO

MAKING CONNECTIONS

As the telegraph served to link railroad lines and other businesses, the telephone served to connect individuals. When the new invention called radio emerged at the turn of the century, the first electronic mass medium was ready for interested audiences.

Radio is the most pervasive electronic communications medium. The average home in the United States has five radio receivers. Technological development leading to the invention of radio coincided with improvements in telegraphy and telephony. As a result, the emerging industries influenced each other's business practices, audiences learned how to use aural media, and governments around the world made decisions about radio use that reflected various philosophies about how information should be shared.

This chapter examines the radio industry in the United States. The chapter covers:

- how the new radio industry established a foundation for future electronic communication industries

Chapter

- how technical developments led to institutional practices in the radio industry

- how radio content developed in response to other news, information, and entertainment media

- how amateurs, experimenters, electricians, and inventors each influenced the burgeoning radio industry

- how radio networks and program distribution developed

- how the public began to use radio and to understand its role in society

- how new developments in radio technology and the practice of audience segmentation influenced programming

- how the popularity of radio influenced the television industry

---

Because radio waves can transmit information from a sender to a receiver with no discernible physical connection, radio messages have been received in some very unusual places! The FCC's archives are filled with amusing stories of people picking up radio signals in a newly filled tooth, or how signals "mysteriously" appear in unusual places, such as telephone signals or electrical outlets. In the beginning of the twentieth century radio was so radically different from any previous communication technology that it was accused of causing all sorts of strange things, including dizzy spells, weather changes, and creaky floorboards (Barnouw 1966, 103).

Radio as an industry provided a model for other communication technologies to follow. The formation of the FCC was a response to this new electronic form, and many later FCC commissioners have maintained the legacy of radio's growth as they consider new technologies. (See for example, Fowler and Brenner, 1988; "Interim head," 1993; Sikes, 1991).

Radio broadcasting is also an effective means of international communication. It is low-cost, and it can by-pass some topographical barriers to broadcasting. Amplitude modulation (AM) can overcome mountains; frequency modulation (FM) is effective over distances covering flat land. Regions with geographical features such as rainforests or dispersed populations can be reached by the directional signal of short wave (SW). Through different transmission systems using AM, FM, or SW signals, broadcasts can be sent to many hard-to-reach places.

In industrialized nations radio has become so popular and so inexpensive that many homes have several receivers. The average home in the United States has more than five radios, often including portable, wired, and car units (U.S. Bureau of the Census 1991, 556). There are almost 5,000 AM radio stations in the United States today, and close to 5,700 FM stations. The result is a tremendous variety of programming that is directed to virtually every age group, ethnic group, and life-style.

This chapter discusses radio's evolution, including the technical elements behind radio's development, the development of regulation, and the social aspects of radio listenership. These have determined many of the media patterns that are in place today.

From Experiment to Phenomenon

Experiments with electrical energy started in the 1700s and continued into the 1800s. They produced several related findings. Ben Franklin's development of the battery in 1752 contributed to the understanding of how electricity could be stored. Michael Faraday's discovery of the electromagnetic field in 1831 contributed to the notion that different segments of air waves could be broken down into discrete units, therefore providing the concept behind sending signals in different frequencies, such as shortwave, AM, and FM. Faraday also contributed to the theory behind the electromagnetic spectrum through experiments that proved electrical energy could be converted into mechanical energy, but it was James Clerk Maxwell, experimenting from 1865 to 1873, who discovered that signals in the electromagnetic spectrum could be broken into different speeds. When Heinrich Hertz began to test Maxwell's theories, the actual propagation of air waves into cycles became useful as a mathematical model for using the electromagnetic spectrum. The use of radio waves for electronic communication finally became a practical reality.

Although there were many inventors working on similar principles of wireless communication, the credit for inventing the radio is generally given to Guglielmo Marconi, who developed what he called the Black Box Wireless (see figure 4.1). This invention could transmit high pitched bursts of sound over a distance of one mile, and in so doing, provided a wireless transmission of the same type of information transmitted by telegraph. When Marconi first developed his device in Italy in 1888, he was unable to obtain sufficient financial backing to support adequate testing.

In 1896 he traveled to England in an effort to find backers, but upon his arrival, the Black Box was smashed by customs agents who suspected it was a bomb. Marconi set about reconstructing the Black Box, and was granted a patent in England in 1897. A few investors formed a small company known as the Wireless Telegraph and Signal Company.

Figure 4.1 *Guglielmo Marconi and the Black Box.*
Picture Source: AT&T Archives

The Father of Radio

Box 4.1

Guglielmo

Marconi

(1874–193

Marconi was born to a wealthy family. His Italian father and Irish mother encouraged their son to study at the University of Bologna. There his interest in Hertz' experiments in electricity led him to an obsessive fascination with sending sound waves through the air.

At the age of 20 he conducted his first successful experiment by ringing a bell in his home by means of a wireless message using Herzian waves. By 1895 (when Marconi was 21), he could operate the "Black Box" with the use of a Morse telegraph key that could transmit a message over one mile.

With the help of the investors he found in Britain, Marconi began to experiment with sending signals over greater distances. On December 12, 1901, he successfully transmitted Morse code for the letter *s* across 2,000 miles, from Poldher, England, to St. Johns, Newfoundland.

After his successful transatlantic experiments, Marconi focused his efforts on building a commercial enterprise. His contributions to the field of wireless telegraphy earned him the Nobel Prize in 1909.

Soon after, it was renamed Marconi's Wireless Telegraph Company, Ltd., and with the support of the British Post Office System, the company set about experimenting with signals in the London Post Office and on Salisbury Plain. Soon Marconi was experimenting with sending signals from the Isle of Wight to ships at sea.

As she had supported the development of telephony, Queen Victoria played a role in the emergence of wireless. Her son, the Prince of Wales, was recuperating on his yacht from a wrenched knee. In an effort to stay in touch with him, the Queen commissioned Marconi to fit the ship with an antenna and set up a land station at Osborn House, where she resided part of the year.

The Marconi Company invested in the development and improvement of various components. One of the most significant came from Ambrose Fleming, a consultant to the company, who developed a valve that permitted electrical energy to flow in one direction. This channeling function served to control the amount of electricity that flowed from one component to another. Called the Fleming valve, this invention is now known as the vacuum tube, and its development was critical to radio and eventually to television and computers. While Marconi's invention had made wireless telegraphy possible, the vacuum tube opened the field to other types of transmission, including voice transmission.

Marconi came to the United States to establish the Marconi Wireless Company of America in 1899. He incorporated under the laws of New Jersey for the use of Marconi patents in the United States, Cuba, and other U.S. protectorates. He required all of his employees to be nationals of the country in which they worked, and one of the first employees at American Marconi was Reginald Fessenden, born in Canada, but raised in Massachusetts.

Reginald Aubrey Fessenden (1866–1932) had worked as a tester at the Edison Machine Works company for a year when his work came to the attention of Thomas Edison himself. In 1887, Edison made him the chief chemist at the Edison Laboratory in New Jersey, where he worked on projects dealing with electrical conductivity. In a few short years Fessenden became chief electrician for the Westinghouse Electric & Manufacturing Company, and by 1883 he had accepted the position of professor of electrical engineering at the Western University of Pennsylvania (later to become the University of Pittsburgh). There he conducted his most influential experiments on wireless communications.

Fessenden originated the radical notion of sending voices over the wireless, changing Marconi's patterns of interrupted bursts to patterns of continuous electrical waves that were modulated for vocal intonation. His experimental 1906 Christmas Eve broadcast to ships at sea included a recorded version of a soprano singing "Silent Night," the reading of a poem, a speech, and Fessenden himself playing a violin solo, reading a few quotations from the Bible, and wishing everyone within range a Merry Christmas.

Another inventor who made important contributions to wireless communication was Lee De Forest (1873–1961). With the proceeds of his first invention, the "sponder," a technology that improved the sensitivity of the telegraph, he established the DeForest Wireless Telegraphy Company to compete with Marconi.

De Forest also invented the **Audion tube,** a device that could amplify the strength of signals and produce continuous electromagnetic waves that were capable of transmitting high frequencies necessary for the transmission of voice and music. But De Forest failed to understand how useful the Audion could be. In 1913 he sold the rights to use the Audion to AT&T, for use in long-distance telephony, for a fraction of its worth. A year later, American Telephone acquired the right to use the Audion for radio transmissions, and used it to improve the Fleming valve. The combination of the two technologies led to the development of the all-important vacuum tube.

De Forest was a flamboyant inventor who was destined to do battle over the rights to a number of inventions that improved the major communication technologies of his day, including telephone, radio, and film (see box 4.2).

Another invention, the alternator, was originally developed by Fessenden and built by General Electric. When General Electric felt that the alternator

Box 4.2   Competition for Technical Improvements

In the early days of telephone and radio experimentation, the work of several inventors seemed to run in parallel lines. Some of Fessenden's and De Forest's work was remarkably similar.

De Forest's work also overlapped with that of Armstrong, and he battled Armstrong in a lengthy controversy over patents for inventions used in radio amplification. More than a dozen courts were involved over a period of 12 years.

The controversy over De Forest's and Armstrong's patents consumed huge amounts of emotional energy, and highlighted the difficulty of protecting an individual's inventions. The De Forest-Armstrong conflict was finally settled at the level of the Supreme Court, where De Forest was declared the winner, but it later became apparent that the justices had misunderstood the technical issues. Later, the real inventor was determined to be Armstrong, but the Supreme Court had already awarded the patent to De Forest.

The Institute of Radio Engineers had awarded Armstrong with a medal for his work, but after the Court decision, he tried to return it. The members of the Institute were aware that justice had miscarried and refused to accept the medal back from Armstrong.

could be further improved, it assigned the task to 28-year-old Ernst F. W. Alexanderson (1878–1975). The Alexanderson alternator was the first machine to regulate the cycles of energy needed for radio, and it produced smooth, continuous waves that made transmission signals more stable. In a long, successful career, Alexanderson developed several other communication technologies, including the 1955 RCA Color Television System.

Another great radio pioneer was Edwin H. Armstrong (1890–1954), who developed the **superheterodyne,** a feature that blended two frequencies together for better sound quality in the radio receiver. While this 1918 development improved sound quality, Armstrong's greatest accomplishments occurred later, in 1933, with his pioneering efforts to test and improve technologies for the broadcast and reception of FM signals. When World War II interrupted his radio inventions, his success turned to tragedy. After the war, 21 corporations fought him over control of the development of FM transmissions.

His energies spent by endless legal battles, he committed suicide in 1954. Ultimately, his family pursued the rights to FM development, and were awarded $10 million in damages.

Figure 4.2 *Edwin H. Armstrong and the "Portable" Radio.*
Picture Source: *The Bettmann Archive*

Radio and the Military

From their inception, the military was keenly interested in the communications industries. Before World War I (1914–1918), the U.S. Army and Navy had been involved in radio, and along with amateurs and manufacturing companies, they experimented with broadcasting.

When the United States entered World War I, all civilian radio operations were prohibited by the government, but those companies involved in the manufacturing of components had a burgeoning business supplying transmitters, receivers, mobile transmitters, and other elements to the military. In particular, Westinghouse, General Electric, and Western Electric benefited from wartime demand, and began to expand into manufacturing giants.

Having experienced success with radio during World War I, the U.S. Navy became increasingly interested in wireless technology, particularly for its ability to communicate from ship-to-shore. As British Marconi became stronger in the international radio area, the Navy feared that the combination of British and American Marconi, both owned by foreign interests, would become too strong, and that U.S. manufacturers would be forever relegated to a secondary role in radio telephony. When General Electric entered into negotiations to sell the Alexanderson alternator to the Marconi Company, the Navy attempted to block the sale, fearing that American manufacturers that owed their success to their involvement with the military would be financially weakened if foreign interests became too strong.

Recognizing the need to create competition for the Marconi companies, General Electric attempted to establish its own international communications company by setting up the Radio Corporation of America (RCA) on October 17, 1919. GE invited other companies to be partners, and soon after RCA was established, AT&T, Western Electric, and eventually Westinghouse, bought shares in the new firm.

Each of the investors had its own patents but it was clear that some system of cooperation had to be developed if radio transmission and reception equipment were to become standardized. From 1919 to 1921, a series of cross-licensing agreements was developed to establish fair use of over 200 different patents. RCA became the company responsible for licensing the patents as well as the sales agent for receivers manufactured by Westinghouse and General Electric. AT&T took the role of manufacturing, selling, and leasing transmitting equipment. Eventually, RCA became the parent company of a fledgling radio network called NBC. Many years later, in 1985, in an interesting intersection of business and fate, GE would become RCA's parent company.

 ## Early Regulations

During the experimental years of radio broadcasting no legislation existed to regulate operation or growth of the industry. All stations broadcast on the few available frequencies and competing signals easily jammed each other. To create some rationale for controlling stations, Congress passed the Radio Act of 1912, but it did little to address the growing problems of radio transmission other than giving the Secretary of Commerce the right to grant licenses for point-to-point installations.

Herbert Hoover, Secretary of Commerce in 1921, recognized the potential power of radio, but he also realized that establishing a regulatory structure would be unpopular with manufacturers. Hoping to encourage the industry to regulate itself, he urged broadcasters to share the amount of time they spent on the air and establish their own rules and regulations for doing so.

Later Senator Clarence Dill and Representative Wallace White sponsored the Radio Act of 1927, which established the Federal Radio Commission (FRC) for the purpose of screening applications for radio licenses, and suggesting procedures for effective operations. This remained the predominant regulatory body for all radio communications until 1934, when the Commission was reconstituted and renamed the Federal Communications Commission (FCC), with responsibility for overseeing all forms of electronic communication.

How Radio Works

Because of the work of the great inventors and subsequent improvements made by others, radio is now a part of our everyday life. The principles behind radio

---

Box. 4.3   Station Identification

The combinations found in radio stations' call letters have an interesting history. When the Department of Commerce began to issue radio licenses in 1921 it planned to identify each station with a series of three letters. But by 1922 there had been so many applications made and licenses granted that the Department had to move to four letter combinations.

The decision to designate "W" as the first letter for stations east of the Mississippi river, and "K" for those west of the Mississippi, helped identify station location and allowed the same frequencies to be used in each of the two sections of the United States. The only exceptions to this practice were stations KDKA from Pittsburgh, and KYW from Philadelphia, both of which began using their call letters before 1921.

Information taken from: Erik Barnouw, *A tower in babel* (New York: Oxford University Press, 1966).

broadcasting are fairly simple, once some basics of electronic communications are understood (see figure 4.3).

When sound (voice, recorded sound, etc.) is fed into a microphone, its energy is transferred to electrical power and the energy is amplified and boosted. It is then transferred to a **transmitter,** where energy goes through a second conversion to radio waves. The wave that carries the sound is called the **carrier signal.**

At the receiving end the signal is reversed. Radio waves are received at an antenna which produces electrical carrier signals that activate the receiver's **tuner,** so that the desired channel can be adjusted. The signal is then amplified and transferred to the loudspeaker in the receiver. In stereo broadcasts, left

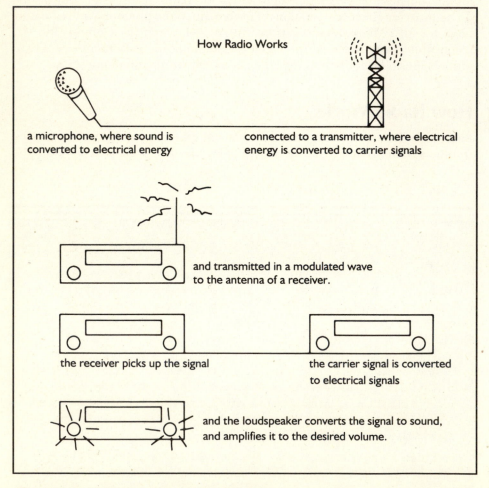

How Radio Works

a microphone, where sound is converted to electrical energy

connected to a transmitter, where electrical energy is converted to carrier signals

and transmitted in a modulated wave to the antenna of a receiver.

the receiver picks up the signal

the carrier signal is converted to electrical signals

and the loudspeaker converts the signal to sound, and amplifies it to the desired volume.

Figure 4.3 *Components of Radio Transmission.*

and right channels are combined and broadcast on one carrier wave. A stereo receiver has a decoder that splits the signals into each sound channel.

Perhaps the most remarkable aspect of radio broadcasting is that so many signals can be transmitted simultaneously. This is made possible with the effective use of the **electromagnetic spectrum** (see figure 4.4).

The Electromagnetic Spectrum

Electromagnetic radiation is energy that travels in the form of invisible waves. The electromagnetic spectrum is the range of wavelengths or frequencies at which electromagnetic energy travels. The human ear is capable of hearing sounds between about 16 cycles per second for a low bass noise, and 16 thousand cycles per second for high treble noises. This means that a very low bass noise makes 16 waves per second. The rate is measured in hertz, in honor of the early radio pioneer Heinrich Hertz. One hertz is one cycle per second, so a low bass note would be at the frequency rate of 16 hertz, a higher note would be at 100 hertz, and a very high note would be at 16,000 hertz. As the number becomes larger, prefixes are added to the word hertz so that the zeros don't become unmanageable. One thousand hertz is referred to as one kilohertz

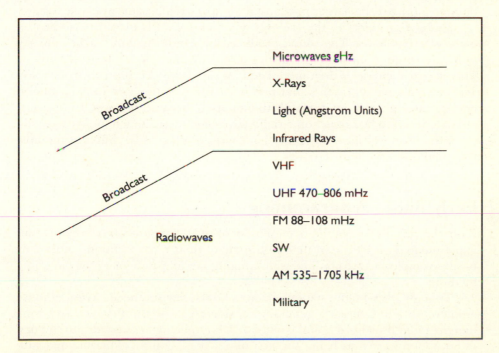

Figure 4.4 The Electromagnetic Spectrum.

(kH), one million hertz is one megahertz (mH), and a trillion hertz is one gigahertz (gH).

Radio waves that are part of the electromagnetic spectrum also have frequencies and are measured in hertz, but their frequencies are higher than sound waves and they can be neither seen nor heard, though they are capable of carrying sound that can be converted to a form that can be heard. The use of a variety of these radio waves increases the number of information channels.

The radio wave portion of the electromagnetic spectrum is divided into eight sections, each of which has a band of frequencies that are measured in hertz. Most radio and television transmission takes place in this area, called the C band of the electromagnetic spectrum. Higher than radio waves on the electromagnetic spectrum are infrared rays and then light waves, and higher still, microwaves.

The position of the C band at which a particular service is placed depends partly on the needs of the service. The lower frequencies have longer ranges in the earth's atmosphere, so long range military communications appear on the very low frequencies while services needing to broadcast over only a short range appear on the ultra high frequencies. Many placements, however, are accidents of history; the lower frequencies were understood and used earlier than higher frequencies. In fact, in the early days of broadcasting the higher frequencies existed, but were unusable because of lower grade transmitters. As technology became more precise, larger portions of the spectrum became available for use.

Modulation refers to the method by which sound is placed on radio frequency carrier waves. The sound produced by a radio station reaches the station's transmitter and antenna in the form of variations in electrical energy. The electrical energy is then modulated, or superimposed onto a carrier wave. The carrier wave represents that particular radio station's frequency. Sound energy can't go very far through the air itself because it doesn't move fast enough; it has to be carried on a radio wave which has a much higher frequency. Different waves have different characteristics created by different modulation methods (see figure 4.5).

Early Radio Programming

From the earliest days of radio, employees of related manufacturing companies experimented on their own time with some of their new inventions, and many of those employees are credited with bringing new innovations to the emerging medium.

Though several radio stations claim to be the first on the air, Westinghouse employee Frank Conrad is generally considered to be the first licensed commercial radio broadcaster, and could lay claim to being associated with the first radio station as well as being the first disc jockey. Conrad experimented with equipment in his garage as well as at the Westinghouse factory in Pittsburgh.

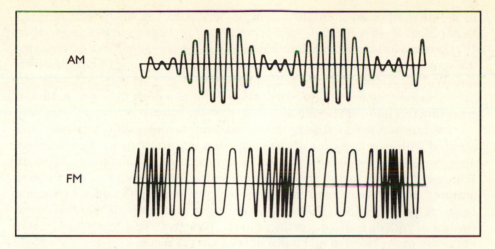

Figure 4.5 *AM & FM Signal Patterns.*
The different carrier waves are modulated so that the energy level of the carrier wave corresponds to the same frequency as the changing energy. AM waves are modulated so that the height of the waves varies with the energy source. FM waves are modulated to have a more even correspondence with the sound signal.

Using the designation 8XK, Conrad tested voice transmissions and records and live banjo music played on the air. When the official Westinghouse radio station was inaugurated on November 2, 1920, with a broadcast of the Harding-Cox Presidential election returns, the station used the call letters KDKA. It pioneered broadcasts of public service announcements, church services, news, sports, drama, and both live and recorded music. The only thing it did not program was commercials.

As other radio stations around the country attempted to experiment with broadcasting at the same frequencies, a "silent night" was instituted each week so that listeners in various locations could hear the experimental broadcasts of other stations. Radio experiments began to be covered in newspaper reports, and the public's awareness of the new medium began to rise. To demonstrate radio, and to sell receivers, some department stores tried to lure customers with the promise of hearing something special. Horne's Department Store in Pittsburgh featured demonstrations of radio receivers, picking up KDKA's signal as well as others on KDKA's silent night. It also sold radio receivers starting at $10.

The year 1922 was a banner year for radio. Over 200 stations were on the air, licensed by the FRC, and over 100,000 sets were sold in that year alone! Radio appeared to have passed the experimental stage and was on its way to becoming a major form of media. Many enterprising individuals would shape content for the new technology.

A young man who worked for Westinghouse, Tommy Cowan, was assigned to monitor an experimental transmitter set up on top of the Bamberger's Department Store in Newark, New Jersey. When he began the task in October, 1921, he had little hope that anyone was listening to the signal, but he repeated the spoken message, "You are listening to the radio telephone broadcasting station WJZ, in Newark, New Jersey." Both Cowan and Westinghouse were surprised when they began receiving letters from places as far away as Illinois reporting reception of the signal.

Cowan's job was to modify the transmission facilities, but he also experimented with various types of programming. He went to his former boss, Thomas Edison, and asked to borrow one of Edison's phonographs. Though Edison purportedly had a sign on his door saying "I do not want to talk radio to anyone," he did allow Cowan to borrow the phonograph. Cowan set it up and began to broadcast from the top of Bamberger's Department Store. He even convinced friends and acquaintances in the theater in New York City to come to the top of the building and transmit live entertainment.

As these experiments continued, the manufacturers of radio transmission and receiving equipment struggled to find what they thought would be an appropriate outlet for the new medium. The patent-sharing consortia that resulted from the cross-licensing agreements made between 1919 and 1923 had formed two groups with different philosophies of how radio should be used.

The group comprising General Electric, Westinghouse, and RCA, which included radio station WJZ under its umbrella, became known as the Radio Group. These manufacturers saw radio broadcasting as a means of selling and promoting other products they manufactured. They produced their own programs and ads for broadcasting, but did not offer to sell advertising time to anyone else. In fact, the members of Radio Group originally thought that radio stations would multiply as different companies established them to advertise their own goods. Soon this was revealed to be an impractical plan, since there were too few products to constitute a full advertising day. Then too, the group saw its competitors receiving advertising money from other manufacturers.

The other broadcasting group, which included AT&T and Western Electric and their station, WEAF (established in August, 1922), believed radio should be a **common carrier**. That is, their group planned to do no program production, but instead would lease time to advertisers who would be responsible for filling airtime with programming. Because AT&T and Western Electric dominated the telephone industry, this group became known as the Telephone Group. They connected their stations by hooking up telephone wires and transmitted their signal through these lines for regional distribution. The sound quality of the Telephone Group's shared programming through wires was far superior to the radio group—which relied on broadcast transmission from one station to another.

The Telephone Group established a system of filling airtime that became known as "toll" broadcasting. With this system, the telephone company would provide no programs, but would make radio service available to anyone who paid a "toll" to use the service. This system proved to be the foundation for commercial broadcasting's financial success.

Advertising and Radio

WEAF became the first toll station, but the use of the medium for advertising met with outrage and indignation from many prominent individuals and corporations. Secretary of Commerce Herbert Hoover warned that it would be "inconceivable that we should allow so great a possibility for service . . . to be drowned in advertising chatter." He later warned that broadcasting would be destroyed if presidential messages ever became "the meat in a sandwich of two patent medicine advertisements" (Barnouw 1978, 15).

As the largest member of the Telephone Group, AT&T insisted that all advertising agencies working with companies that chose to use toll broadcasting be paid a 15 percent commission—the same amount paid by print advertisers. The 15 percent was the standard rate print media returned to agencies, which encouraged them to place clients' ads in their publications. Agencies, operating as "middle men" between clients and print media, assumed the 15 percent as part of their profit. This encouraged advertising companies to place messages on the radio and to persuade their clients to think about radio broadcasting.

Early ads took many forms. One was the use of informative talks about the history of the product being advertised. An ad featuring the history of beards led to the successful marketing of the safety razor by Gillette; another describing the history of Christmas cards was sponsored by an association of greeting card manufacturers. By April, 1923, the idea of program sponsorship as a form of indirect selling had become popular. The first one-hour program to try to cash in on trade-name identification was the Browning King clothing firm's Browning King Orchestra. Soon after, several other firms followed the model, sponsoring the, "Cliquot Club Eskimos," the "A&P Gypsies," the "Lucky Strike

---

Box 4.4   WEAF Advertisement

"On August 28 the Queensboro Corporation paid $50 for a late-afternoon 10-minute period on WEAF, and used it to extol suburban living and promote the sale of apartments in a housing complex in Jackson Heights, Long Island." Three weeks later the "Corporation reported sales amounting to $127,000, directly traceable to one speech."

Source: Erik Barnouw, *The Sponsor* (New York: Oxford University Press, 1978) 15–16.

Orchestra," the "Ipana Troubadours," and the "Kodak Chorus" (Barnouw 1966, l58; 1978, 17).

From 1922 to 1926, however, only the Telephone Group was supported by advertising. The original philosophy of the Radio Group, to support only products manufactured by station owners, was impractical, and WJZ was making no profit for the Radio Group at all. WEAF, however, was making $750,000 each year for the Telephone Group.

The Formation of Networks

The Telephone Group also claimed that the cross-licensing agreements of 1919–1923 prohibited any other broadcasters from connecting broadcast equipment through telephone lines, and in 1923, they established the first permanent link between two of their own stations, WEAF and WMAF in South Dartmouth, Massachusetts. This was the first interconnection, though telephone lines, that permitted two stations to share the same programming. WEAF fed WMAF toll programming (commercial) and non-toll programming (called sustaining programs), for which WMAF paid a fee. These sustaining programs were not sponsored by commercial enterprises, but rather, were produced so that the station would have continuous sound, even when commercially sponsored programs were unavailable.

The Telephone Group quickly began to add more of these types of interconnections, and by October 1924, it had 22 stations across the country that were connected by phone lines to carry a speech by President Calvin Coolidge. This was the first "coast-to-coast" broadcast. Though not all 22 stations were linked together at all times (only six stations were regularly connected to WEAF for about three hours of programming each day), the power of a radio network had become apparent to everyone.

WJZ had been prevented from using telephone lines for interconnections by the cross-licensing agreements, but it attempted to connect other stations through Western Union's telegraph wires for the same effect as the Telephone Group's. Unfortunately, telegraph lines were not as sophisticated as telephone lines and could not carry the same frequencies, so the sound quality of the Radio Group's interconnections was far lower than the Telephone Group's connections. Nevertheless, WJZ opened another station in Washington, D.C., in 1923, and by 1925, had organized connections among 14 different stations.

By 1926, the problems stemming from the first cross-licensing agreements had come to a head, and various radio manufacturers sought resolution in the courts. Radio broadcasting and the manufacture of receivers had become big business. Various interests within the industry had clashed repeatedly with the Department of Commerce, resulting in a series of impromptu resolutions. The department and the broadcasters revised these resolutions into a set of radio agreements that passed in July 1926. The department intended the actions to encourage greater participation of different owners and manufacturers in the burgeoning radio industry. The broadcasters viewed the agreements as opportunities to diversify in areas of manufacturing and programming.

As a result, AT&T agreed to sell WEAF and all its other broadcasting assets to the Radio Group, to prohibit Western Electric from manufacturing radio receivers, and to surrender patents on the manufacturing of radio transmitters. In return for the exclusive right right to telephony and nonbroadcast services, AT&T agreed to stay out of commercial radio broadcasting.

The big winner in the contest was the Radio Group, because it was given the power to shape the direction of commercial radio broadcasting for the future. The only major concession it made was an agreement to lease network relay facilities from AT&T. This arrangement allowed the Radio Group to operate with improved sound quality and participate in advertiser-supported programming to obtain funding. AT&T also saw a financial advantage in leasing its lines for radio networking, which gave it an incentive to accept the agreement.

NBC   Within a few months of the agreement the Radio Group organized a new subsidiary called the National Broadcasting Company (NBC), headed by David Sarnoff (see box 4.5). NBC offered two services: the former Radio Group, with the anchor station WJZ, became known as NBC Blue; and the old Telephone Group, anchored by WEAF, became known as NBC Red. The Blue and Red designations were supposedly provided by a radio engineer who christened the two networks according to the two dominant colors in the electrical

---

Box 4.5   David Sarnoff

One of the great pioneers of the radio industry was David Sarnoff, who began his radio career at an early age as a telegraph operator at the Wanamaker's Department Store in New York City. Sarnoff wrote the legendary "Music Box Memo," which predicted that radio would someday be used to transmit music. His success as the first general manager of the newly created RCA and his rise to the leadership of NBC radio and television provide the sources for many interesting stories about his ability to turn ideas into profitable enterprises.

A visionary in the business, Sarnoff correctly predicted the power of broadcasting. Even though he was a skillful businessman, he always claimed that broadcasting should be responsible to its audiences, and that this was more important than the profit motive.

Information taken from: Kenneth Bilby, *The General* (New York: Harper & Row, 1986).

Figure 4.6 *David Sarnoff Examining the RCA Videotape System.*
Picture Source: UPI/Bettmann

wires that fed each system its programming. Eventually, WJZ's name was changed to WABC and WEAF became WNBC.

CBS   In 1927 another network was established through the efforts of a group called United Independent Broadcasters (UIB). It was launched by the Judson and Coates Talent Agency to serve as a vehicle for the agency's performers. The leaders of the network had little knowledge of radio operations and small stations showed little interest in affiliating with UIB. As a result the network had a slow start. But within months it changed its name to the Columbia Phonograph Broadcast System, and in 1928 William S. Paley took over the operation and changed the name to the Columbia Broadcasting System (CBS). He established a new practice called **free sustaining service**—a system that guaranteed affiliates 20 hours of programming each week and allowed them to share commer-

Figure 4.7 *William S. Paley Addressing the CBS Radio Audience, 1934.*
Picture Source: UPI/Bettmann Newsphotos

cial programming time. While some of the ads were placed by the network, the stations were allowed to sell time slots in their own regions. This allowed stations to obtain more revenue for themselves. Additionally, the network had exclusive rights for broadcasting through the affiliates, and the stations were required to identify themselves with the CBS name.

This practice not only provided CBS with more recognition, but gave free programming to the affiliates, enabling them to reduce the costs entailed in producing original programming or leasing content from other sources. Paley also established a flagship station in New York, which was eventually called WCBS.

MBS   During the 1930s, another network attempted to become involved in radio broadcasting and, for a short while, experienced moderate success. The

---

Box 4.6   William S. Paley

Born to an affluent family, William Paley was a broadcasting genius who recognized the importance of programming. Among other accomplishments, he brought big name stars to the CBS line-up and promoted them heavily. He also created a news bureau that featured one of the most outstanding teams of broadcast journalists in history. Its members included Edward R. Murrow, Robert Trout, and Hans van Kaltenborn.

Paley acquired other media companies on behalf of CBS, including a record company, (Columbia Records), a publishing company (Holt, Rinehart and Winston), and an educational toy manufacturer (Creative Playthings). For a time CBS also owned the New York Yankees baseball team. Most of the CBS holdings were divested in the 1970s and 1980s, with the most controversial divestiture being the sale of Columbia Records to the Sony Corportation of Japan.

Information taken from: Lewis J. Paper, *Empire* (New York: St. Martin's Press, 1987).

Mutual Broadcasting System (MBS) began operation in 1934 and by 1948 had more affiliated stations than any of the other networks. Using several innovative practices, Mutual positioned itself to be the network that encouraged broadcasting on a local level. In addition to its stations, many of which were outside major urban areas, Mutual started the system of **cooperative advertising,** which served local advertisers and used local ad revenues to help support network programming. Cooperative advertising involved a business arrangement in which both the station and the advertiser agreed to underwrite a part of the cost of the ad.

Cooperative broadcasting operated in a similar way. A typical cooperative broadcasting venture might include a nonprofit sponsor who would pay for the cost of the production of a program, but would not pay for air time. The station would donate air time to the program.

The big difference between MBS and the other networks, was that MBS owned no stations of its own. The four stations producing most of the programming for the MBS network and forming the core of MBS activity included WOR (New York), WLW (Cincinnati), WGN (Chicago), and WXYZ (Detroit). In serving the populations of these large cities, MBS developed programming that would appeal to diverse audiences. Still, the power of its system could not rival the extensive networks of NBC or CBS.

Box 4.7   Roosevelt Establishes the FCC

When Franklin D. Roosevelt became President, he was concerned about the lack of systematic regulation of the country's communication industries. He urged Congress to form a commission to establish such regulation, and the result was the passage of the Communications Act of 1934.

The act created the Federal Communications Commission (FCC), which comprised seven members who regulated interstate electrical communication, including broadcasting. Commissioners were to be appointed by the President. The new commission replaced the old FRC, but parts of the Radio Act of 1927 were incorporated into the 1934 act.

In 1987 the FCC's membership was reduced to five members, but all members are still appointed by the President. The Commissioners then choose their own Chief Commissioner.

There have been many attempts in recent years to disband the FCC as a result of complaints that it no longer operates effectively as a regulatory body because so many technologies today include advanced distribution systems that no longer neatly fit the original mission of the FCC. At the same time, moves toward less government involvement in telecommunications have required that legislators carefully consider the role of a governmental body in a free market economy.

The chain broadcasting investigation   By 1938, 98 percent of existing radio stations were hooked up to either NBC or CBS at night. MBS claimed that these networks had an unfair advantage, and took its complaint to what by that time had become the FCC (see box 4.7), where the Chain Broadcasting Regulations were established to limit the power of the large networks and give a better chance of survival to fledgling operations like MBS. "Chain broadcasting" was the description given to networks that were linked together and controlled by one of the major groups. Though NBC and CBS fought the FCC's ruling, a review by the Supreme Court supported the FCC's decision.

The most significant result of this legal action was the requirement that NBC divest itself of one of its networks. NBC Blue had long been considered the weaker network, and NBC sold it in 1943. Its new owner renamed it the American Broadcasting Company (ABC).

ABC   NBC Blue had been for sale, with only a few serious potential buyers bidding for control, for several months when Edward Noble, a financier who

111

had made a fortune in the Life Saver candy business, bought the network. The $8 million sale was approved by the FCC, a decision expedited by the fact that Noble had agreed that Blue, which he would rename the American Broadcasting Company (ABC), would serve primarily the needs of working class people by developing programming for them.

The three new networks proved to be too much competition for MBS, and when that system was dissolved, ABC jumped at the chance to take over the advertising business that MBS had fostered. As a result, ABC quickly became more powerful than NBC Blue had been, though it remained in third place among the networks in terms of ratings and revenues.

Social Acceptance of Radio

Part of radio's success had to do with its maturing at a particular time in history. Throughout the 1930s Americans went through long periods of social stress. During the Depression a third of the nation's workforce was unemployed, but a radio receiver could be purchased for as little as $15, and radio became one of the most popular ways to pass time. By 1938 three-quarters of the public had access to radios.

By the time the Second World War broke out radio was an established medium that brought news, information, entertainment, and more importantly, the idea of a unique "American" identity into the nation's homes. Throughout these years, radio was a friend to the friendless, a link to the world, and a connection to the national community.

As the radio industry grew, it inspired greater efforts to understand the power and potential uses of the medium, and it served as a foundation for other industries such as television. Twenty-five years after radio became a household word in the United States, the field of media research had been given little consideration by either the academic community or the industry. Other than the Payne Fund Studies (a series of research reports conducted from 1929 to 1932), which investigated the way Americans used and were affected by motion pictures, there were no major attempts to understand how and why people listened to radio until the 1940s. But social scientists had been experiencing a growing concern to understand modern technologies. In the late thirties Paul Lazarsfeld began his pioneering efforts to give a structure to the way people used radio. Lazarsfeld's operation at the Columbia University Office of Radio Research was created in 1937 by a grant from the Rockefeller Foundation "to study what radio means in the lives of the listeners" (Lazarsfeld and Stanton 1944, vii). Most of the studies used a survey methodology and focused on aspects of listeners' behavior, such as their exposure to different forms of media, their susceptibility to persuasion and their attitude formation. His research was of interest not only to academics but also to executives in the radio and advertising industries, who began to take notice of people's media habits. The earliest studies laid the groundwork for more sophisticated techniques for measuring listener ratings and establishing advertising rates. The studies also explored how radio might be practically integrated into a person's life and with what effect.

In the 1940s the organizations most interested in assessing radio's impact in the United States were the federal government and the Radio Bureau, a newly created division of the Office of War Information. The Radio Bureau was particularly interested in understanding the ability of radio to persuade people to do things, such as vote, buy products, and think about new issues. Much of the early research into radio's impact came from the Office of War Information, which began funding its Radio Research series of reports in 1941. Though the efforts of the organization to understand the possible propaganda function of radio were terminated for the duration of the war, other agencies and organizations expanded this avenue of research to further investigate how individuals were using radio. The office of War Information began applying what it had learned to short wave broadcasts to foreign countries, and to programs within the United States to support war efforts.

Habits During the War Years

A study that took place in the war years of 1942 and 1943 involving 3,529 persons focused on subjects' media habits. Researchers found that only a small segment (5 percent) of Americans reported that they seldom or never listened to the radio. Twenty-one percent said their evening listening was confined to less than an hour, but 49 percent listened one to three hours, and 25 percent listened in excess of three hours each evening. Ninety percent said they usually read the daily newspaper. A radio fan was likely to be a movie fan as well. This led researchers to believe that "The more easily available a medium is, the more people will expose themselves to it" (Lazarsfeld and Stanton, 1944, 13). Clearly, radio had demonstrated that it could interest audiences. This type of research fueled the development of the industry.

What Were People Listening To?

The 1930s saw the development of new radio production techniques and program formats including variety shows, game shows, and documentaries. The decade also saw an extremely skillful communicator, Franklin Delano Roosevelt, become the first politician to consistently use radio as a means of personally communicating with the country. His 1933 inaugural address gave us one of the first "sound bites," or memorable phrases, in radio history: "The only thing we have to fear is fear itself." His regular "fireside chats" exuded warmth and informality, and did much to reassure Americans that they would survive the economic, political, and military problems besetting the country.

One popular radio format was comedy. It was so popular, in fact, that during the most listened-to network program, "Amos 'n Andy," which ran five nights a week for 15 minutes at a time, movie theaters would stop their shows to play the program, and traffic would stop on the streets as people listened to the program (Head and Sterling 1987, 71).

Radio news   The first radio network to establish its own news bureau was NBC. Abe Schechter, who was originally hired to write publicity, was given the task of developing a news organization. Despite poor facilities (his office was a converted broom closet), he put together the first version of what would become a staple of radio broadcasting: the news.

The first regularly scheduled radio newscast went on the air in 1930, with NBC's Lowell Thomas as announcer. Schecter's experience with publicity had given him a clear advantage in knowing how to obtain a good story. Press agents often fed him tips, and he responded with tickets to popular radio personality broadcasts. Occasionally the information he was provided supplied Walter Winchell's Sunday evening gossip program with interesting features (Barnouw 1968, 19).

With NBC's radio news proving to be a popular radio format, CBS turned its attention to news gathering. Its first news triumph took place when it devoted a half-hour newscast to the Nazi invasion of Austria. The program originated live from locations in London, Paris, Rome, Berlin, and Vienna, which constituted a technical coup. Audiences had never heard a live broadcast compiled from short wave reports before, and the planning and implementation of this news event took a year (Murrow 1967, 3). Anchored by Robert Trout, the program featured a reporter who was destined to become one of the greatest newscasters in broadcast history. His name was Edward R. Murrow, and he became the first broadcast anchor to report from the scene of many conflicts. Later, he also hosted an influential television news feature program called "See It Now" for CBS.

Drama   Radio dramatists learned how to work with the unique characteristics of the audio medium. Not only did writers learn how to construct original stories that could be enhanced with sound effects and suggest images that listeners could see in their imaginations, but a number of dramatic companies developed their own programs for which they would often produce radio dramas of well-known stories, literary adaptations, or original materials. One of the most memorable companies was the Mercury Theater on the Air, directed by Orson Welles and John Houseman. Their October 30, 1938, radio broadcast of "The War of the Worlds" was a landmark in radio drama, and has justifiably earned the Mercury Theater a place in broadcasting history (see box 4.8).

Soap operas   Other popular radio dramas fell into the category of soap operas, so named because the sponsors of the programs were often soap companies, such as Lever Brothers and Proctor and Gamble. Some of the soap

Box 4.8   "The War of the Worlds"

When the Mercury Theater on the Air presented "The War of the Worlds" on October 30, 1938, the broadcast created an uproar that has since been called "mass panic." The public had become familiar with radio style, and the program was organized to intersperse the type of music usually heard on the radio with what sounded like authentic news reports of Martians landing in Grovers Mill, New Jersey.

Many of the listeners who panicked attempted to reduce their uncertainty by contacting friends—many of whom had heard the same broadcast. The CBS switchboard was inundated with telephone calls from listeners asking if the "news" reports were true. Many of the listeners believed that the United States was being invaded by aliens from outer space.

In a study on the effect of the broadcast, the Office of Radio Research at Princeton University found that 28 percent of the audience (1.7 million people) thought the program was indeed a real news report, and, of that group, 70 percent (1.2 million people) were frightened or disturbed. The broadcast afforded the first large-scale study of how the medium of radio could create panic, and who might be prone to this type of behavior.

While it seems that such a response to a radio program could not happen today, radio broadcasters who replay the "War of the Worlds" broadcast on its Halloween Eve anniversary often report phone calls from individuals who wonder if it's real. And, in recent television specials that have capitalized on the same format of presenting frightening material, such as "The Day After," about the day after nuclear holocaust, similar reports indicate that at least a segment of the audience believes it to be real.

These events suggest that the media has a tremendous power to influence audiences, even though we might expect more sophistication on their part after living with radio and television for so long.

operas that survive on television today originally started on radio, including "The Guiding Light," which began in 1937.

The soaps were original radio dramas that turned personal tragedy and human emotion into images that exploited the unique ability of radio to stimulate the listener's imagination. Recognizing that radio programming needed to allow for the habits of the typical listener, who research reported was likely to be a woman working in the home, the soaps developed a format in which key elements of the story were repeated frequently. Women working in the home were likely to be busy and might not pay much attention to each daily or weekly broadcast, so the typical soap opera would remind the occasional listener of past events in the story. Listeners were less likely to lose interest in the ongoing stories if they could pick up what they had missed.

Another feature of the soap opera was that the content was appropriate to the calendar. Christmas was celebrated on December 25, characters talked about the heat in August, and events were always presented to give the illusion of reality. This combination of reality and fantasy presented listeners with a unique combination of technological possibility and fictional content.

New Developments in Radio

As the same companies that had dominated radio began to dominate the new television industry from 1947 onwards, radio began to feel competition from the new medium. Many popular radio stars made successful transitions to television, and programs in all areas, including drama, variety shows, game shows, and documentaries, were picked up from radio by television. Radio stations were left with declining income, and throughout the 1950s they scrambled to find other ways of maintaining audiences.

With some of radio's most effective genres, like comedy and soap opera, migrating to television, radio executives sought to exploit the medium's unique ability to transmit instantaneous information and entertainment. Talk shows, news, and music were the features that radio could still effectively use to reach audiences.

FM   The major technical innovation in radio during the late 1950s and early 1960s came from the effective application of frequency modulation (FM) broadcasting. The FM wave pattern interweaves two signals that can be split into channels in a receiver, making two-channel, stereo sound possible. In addition, the FM signal is sent from the transmitter in what is called "line of sight" direction, meaning that it is sent at an angle parallel to the earth.

Since the invention of AM radio, FM had been a technological possibility, with Edwin H. Armstrong having provided much of the original research. At the time, however, Congress and first the FRC, then the FCC, felt that more attention should be given to AM, and that additional experimentation in FM would hurt AM's potential to develop a following. FM licenses were not available until the FCC began approving requests in 1961.

FM was finally approved because the AM frequencies were becoming crowded, but in addition, its superior sound quality made it a perfect vehicle for music. Today, there are more FM stations in the country than there are AM stations, but no station or network is as powerful as it was in the days prior to television. Many of the original FM licenses were granted to broadcasters who already had AM stations, and often, broadcasters transmitted the same programs on AM and FM. However, FM's superior sound quality and stereo capacity made it more suitable than AM for musical formats, and within a short time, several FM stations began playing entire albums of music, interspersed with introductions and comments by clever radio personalities. FM music broadcasting began to focus on a particular audience, the youth market.

Contemporary Radio

Since the development of FM broadcasting, radio has become increasingly concerned about competition from other forms of media. First television robbed radio of many of its key performers and adapted radio formats like news, dramas, and soap operas to the new visual form. Today, portable audio tape players and compact discs (CDs), compete for audiences that seek to fill listening time. In the future digital audio tape (DAT) will do the same. Many radio stations have responded to this challenge by developing different formats that appeal to diverse groups. The listening audience now represents a greater number of ages, ethnic groups, and local concerns than it did in the days when service was primarily national. Different stations offer a greater variety of content, and programming services offer syndicated material to similar-format stations around the country. Programming is often transmitted by satellite rather than telephone cable. These developments, plus a need to reduce broadcast costs, have created changes in radio programming and the way radio stations use technology.

Formats and Programming

Contemporary formats and programming reflect competition from other media, but they also use radio's unique ability to transmit instantaneous entertainment and information, and to create images in the audience members' minds. Some of the most successful contemporary radio programs are talk shows that explore a variety of interests, values, and issues. Audiences for traditional musical formats have generally dwindled in size, but the formats have increased in number and diversity. Each of these formats suggests a different connection between audience interests and appropriate use of radio in an era of increased competition for audience attention.

Talk radio   One of the few formats to have increased its national audience is talk radio. Popular personalities like Larry King, Rush Limbaugh, and Howard Stern have all developed loyal audiences in locations around the country. Part of the success of talk radio results from the syndication of some programs, and audience interest in call-in programs.

   Syndication is a means of distributing recorded programs to many stations,

117

which then broadcast them in their own chosen time slots. Call-in programs allow interested listeners to phone questions, comments, or criticism to the program moderator, who often has an identifiable personality. Even these programs may be syndicated, but their primary appeal is at the local level where

Box 4.9 Examples of Musical Formats and Their Audiences

Format	Style	Target Audience
Top 40	Best-selling records	12–17 18–24
Top 100	A little slower tempo than Top 40, broader range	12–17 18–24 some 25–34
Adult contemporary	Contemporary music with commentary	some teens 18–49
Classic rock	Popular early rock	men 18–34
Album-oriented rock (AOR)	New music and oldies	18–34 more men than women
Urban contemporary	Rap, R&B	African-American and Hispanic women and men 18–24
Beautiful music	Soft, background music	35+
Heavy Metal	Hard electric sound	men 18–35 women 13–24
Classical music	Educated	25+
Oldies	Rock from the 50s and 60s	25–49

Source: (In part) Jonne Murphy, *Handbook of Radio Advertising* (Radnor, Pa.: Chilton Book Co, 1980) 13–15 (updated, by author).

the listeners call in to a live show that reflects their interests and values.

Talk radio demonstrates how broadcasting can become a public forum when members of the audience can express their opinions to the moderator in the hearing of a large number of listeners. In some cases, the controversial nature of the interactions is what makes the show popular.

Musical formats   Both AM and FM radio program a significant amount of music, but as indicated above, they target the interests of segments of the population. In this way, the audience interests are met, and the effectiveness of advertising is more accurately assured. Music programming may serve the greatest variety of audience segments (see box 4.9).

In the 1980s radio broadcasters became increasingly alarmed at the drop in radio listenership across the country. The only musical format that has made significant gains in recent years is country music. Originally called "hillbilly" music, today's country music is less concerned with rural America and more concerned with the feelings of individuals. Many have called today's country music a combination of "red-neck rock" and contemporary rhythms.

The diversity of the population in the geographic United States creates small groups in different areas who are interested in similar programming services. Commercial satellite distribution is now the primary method of delivering programming to over 1,000 stations across the country. The services that package and distribute radio programs are often divisions of larger broadcasters, such as CapCities/ABC's services for entertainment, music, and informational programming, and NBC's interests in news, information, and talk radio. Still other organizations with special interests, such as the Sheridan Corporation, which specializes in Black entertainment, or Caballero, which carries Hispanic entertainment, have found it profitable to distribute their signals over satellites.

Technical Changes

While many radio stations continue to broadcast original programming, the realities of smaller audiences and lower revenues have encouraged some radio operators to reduce payrolls by automating many of the station's operations. In recent years, **automation** has increasingly been used to run pre-recorded programs, many of which are syndicated to various radio stations. Automated stations operate by connecting their local broadcast transmitters to the delivery service, which may come via satellite or computer. At certain times of the day news, weather, or a programming service can be broadcast with no disc jockey or engineer standing by.

There are different types of automated services, including fully operational **turnkey stations,** which are entirely automated, or **semi-automated stations,** which use some automated programming. Each type requires fewer radio personnel because interactions between programming services and local stations are accomplished by computer.

Technological connections currently in use influence types of programming and the number of personnel necessary to run a radio operation, but new distribution forms are being developed that will present the radio industry with further challenges. Digital Audio Broadcasting (DAB) is the next technical advance on the horizon.

Digital Audio Broadcasting

A new technology currently being considered by the FCC, the National Association of Broadcasters (NAB), and Congress is Digital Audio Broadcasting (DAB). In this new method of broadcasting traditional analog radio waves are converted to digital waves that can be transmitted by either satellite or terrestrial relay systems called Multipoint Microwave Distribution Systems (MMDS or MDS). While this system is still under scrutiny by all parties involved, DAB could ultimately revolutionize the distribution of radio and make our present forms obsolete. Because DAB would offer superior sound quality it could negatively affect those stations that currently broadcast in AM or FM.

The FCC officially began to investigate the viability of DAB on August 1, 1990, with their Notice of Inquiry into DAB, based on the potential of the technology to reproduce sound with greater fidelity than either AM or FM broadcasting. Since that time, broadcasters and common carrier companies have become very interested in DAB rather than traditional broadcasting means. The most significant effect of DAB, however, is that it would take more electromagnetic spectrum space for transmission than either AM or FM requires. Until this problem is solved, the FCC is unlikely to make it widely available .

To ameliorate the spectrum problem, the National Association of Broadcasters (NAB) has suggested that DAB be relegated to the Long wave frequencies in the electromagnetic spectrum, which are currently not crowded, and used primarily for military purposes. This would place DAB in the domain of terrestrial broadcasting rather than satellite distribution, and its range over geographical space would be severely limited.

CONCLUSION

Though nowadays many people regard radio as background sound, and virtually everyone in industrialized nations has grown up with exposure to radio, the medium is still evolving. From the earliest days of amateur operators and experiments in technical, programming, and business operations, radio grew from a specialized industry to the medium most capable of uniting an entire nation in instantaneous communication. Over the years, radio's power has been somewhat eclipsed by other communication technologies, forcing the radio industry to become more locally oriented.

Though many stations have begun to cater to local audiences, there are still some national services and nationally syndicated programs that have maintained the traditional approach to radio as a pervasive means of reaching audiences. Some of these services, like National Public Radio, and the syndicated shows that feature personalities, like Rush Limbaugh, Larry King, and Howard Stern, appeal to specific types of audiences. That audience may be found throughout the country, but does not include all listeners in every locality.

With new technology on the horizon, we may see a return to more nationally oriented services through DAB, or we could see further splitting of the industry into local, regional, and national services. Whatever the outcome, radio will remain one of the most pervasive forms of communication because reception technology is inexpensive, the medium can broadcast instantaneous information and entertainment, and radio has a unique ability to capture the imagination.

SUMMARY

Radio, like most electronic communication technologies, was the result of efforts by many scientists, inventors, and experimenters. In the growth and development of the industry:

- regulation was originally enacted to maintain the airwaves as a public trust
- content was adapted from other forms of media, and later, developed in response to audience segmentation
- the entrepreneurs of the radio industry often became the leaders in subsequent communications businesses, most notably, television
- radio has become an important and pervasive form of communication, but it seldom reaches a single national audience
- radio's popularity today can be seen as a part of the changing communication environment as more technologies compete for audience attention and different audio communication technologies usurp the power of radio to reach audiences.

DISCUSSION QUESTIONS

1. Try to imagine a world with no form of electronic communication. Suddenly, you have the power to receive signals from other parts of the country. How might your view of the world and your understanding of your place in it be challenged by the new source of information and entertainment?

2. Audiotapes of old radio programs are now readily available. Buy one, or borrow one from a library, and recreate the experience of listening to the radio the way people did when the program was recorded. Dim the lights, reduce distractions, and focus on the sound. Discuss the qualities of the program and the experience of listening to it in this way.

3. Have different members of the class listen to radio stations with different formats, and chart the amount of time spent on each segment, including the commercial breaks. How much information or entertainment does each format present?

4. Compare the discussions that take place on various types of radio talk shows. How are callers treated? How are guests treated? What topics are covered, and how well? Who do you think the target audience is for each of these programs?

5. Discuss individual students' preferences for listening to radio, records, tapes, or CDs. Why does choice play such an important role in determining what you listen to?

6. Examine trade publications such as Billboard, Record World, and Variety. How much attention is given to the radio industry? How much attention is given to the impact of musicians and styles that have crossover appeal to video, television, and film?

7. If students in your class come from many places, discuss the most popular radio personalities and formats from their areas. What contemporary values do these people and radio formats reflect?

REFERENCES

Barnouw, Erik. 1966. *A tower in babel; A history of broadcasting in the United States.* Vol. 1, To 1933. New York: Oxford University Press.

———. 1978. *The sponsor: Notes on a modern potentate.* Oxford: Oxford University Press.

Bilby, Kenneth. 1986. *The general.* New York: Harper & Row.

Dunlap, Orrin E., Jr. 1927. *The story of radio.* New York: The Dial Press.

Fowler, Mark S. and Brenner, Daniel L. 1988. A marketplace approach to regulating broadcasting. *Texas law review* 60 (February): 209–257.

Head, Sidney W. and Sterling, Christopher H. 1987. *Broadcasting in America,* 5th ed. Boston: Houghton Mifflin Co.

Interim F.C.C. head (James H. Quello). 1993. *New York Times,* February 8, D8.

Kaplan, Michael. 1991. Three men and their little empires. *Mediaweek,* January, 22.

Lazarsfeld, Paul F. and Kendall, Patricia L. 1948. *Radio listening in America: The people look at radio—again.* New York: Prentice-Hall, Inc.

Lazarsfeld, Paul F. and Stanton, Frank N., eds. 1944. *Radio research 1942–1943.* New York: Essential Books.

Murphy, Jonne. 1980. *Handbook of radio advertising.* Radnor, Pa: Childton Book Co.

Murrow, Edward R. 1968. *In search of light: The broadcasts of Edward R. Murrow, 1938–1961.* London: Macmillan.

Paper, Lewis J. 1987. *Empire: William S. Paley and the making of CBS.* New York: St. Martin's Press.

Sikes reaffirms preferences for simulcast HDTV. 1991. *Broadcasting,* Oct. 28, 27

United States Bureau of the Census. 1991. *Statistical abstract of the United States.* 111th ed. Washington, D.C.

Five

BROADCAST SYSTEMS
TELEVISION

MAKING CONNECTIONS

While radio had introduced news, information, and entertainment to the home, television threatened radio's popularity by robbing it of some of its most successful talent, and by providing images that no longer required the audience to imagine what their favorite performers looked like. As a result of television's success, the print, theater, radio, and film industries began to look for ways to recapture or hold on to their audiences. But in spite of using creative ways to gain attention, most of the other media forms had to acknowledge that first radio, then television, had ushered in a revolution in home entertainment.

The chapter on radio introduced individuals and industries that shaped the emerging field of broadcasting. Television followed the same pattern of development, but soon became a more controversial forum for the expression of social ideas.

This chapter discusses the growth of television and how it has dominated the media environment. Connections will be made among the following issues:

Chapter

- how the content of other media was adapted for television

- television's unique characteristics

- how viewers relate to the presentation of television images

- how industry practices have been influenced by regulatory trends

- how television's success is measured

- how significant a medium of communication television has become in our society

---

When television was marketed to Americans, it seemed that there were two groups of people: those who couldn't wait to see what television had to offer, and those who feared that whatever it did, it would further contribute to the diminishing of human interaction, introduction of radical concepts, or otherwise corrupt society. Despite the adoration and the fear that accompanied television's entry into the home, it has become one of the major communication technologies in our society, providing audiences with a forum for public ideas, an opportunity to share in communal information, and a release from other activities. It seems that television always has and always will invite positive and negative criticism. Perhaps a reason for this is that television is used for so many different purposes and is open to so many different interpretations. It provides services to its audiences, but can also enslave its viewers. Whether it is seen as good, bad, or neutral has to do with who is using it and for what purposes.

Since its successful mass marketing, television has become one of the most powerful communication technologies in our society. Almost everyone (98.2 percent of the population) has access to a television set (U.S. Bureau of the Census 1991, 556). More people have access to a television set than a telephone. The Nielsen Company reports that sets are on in the average American household more than 7 hours each day. Children typically watch 32 hours of television per week (Winn 1987). It seems only logical to think that because people spend so much time with television, the medium must have an effect on individuals and their knowledge of what issues are important in society. This relationship has been closely studied by academics, the government, and the communications industries. In this chapter television is the focus for the connections among these groups.

Early Television Developments

As indicated in previous chapters, many electronics firms experimented with sending television signals over the air. Philo Farnsworth successfully transmitted an electronic television signal in 1927, and patented both the television system and the receiver necessary to show the image. A few years earlier, in 1923, Vladymir Zworykin, an electronics technician who had been associated with both Westinghouse and RCA, attempted to patent his own television system. The controversy over who owned the idea behind a workable television system and receiver resulted in court conflicts that lasted until 1934.

Despite the litigation, Zworykin also patented another improvement for television picture scanning, the **iconoscope.** It was one of the first picture tubes, and it was an important invention because it regulated the flow of electricity and provided the necessary mechanism for the recording and presentation of images.[1]

The system Zworykin developed (working with a team of engineers) had a picture quality of 441 lines per frame. These "lines" of information reflected the scanning process of television, which uses **interlacing,** a system of picture composition that separates the image into two patterns. The picture tube then reconstructs half the set of lines, and before they disappear on the tube, the second set is assembled. This system debuted at the 1939 World's Fair, but it attracted relatively little attention.

Echoing the development of radio before the cross-licensing agreements of 1919, television needed a technical standard that would make all experimental systems compatible before it could be developed for a mass market. By 1941, the FCC endorsed the transmission standard of 525 lines per frame and 30 frames per second established by the National Television Standards Committee (NTSC), an organization made up of 15 major electronics manufacturers. This was the most sophisticated technical standard available at the time. It is the system currently in use for regular television broadcasting in the United States.

While television patent wars were being fought, new plans for the television industry began to take shape. Some entrepreneurs, anxious to profit from television and wrest control over it from the radio industries, embarked on a plan to centralize television operations in the United States. A center for television broadcasting, which would become "Television City," was proposed for Chicago's Navy Pier. Since New York had become the center for theater and radio and Hollywood was the film capital, a central location in the Midwest was

---

[1] *The iconoscope was the first technology used to convert electricity to an image, but shortly after its invention, the image orthicon tube was developed. This was eventually replaced by vidicon and later, plumicon tubes. Today, many cameras use computer chips to process information.*

thought to be the perfect place to house the new television industry. Broadcast signals would emanate from the Chicago transmitters and be rebroadcast to other parts of the United States, or be distributed through **coaxial cable.** AT&T controlled the coaxial cable, and would act as a common carrier, following the model established in the resolution between the Radio and Telephone Groups.

Unfortunately for the entrepreneurs, the country was moving toward war, and soon development of the unique broadcast center ceased. By the time the war was over, the television industry had become entrenched in New York, where successful talent and the radio powerhouses were already located. Navy Pier was abandoned, and the idea of central television broadcast facilities for the country was dropped.

By 1945, 95 percent of all radio stations in the country had become affiliated with one or more of the four national radio networks. With their extensive experience in programming and large talent pools, these stations paved the way for the growth of television at the end of World War II.

Creating Networks

Since radio networks already had distribution systems in place for transferring programming from one station to another, the pattern was repeated for television. Unfortunately, linking television stations for networking was not as easy as it had been for radio stations. The television image took up a larger portion of the telephone wire, and therefore overburdened telephone distribution systems.

The first coaxial cable designated specifically for television networking was laid in 1946. It connected New York, Philadelphia, and Washington, D.C. By 1947 coaxial cable was extended north from New York to Boston, and by late 1948, cities of the Northeast were linked with cities in the Midwest, including Chicago, Milwaukee, St. Louis, Detroit, and Cincinnati.

The Southwest and West Coast were connected in 1950. The first coast-to-coast link connected by both coaxial cable and microwave relay transmissions reached about 95 percent of the country's television sets. It occurred, auspiciously, on September 2, 1945, when President Truman addressed the peace conference recognizing the Japanese surrender. All 94 television stations (all that were then in existence) carried the speech, and the event signaled the official start of nationwide television broadcasting.

The end of the war signaled a turning point for television. From 1947 to 1951 the number of television sets purchased grew by 500 percent, increasing the number of television receivers in use to over 17 million.

Applications for independent television stations were also increasing as would-be broadcasters flooded the FCC with requests for licenses. With only 12 VHF channels available to serve the entire country, the FCC monitored areas

---

Box 5.1   The DuMont Network

From 1946 until 1955 a fourth network, owned by Allen B. DuMont, was in existence. DuMont was an electronics expert who pioneered improvements in television receivers. Although his company, Allen B. DuMont Laboratories, did much to improve television technology, it lacked a background in radio programming and broadcasting. As a result, the DuMont Network was always a poor cousin to the big three: CBS, NBC, and ABC.

The DuMont Network tried nobly to succeed. During the "Golden Age" of television (1948–57), DuMont produced some of the most innovative programs—they pushed the limits of what could be done in television broadcasting. But good ideas and innovative approaches were not enough. The licensing freeze effectively put an end to the DuMont network, since smaller stations preferred to sign with the more powerful networks, and DuMont could not maintain its network with so few stations.

---

to make sure signals were not jamming each other, ensuring geographic separation between license holders.

License freeze   On September 29, 1948, the FCC imposed a freeze on processing further television station license applications until the available channel capacity could be studied. The FCC also wanted to review debates over color television systems and the number of channels necessary to meet the perceived future needs of the television industry.

The resolution to the freeze occurred on April 14, 1952, with the FCC's *Sixth Report and Order* (41 FCC 148). The FCC decided to limit the number of stations allowed to operate as networks to those already in operation. To accommodate future demand, the FCC broke available airwaves into two types of frequencies: VHF (very high frequencies), consisting of channel numbers 2 through 13, and UHF (ultra high frequencies), including channel numbers 14 through 83.

By the end of the license freeze, CBS and RCA both had patented color television systems, but these systems were incompatible. In 1950 the FCC approved the CBS color system, even though it was incompatible with black and white transmission and reception technology already available. Consumers would have to purchase new receivers to receive the CBS color system.

After heated discussions in which the RCA system was overwhelmingly supported by manufacturers like DuMont and Philco, the FCC reversed its decision in 1953, and approved the RCA color system. This allowed manufacturers to make new television receivers that could receive both the black and white, and color signals. Still, color television did not catch on quickly. Advertisers were unwilling to pay for the high production costs of color programming. NBC (owned by RCA, the maker of the color system) was the only network to produce any programs in color. The three networks did not shift to all-color prime time programming until 1966. Even so, consumers did not want to part with their old black and white television sets. By 1972, only about half of the nation's television sets could receive the color broadcasts.

How Television Works

The principles behind television transmission and reception can be more easily understood if they are related to radio. Add a camera and picture tube to the broadcast transmission of electronic signals, and you have the framework of the system.

In a television camera, the lens acts as a mechanism to direct different wavelengths of images to the three color tubes in the camera (see figure 5.1). At the same time, the images are broken into **pixels,** which are mathematically constructed and transferred into a pattern of electrical impulses. The signals separated by wavelength in the three color tubes (red, green, and blue) go to a color mixer which produces a **luminance** signal. This signal processes the brightness of each of the parts of the picture scanned by the different color tubes. These signals are then combined in a color encoder to process **chrominance,** the quality of the colors. The signals are synchronized so that signals from all three color tubes are combined into one video signal, and the audio is synchronized with the image.

At the receiver, the reverse process takes place; luminance, chrominance, and synchronizations in the video signal, as well as the accompanying audio signal, are separated and routed to different parts of the receiver. The chrominance decoder splits the three color signals and the picture tube controls the scanning of images on the inner surface of the screen to form a picture. When the images are projected onto the screen, a layer of phosphors, which may be thought of as electronic "dots," illuminates the red, green, and blue colors. A shadow "mask" allows only the correct colors to reach the screen, and the phosphor coating of the screen reflects the colors that pass through the mask. The interlacing of these images presents, in combination with controlled brightness and contrast, images that appear to move in real time.

Ownership

After the FCC's 1953 ruling on ownership, broadcasters were limited to owning seven AM stations, seven FM stations, and seven VHF television stations. The

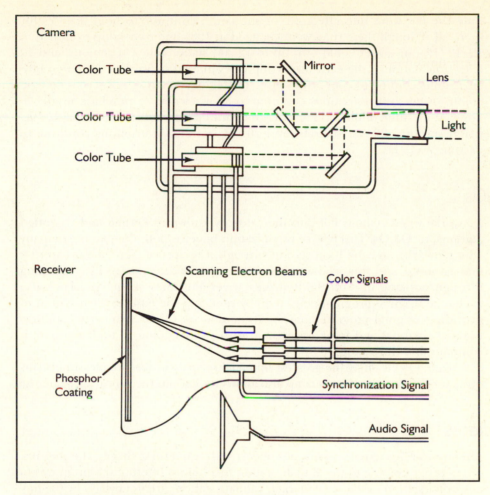

Figure 5.1 *How a Television Transmission Works.*
The image is registered by the camera where the information is broken into pixels and converted to electronic impulses. In color television, the colors are separated by red, green, and blue tubes. Colors are controlled both by luminance and chrominance signals and then transmitted. When they reach the receiver, the reverse process takes place and the image is "re-scanned" for visual presentation.

FCC's **duopoly rule,** stemming from a 1940 decision, limited any broadcaster from owning more than one station of the same type in the same market. One owner could, however, hold licenses for one AM radio station, one FM radio station, and one television station within the same market. In addition, the law contained a **grandfather clause;** if someone owned more stations prior to the time the law went into effect, he or she could continue to hold licenses for them all. Though these rules were changed in 1985 and ownership extended to 12/12/12 (an owner could own up to 12 AM stations, 12 FM stations, and 12 television stations), the early ownership rules limited networks and station buyers from becoming too powerful within any region. As a result of recent deregulation, ownership restrictions continue to allow owners to purchase more stations. At the time of this writing FCC guidelines permitted ownership of 12 television stations, 20 AM stations, and 20 FM stations; restrictions continue to become more lax.

O&Os

Network-owned stations fall into the category known as **Owned and Operated Stations,** or **O&Os.** This type of organization benefits both the parent company (the network) and the local station through a reciprocal agreement covering management and financial accountability. O&Os often share programming through hooking up with the networks at certain times of the day. They also exchange original programming, thereby reducing the costs to each station of providing original programming for its audiences. O&Os also carry combinations of national and local advertising, with profits going to both the parent company and the station.

While O&Os enjoy the greatest financial security in the broadcasting structure, another system of ownership also allows for certain reciprocal agreements.

Affiliates

Affiliate stations agree to work in concert with a network; that is, the network offers programming to the affiliate station first before offering the programs to any other station in the same market. Affiliate stations are not owned by the networks, but rather, have exclusivity arrangements with networks for programming on contractual cycles.

Almost three-fourths of the commercial stations in the United States are affiliated with at least one major network, and most of them operate as distribution agents for only one major network at a time, although there are stations (particularly in smaller markets) that affiliate with more than one network.

The Independents

For many years, independent television stations were the poor relations of the more powerful affiliates and O&Os. Without the financial support of network advertisers, independent stations had to raise money from local ads and pay for their own programming. Because of the power of demographics and markets, small independent stations often had a difficult time providing programming that would interest audiences and take attention away from the larger broadcasters. But since the Association of Independent Television Stations (INTV) was established in 1977, independents have gained power and a financial foothold in the broadcast marketplace. Effective lobbying efforts and INTV pressure on the FCC have given the independents more autonomy and control.

The majority of independent stations broadcast on the UHF frequencies, but as broadcast markets began to experience changes caused by the influx of cable and the localization of advertising, independents have found a niche. Many of them specialize in programming that serves a segment of the population not served by networks, O&Os, or affiliates. Special language, all news, all sports, and other programs targeted to specific segments of the viewing audience have become increasingly popular, especially now that cable delivers an improved signal. The specialized nature of the audience makes advertising more effective for certain products. Those targeting a male audience on a sports channel provide one such example.

The Fox Network

Perhaps the biggest challenge to network dominance has come from the Fox Broadcasting Company. Fox began to attract a number of independent stations, most of which were new and in the UHF frequencies, in 1986. Originally, Fox produced original programming only two nights a week, but by November 1989 it had picked up 128 affiliates and could reach (through cable) about 90 percent of the homes in the United States (Block 1990, 38). By 1991 it transmitted original programming seven nights a week.

The Fox Network's key to success was targeting a young audience and coming up with programs that would appeal specifically to them. Programs such as "Married . . . with Children," "Beverly Hills 90210," "The Simpsons," "Roc," and "In Living Color" were only a few of the original programs produced for an audience that advertisers truly desired—young people. Fox then offered advertising time at a lower cost than the rates charged by networks. Advertisers, happy to pay lower rates for an audience they felt certain to reach, flocked to the independents affiliated with Fox. The fledgling network quickly became profitable. The independents were delighted to have so much business. Fox can now truly be considered a fourth network.

Programming

The history of television programming reflects the technical skill and knowledge of the people working with the emerging visual form, but it has also been influenced by the interests of television creators and their understanding of what would interest the audience. If it is true that American values can be monitored by looking at television's content, programming during the early days of television indicate that the audience was willing to accept a wider variety of styles, formats, and ideas than are seen today.

From 1948 to 1957 television programming blossomed. Virtually all the production in those days was live, which meant the technical features of the medium were made to adapt to real time. In live TV any mistakes that were made went out over the airwaves. Directors learned how to exploit the intimate nature of a camera close-up; writers developed stories about families, morals, and social consciousness; and actors learned how to communicate in the small confines of a television studio for an audience that could only be imagined through a camera lens. This time of creativity has become known as the Golden Age of television.

The effective use of time slots for popular programs was a difficult obstacle to overcome at first. Since the United States is divided into time zones, the only way an audience on the West Coast could see a program broadcast live from New York at 8:00 P.M. was to tune in at 5:00 P.M. NBC, CBS, and ABC were eager to find a technology that could reliably record their programs for later broadcast. By 1955 a system of recording had been developed that met some of the broadcasters' needs.

The new technology was called the **kinescope.** It required either 16mm film or 35mm film to record live images as they were broadcast to a television set. Programs were recorded in 20-minute segments and the film rushed to be developed. The film could be processed and broadcast to West Coast audiences in three hours (Nmungwun 1989, 109).

The kinescopes that have survived time are often the only records we have of early live broadcasts, but the chemical composition of a kinescope is such that the originals become dry and brittle after a few years. The celluloid and the chemicals necessary to process film quickly were not of the quality used to produce feature films. The speed and procedures necessary to record the kinescope produced a product that became too fragile to play, and many of the recordings of early programs have deteriorated so badly they are no longer usable. Most of the existing recordings from kinescopes have been transferred to videotape to preserve the images, but unfortunately, many of the early shows are now lost forever.

Some examples of Golden Age programs still seem extraordinary, while others seem simplistic by today's standards. In 1957, when NBC's Kraft Theater mounted a production of "A Night to Remember," a play about the sinking of the Titanic, 105 cast members, a full orchestra, and 5 separate flats with scenery were crammed into one NBC studio. Two hours of numerous scene changes, musical transitions, and commercials, all in live performance, portrayed both the elegance of the upper decks and the crowding in steerage, dramatizing the influence of class tensions in the tragedy. The cameras were placed inside the round scenery flats. One camera would record one scene, then the director would cut to another camera recording a scene mounted on another flat, and stagehands would tilt and turn the first flat until the next scene could be rolled into place. The response to this program was so great that director George Roy Hill and the company repeated the entire live broadcast the following week.

Today, when we look at surviving kinescopes of "A Night to Remember," the scenes in the program seem tediously long, but the ornate sets and tight coordination are still extraordinarily impressive. When you realize that the pro-

---

Box 5.2   Programming Strategies

David Sarnoff, president at NBC, and William Paley, president at CBS, each placed his personal imprint on his network. Programming strategy at ABC was not as clearly defined as it was at the other two networks in the early days, because the network didn't have the resources available to mount programming as sophisticated or costly as the other two. In part, this was a result of the financial empires amassed by NBC and CBS in the radio industry.

David Sarnoff's interest in television programming was eclipsed by his interest in RCA's technological achievements. His attention focused first on Zworykin's iconoscope, and later on color television and electronic video recording. He left day-to-day decisions to his staff of trusted employees, but on occasion, he exercised his power and ability to persuade others to influence the type of programming NBC developed for television. He was particularly proud of the signing of the New York Philharmonic Symphony and the great conductor Arturo Toscanini to a series of televised concerts. By focusing attention on the power of television to disseminate fine arts programming to its audiences, Sarnoff presented an alternative to the critics who feared that television would be a medium for the basest of programming.

William Paley's contribution to programming involved developing a stable of popular performers and creating genres of television that showcased their talents. With the signing of Ed Sullivan, a popular newspaper columnist, as the host of a variety show, Paley's strategy of presenting well-known names to the public in television programs began to pay off. He located the most popular performers from theater and vaudeville and offered them their own shows. Some, like George Burns and Gracie Allen, Jackie Gleason, and Lucille Ball, ended up with long television careers. Not content to restrict his searches to the East Coast, Paley sent representatives to Hollywood to tap popular film stars.

duction was done live, it gives you a special appreciation for the intricacies of the Golden Age of broadcasting.

The Golden Age also was a time for experimentation with different types of genres for television. One of the most successful was the live-action magazine format. "Omnibus" was the forerunner of today's popular magazine shows like "60 Minutes" and "20/20."

CBS's big venture in drama was "Studio One," dedicated to the telecasting of an original drama every week. "Studio One" mounted productions of *Anna Karenina, Of Human Bondage,* and *Jane Eyre,* to name but a few, directed by such notables as Sidney Lumet, George Roy Hill, and Yul Brynner.

One of the great television pioneers of the Golden Age was Ernie Kovacs, who worked with television technology and used angles, zooms, and special effects to enhance his comedy show. If you tuned into the Ernie Kovacs show, you might see an entire scene apparently shot inside a fish tank, or a gentleman trying to pour coffee from his thermos—except the coffee would pour at an angle. Kovacs had the television camera shoot through a fish tank to simulate being underwater, and had entire sets built on an angle to perfect a 10-sec-

Figure 5.2 *Ernie Kovacs.*
Picture Source: UPI/Bettmann

ond sight gag. The results were a novel approach to producing entertainment for the home, and a better understanding by the television industry of the medium's unique power as a communication tool.

Television and the Film Industry

As television became more popular, the film industry became uneasy about the competition for audiences, and attempted to gain a foothold in television programming too. In 1952 Columbia Pictures formed a television subsidiary called Screen Gems to produce programs and commercials for television. Cooperative agreements were made between ABC and Paramount Theaters in 1953 and Walt Disney and Warner Brothers in 1954, but it was still more economical for broadcasters to produce live television. However, profit-minded programmers were faced with a problem: the longer the broadcast day, the greater the need for content to fill the hours. Therefore, in 1956, Hollywood arranged to release more than 2500 films made before 1948 to television.

From 1956 to 1957, sixty-three percent of all network programming was produced in New York, but some commercials, films, and made-for-TV films were produced on the West Coast. Production procedures for live television were faster than film production procedures. The visual styles of both types of programs encouraged viewers to see television as a distribution medium for both live TV and movies.

Television hurt the film industry by competing for audiences. Though 383 feature films were produced in 1950, the number dropped to 254 by 1955. And only 154 were produced in 1960 (Bohn and Stromgren 1987, 241).

The film industry attempted to be more creative with special technical improvements that emphasized the differences between the two media. They focused on the size of the motion picture screen as the key to success. Big screen technology and multi-camera production produced some interesting visual production styles, but the films had to be shown in specially outfitted theaters. Cinerama emphasized large-scale screen images and stereo sound, and was initially successful. The images projected on the screen were three times as wide as the earlier film image size—an improvement made possible by a process of filming with three cameras and projecting the film on a wider screen. Unfortunately Cinerama could only be shown in theaters that possessed a special projector and a special wide screen, so the new style was limited from the start.

Cinerama did stimulate more experimentation with other methods of production. Cinemascope was created by squeezing the images recorded by film into a smaller frame, but projecting them onto a screen that was two and two-thirds times as wide as it was high! This too required a wide screen, but movie theaters needed to invest only in a new lens rather than a new projector in order to show the film.

137

Figure 5.3 *Film Audience with 3-D Glasses.*
To "see" three dimensional images, special glasses with one lens made of red cellophane
and the other of green were dispensed to those who bought a ticket. The cinematography
used a special device to record images that, when viewed with the glasses, appeared to
have three dimensional images.
Picture Source: Museum of Modern Art/Film Stills Archive

Three dimensional images and 70mm film followed, as well as more films
produced in color (see figure 5.4). At the beginning of the television era, only
12 percent of the films produced in Hollywood were in color. In an effort to
attract audiences, the film industry boosted the number of color films to 58 percent by 1954.

Even though film survived as a major medium in its own right, the film
industry lost regular theater patrons consistently for years as the television audience grew.

Hollywood's path to survival was to get into the business of producing
prime-time television programs. Independent producers like Norman Lear,
Aaron Spelling, Leonard Goldberg, and Steven J. Cannell established their tele-

vision production facilities in Hollywood to take advantage of the film industry's infrastructure.

Syndication

The number of distribution outlets for television content has seen spectacular growth with the advent of cable, and this has opened the door to a more sophisticated pattern of program distribution. One area of tremendous growth has been the development of **syndication.** Syndicators are brokers for television content that includes packages of movies, game shows, reality programs, and television series that were originally broadcast by the networks during prime time. Syndicators sell entire packages of programs to other distribution outlets for presentation. Because syndicators generally broker programs that have already been broadcast and ratings information is available to estimate the size of the audience interested in the program or series, syndicators negotiate their contracts with a good amount of information to back up their sales strategies.

A syndicator may purchase packages of programs from production companies or may raise a part of the capital required to finance a new pilot or number of episodes. In return for its contribution to development the syndicator retains the rights to distribute the series nationally or internationally. Syndicators then charge an additional fee for their services that becomes pure profit when all costs have been paid. One of the most lucrative operations in media, syndication has increased its revenues approximately $1.2 billion each year since 1980, with projected revenues reaching $2 billion in 1993 (Growing Sales 1992).

The most successful syndicated program at the time of this writing is "The Cosby Show," which in its first year of syndication (1990–91) earned over $1 billion (Carter 1991, B-1). The highest rated television series of the 1980s, "The Cosby Show," made Bill Cosby the highest paid star on television. Even before he began his new series, "You Bet Your Life," a revival of a classic game show hosted by Groucho Marx, arrangements were made to put the new show into syndication, bypassing traditional network delivery for first run shows. The move of television's biggest star from network television to immediate syndication may provide a glimpse into the future. As the big three networks face competition from cable and other distribution forms, syndication may become the primary means of distributing content.

Generally, a television series becomes possible syndication material when there are 48 finished episodes. This is why you can often see reruns of a program that is still enjoying a long-running contract in prime time. Cable operators are the primary users of syndicated programs, but O&Os and affiliates often contract for syndicated content too. Station programming schedules can easily be filled with syndicated programming that is cheaper than original material.

139

Box 5.3   Senator Joe McCarthy and the Red Scare

Senator Joseph McCarthy of Wisconsin was an ambitious man who saw the spread of Communism in the world as a way to advance his own career. In the 1950s he persuaded Congress to establish a committee to "weed out" Communists and Communist sympathizers in the United States. He focused his attention on the entertainment industry because many Hollywood personalities and production personnel had taken part in leftist activities. Some were associated with the Communist Party, others were not. In his zeal to expose the members of the entertainment industry, McCarthy began what has often been called a "witch hunt," or the "Red Scare."

McCarthy knew his focus on the entertainment industry was guaranteed to give him maximum exposure by the press. By capitalizing on the power of television to reach audiences, and audience interest in entertainment personalities, McCarthy attempted to cast himself as a new American hero. In the end, however, a master reporter exposed his campaign as an effort to win personal attention.

Edward R. Murrow was one of the radio reporters who made a successful transition to television. On his interview program called "See It Now," Murrow grilled McCarthy on his motives. The interview revealed the inconsistencies in the Senator's motives and his use of third-party allegations to accuse suspected Communists. Murrow's careful questioning made McCarthy appear to be a babbling fool. Soon the audience lost interest in his mission and Congress dropped its inquiries into the Red Scare.

Fin-Syn

The FCC dealt a major financial blow to the broadcast networks with the **Financial Interest in Syndication** rules, known as Fin-Syn. These rules prohibit networks from syndicating shows that they originally aired. Thus, networks cannot benefit from the long-term revenue that syndication provides.

Networks produce only news, some sports, and a few other formats. None of these lends itself to syndication, since each has only temporary value. Networks pay license fees to production companies that produce entertainment shows, dramas, sit-coms, made-for-TV movies, and other specials. The production companies retain the right to syndicate their shows and sell time to advertisers. Because other media have been deregulated, the networks would like to see an end to fin-syn rules, so that they too can compete in producing and selling programs in syndication.

As other types of distributors have been allowed to engage in greater program distribution activities, the networks have begun to lose their control over the viewership of the United States. Knowing that audiences are tuning in more often to cable and less often to the broadcast networks, advertisers have begun to move their money to where the audiences are—cable.

 ## Television and Values

As television gained an audience, a new agenda emerged for viewers. Television unified the nation even more than radio had, and it addressed new issues emerging in society. Today the 1950s are often remembered for the good, simple values we've come to know from television programs produced in the 1970s like "Happy Days," and films like *American Graffiti,* but the reality was somewhat different.

Throughout the fifties the United States was experiencing a postwar adjustment that challenged many deeply held values. The national economy was not stable, and housing and jobs were in short supply. The growth of Communism around the world charged the political atmosphere. The United States sent its first advisors to Vietnam, and Senator Joe McCarthy's "Red Scare" became a part of the national agenda (see box 5.3).

The Civil Rights Movement was born in 1955 in Montgomery, Alabama, when black citizens boycotted a local bus company. Integration became a theme that would extend into the future. Blacks, who had been virtually non-existent in television, were becoming the subject of news and politics. Martin Luther King's famous "I Have A Dream" speech was heard nationwide, and white America was exposed to the reality of racism in a way never before seen in mass media.

Television played a large role in bringing these events into the homes of Americans through news broadcasts and drama presentations. While these images were making people more aware of the differences in society, quite different images of affluence, productivity, and the "good life" were being presented by television advertisers. The powerful medium of television was changing the audience's perception of the world.

The reflection of social values can be determined by looking to the way television treats some basic subjects. When Lucy gave birth to Little Ricky (see box 5.4), audiences responded to the joyous event with gifts and cards. Images of sexuality were not allowed on television in the 1950s, but because Lucille Ball and Desi Arnaz, the two actors in the show, were married, the program was allowed to focus on the outcome of a sexual relationship.

Box 5.4   Family Values

Ever since former Vice President Dan Quayle raised the issue of family values in the 1992 presidential campaign, exactly who and what constitutes a family has become a major topic of social discourse. For years television has portrayed families from all walks of life in a wide variety of circumstances.

When the actress Lucille Ball was pregnant, the character she played on television, Lucy Riccardo, was also written to be pregnant so that Ms. Ball could continue to play the part. The entire baby sequence for television was shot eight weeks before the birth of Ms. Ball's baby so that she would have time to rest before her delivery. Showing impeccable timing, Ms. Ball gave birth to a son on the morning of the day the fictional Lucy was going to have a baby boy. On January 19, 1953, the morning press reported the birth; in the evening viewers watched "I Love Lucy" and saw the fictional family welcoming a new baby. Viewers responded by sending gifts, flowers, and cards. Clearly, some viewers confused the real birth with the fictitious one, but most of the viewers were genuinely happy to celebrate the birth of the child of one of their favorite couples.

When the fictitious unwed mother Murphy Brown gave birth to a baby in 1992, viewers again celebrated with baby showers and parties. Did these viewers know that Murphy Brown was a fictional character and that the actress Candice Bergen had not given birth? Most accounts indicate that viewers realized there was a difference, but enjoyed having a reason to celebrate.

Parenthood, within marriage or without, and children, born within a marriage or without, still appear to be reasons for celebration, and perhaps this fact is a core component of "family values."

The Unique Qualities of Television

As indicated before, television was a powerful medium in part because it reached audiences in the home. The relaxed atmosphere in which audiences watched television, and the small size of the picture screen, which presented close-up images to their best advantage, made television seem to be an intimate medium. Television, it seemed, could create relationships that touched audiences personally. Occasionally, some programs that introduced popular characters also introduced new technical innovations that influenced the medium (see box 5.5).

Technical developments in video production and the development of videotape in the 1970s extended further options to broadcasters for the distrib-

Figure 5.4 *Lucille Ball and Desi Arnaz warm up the audience on the soundstage of their show,* I Love Lucy.
Picture Source: UPI/Bettmann Newsphotos

ution of their programs. Video technology, which is discussed extensively in Chapter 6, enabled new genres and styles of television to emerge. Not only did videotape prove effective in news and information programs, but studio production also used the multi-camera setup with video recorders.

In 1972 Norman Lear produced the first television situation comedy (sitcom) using multi-camera video production. "All in the Family" pushed the limits of traditional television comedy with its style of writing and characterization, and its "real" look provided by videotape.

Video production was cheaper than film, and quickly became a popular means of recording talk and game shows, too. As portable video technology improved over the years, video also began to be used for tabloid shows that relied on "reality" programming, a format that blurred the distinctions between news and entertainment. Programs like "Hard Copy," "Rescue 911," and "America's Most Wanted" received large shares of the viewing audience and

Box 5.5 Desilu Productions

One of the most popular television series both in its first run and in syndication has been "I Love Lucy," produced by the Desilu Production company, a creative group with Desi Arnaz as president and Lucille Ball as vice president. Arnaz had been a moderately successful bandleader and actor, but his greatest talent was as a producer. On television the star was his real-life wife, Lucille Ball.

Ms. Ball was an actress who was just starting to attract Hollywood recognition when CBS asked her to bring her successful radio show, "My Favorite Husband," to television. She agreed, but only if her real husband, Desi Arnaz, played the title character. CBS was skeptical. Desi was Cuban and Lucy was an American redhead. Would the audience believe they were really married? After several successful tests in which audiences were asked whether they believed the two were really a couple, CBS agreed to the arrangement. Desi wanted to change the format of the program to highlight Lucy's comedic talent with the use of slapstick humor. He became the straight man for her jokes. The battle of the sexes became the theme of the program, which was named "I Love Lucy."

But the show was more than just a comedy. When it debuted in 1951 it introduced a new style of television. Until then programs were either broadcast live from New York or shown in other time zones on kinescope. If a program had a live audience it was confined to a theatrical stage where only one camera could shoot the action. Desilu Productions wanted to shoot their program in Hollywood, on film, on a soundstage, and with a real audience. To accomplish this, Desi hired some of the most talented photographers, sound technicians, lighting designers, and support staff in the television industry.

A soundstage had to be remodeled to accommodate an audience of about 300 people, and cameras and lights had to be operated so the audience's view would not be blocked. Special technical apparatuses were developed for the show, many of which are still in use today. Most importantly, the process of shooting film with several cameras, all running simultaneously, and the recording of sound had to be controlled so the program could be edited efficiently. The end result was one of the most popular television series in history, and a style that revolutionized television comedy production.

were relatively inexpensive to produce (see box 5.6). In 1991 "Entertainment Tonight," which combined a magazine format with news techniques and flashy computer graphics, became the most popular program in television history.

Box 5.6   Connecting with Jo Holz, Director, NBC Audience Research

As Director of Audience Research for NBC's network news, Josephine Holz has an insider's view of what the audience expects and will watch. In a discussion focused on the current state of news research and the popularity of the new genre of programs that mix elements of news and features, called reality programs, Holz shared her views on the current state of the media. When asked what went on in news research, she said:

[There are] two sides to network research. One side is the ratings side and that's probably the primary research activity in any network . . . crunching numbers, analyzing data, identifying trends, making sales projections, and that kind of thing. . . . The primary activity of the research department is dealing with ratings. Then there is a smaller side which does primary research to try to make recommendations to improve the ratings. . . . There is a different amount of emphasis on primary research . . . at the different networks. Some rely on it a little more than others. There's quite a bit of research that goes into entertainment programming because that really is the bread and butter of the networks. And we also conduct some research on our news programs, which are becoming a more important part of the network schedule.

Q. Has CNN significantly affected the way you produce news or think about news?

A. Somewhat . . . it's not just CNN but all of the other sources that are out there for people. . . . People think of CNN as more of a headline-breaking sort of news service. CNN has not significantly affected the ratings for the evening newscast. That's the lowest rated period for CNN—when they compete with the network newscasts. . . . CNN does very well when there's an emergency, or a major story they can cover intensely, but then after that, when the story is over, their ratings fall back down to where they were originally, which is really quite low.

Q. What about the audience for reality shows?

A. The audience for reality shows is different than the audience for traditional evening news or even the morning shows, like "The Today Show." The audiences are basically younger. The majority of the traditional news audience is over the age of 50. And that's always been the defining characteristic of news programs in terms of the audience.

Reality shows are somewhat different. Their audience is more similar to the afternoon talk shows, although the talk shows have more women during the daytime. Evening shows appeal to men a lot, too, and more to people under 50, so there's an age difference. There's also a bit of an educational difference. The reality shows appeal more to less-educated segments of the audience.

Measuring the Audience: Ratings

Ratings are report cards for the mass media, but they also act as a standard by which the rates for advertisers are judged against the possible audience. Critics claim that ratings are often misused, relied on too much, or that they encourage television to cater to the interests of the "lowest common denominator." Although there is evidence to support each of these claims, the existence of ratings is tied to the fact that the mass media in this country are supported by advertisers. Ratings primarily serve the purpose of helping advertisers make decisions about how to reach their target audiences. Mass media rely on mass audiences, and though ratings may be controversial, no other method of measuring the size of an audience has proven successful.

The earliest rating system was devised by Archibald Crossley in 1929. Crossley randomly telephoned radio listeners to ask what programs they recalled hearing the previous night. When the American Association of Advertising Agencies (AAAA) found out about Crossley's information, they formed the Cooperative Analysis of Broadcasting (CAB) organization and in 1930 hired Crossley to inform them of his findings.

In 1934, C. E. Hooper, Inc., an organization that had traditionally conducted studies of magazine and newspaper advertising effectiveness, began doing radio surveys, which eventually became known as Hooperatings. The big difference between the Crossley and Hooper ratings was that Hooper saw advertisers as its clients just as much as it regarded the broadcasters as clients. Hooper's methods have been criticized for reporting findings that both organizations would find useful.

In 1942, A. C. Nielsen, Inc., began using an **audimeter** to conduct its Radio Index. The audimeter was hooked directly to the receiver in someone's home and recorded what channel was tuned in, and what time it was being heard, on paper tape (and later, on 16mm film). At the end of the week, each Nielsen family would replace the paper or film and send the coded information to Nielsen headquarters. Nielsen would then send them fifty cents for their trouble. The ratings took about six weeks to determine.

In 1950 Hooper sold its operation to Nielsen, Inc., and Nielsen began using a combination of Hooper's and its own ratings systems to record television viewing. By 1961, improved measurement and analysis procedures had decreased the turn-around time to 16 days, and, in 1967, to nine days. By 1973 the time was reduced to one week, and now, reports are issued overnight.

In 1987 Nielsen introduced **peoplemeters,** an audience measuring device that requires viewers to punch in personal code numbers when they start and end their viewing. Unfortunately, people often forget or don't bother to do so. Broadcasters were upset that their ratings appeared to drop considerably as soon as the peoplemeters were in place. Peoplemeters, like audimeters, do not tell the ratings company whether people are really watching television, or if the set has merely been turned on. In the future a **passive peoplemeter** may be used, which will have an infrared sensor to detect who is really in the room when the set is on. The organization most interested in using passive peoplemeters is Arbitron, Nielsen's primary competitor.

While the term *ratings* is commonly used to identify audience measure-

---

Box 5.7   Computing Ratings

When ratings and shares are computed, the numbers are always relative to the number of households that own a radio or television set and those with the set "on" at any given time.

There are currently 92 million television homes in the United States. If 30 million homes are watching a certain show, the **rating** is computed by dividing 92 million into 30 million.

$$30,000,000 \div 92,000,000 = 32.6 \text{ rating}$$

To determine a program's **share,** the number of homes using television HUTs (homes having the television *on*) is divided into the number of homes tuned to a program. If 25 million televisions are tuned to CBS, and 60 million televisions are on at that time:

$$25,000,000 \div 60,000,000 = 41.6 \text{ share}$$

ment, the media industries use specific terminology to indicate parts of the overall reporting process. A rating is an estimate, given as a percentage, of the total number of households tuned to a specific station or network at any given time. It relies on the count of the number of receivers that could possibly be in use. The number of receivers tuned to a channel is divided by the total number of receivers in the United States, whether they are on or not. The number of households with television sets in the United States is approximately 92 million. A share reports the percentage of the total households that are actually using television during a specific time tuned to a specific channel. The share then, indicates the percentage of users of the medium rather than the percentage of receivers. Ratings are used by sales staffs to help them set ad rates, while shares are more often used by programmers who want to see how well one program is doing compared to others shown at the same time.

While past investigations into the validity of ratings systems have proven that they do reliably judge audience size, there are several questions that ratings do not answer. Ratings cannot address subjective questions, such as:

- What is it about a specific program that interests a viewer?
- How important is program quality to the viewer?

Technological improvements that speeded up ratings reporting allowed programmers to respond more rapidly to a program's success or failure. While in the past a network might have "optioned," or paid for exclusive rights to a show for 13 episodes in one season, the quick turnaround time of ratings reports has encouraged programmers to option to fewer episodes. By 1980 networks were ordering only four to six episodes of new shows. If overnight reporting showed two or three bad weeks of ratings, a show could be canceled before it had time to cultivate an audience.

Quick cancellations of programs became the second area of complaints about ratings services. Advocates of giving programs time to develop audiences cited popular, long running shows like "All In the Family," "The Mary Tyler Moore Show," "M*A*S*H," and "Lou Grant" as evidence that it takes time to build an audience. But the networks turned deaf ears to the complaints, arguing that they could not afford to lose viewers when the cost of supporting shows was so high and advertisers were unhappy with slow results.

In the 1980s, network revenues had slumped in reaction to the growth of competing distribution outlets like cable and videocassette recorders. From 1981 to 1990 each broadcast network's share dropped as shares for cable increased. By 1990 a mere 63 percent of the viewing public was tuning in to the broadcast networks. In 1991, for the first time in its history, NBC posted no profit at the conclusion of the year. CBS and ABC posted moderate profits, but it appeared that the era of network domination of the airwaves had come to an end (see figure 5.5).

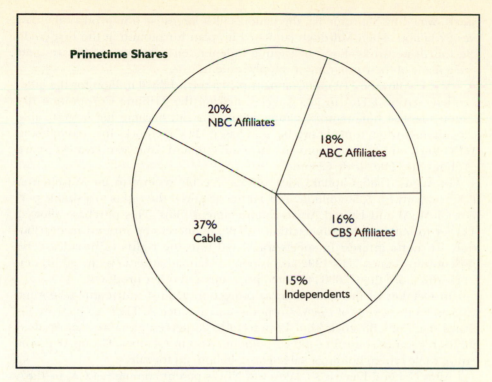

Primetime Shares

20%
NBC Affiliates

18%
ABC Affiliates

16%
CBS Affiliates

15%
Independents

37%
Cable

Figure 5.5   *Network and Cable Shares.*
Cable receives the larger share of daytime programming (42 percent), with the overall day share of viewing at 15 percent.
Source: "Cables's Audience Share Rises Year 'Round " (Advertising Supplement) Advertising Age (February 11, 1991) C24.

Changes in Ownership and Power

During the 1980s changes in ownership transformed the television business. No longer could a few individuals—such as NBC's David Sarnoff and CBS's William Paley—influence an entire industry. Now there was a host of powerful new players.

Nineteen eighty-six was a banner year for mergers, takeovers, and purchases. In March, the largest merger in the United States outside of the oil industry occurred when Capital Cities Communications purchased ABC for $3.5 billion. That same month, Ted Turner tried—and failed—to take over CBS. Rupert Murdoch's News Corporation paid $162 million for 50 percent ownership of Twentieth Century Fox Film Corporation. In May, Murdoch and Marvin Davis, another media entrepreneur, together purchased seven television stations formerly owned by Metromedia, the nation's fifth largest station group—the cost was $2 billion. Then Murdoch launched his plan for mounting the first credible fourth network—Fox—by signing independent stations as affiliates and using many of their programs to supply content.

Also in May, the Tribune Company paid a record $510 million for the independent station KTLA in Los Angeles, making the Tribune Corporation the nation's largest non-network station group. Viacom became the largest cable programmer when it made two big purchases: MTV Networks Inc. (comprising MTV, VH1, and Nickelodeon) for $690 million, and American Express' share of Showtime/The Movie Channel.

In August 1986, Capital Cities sold its 53 cable systems to the Washington Post company for $350 million. Ted Turner acquired the rights to a sizable portion of MGM and United Artists Entertainment films. This purchase allowed Turner to build up his superstation, WTBS, by increasing interest in distribution. Turner's interest in sports translated into the rights to broadcast the "Friendship Games." His 1992 acquisition of Hanna-Barbera enhanced his network with more than 3,000 animated programs and other products.

In October of the same year, as protection against unfriendly takeovers, CBS asked the owner of Loews Corporation, Laurence A. Tisch, to increase his firm's share of CBS stock from 12 percent to 25 percent, a move that resulted in Tisch gaining control of the corporation. Also in October, Group W put its entire cable system holdings, valued at $2 billion, up for sale.

After General Electric's takeover of NBC's parent company, RCA, in 1987, the transformation of the U.S. television industry had left no network untouched. Each of the new corporate leaders pledged to improve business practices in their networks. They would implement fewer frills, fewer executive perks, smaller staffs, greater cost control, and strict attention to profit margins.

These new business arrangements changed traditional organizational structures. The type of control over programming, distribution, and syndication rights exercised by the diversified companies created by mergers is called **vertical integration.** This means that a program produced by one production company can be syndicated by a division of the parent company. Arrangements may be made to distribute a program simultaneously in first run to broadcast television, in syndication nationally and internationally, and in home video. Vertical integration is also demonstrated by Hollywood studios like Universal (MCA Inc.) and Lorimar Telepictures, which have purchased television stations, and Walt Disney Productions, which has established a successful pay cable network, The Disney Channel.

The Networks in Decline

Alternative distribution channels for television material, like cable, videocassettes, and pay services (discussed in Chapter 7) have all contributed to the networks' decline. Most of the activity is attributable to the decentralization and deregulation of the media industries that occurred throughout the 1980s, and the networks' inability to kill the fin-syn rules in Washington. With their highly paid lobbyists mounting the battle for network parity, the networks were over-confident about their ability to put pressure on the FCC. Their efforts failed, and when the FCC continued to bar the networks from getting into the production business, film studios seized the advantage and moved into television station ownership.

A 1991 FCC paper from the Office of Plans and Policy (OPP) predicted a gloomy future for broadcast television. Pointing out that the broadcast industry "has suffered an irreversible long-term decline in audience and revenue shares which will continue through the current decade" (Setzer and Levy 1991), the report continued:

> . . . the decline in audience share will probably slow over the next decade as cable matures. . . . One could speculate that by 1999, average network prime-time viewing shares might fall to 15 percent, while the average all-day viewing shares could well sink to 8 percent.

Television and Ethics

There are several ways to approach the relationship between television and ethics. Does television mislead audiences for the sole purpose of getting them to buy the products advertised? Does television mislead them by allowing us to think that the values expressed in its programming are those of mainstream America? Does the television industry operate solely by the profit motive, or is there a real interest in delivering a variety of viewpoints and styles of information to audiences?

Obviously, the answers are complex, but they are well worth considering. Television is a business, but it is also a powerful mediator of ideas and images. Should the television industry exercise a measure of responsibility toward its audiences, or only toward its stockholders?

One way to address the ethical dimensions of television in our society today is to examine the role of the industry, the power of the visual image, and the role of the audience. If the industry were to act responsibly toward the audience and show a sense of responsibility in the images it constructs, and audiences were to develop a degree of media literacy so that they could better understand television images within a larger context, the ethical issues might not be so controversial. Mere acceptance of things "as they are" does not address the complexities created by the interaction between images, values, attitudes and beliefs.

There will always be surprises in how audiences react to content, in who is affected more by certain types of content, and the long-term effects of certain images. Developing critical standards to better understand how television operates within its usual contexts is the best way to operate in good faith. The industries that respond to these needs will act more ethically toward their audiences. The audiences that exercise critical standards and ask more of the television industry will also be acting in a more responsible, and ethical manner.

CONCLUSION

The structure and ownership of television has changed quite a bit since the medium was inaugurated, but public opinion has changed far less. When television was a new technology, many people expressed fear about its power over the audience—particularly over children. These fears continue today. Television has been called "the idiot box," "the boob tube," and "the vast wasteland."

Despite the derogatory terms leveled at television, it remains one of the most pervasive and available technologies of communication today. Television has evolved from a medium that relied on the mass audience, to one that can serve many different interests and target audiences simultaneously. Television's power to act as a national medium still emerges from time to time, such as when it covers war, disaster, or celebration.

Television has represented the values of our society, introduced new issues and ideas, and has proven to be effective at keeping tradition alive. Through connections with satellites and video technology, it provides images from around the world.

Like any technology, it can be abused. When television becomes a replacement for discussion, personal interaction, or intellectual inquiry, it may become restrictive. Viewers need to pay conscious attention to how and why they use television in order to live with it successfully.

The television industry has changed. Once the networks were Goliath and the cable companies were David. But federal deregulation of other media industries has changed the situation to the point where we now have two Goliaths: the networks and the cable companies. It will be some time before we see whether the two Goliaths can live together, or whether one will eventually slay the other.

SUMMARY

Television has become an important medium of communication primarily because it is in the home, where audience reactions are conditioned by the informality and comfort of their surroundings. As a powerful medium, it has also undergone many changes:

- television has challenged the prominence of earlier technologies, but is now challenged by newer ones
- the industry developed out of the radio industry, and conflicts over incompatible technical standards have been common
- television reflects national values, introduces new ideas, and brings new concepts to the home
- threats by alternative media forms and changes in corporate ownership have changed the nature and operation of the television industry

DISCUSSION QUESTIONS

1. Discuss the television programs that were most important to you as a child. What made them attractive to you? Do members of the class share your perspective? Can you trace any values you currently hold to television?

2. Write down what television programs you would hate to miss during the week, and those you think would be a good example of bad television. Share the two lists with the class and discuss what factors appeal to you in your favorite programs, as well as what factors constitute bad television. Find areas of agreement on what constitutes bad television.

3. For one evening, watch two hours of television that you normally would not watch. What are your observations? Why did you choose these two hours? Do your perceptions match those of other class members? To whom do you think these programs were directed?

4. If possible, watch some television programming from another country. Even if there is a language barrier, what elements of the program communicate to you? What do they communicate?

5. Collect television reviews from newspapers and magazines. What critical standards have the reviewers/critics used? Are they appropriate?

6. Pretend that your class has been asked to cast a soap opera. Budget is no problem in hiring the actors you want to play certain roles. Define the roles, and suggest one actor or actress to play each part. When several roles have been "cast," discuss the reasons for the names that have been suggested. Were the actors typecast? Does your cast represent the real ethnic, racial, and gender division in society, or the picture of the television world? How are they different?

7. If you were a television programmer, how would you create programs that exploit the unique features of the medium but also guarantee large audiences for your advertisers? Are these two goals incompatible?

153

REFERENCES

Abramson, A. 1955. A short history of television recording. *Journal of SMPTE* 64.

Auletta, Ken. 1991. *Three blind mice: How the TV networks lost their way.* New York: Random House.

Barnouw, Erik. 1970. *The image empire: A history of broadcasting in the United States from 1933.* New York: Oxford University Press.

Block, Alex Ben. 1990. Twenty-first century Fox. *Channels,* Jan., 36–40.

Bohn, Thomas W. and Stromgren, Richard L. 1987. *Light and shadows: A history of motion pictures.* 3rd ed. Mountain View, CA: Mayfield Publishing Co.

Cable's audience share rises year 'round (advertising supplement). 1991. *Advertising Age,* Feb. 11, C-24.

Carter, Bill. 1991. Cosby sidesteps networks in big TV deal. *New York Times* (October 28): D1, D8.

Growing sales. 1992. Advertising Syndicated Television Association. *New York Times.* (January 28): A1.

Holz, Josephine. Interview with author. New York, August 14, 1992.

Nmungwun, Aaron Foisi. 1989. *Video recording technology: Its impact on media and home entertainment.* Hillsdale, New Jersey: Lawrence Erlbaum Associates.

Setzer, Florence and Levy, Jonathan. 1991. Broadcast television in a multichannel marketplace. *OPP working paper no. 26.* Office of Plans and Policy, FCC, Washington, D.C.

United States Bureau of the Census. 1991. *Statistical abstract of the United States, 1991.* 111th ed. Washington, D.C.

Winn, Marie. 1987. *Unplugging the plug-in drug.* New York: Viking.

IMPROVEMENTS IN VIDEO TECHNOLOGY

MAKING CONNECTIONS

The software and technology for the distribution of video, whether by television or other means, is one of the most revolutionary developments in the world of information and entertainment in the 20th century. Though not always as obvious as one would think, video technology, including the recording, editing, and presentation processes, has made the television, cable, and home video entertainment industries what they are today.

An examination the connection between the technological growth of the television industry (covered in Chapter 5) and advancements in video technologies yields a better understanding of the future of visual communication. New technologies and techniques will undoubtedly lead to new uses and new ways of perceiving and understanding visual images.

This chapter focuses on major changes in the television industry resulting from the development of improved video technologies. The following issues are discussed:

- how the unique characteristics of videotape and video technologies influence media con-

Chapter

tent and business practices

- how the instantaneous image produced by video influences viewers' perceptions

- how portable video technology has revolutionized television news and entertainment

- how home use of video has become big business

- the future of video, including high-definition and three-dimensional television

An apocryphal story says that David Sarnoff asked RCA for three presents to celebrate his 50th year in broadcasting: an electronic air conditioner, a light-weight device that could record signals off television, and inexpensive tape to record the signals (Gerson 1981, 54). It took several years for these developments to occur, but each has had a significant impact on society. Only two of Sarnoff's wishes will be discussed in this chapter; the development of the **video-cassette recorder (VCR),** and the invention of videotape, necessary for recording signals. While the two were being developed simultaneously, the knowledge necessary for the invention of videotape preceded the possibility of a light-weight recorder for its use.

The Development of Videotape and Video Technologies

While cable and satellites continued to change the nature of the distribution of television and other video-based information services, new developments in the production of television and video content began to affect programming and the operation of the broadcast industry. Most significant was the development of videotape, which could be edited efficiently and electronically. Ultimately this invention would reduce the cost of television production and open the door for a host of new distribution forms and media uses. The improvements in video technology discussed in this chapter all began at about the same time television was becoming popular in the United States. The result is a history of improvements in television and video that grew from infancy to maturity simultaneously with the audience's acceptance of home video technology. This may explain why audiences have so readily adopted new video technologies.

The Invention of Videotape

The technical development that most changed television industry practices was the invention of videotape. It was a technical possibility only because there had been earlier refinements in magnetic audio recording tape (see box 6.1). Videotape had its debut on November 11, 1951, when the Electronics Division of Bing Crosby Enterprises first demonstrated its ability to record images in black and white. Two years later RCA successfully demonstrated videotape recording in black and white as well as color but the recording technology was not well developed. A 19-inch reel was necessary for the half-inch wide tape, and the entire reel could record only 15 minutes of a program (Adams, 1956).

Box 6.1   Development of Magnetic Tape

Some of the earliest experiments with reproducing sound were done by a metallurgist, Oberlin Smith, in 1888. Many of his theories were tested by Thomas Edison and his staff during the development of the phonograph. While Edison thought the best medium for storing and reproducing sound was a wax disc, Emile Berliner, the young salesclerk who eventually became an employee of Alexander Graham Bell's, discovered the possibility of recording sound on a disc made of shellac in 1888.

For several years many scientists in several countries attempted to improve sound recording and reproduction. A major breakthrough in Germany in 1946 paved the way for recordings on tape. The chemical firm of I.G. Farbenindustrie A.G. and one of its subsidiaries, BASF, developed a magnetic tape that could record sound and be played on hardware manufactured by another company, Allgemeine Electricitaets Gesellschaft. One final development, the magnetophone, which produced high-fidelity sound, completed the system required for magnetic recording and quality sound reproduction on audio tape. Also originated in Germany, the magnetophone provided the critical tool for effective sound reproduction while screening out background noise.

During World War II, a young serviceman named John Mullin who was stationed in Germany heard and observed the effective sound quality produced by the magnetic tape. When he returned to the United States in 1946 he found several investors, and established contact with the Ampex Corporation. The first U.S. demonstration of audio recording on magnetic tape was on May 16, 1946, in San Francisco. The magnetophone and Ampex development specialists worked together to perfect first audiotape, then videotape.

Source: Aaron Foisi Nmungwun. 1989. *Video recording technology: Its impact on media and home entertainment.* Hillsdale, New Jersey: Lawrence Erlbaum Associates.

The big news in videotape came in April, 1956, when the Ampex Corporation demonstrated their new videotape recorder at the CBS-TV affiliates meeting. This recorder was more portable and made more precise starts and stops than earlier records. Finally a technology had been developed to effectively use the videotape that was then available. The videotape used by the Ampex system was two inches wide, and the equipment needed to record, edit, and play it was large and cumbersome.

Videotape has a dull black side on which the recording is made. The dull appearance results from a coating of oxide particles that "hold" the electronic impulses that make up the information on the tape. On one edge of the tape an audio (sound) band records sound simultaneously with the visual images being recorded in the largest portion of the center of the tape. The control track on the other edge of the tape regulates the speed and stabilizes the tape as it passes the audio and visual heads, which record or play back the information to the tape (see Fig. 6.1). Impulses are electronically recorded on the oxide particles of the tape. When the tape is played, the information recorded on the tape is reproduced in a pattern that scans two "fields" of information per frame (see Chapter 5). One field is scanned from top to bottom, then another field begins. The system of "overlapping" fields is called **interlacing.** When the two fields of information are completed, a "frame" has been created. In the United States, the technical standard used for television (and, therefore, also for videotape) is the presentation of 30 frames per second, for a pattern of 525 lines of resolution (picture quality) per frame.

Much of the success of finding applications of videotape can be credited to the Sony Corporation, which, in 1964, introduced a new machine that

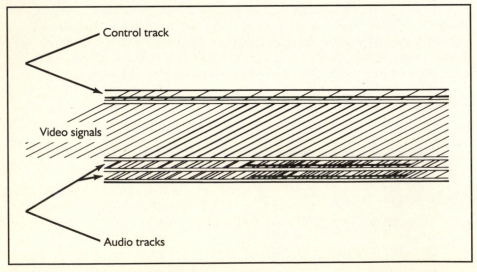

Figure 6.1   Electronic Signal Registration on Videotape.

improved on the scanning design of the previous recorders. The Sony machine enabled the user to stop the action and advance the tape in slow motion. Ultimately Sony advanced the technology so that portable videotape equipment could be used.

Early videotape was edited like film, but it took longer to splice tape and cement it for a change in scene, because the editor could not see the image on the videotape the way he or she could on film. Editors had to use their best judgment to physically cut and cement two pieces of tape together to make an edit. Occasionally the edit would be incorrect, causing a **glitch** or visual imperfection when the tape was shown.

Outdoor activities, specifically sports, offered the best opportunity to exploit the immediate response of videotape, but moving the heavy videotape equipment outdoors posed a serious logistical problem. Once this problem was overcome, the presence of the videocamera at sporting events and the instant replay of action in a game became commonplace.

Instant replays focused audience attention on details of the sport. At the Army-Navy football game on New Year's Eve, 1963, the instant replay was used for the first time, and by 1964 the instant replay became a common sight in televised football games. Football became a popular component of sports programming on television (Barnouw 1970, 245).

Videotape and Perception

Though the average person may not know whether what he or she is watching on television is live, recorded on videotape, or recorded on film, each presentation form creates a different relationship to the viewer. Many people, with a little coaching, can tell the difference between film and videotape. It is virtually impossible to tell the difference between a live presentation and one recorded on videotape. Each has an identical quality or "look."

Does this really matter? The differences between the two forms are so subtle that many viewers do not care. Even if the difference is brought to their attention, it may have no significance for their appreciation of the content, but studies show that the viewer's perceptions are influenced by the form of technology used to present an image. As discussed in Chapter 2, the audience's perception and cognition is profoundly affected by the different presentation of images.

Videotape compared to film   The use of film on television was so firmly established by the time videotape was developed that many viewers did not suspect that a change was taking place in the software used in television production. But film had definite drawbacks. For one thing, film required time for processing. Feature television content intended for entertainment purposes could be recorded on film, since shooting schedules could be planned around

159

the film processing time. If a scene didn't look right, or if something went wrong in processing the film, the scene could be re-shot at a later date and edited to produce a smooth flow of content. But this technique was costly, because actors and production crews had to be hired for another day's shooting and sets might have to be reconstructed or rental fees paid for use of a location. These costs increased the budget for each television film. Production houses and giant studios could support the costs, but smaller television operations didn't have the same financial resources.

Film was particularly inappropriate for news stories, which had to be as current as possible. If the production crew failed to shoot an important image, there was no time to go back and shoot it again. When video was used, the tape could be rewound and images checked before sending it to the studio for broadcast. Film also required that more control be exercised over the lighting necessary for production. This meant a crew member had to be assigned solely to control artificial light and in doing so, made the production more artificial for the recording of people unused to the production process. Many people unaccustomed to media presentations found themselves staring into bright lights beamed at them by an electrician while a camera operator pointed a camera and an audio technician extended a microphone. The costs of sending a two- or three-person crew to cover a news event were prohibitive, and the processes necessary for shooting a good quality film image were eliminated, which made some news stories appear staged or artificial. In many major news centers the crew carted several hundred pounds of equipment. Some news programs, such as the 1953 "Camel News Caravan" on NBC, shot material on 35mm film. Others, like the "CBS Television News with Douglas Edwards," used 16mm equipment, but were considered second rate for this very reason (Barnouw 1970, 42). Larger stations often had messengers standing by to rush the film to the processor in hopes of getting footage on the air before any other station.

Before the advent of videotape, the "look" of most television programming was virtually the same, whether the program was an action/adventure story or a filmed report of a local accident. Coverage of news events was evaluated by the same set of standards as entertainment programming, and the look created by film made news reports appear to have been staged. These factors gave American television an overly finished, or "slick" look. To look professional, television had to project the appearance of total control over its content. Any deviation from what the American public had come to expect from feature films was unacceptable.

Improved Portable Video Technologies

Throughout the 1950s and 1960s, all major networks were conducting experimental projects with video. One of the first successes of the 1960s was claimed by CBS, which, while working with a Japanese firm, developed the first "portable" video camera, weighing "only" 120 pounds. In 1968 CBS introduced the first video cassette system, called Electronic Video Recording (EVR).

In 1974 CBS contracted with the Japanese firm Ikegami to produce the first truly portable minicam video camera. The result was the HL33 camera—a 33-pound "handi-lookie." After this improvement video could be used for live, on-the-spot coverage. The new camera could also be used with a recorder to record on videotape and play back instantaneously.

By 1975 Sony had developed a recorder and portable editing deck that could edit three-fourth-inch videocassettes. Finally, a combination of camera, recorder, and electronic editor had become portable enough for the needs of news programs.

ENG and Field Techniques

The next few years saw video technology grow rapidly. News was a natural subject for an instantaneous medium. Video coverage of news events was called **electronic news gathering (ENG)**. (This term is often used synonymously with electronic field production, or EFP.)

By 1974, ENG was being used extensively in coverage of the Vietnam War, sometimes called the first "television war" because it was brought to millions of Americans in their homes via television (MacDonald, 1985). The first station in the United States to use ENG exclusively was KMOX, a CBS O&O in St. Louis, which started using the technology in 1975.

Within a few short years, the major networks reduced their news film crews to one or two persons, who were now a "video" crew. An electrician was no longer needed since video equipment could operate in natural or indoor artificial light without the addition of extra brightness. Video equipment could also record audio simultaneously, making audio-technicians unnecessary. One person could carry or "wear" all the equipment necessary for on-the-spot recording. Most major operations continued to have a crew of at least two to help with details and to carry equipment, and also to appease the technical unions, who were resentful about the use of fewer workers.

The reduced costs of using ENG were a benefit to broadcasters. While film equipment was cheaper than video technology, operational costs were less with video production. The overall cost factor was a major strength of ENG technology. Only three percent of the commercial television stations used ENG in 1973, but by 1979, 86 percent were relying on it (Stone 1980, 5).

More studio developments
As video technology developed, a time base corrector (TBC) was added to the system. This device adjusted the control track on the videotape to run at more precise speeds to facilitate the electronic editing process. An uncorrected tape could have an uneven control track that

would create a **glitch,** or visual imperfection, in the edited tape. The TBC corrected the control track so that it could ride past the heads of the editing machine far more easily, and edits could be more controlled.

Computerized editing further decreased the amount of time it took one person to edit a piece of tape. A computer code could be imposed on a segment of the control track, and the computer editor could use it to find the "in" and "out" points. This type of electronic coding for edits made the entire electronic process more effective.

In addition, special effects generators (SEGs) and **character generators (CGs)** were developed to enhance videotape either as it was being recorded or in post-production. SEGs are used to create interesting visual effects such as wipes, dissolves, and moving computer images. CGs create text to accompany the visual images. These technologies make the finished project look sophisticated and professional.

The speed with which video technology developed has allowed for greater experimentation with the medium in other fields. While video pioneers in the television broadcast industry have continued to encourage development of video and related technologies and to exploit the video form in various broadcast modes, the portability of the equipment and the cost-effectiveness of video technology have allowed it to be adapted for even broader uses.

SATCOM   As the capability for satellites to connect with studio technology was developed in the late 1970s, the instantaneous transmission of visuals and sound from virtually anywhere in the world offered another possibility for newsgathering. Called satellite communication, or SATCOM, the connection of video and satellites made it possible to bring live action from around the world to the studio setting.

We can see how the news and information industries changed over the years by focusing on leaps in technological applications. When video became an accepted source of instant information and an established component of news production, it was just a matter of time before videotape, satellite, and broadcasting technologies would be connected to create yet another breakthrough in news style.

During the Iran hostage crisis that lasted from 1979 to 1981, these technologies came together in ABC's program "Nightline," hosted by Ted Koppel. When the American Hostages were seized in Iran, foreign journalists were expelled from the country. Rather than go to the expense of having special reports produced elsewhere and fed into the "Nightline" broadcast, or of flying experts to the ABC studio, "Nightline" producers established satellite links with experts located around the world and allowed Ted Koppel to interview them via satellite from the ABC studio. Live, long-distance interviews presented a new visual aesthetic, and a new interview format was born.

Figure 6.2 *Ted Koppel interviews UN Secretary General Boutros Boutros Ghali, via satellite.*
Picture Source: ABC News

Clearly, the capability of video technology to capture and transmit images instantaneously was an advantage in the newsgathering process. Not only was it cost-effective, but the process and techniques were vital to producing timely news. The techniques have become so popular today that entire genres of programming have been produced on videotape rather than live in a studio or on film.

Another key area of videotape and video technology is the boom in home use of video. VCRs, and more recently, camcorders, are bringing new communication possibilities to the home.

Videocassette Recorders

Videocassette recorders (VCRs) have gained in popularity throughout the 1980s and 1990s, contributing to changes in television viewership and home entertainment patterns. It is almost surprising how quickly VCRs spread throughout the United States. In 1984 about 30 percent of U.S. homes with television sets also had VCRs, and, by the end of 1992, that figure had grown to 58 percent.

163

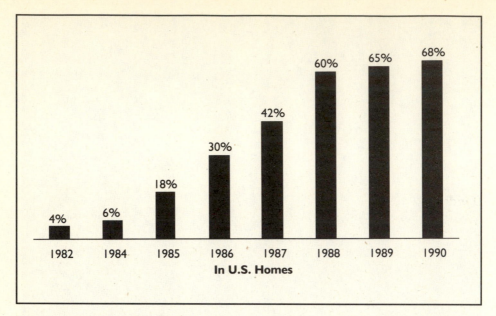

Figure 6.3 *Growth of VCRs.*

Prior to the development of home technology, videotape came in two sizes, which was a significant impediment to using it for many purposes. The Sony Corporation was reluctant to change format from their U-Matic VCR designed for professional use, which required tape that was three-fourths-inch wide. The picture quality and the durability of the U-Matic had given Sony an edge over others in the VCR marketplace, but the U-Matic cassettes had only enough tape for one hour.

While VCRs had been used in television studios and in educational and business settings since the 1950s, the year usually given for the birth of the home video market was 1975, when Sony introduced the Betamax machine to the home consumer in the United States. Prior to that time the video recording business had been dominated by Ampex in the United States and by the Sony Corporation in Japan. Soon other firms in Japan, the United States, Great Britain, the Netherlands, and West Germany were all competing in the home video market.

Though not totally committed to the idea of one-half-inch tape for home consumers, Sony allowed one of its engineers to develop a prototype recorder, the Betamax. He used a patent from a firm originally owned by RCA called JVC (Victor Company of Japan), which had been sold to Matsushita. Sony tried to persuade JVC to cease development of its own 1/2-inch format, VHS, but the firm refused. It entered the market with the VHS system soon after the

Betamax was introduced. A valuable feature of the VHS recorder was that it could record at variable speed, up to four hours at a time.

At first home VCRs were touted as a means of time shifting—recording programs and viewing them at a different time. But by 1977 VCRs had spawned another industry—the rental of pre-recorded videotapes. This successful marketing venture was the brainchild of a Detroit businessman, Andre Blay, who formed a mail-order club, called Video Club of America, to distribute feature films. Soon the motion picture companies realized that the distribution of feature films could provide them with a new and lucrative source of revenue. The capacity of the VCR to shift time by recording TV and cable programs reached its peak just in time for the beginning of the home video rental business (Lindstrom 1989, 45; Marlow and Secunda 1991, 130), and the home video market exploded. According to the Nielsen ratings company, the use of pre-recorded videocassettes constituted 49 percent of VCR use in 1982. By 1985 that figure had risen to 80 percent, and by 1986 it was up to 90 percent (cited in Lindstrom, 46).

Industry analyses now indicate that people who have VCRs rent about 51 videocassettes each year (Veronis, Suhler & Associates 1991, 116); spending approximately $100 a year on videocassette rentals. The same families may spend as much as $67 on purchases of videocassettes (see box 6.2).

The videocassette sale and rental businesses have surprised many people in the electronics industry. In the five years between 1985 and 1990, video user spending increased over 32 percent, making this the fastest growing sector of the communications industry. Prices of videocassettes for sale have also declined in recent years. The average price of a pre-recorded tape in 1985 was $29.55; by 1990, the cost had dropped to $21.50.

While the VCR has been widespread for several years now, we have just begun to understand how it changes people's viewing patterns. What we have

Box 6.2 Videocassette Spending Per Household

Year	Retail Purchases ($)	Rentals ($)	Total ($)
1985	$27.08	$ 83.33	$110.42
1990	66.67	102.33	169.00
2000 (projected)	75.00	121.74	196.74

Source: Veronis, Suhler & Associates, *Industry Forecast.* (June 1991): 116.

learned so far is that it has not changed the amount of time people spend viewing television. But it has changed the amount of time spent with other communication technologies. Fewer people go out to the movies today than in the past, and the VCR is largely responsible for bringing the movie-viewing experience into the home.

Camcorders

The development of the camcorder, a low-cost, portable camera that records images on videotape, has replaced traditional "home movies" on 8mm film. But camcorders have been adopted by home consumers at a slower rate than VCRs.

In 1981 Sony introduced a small combination video camera and recorder that created a "videomovie" (Nmungwun 1989, 194). Other manufacturers like RCA and Panasonic entered the market soon after, but consumer interest remained low. In 1982, the Video Standardization Conference, established by 122 companies interested in the future of home video recording, agreed on a technical standard that would require the use of 8mm tape in a cassette.

Part of initial low consumer interest in home video recording had to do with the cost of camcorders (over $1000 in 1983, dropping to $700 by 1992) as well as the weight of some of the earlier models (as much as 12 pounds). The expense and weight were more prohibitive than that of other technology like still cameras or Super 8 film. Still cameras could effectively reproduce objects that don't move. Super 8 technology was cheaper than video technology, and the slow processing time for the film didn't seem to bother home consumers. Until the costs of home recording equipment came down, there was simply little interest in home video. Today, however, interest seems to be rising as costs for camcorders have become lower, and the units themselves more portable. The newest camcorders, Super-VHS (S-VHS) and Super-VHS-Compact (S-VHS-C), both with a superior picture quality to earlier cameras, are still more expensive than the most pervasive format, VHS, but the lightweight feature of the technology has interested consumers who have become more accustomed to having videotape available for immediate viewing.

 ## Future Video

The biggest change in broadcasting technology in the future will be the availability of **high definition television (HDTV)**. HDTV offers a much clearer image than present-day television sets, replicating the visual clarity, color range, and screen size of 35mm film. It provides audio quality similar to that of digitally recorded sound. The most obvious physical difference between HDTV and current technology is the size of the screen, which increases the aspect ratio (dimensions of the picture) from 4:3 to 5:3 (see figure 6.4). The HDTV picture quality is far superior to any other home video technology to date.

Figure 6.4 *Spectrum Compatible HDTV Compared to a Traditional Television Receiver.*
Picture source: Zenith Electronics Corporation

HDTV development has been slow because many competing technical systems have been researched by different companies and different nations. In the United States at least 20 format variations have been considered by competing manufacturers. Some of those companies have established consortia to develop different components of the HDTV system.

In 1990 the FCC and Congress approved the HDTV system proposed by Zenith and AT&T, called "Digital Spectrum Compatible" (DSC-HDTV) television. Using a progressive line scan system that "paints" images on the screen rather than using the interlacing system, DSC-HDTV presents an entire image in one-sixtieth of a second rather than one-thirtieth of a second.

What makes DSC-HDTV so attractive is that it meets the FCC's requirement that any new HDTV system be able to simulcast regular NTSC signals for use by older receivers. Through signal compression, DSC-HDTV will not require a larger bandwidth in the electromagnetic spectrum. Special filters will prevent the HDTV transmissions from interfering with conventional broadcasts.

The slow development of HDTV in the United States has little to do with the cost to broadcasters wishing to send HDTV signals, but rather with the cost of home receivers. These currently range from $2,000 to $5,000, but prices are expected to drop to approximately $1000 to $1500 by the mid-1990s.

The system developed in the United States is visually similar to the HDTV systems developed in Japan and Europe, but differs most in wave form and method of distribution. The Japanese HDTV signal provides 1,125 scanning lines, but is distributed via satellite in analog waves. Since November, 1991, NHK, the Japanese broadcasting system, has been experimenting with transmission to a variety of locations outfitted for HDTV reception. The Japanese have also signed agreements with Hollywood to purchase several film packages, which conveniently fit the new aspect ratio of HDTV and will provide hours of HDTV compatible programming. The Eurikon system, created by a consortium of European companies, also uses satellite distribution and operates in an analog mode. Its picture resolution operates at 1250 lines.

DSC-HDTV in the United States would be capable of 1,575 lines of resolution, and could be transmitted over traditional terrestrial carriers, including microwaves, cable, or optical fiber. A digital technology, it would take less energy to transmit than analog formats, and therefore, could use smaller transmitters and antennas.

It is important to remember that each of the systems under development is not compatible with the others. It will not be possible to create content in one HDTV format for use by others unless the signals are converted the way different international signals must be converted to fit different technical standards.

Why are there competing systems? Each nation or development consortia hopes that its system will become a world standard. If so, that nation or group will stand to make a great deal of money from the manufacture of receivers and broadcast and production equipment.

For European countries that are geographically close to each other, one system for all of Europe would not crowd the usable frequencies, and could be accommodated more effectively by satellite signal distribution or cable. But if the Eurikon system becomes the standard for the whole world, the available bandwidths for video transmission will be increasingly crowded because the system requires more frequencies, causing potential jamming in areas now used for satellite coverage. Similarly, signals could bleed into other FM frequencies. For these reasons, alternative systems and other forms of distribution are currently being considered for more effective signal transfer.

The cost and problems associated with HDTV mean it is unlikely that home consumers will soon have HDTV systems. Prototype displays and experiments may soon be available to a wider audience, and HDTV is currently being used for some types of television production, which are later converted to the 525 NTSC standard. Toronto, Canada, has become a center for HDTV production that provides film-image-quality product for television broadcast, and uses the capacity to transfer standard formats for presentation of high-quality images shot on HDTV to other systems currently in use.

Signal Compression

Another technical advancement that will allow more programming to be transmitted via satellite or cable is the newly developed ability to compress signals into smaller space. Digital compression uses computer techniques to squeeze three to ten programs into a single channel. Using this technology, DSC-HDTV can be made more precise, and it will take up far less room in the electromagnetic spectrum, while at the same time using less power.

Three-Dimensional Television

While it may be a long way off, three-dimensional television could become a consumer gimmick. If you've ever been to Disneyland or Disney World's Haunted House, you may have been surprised to see yourself sitting next to a filmy ghost-like figure. The apparitions in the Haunted House are holograms that are projected from light sources placed strategically at different angles to "mix" into a three-dimensional image. To make these ghosts "move", the light sources change angles. These holograms are not very different from the simple holograms you can see on a credit card. When you tilt the card to one angle you see one image, but when you tilt it another way you see something different. In this case, you provide the angle, the card has the emulsion base with different images etched at different angles, and the light is reflected from the emulsion giving the appearance of movement when you change the angle.

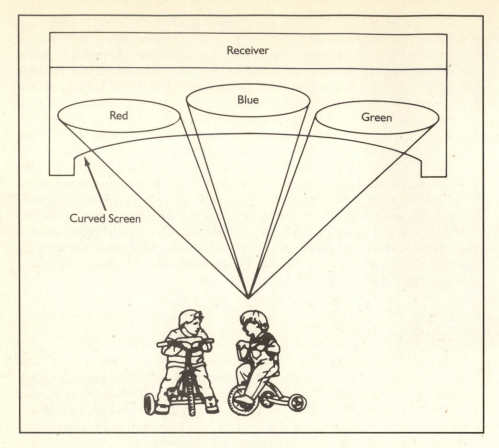

Figure 6.5 *Curved Screen and Angles for 3-D TV.*
In this prototype system the 3-D image would be projected in front of the screen. Two-dimensional images would remain in the background.

It is not difficult to simulate a three-dimensional image with television, too, but at this time the images would also appear filmy or gauze-like. The only way you could see them well would be to center yourself in front of a special curved television screen. (see figure 6.4).

Three things are currently necessary for the creation of a three-dimensional image on a television set: angles, light sources, and a special thick emulsion base that can register and record projected images. Light sources projecting red, green, and yellow beams converge at a point in front of the screen, giving the impression that the image is "mixed" in front of the screen, even though traditional two-dimensional images can still be seen on the screen. The result might look as though Joe Montana were throwing a football to you in your living room, or the advertiser was extending an arm to tempt you to try a bite of a new food product.

Three-dimensional TV is available in some experimental facilities like museums or specially adapted theaters, but it is unlikely that this technology will move quickly into the home because: (1) it is expensive, (2) no regular broadcasts transmit 3-D signals, and (3) it requires a viewing space larger than that available in most homes. At this point, one entire room could be taken up with the technology, and only one or two people would be able to sit in the best position for viewing the image. Of course, if HDTV becomes the norm, the picture quality and size of 3-D technology could become more popular, and the increase in visual information packed into the signal would require more complex receivers to present the images. When people purchased new sets, they would have the technology necessary for reception.

CONCLUSION

From the industrial setting to the home environment, new developments in video technologies have revolutionized traditional practices. Within the broadcast industry video has enabled the production of a wide variety of genres including new news formats. VCRs have permitted time shifting and have given more entertainment options to both industry and the home, and have provided yet another element of competition to traditional broadcast networks.

Video technology exploits the unique characteristics of an instantaneous image that simulates live broadcasting. Video recording capacity and additional technologies make it possible to enhance, change, and edit images quickly and effectively.

With more video developments coming in the future, the images we will see may have the capacity to manipulate our perceptions even further than they do now. What is most remarkable is that we will feel their presence in the intimate environment of our homes. These new technologies and services could well require new home viewing arrangements, including rooms that will accommodate larger screens, present the maximum effect of 3-D presentations, and disseminate digitally perfected sound. If we have grown up with television, how will we respond to these newer video technologies?

SUMMARY

The new technologies discussed in this chapter share several characteristics:

- they rely on the development of video-related hardware and software
- at the level of industrial use, video technology has revolutionized the way some programs are produced
- the unique qualities of the video image, portable video technology, and the storage mechanism provided by videotape have allowed video technology to be used for a variety of purposes
- portable recording devices have created opportunities to make connections between other media industries such as film and the home market
- the availability of video technologies to the home consumer has given audiences greater opportunities to manipulate and understand the instantaneous nature of video
- new developments in video technology are likely to change our relationship to video content in very interesting ways, creating entirely new viewing experiences

DISCUSSION QUESTIONS

1. Can you tell the difference between video, film, and live television? How do you describe the visual image? Do you feel that different "looks" contribute to your perception of the type of program you watch?
2. View a typical newscast and attempt to determine how many different video technologies are necessary for the presentation of the various images. Include CGs, SEGs, and any SATCOM images you see. How much of the newscast is made up of electronically created special images?
3. Discuss typical uses of VCRs in class; do many people still use them for time-shifting, or are they used more often for playing prerecorded cassettes? What are the class' spending habits regarding VCR use?
4. If possible, obtain a videotape or film produced in another country. Are the same styles, techniques, and technologies used? Can you infer any cultural biases in the way the programs are produced?
5. Put yourselves in the role of media executives trying to determine which programs you will broadcast first with HDTV and possibly 3-D systems. Which programs would work in these different formats? Which ones would suffer?

6. If possible, use a camcorder to record an event on campus or at home. When viewing it, be critical about the styles and techniques used in producing the tape. How are our critical standards for viewing television brought into play when we take on the task of producing low-budget video?

7. Watch and critique an episode of one of the home-video television programs, such as "I Witness Video," "America's Funniest Home Videos," etc. How aware do you become of the role of the camcorder in determining what we see, and how we see it?

REFERENCES

Abramson, A. 1955. A short history of television recording. *The Journal of The Society of Motion Picture and Television Engineers* (February) 64: 250–51.

Adams, Val. 1956. TV is put on tape by new recorder. *New York Times,* (April 15):1, 76.

Barnouw, Erik. 1970. *The image empire: A history of broadcasting in the United States from 1933.* New York: Oxford University Press.

Gerson, Bob. 1981. Happy birthday videotape! *Video review.* (January) 1: 54–55.

Henke, Lucy L. and Donohue, Thomas R. 1989. Functional displacement of traditional TV viewing by VCR owners. *Journal of advertising research* 29(April/May): 18–23.

Lindstrom, Paul B. 1989. Home video: the consumer impact. In *The VCR age: Home video and mass communication,* ed. Mark R. Levy. Newbury Park, Calif.: Sage. 40–49.

MacDonald, John F. 1985. *Television and the red menace: The video road to Vietnam.* New York: Praeger.

Marlow, Eugene and Secunda, Eugene. 1991. S*hifting time and space: The story of videotape.* New York: Praeger.

Nmungwun, Aaron Foisi. 1989. *Video recording technology: Its impact on media and home entertainment.* Hillsdale, N.J.: Lawrence Erlbaum Associates.

Rosenbloom, Richard S. and Cusumano, Michael A. 1987. Technological pioneering and competitive advantage: The birth of the VCR industry. *California management review* 29 (4): 51–72.

Smith, Marvin. 1985. *Radio, TV, Cable: A telecommunications approach.* New York: Holt, Rinehart, and Winston.

Stone, Vernon A. 1980. ENG growth documented in 1979 RTNDA Survey. *RTNDA Communicator* 34 (January): 4–15

Veronis, Suhler & Associates. June 1991. *Industry Forecast.* New York: Veronis, Suhler, & Associates, Inc.

Seven

CABLE DISTRIBUTION AND INTERACTIVE SERVICES

AKING CONNECTIONS

Cable television in the United States has had a significant impact on the broadcasting industry. From a humble beginning, cable has grown to become a major media distribution form. Part of its success is the result of technical advances in video technologies and distribution forms, but another important part lies in its development during a time in history in which deregulation influenced the industry, and the FCC actively sought to encourage alternative television delivery. Originally considered a poor stepchild of the broadcast industry, cable's growth has been phenomenal.

Now, however, as the government seeks to reregulate cable, the entire industry is poised on the threshold of monumental change. Will cable maintain its audience as other alternative delivery systems challenge it in the way it once challenged the broadcast networks?

In this chapter, the development of cable is viewed as an alternative to the broadcast industry. Because of its introduction to consumers and its ascendancy at a specific

Chapter

period in history, the events associated with its growth could provide a lesson for other emerging distribution forms. This chapter focuses on:

- the origin of cable as an alternative means of receiving broadcast signals

- the competition cable has given the broadcast industry, and the challenges it now is experiencing from other industries

- how the cable television industry benefited from developments in satellite distribution and alternative services

- how programming has addressed the interests of specific target audiences

- experiments in home distribution that use connections between broadcast and narrowcast technologies

- how the deregulatory climate gave cable a competitive edge over the broadcast networks

---

From its infancy, television operated in a broadcast mode and was scrupulously regulated. Though new technologies such as portable video enabled television to experiment with different types of production and content, distribution technologies have also dramatically affected the types of programming available.

From the beginning, cable was viewed as a practical alternative to the dominance of the broadcast networks. Because the industry had the option of programming several channels, the FCC considered cable a way of encouraging multiple viewpoints and a variety of programming to meet the interests and needs of a diverse audience. Since the characteristics of the cable audience were somewhat more identifiable (through subscription information that provided the address and the types of programs to which individual households would be interested in subscribing) than those of the broadcast-programs audience, advertisers quickly turned to cable. Even better, from their perspective, was the fact that cable advertising was significantly cheaper than broadcast advertising, since cable companies received much of their revenue through subscriptions.

Cable and other technologies (such as VCRs and videodiscs and services like pay-TV and text-based content) distributed to smaller audiences are sometimes referred to as **narrowcasting.** When cable and other technologies are connected through a variety of distribution forms, including satellites and microwaves, they may change the concept of mass communication as they attempt to reach smaller groups.

This chapter explores cable, the primary alternative television-distribution form. With its attention to the interests of smaller audiences, cable may be viewed as a stepping-stone to more personal communication environments. (For more on this, see Chapter 8.)

The most obvious difference between cable and the broadcast industry is the way the messages reach the audience. This distribution form is reminiscent of wired communication technologies and reflects some similar concerns; cable can be a direct link to a specific audience, but it also can be subject to the problems of wired communication. To better understand how cable began to be regarded as both an alternative television-distribution form and a method of direct delivery, the original purpose of cable television should be addressed.

Cable's Humble Beginnings: Wired Television

Cable television started in the late 1940s as community antenna television (CATV). Rural communities located in mountains, valleys, or other areas where topographical barriers interfered with reception had difficulty receiving broadcast signals. With the goal of delivering signals to these communities, a number of enterprising individuals began to connect antennas in locations that could

---

Box 7.1   Early Cable

One of the first cablecasters was a radio and television receiver sales representative, Robert J. Tarlton of Lansford, Pennsylvania. Lansford, a town 65 miles from Philadelphia, received only weak television signals because the Allegheny Mountains interrupted the signal. In 1949, Tarlton tried to set up individual antennas for the people of Lansford, but it didn't take him long to realize that the eventual outcome of the plan would be a jungle of antennas. As an alternative, he and some friends invested in a company called Panther Valley Television, and they hooked up homes to a single mountaintop antenna for an installation charge of $125 plus $3 per month. With the community able to receive three clear stations, Tarlton quickly began selling television sets.

Source: Thomas Baldwin and D. Stevens McCoy. *Cable Communication* (Englewood Cliffs, N.J.: Prentice-Hall, 1983), 8.

receive clear broadcast signals—for example, the top of a mountain—and relay these signals to hard-to-reach areas by cable (see box 7.1).

In the early days of CATV, the cable connections were made through arrangements with local governments. The most sensible arrangement appeared to be the granting of a **franchise** agreement, wherein the cable operators were given permission to operate as a monopoly in the area for a designated number of years.

The cablers attempted various schemes to attract subscribers. One approach proposed to black out television commercials. It was assumed that people who were likely to have their homes hooked up to cable for better reception would not want the intrusive commercials; but the alternative was a few minutes of blank screen, which was just as annoying as the regular commercial fare. Though blacking out of commercials did attract subscribers, cable companies quickly found that audiences were not happy with the holes in their programming. Within a few months, most companies that had promised to black out commercials were filling the time with local advertising spots.

Most of the other attempts to gain subscribers involved promises of more television channels, clearer reception, and the possibility of uncut movies to be shown in the future. Though clear reception was one thing cable could provide, the increase in the number of additional channels was slow at first, and the uncut movies lasted only a short time until most cablecasters found that it was more profitable to run commercials during films. Audiences were accustomed to commercial breaks in films shown on television, so few registered any complaints.

Government Interest in Cable

In the early days when CATV and cable operations were small and operated on the local level, the FCC had little interest in interfering with their operations. Taking the position that cable was not using the airwaves, the FCC declined to accept any authority over the new form of distribution. But as cable companies looked for ways to increase the number of subscribers, they turned to **augmentation,** a means of adding services such as importation of distant signals or locally originated programming.

Independent broadcast stations, most of which were on the UHF band, felt threatened by the new competition from cable for viewers. Many of the independent stations had small audiences (compared to the networks) and had learned how to cater to the specific interests and needs of their viewers. These stations also had cultivated relationships with local advertisers and worried that increased competition would pull viewers and advertisers away from their programs.

The FCC had tried to protect UHF stations for years, acknowledging the competitive edge of the networks and clinging to the principle that UHF at least offered viewers some diversity of programming. Even network affiliates began to feel cable's power when cablecasters duplicated their broadcast signals in service packages.

Then cable companies began to use microwave relays to transmit their programs over distances to other carriers, and the FCC stepped in to impose restrictions on a case-by-case basis. From 1962 to 1966, the FCC decisions were made in an ad hoc manner, but, in 1966, the regulations were extended uniformly to all cable operators.

After 1966 the FCC heavily regulated cable television. Not only were cablecasters required to carry local television stations, but they were not allowed to duplicate network programs on the same day that the network aired them. Furthermore, cable operators in the top hundred markets were required to demonstrate how their operations would not endanger the financial stability of the existing television stations in those markets.

To further differentiate cable from broadcasting, the FCC mandated that cable prove its commitment to local communities by providing a **community access channel.** In every application for a franchise, a cable company had to promise that one channel would be reserved for community activities, such as high school sporting events, town meetings, or even talent shows from a senior citizen's center. Any individual or group that wished to produce a legitimate program was to be given the support facilities to do so.

The problem with community access, however, was that the resources necessary to maintain a vigorous program were costly to the cable companies. Maintaining equipment that could be used for public purposes and training individuals to operate cameras to produce something that looked good enough for the cable channel were time-consuming, frustrating, and often expensive. For this reason, many cable companies did not actively promote their community access channels. When the channels weren't used by the community, the cable companies used them to transmit text material or low-budget programming from other sources. As communities relicensed cable franchises and the government moved toward deregulation, the community access requirement was dropped, although some communities chose to retain it in their relicensing contracts.

As cable entered the 1970s, the industry experienced a variety of challenges. Most notably, the number of subscribers began to grow (see figure 7.1), largely because of the new services cable was offering. By 1971, 2750 systems served almost six million homes.

Other distribution technologies also were becoming available, and these provided yet another wealth of material for cable programmers. Prior to 1972, satellites could be used only by private firms or the government. The FCC's "Open Skies Policy" allowed satellite companies to rent their services for the distribution of signals to commercial enterprises. The first company to take advantage of satellite distribution of television content was Home Box Office (HBO).

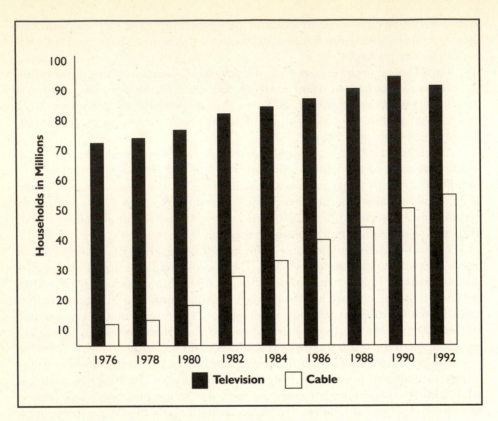

Figure 7.1 *The Growth of the Television and Cable Industries.*
Source: Cablevision *(September 21, 1992) 25.*

How Cable Works

Cable television companies combine program services, technical facilities, and billing services. At every cable franchise in a community, satellite dishes receive signals beamed from the program providers for distribution via cable to the homes of subscribers. At the facility engineers route the "packages" of channels to homes that have contracted for different services.

In addition to community services, which may include community access facilities and local-origination programming for the people of the area, cable companies sometimes offer customers special services such as **pay-per-view,** specific one-time, one-charge viewing opportunities. Examples of pay-per-view include the Olympic coverage of 1992; special first-run movies; sporting events such as boxing; or performance programs such as rock or jazz concerts.

Cable companies also arrange for the wiring of subscriber homes. The connections made between home and company are maintained and monitored by the cable franchise operator.

Billing and additional charges (for services such as pay-per-view) also are monitored and handled by the company. Sometimes franchises are part of larger organizations known as **multiple systems operators (MSOs)**. These companies act like cable networks to contract for programming services and the distribution of content throughout the member companies. More on multiple systems operators follows, but in the meantime, the content of cable television needs to be discussed for better understanding of the services cable provides.

Pay-TV

Knowledge of the way cable companies obtain their programming is essential to understanding how costs for certain services are determined. While basic services may include the broadcast networks and a few additional channels, premium services known as pay-TV make up a significant portion of cable programming.

Home Box Office started in 1972 as a service of Time, Inc., to distribute movies and special events to subscribers. At first, HBO signals were distributed through microwaves in the UHF frequencies, but the signals were scrambled so that individuals could not easily receive a clear image on their television screens unless they paid for decoders. The scrambling did not provide effective protection, however, because a rash of entrepreneurs learned how to make cheap descramblers, which they marketed for as little as $10.

The financial turning point for HBO occurred in 1975 when the company began using a satellite service to distribute its programming to cable companies. HBO's popularity grew quickly because Time, Inc., owned a number of cable stations, and they all invested in receiving dishes that would pull the HBO signal from the satellite and retransmit it to cable homes. Soon other pay-TV services became available. Different distributors, such as Viacom's Movie Channel, Showtime, Warner-Amex's Movie Channel, and Times-Mirror's Spotlight, offered 24-hour film services on a subscription basis. Within a short time, the Disney Channel, Playboy, Bravo, the Entertainment Channel, and special language services like Galavision, a Spanish-language movie service, all entered the programming-services arena.

The Rise of Superstations

Independent stations that produced their own programs had a wealth of content available for cable packages. Cable and satellite provided convenient distribution outlets, and cable companies quickly found that the successful independent stations attracted a number of viewers for their programs. Those independent stations that contract for satellite and cable distribution of their programs are called **superstations.**

In general, the term *superstation* means that the station is distributed by satellite. The five largest superstations currently in existence are WTBS, Atlanta; WGN, Chicago; KTVT, Los Angeles; WWOR, Secaucus, New Jersey (carrying programming that comes from New York City); and WPIX, New York.

Each of these powerful independent stations had developed a full programming schedule; most had gained exclusive contract rights to sporting events of popular teams. This meant that in each case, the superstations offered cable companies not only local-origination programming and full services, but sporting events that viewers would not have been able to see otherwise.

 ## Services to Communities

Growth of suburbs in the 1970s was part of the key to cable's success; cable companies found it easier to lay cables in communities with few physical obstructions. In newly created suburbs, cable could be laid as the homes were built. Cities and older communities—with their already-paved streets and driveways—prevented easy access to homes, often requiring excavation and replacement of pavement; they cost the cable companies more to wire than did newer developments and suburbs.

Box 7.2   Cable Packages

Basic Service:	local broadcast stations (including O&O stations or affiliates of the networks); some distant stations (like superstations); and community access
Limited Satellite Service:	(often in conjunction with basic service) including such general interest services as CNN, Headline News, C-SPAN
Expanded Satellite Service:	(often in conjunction with basic service) including additional programs (5–36 channels)
Premium Pay Services:	such as HBO, Cinemax, Showtime, the Disney Channel, Sportschannel, ESPN, or other sports services

Every franchise puts together packages to appeal to the greatest number of subscribers, but this breakdown provides general information for most subscriptions available today.

Suburbs also had many residential neighborhoods concentrated in areas that were relatively inexpensive for cable companies to reach (compared to rural areas), and the similarities in socioeconomic status of suburban residents allowed cable companies to streamline the variety of programming they felt would be most appealing to subscribers (see box 7.2).

TVRO

Cable saturation in the United States is not likely to ever reach 100 percent because of the high costs of running copper cable—or even optical fibers— over areas with small populations. An alternative to cable is television-receive-only dishes (TVRO), more commonly called home satellite dishes or backyard dishes. These units receive the signals that are transmitted from satellites to cable companies, bypassing the cable operator or subscription charges.

While home dishes initially were expensive (about $2500) and large (8 to 10 feet in diameter), dishes now can be purchased for under $500 and are less that two feet in diameter. Since the cost has diminished, the number of dishes in operation has increased (see box 7.3). From 1987 to 1991, cable subscription rates grew by 60 percent; if subscription rates continue to rise and the cost of TVRO units continues to drop, we may well see more TVRO units in use.

Box 7.3   Sales of TVRO Dishes in the United States, 1985–1992

1985	735,000 units sold
1986	227,500 units sold
1987	268,500 units sold
1988	346,000 units sold
1989	352,000 units sold
1990	265,000 units sold
1991	412,000 units sold
1992	628,000 units sold

The drop in TVRO sales from 1985 to 1986 was the result of cable deregulation; the cable industry mounted a significant challenge to other new forms of distribution. Continued growth from 1986 (with the exception of a loss in 1990, perhaps due to the state of the national economy) reflects the drop in dish costs and the increase in cable rates.

Source: Sales of TVRO Dishes. *Television & Cable Factbook* 58 (Washington, D.C.: Television Digest Inc., 1990), with author's projections for 1991 and 1992.

Pay-per-view

As mentioned earlier, pay-per-view is a popular new cable service. Pay-per-view distributes programs to highly specialized target audiences. The service may be distributed via satellite to the cable company, which in turn routes it to the home that agrees to pay for the service—whether anyone really watches it or not!

One reason pay-per-view can be distributed by cable companies is that they usually reserve some channels for additional material. These channels have full capacity for distributing programs but generally are not included in service packages.

As cable technology advances, it has become possible to include more programs in the traditional coaxial cable. While some companies offer a number of pay channels for subscribers, others offer only what their general subscribing public seems willing to pay for (see box 7.4). Most cable companies offer approximately 35 channels in their most common program package, but some offer far more—in some areas, as many as 150 different channels.

The ability to deliver the increased number of channels and services raises the question of how many channels a customer needs. In the past, a greater number of channel outlets has not significantly increased the quality of programming, but it has facilitated **strip programming**—full-day or time-segment continuity that is devoted to the interests of smaller target audiences. For example, MTV targets teenage boys; Lifetime, adult women; and ESPN, adult men.

Box 7.4 Cable Channel Capacity

Channel Capacity	Systems	% of Total	Subscribers	% of Total
54 & over	1,133	10.22%	17,347,573	33.01%
30–53	5,984	53.98%	31,660,428	60.24%
20–29	1,307	11.79%	1,988,720	3.78%
13–19	337	3.04%	122,496	0.23%
6–12	800	7.22%	335,595	0.64%
5 only	18	0.16%	4,054	0.008%
Sub-5	6	0.05%	789	0.002%
Not available	1,501	13.54%	1,097,727	2.09%
Total	**11,086**	**100.00%**	**52,557,382**	**100.00%**

Source: Channel Capacity of Existing Cable Systems. *Television & Cable Factbook* 60 (Washington, D.C.: Television Digest Inc.,1992).

Cable Programming

While many people are critical of the number of channels and what they are used for, cable has developed a few unique services that probably would not have been successful if left to the broadcast networks. The three services that have made a considerable impact are MTV, CNN, and C-SPAN.

MTV

In the early 1980s, MTV, a division of Warner Communications, brought radio with pictures to television. Though there have been other cable music formats, like VH-1 and Ted Turner's short-lived Cable Music Channel (in existence for only 36 days in 1984), MTV has been the most effective and the most popular, particularly with teenaged males.

MTV has had a major impact on both the radio and recording industries as well as cable television. Performers now think of the video in the same way they plan promotional tours and album covers. Some of the most creative directors in Hollywood and New York's commercial production center now spend their time directing MTV videos that are, in essence, commercials for the music, the performers, and any promotional tours they may have scheduled.

The commercial venture by Warner Communications proved profitable, but Warner decided to invest in other areas of the entertainment business. In 1985, Viacom purchased MTV, VH-1, and Nickelodeon, and became the largest cable programmer in the country. With Viacom's success as a syndicator, MTV and its other programs will be packaged and sold to domestic cable companies and to the international market as well.

CNN

The real surprise in cable programming, however, came with Ted Turner's Cable News Network, which, after a painfully slow start, toppled competition from the networks in 1991.

The Persian Gulf War in 1991 firmly established CNN as the dominant news channel, hurting the news operations of the big three networks. Because the networks decided to broadcast live with a total concentration on the Persian Gulf, they did not run advertising during the first week of the war. This was not entirely an altruistic decision. Advertisers did not want their products associated with the war. During that first week of the war, the networks lost $6 million in advertising revenues. As a cable station, CNN's costs were underwritten by their subscriptions, so even without advertising, some revenue continued to support the 24-hour coverage of the conflict.

Box 7.5   The Rise of CNN

When Ted Turner borrowed more than $100 million to launch CNN in June 1980, the new network was considered by many to be a joke. Though he had hired a few leading journalists and correspondents (for far less money than they had earned previously), most of the staff was fresh out of college.

Between 1980 and 1985, CNN lost $77 million, averaging a loss of $2 million a month. The turnaround began in 1984 when CNN had an anchor booth on the floor at the Democratic Convention along with the networks. In June 1985, Shiite terrorists hijacked a TWA jet, and CNN commanded a large portion of the news audience for days; viewers could see the drama unfold at any time of the day—not just when the network news programs were broadcast.

Seeing the growing popularity of CNN, the networks began to get nervous. ABC invested in the Satellite News Channel (SNC), a short-lived alternative to 24-hour news. CBS abandoned plans for a similar network, but NBC launched CNBC, though cable operators have been reluctant to pick up another all-news channel.

CNN's popularity soared after it purchased a "fly-away uplink"—a portable transmitter, which came in handy when the student confrontations erupted in Beijing; CNN was the only news organization that did not have to depend on government-controlled satellite stations to transmit its signal back to the United States.

In 1989, CNN expanded with a Spanish-language news program for the global Spanish network, Telemundo. By 1990, CNN had 18 overseas bureaus. It plans to deliver news to virtually every nation in the world.

The all-news channel is now available in over 33 million cable homes in the United States. In 1981 Turner started a second cable service, CNN-2, now known as Headline News, which updates news stories every 30 minutes.

C-SPAN

The Cable Satellite Public Affairs Network (C-SPAN) was developed to provide live coverage of the House of Representatives. On C-SPAN, viewers can witness the debates in the House, as well as special addresses by political leaders to members of Congress or special-interest groups. Talk shows in which the significant issues of the day are discussed by influential people from all walks of life serve to provide additional viewpoints on issues of public concern.

C-SPAN has served not only the community of politically motivated individuals; it has proven to be a useful adjunct to educational courses that focus on current events. It also has provided an in-depth view of significant milestones in our country's history, such as coverage of the Clarence Thomas–Anita Hill hearings and the inauguration of President Clinton.

Cable Diversity

Many experts claim that the greater the number of channels offered, the greater the potential for program diversity. This may be true, but business practices including syndication and program distribution tend to recycle what has already been popular, rather than seek a greater diversity of information.

In addition to its ability to deliver a number of channels, regardless of the diversity of the content, the fact remains that in some parts of the country, people cannot receive television signals without cable or a TVRO dish. Still others may not be able to afford the high costs of even basic cable service. Should individuals in these areas do without access to television? The question has prompted the FCC and Congress to consider whether deregulation of the cable industry has been in the best interest of the general population.

Box 7.6   The Largest Multiple Systems Operators

1. Tele-Communications Inc.
2. American Television & Communications Corp.
3. UA Entertainment
4. Continental Cablevision
5. Warner Cable Communications
6. Comcast
7. Cox Cable Communications
8. Storer Cable Communications
9. Cablevision System
10. Jones Intercable/Spacelink

Source: Cable Television and Advertising Bureau, "Multiple Systems Operators," *Advertising Age*, 11 Feb. 1991, C-28.

Cable Deregulation and Re-regulation

In 1984 the FCC deregulated the cable industry by amending the Communications Act of 1934 with the Cable Communications Policy Act of 1984. The most important part of the document was section 601, item 6, which "promoted competition in cable communications" and restricted any actions that would impose "undue economic burdens" on cable systems. "Undue economic burdens" has been broadly interpreted to mean that little if any action can be taken to restrict what cable operators can do for profit. It is the key concept used to justify deregulation.

Claiming that new distribution forms such as cable, satellites, videocassette recorders, and pay services offered the diversity that was necessary for television, the FCC viewed deregulation as a way to let businesses operate in their own interests. This generally is referred to as letting the marketplace rule.

As cable was allowed to grow free from governmental restrictions, three things happened: (1) the number of multiple systems operators (MSOs) began to buy up cable, distribution, and production companies, **vertically integrating** the market and profiting at both program production and distribution levels (see box 7.6); (2) the costs of cable subscriptions grew dramatically from 1984 to 1992; and (3) over-the-air broadcasters were restricted from equal arrangements by government controls, like the fin-syn rules.

Clearly, deregulation of the cable industry had allowed cable companies to become profitable, but the goal of encouraging competition in the marketplace was not accomplished. As more multiple systems operators controlled cable companies, the diversity of programs actually began to diminish. Additionally, the rise in the cost of subscriptions and premium services began to place cable service out of the reach of lower-income or fixed-income consumers.

For years, concerned legislators in Congress had been advocating a reregulation of communications industries, especially cable. On October 5, 1992, both the House and Senate overrode a presidential veto and enacted the Cable Television Consumer Protection and Competition Act of 1992, usually referred to as the Cable Act. The override of the presidential veto marked the first time that Congress had overridden one of President Bush's vetoes.

The Cable Act outlined a plan of action toward controlling the high costs demanded by cable companies, and mandated that the FCC protect cable subscribers in a number of key areas. Among the critical issues were:

- the power of the FCC to establish and regulate "reasonable" rates for basic cable service and to review other rates
- a requirement of cable companies to carry broadcast signals in the basic service

- competition in franchise areas of a specified size
- an allowance for cable operators to offer differentially priced rates to the elderly or other economically disadvantaged groups
- protection of subscribers' privacy by requiring that cable companies prohibit outside access to information about the subscriber

The reregulation requirements specify a timetable for each of the actions (those mentioned above and others), most of which were to be completed by October 5, 1993. While it may take some time to evaluate the real impact of reregulation, cable companies have been concerned that these steps will limit their ability to engage in other enterprises central to cable delivery.

Cable companies are well aware of the competition that could result from other communications industries benefiting from deregulation or advanced technology, and they are particularly concerned about telco entry into video dial tone services, and the possibility of direct satellite services. Since cable's inception, experiments have been conducted to measure its potential for more than just television delivery. In the section that follows, some of the early experiments show how the unique qualities of cable could be developed for other purposes. Whether re-regulation will affect the development of the cable industry to engage in future experiments is yet unknown.

Experiments with Interactive Cable

Because cable is uniquely suited to controlled information from one source to a specific user, it has been the vehicle for many new experiments. Some of the goals were established from models of earlier experiments to transmit more information over broadcast airwaves and to pack the video screen with more information that consumers could use with the purchase of a descrambling unit, as in the early days of HBO.

Though there have been several experiments with controlling the amount and direction of information on a television screen or in a cable system, some of the most innovative came from the laboratory of a British Post Office Research Center engineer, Sam Fedida. In Great Britain, communications are regulated by the Ministry of Posts and Telecommunications. Fedida's experiments with signal transfer were appropriately targeted toward enhancing **picturephone**—sending visual images through telephone lines.

In 1966, Fedida came up with two different systems of information transfer, **teletext** and **videotex.** Though each system is now used for different purposes and operates in different modes, both forms have found markets in many countries in the area of enhanced communications.

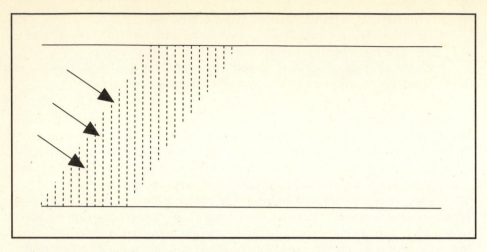

Figure 7.2 *Images in the VBI (Vertical Blanking Interval).*
By inserting extra information in the VBI, engineers can pack more information into a typical television signal. With the aid of a decoder, this information can be extracted from the VBI and shown on the screen. This extra information has been useful for engineering purposes, but has also gained some commercial advantage by coding information for special audiences, such as the "closed captioning" service for the hearing impaired.

Teletext

Sam Fedida's attempts to package more information into a regular television image resulted in the use of what is known as the **vertical blanking interval** (VBI) on your television screen (see figure 7.2). As technology has become more precise, it has become possible to insert extra information between the electronic pulses that make up the visual image.

At the broadcast end, extra information packaged into the VBI can be sent along with the regular broadcast signal. If a television receiver has a special decoder attachment that extracts the information from the VBI, it can be displayed on the screen. This type of **piggybacking** information has been used for years by television engineers who insert special information into the VBI for registering signals in broadcast studios, but the teletext service has made it possible to send extra information to special markets.

One use of teletext in the United States is closed captioning for the hearing impaired. When you see the small icon (see figure 7.3) at the beginning of a program, anyone with a special decoder can extract information from the VBI, and see the program's captions at the bottom of the screen.

Closed captioning was introduced in the United States in 1980 when NBC, ABC, and PBS began to cooperate with the National Captioning Institute's plans to use this teletext service for the hearing impaired. CBS was not one of

Figure 7.3 *Closed Captioning Icon.*
This image indicates that the program has closed captioning available to anyone who has the decoder to extract the information from the VBI.

the first participants in the project, since it was experimenting with its own videotex services. Eventually CBS did participate so that now virtually all television programming is accessible to the hearing impaired.

In 1979, the Reuters news service experimented with a commercial teletext service called News-Views, which was delivered over phone lines to cable companies. Viewers received a printed text on their television screens providing in-depth news coverage.

What prevented greater use of teletext in the United States was the FCC's 1983 decision to consider teletext an ancillary service. That meant that no one technical standard would be mandatory and competing technical standards that would be incompatible with each other could be marketed. A new decoder would be necessary for each technical standard in operation. Though this lack of standardization prevented teletext from growing in the United States, other countries have chosen teletext systems that deliver information on weather, stock prices, local information, and other material. Many of the televisions specially equipped with teletext services are installed in public places for the use of the citizens. In the United States, teletext operates on a small scale in some markets. For example, stock information is displayed in some urban areas, and weather information is carried in others.

The success of teletext in other countries and the realization that closed captioning was indeed a necessity for many consumers led the FCC to require that manufacturers of television receivers to be sold in the United States include a chip that will extract the closed captioning teletext message. All television receivers manufactured and sold after 1993 are required to have this piece of circuitry installed. In the future, this could mean that teletext services (beyond closed captioning) could be offered for a variety of purposes.

Videotex

Like teletext, videotex experiments were conducted almost as soon as television technology was available, but most of the breakthroughs were achieved at the British Post Office Research Center in the 1960s. Videotex turns the television signal into a two-way, or **interactive,** mode. It does not use the VBI to piggyback signals, but it does allow for sending signals back and forth through the use of modems.

To operate videotex, a modified television receiver with a decoder translates data and creates text and video images. The decoder may be plugged directly into a television antenna connection or wired directly into the color beam circuitry of a television set.

Videotex has a multidimensional capacity for storing and retrieving documents, which is suitable for many business applications. It has been used most successfully by the travel industry, providing instant access to a variety of data bases for schedules, fares, and additional information.

Videotex technologies vary in the way in which they display words and pictures on the screen, ranging from simple codes to more complex combinations. Sam Fedida's Prestel was the first operational videotex service. Soon several other countries began limited videotex services for business or consumer information.

Although the United States did not take the lead in developing videotex systems, the sheer size of the American market and its dominance in the computer, telecommunications, and information industries made it inevitable that videotex eventually would reach the United States. Beginning in 1979, a number of limited videotex experiments were conducted to see if the service could be marketed profitably to home consumers. Among some of the early services were Viewtron, owned by Knight-Ridder Newspapers, Inc.; The Source, owned by Reader's Digest; and CompuServe, owned by H&R Block, a division of Sears. These services offered not only news, weather, games, local movies, and other entertainment functions, but also optional electronic mail and banking services.

Qube　One of the videotex experiments that garnered considerable attention was the **Qube** experiment, conducted by Warner Cable in Columbus, Ohio. The experiment lasted from 1977 to 1982. The service was hooked up in test homes equipped with a keypad that enabled users to send signals to the cable company for specific responses. If a political debate were being shown, viewers might be asked by an announcer's voice or a written message on the screen to "vote" by pressing one of the buttons on the keypad.

Viewers could choose specific movies and were billed accordingly, much like other pay-per-view services that have been gaining in popularity. Home-security systems also could be connected to the service for monitoring fire or theft, though subscribers paid more for these additional services.

When it had concluded, the Qube experiment was considered a minor success, but not enough subscribers wished to maintain the service at the cost necessary to keep it in full operation.

What each of the experiments tells us is that cable can be used for more than strictly delivering television programs. Features such as extra information in the VBI, monitoring pay-per-view billing or other record-keeping purposes, and the potential for online interactive services could make cable a more attractive distribution system available for a greater number of services in the future.

Competition for Cable Services

The alternative services just discussed should not be considered solely the domain of the cable companies currently in existence. Cable companies and other communication industries are well aware of the impact of deregulation that might not be so easily remedied by moves toward re-regulation. The entire communication-technology landscape has been significantly altered by the deregulatory movement throughout the 1980s, and not all past decisions will be overturned.

Most notably, cable companies are aware that telco entry into the video programming distribution arena will significantly affect their own abilities to serve as monopolies of wired video systems into the home. On February 9, 1993, the Southwestern Bell Corporation announced its purchase of two cable systems in the Washington, D.C. area. While Southwestern Bell provides telephone service to the southwestern states, including Arkansas and Texas, the cable purchase marks the first time this clause of the Modified Final Judgment has been implemented. The telcos still cannot operate cable companies in areas in which they already have telephone services.

What Southwestern Bell intends to do with its cable companies is what other telcos undoubtedly will do in the future. It will use existing cable facilities to network to cellular telephone systems for PCSs in the D.C. area, bypassing the local telephone company, Bell Atlantic (Fabrikant 1993, D2).

CONCLUSION

From its humble beginnings, the cable industry has grown to a point at which it is eclipsing the networks as the provider of television content. While network industry executives are careful to point out that 70 percent of the audiences subscribing to cable are still watching network programming, the loss of advertising revenue has significantly affected the networks' profits. In 1991, the combined network profit in advertising was $8 billion. In the same year, cable companies' combined subscription rates were $80 billion. This figure does not even include cable's profits from advertising.

There are many predictions about whether the networks will survive, given the competition from cable and other communications technologies. While networks were once Goliath and cable the small David, we have today a situation in which two Goliaths are competing for audiences. It is inevitable that each industry will undergo many changes in regulation, programming, and operations.

Most notably, cable undoubtedly will become a conduit for other types of communication services. Deregulation of communication industries has introduced competition at an unforseen level. Cable television will be only a part of the cable company's domain.

SUMMARY

The cable industry has undergone significant changes since its inception. First unregulated environments saw a period of experimentation that gave way to an extraordinary amount of regulation by the federal government. During the deregulatory climate of the 1980s, cable grew from its relatively secure position vis-à-vis other communication industries.

Cable reregulation may change the role of cable as a television provider, but even more importantly, the number of other industries that are redirecting cable companies and the number of experiments in alternative services via cable could serve to change the industry. All of these changes shift the direction of cable toward more personal communication services.

In this chapter, cable was discussed with regard to:

- its development as an alternative means of signal distribution
- the growth of cable and programming services using a variety of distribution means
- the rise of superstations and their connection to the cable industry
- the deregulation and reregulation of the cable industry

- the unique characteristics of cable and the experiments in which these characteristics lend themselves to new services

DISCUSSION QUESTIONS

1. Look at the programming services provided by your local cable company. Explain how the program offerings do or do not meet the different interests and needs of your community.
2. If you were to package the program services for a specific community, what elements would you need to consider? What would the most acceptable rate structure be for delivering your package? (For reference look at the rates charged by other companies.)
3. If TVRO dishes are prominent in your community, find out how the companies market their product. Do they propose TVRO as an alternative to cable or a solution for those who can't get cable? What other features do they promote?
4. Go to a local retailer who carries videotex products such as Prodigy and discuss the profile of the usual buyer.
5. Discuss the impact of closed captioning for the hearing impaired. What other services would make communication more possible for handicapped or disabled people?
6. Discuss how cable could be used for a variety of interactive purposes. How would cable companies have to modify their present rate structures?
7. What has been the effect of cable re-regulation? Have cable companies lost money, or have they found alternative means of maintaining their stream of revenue?

REFERENCES

Alber, Antone F. 1985. *Videotex/Teletext*. New York: McGraw-Hill.

Baldwin, Thomas and McCoy, D. Stevens. 1983. *Cable communication.* Englewood Cliffs, New Jersey: Prentice-Hall.

Cable television and advertising bureau. 1991. Cable's audience share rises year 'round. *Advertising Age*, Feb. 11, C-25.

———. 1991. Multiple systems operators. *Advertising Age*, Feb. 11, C-28.

Channel capacity of existing cable systems. 1992. *Television & Cable Factbook* 60. Washington, D.C.: Television Digest, Inc., G65

Estimated growth of the cable industry. 1992. *Television & Cable Factbook* 60. Washington D.C.: Television Digest, Inc., G64.

Fabrikant, Geraldine. 1993. Phone company breaks ground by buying into cable television. *New York Times,* Feb. 10, 1, D2.

Pay-per-view services profile. 1990. *Television & Cable Factbook* 60, (May 21).

Sales of TVRO dishes. 1990. *Television & Cable Factbook* 58. Washington, D.C.: Television Digest, Inc.

TECHNOLOGIES AND SERVICES
FROM MASS AUDIENCE TO THE INDIVIDUAL

MAKING CONNECTIONS

The proliferation of technologies and the variety of content have presented
consumers with alternatives to traditional mass communication. As emphasized
in earlier chapters, the communication industries work to make profits. Serving
smaller audiences is not necessarily in the interests of the creators or distributors of messages, unless a creative way of maximizing profits can be built in.
Since audiences have many reasons for choosing to focus their attention on any
specific form of media or content, a tension between industries and audiences
can arise. Industrial response has been to explore alternative distribution forms
to provide for the special interests of audiences.

This chapter describes many of the distribution systems and services that create
new media environments. Each form maintains unique
qualities that make it adaptable for certain types of content. The connections in this chapter address:

- some of the distribution systems that facilitate
  new ways of broadcasting

- the need for using the electromagnetic spec-

Chapter

trum for distribution of broadcast services

- how newer forms influence users' perceptions

- how using media in the home changes the context for some traditional communication options

- how individuals and audiences respond to both the choices and the unique characteristics of the new technologies and services

---

Many years ago, a person would have been hard-pressed to find media that did not reflect the main intent of the industries—to reach the widest possible audience. Logical assumptions about the relationship of the audience and broadcast content could be made through ratings and the popularity of genres and celebrities. Some researchers would argue that national tastes and interests set an agenda for media content; others would say the inverse was true.

Today measurement of audience interest would have to take into consideration a plethora of new consumer options brought about by VCRs, cable, CDs, DATs, and more personal technologies such as portable telephones, audiotape recorders with headphones, or wrist-sized televisions. Think about how a VCR changes the function of a traditional television set. No longer does an audience member engage in receiving broadcast content; instead he or she may tape a program for later viewing, or use the VCR to play a film that several months earlier could not have been seen outside a theater. The new technologies allow people to develop different media habits.

This chapter discusses electronic technologies including distribution forms and services that can be added to traditional systems. The development of some of these technologies raises questions of whether the availability of more media merely supplement older forms, or whether they replace them with new channels of communication for the user, complete with unique characteristics that require new consideration for how the audience uses and makes sense of the content.

There is no one formula to predict the success of a new product or service. Most new media technologies are first adopted by users who can afford the financial risks of experimentation. Only when technologies become inexpensive enough for mass distribution can we expect to understand their possible impact on communication patterns. Sometimes the pattern of adoption (or curve of diffusion) does not meet the expectations of inventors or investors. When videocassette recorders were first developed in the early 1960s, marketers assumed that only the most affluent people would buy them. One of the first VCRs cost $30,000, but within a year, Ampex had developed a home model priced at $1095 (Lardner 1987). While this cost was still far too high to attract many buyers, the people who did purchase VCRs were not the initial target audience; marketers were surprised when they found that most purchasers of VCRs were blue-collar workers. In hindsight, the pattern made sense. Blue-collar workers spent long hours on the job and had relatively little time to spend in leisure activities or at home. The typical consumer of a VCR was a person who worked nights, extra shifts, or a second job, and considered the VCR's time-shifting capability its most attractive quality. With a VCR, favorite prime-time programs could be recorded and viewed later. This pattern of blue-collar consumption remained constant during the big VCR boom of the 1980s when the price finally came down enough to tempt other consumers.

Knowing that the most likely VCR consumers had problems in arranging time schedules that allowed them to do things like go to movies, entrepreneurs began to search for the type of content that would appeal to that audience. The home video market (which previously had been considered small) began to offer movies on tape, collections of earlier TV shows, and a number of special-interest tapes in such categories as how-to, exercise, and comedy performance.

VCRs and home entertainment caught on quickly, and American habits and behavior began to change. The result was that people spent more time at home. The new communication environment in the home seemed easy, simple, and benign. Effects on the industries were far more severe.

New Media Environments

It is easy to think that only the best technologies and services are successful. As previous chapters have shown, this is not always true. Social, political, and economic factors play a large part in determining the potential success of a new product. Consumer decisions to purchase a technology or service may be made for a variety of reasons. Some people are attracted to any new gadget. Some are tempted by advertising and a desire to have the best products despite costs. Still others are skeptical about the rapid developments in particular home communication technologies, and are hesitant to make purchases until the technologies are proven to have staying power. Consumer anxiety over videodisc versus videotape and CDs versus record albums prompted comedienne Rita Rudner to quip that she would buy a compact disc player "only when they promise me they won't come up with anything new!" Perhaps many feel the same way about multiscreen televisions, HDTV, and digital audiotape.

Distribution Systems

As demonstrated in previous chapters, alternatives to traditional broadcast operations are growing in the United States and around the world. Questions raised in issues dealing with telephone service, broadcast television versus cable, and the addition of other new communication technologies pose social and economic problems for people who cannot afford these products or services. If business practices reinforce market principles that make it less profitable for companies to distribute media to audiences in less densely populated areas, must these audiences do without service? If some viewers live in an area that would not be served profitably by cable, but no broadcast television reaches them, should they do without? If elderly people on fixed incomes can't afford telephone service, must they forgo the possibility of calling for help if necessary?

Some advocates of what traditionally has been labeled free TV have encouraged regulators to make other options available, so that we don't end up with a society of media "haves" and "have nots." Ongoing Congressional debates concerning rates charged by deregulated cable and telephone companies specifically address these issues.

While the controversy over access to some communication technologies and their costs continues to concern Congress, customers, and the industries, the FCC has approved the development and use of other forms of message distribution that circumvent some of the traditional problems associated with reaching the most profitable audiences. While each industry also operates with a profit motive, the audiences it serves are smaller. This helps to bridge the gap between the needs and interests of people in smaller communities and their ability to access content that reflects more locally oriented material. As the different distribution technologies are discussed, consider their potential impact and how they might be used for innovative programming.

Low Power TV (LPTV)

One answer to the need for community-oriented television broadcasting is low power TV (LPTV), which generally has a broadcasting range of only 15 to 30 miles. LPTV's signal usually is broadcast in either UHF or VHF frequencies, so any regular home television receiver can receive the message. Because LPTV programmers can determine the interests, needs, and desires of people within such a small vicinity, they have a good sense of their target audience—a particularly attractive feature to advertisers.

When the FCC began offering LPTV licenses in 1981, it assumed that the range of LPTV was so narrow that it would readily serve the interests of the community. The FCC reasoned that it would be difficult to evaluate the number of applications for licenses, so they decided to make LPTV licenses available through a lottery system.

Unfortunately, history repeated itself with LPTV licenses. Just like the rush to reserve channel space in the UHF band when those licenses were made available, many who succeeded in getting LPTV licenses have chosen to do nothing with the broadcast facility until a profitable opportunity arises. Of the many LPTV licenses held today, only about a third of the broadcast operations are actually in use. The content for many stations involves movies, musical programs, community politics such as town meetings, and of course, local commercials.

An interesting approach to using LPTV as a service to the community is Buffalo, New York's Channel 58, which is controlled by Citizen's Action Television, a group sponsored by consumer activist Ralph Nader. At Channel 58, consumers are given free airtime to discuss products and purchasing decisions, issues of manufacturer accountability, and other items of interest to local consumers.

Some LPTV stations in New Mexico have begun programming for the special needs of Native American reservations by offering programming that supports native culture and by spreading information relevant to the community. In parts of Florida, LPTV stations broadcast in Spanish, or program news and information for an older population.

Until the effectiveness of LPTV is determined and the distribution system becomes profitable for license holders, LPTV may be relegated to the position of just another community access channel.

Satellite Master Antenna Television (SMATV)

On a small scale, satellite master antenna television (SMATV) (sometimes referred to as small master antenna TV) can be considered a combination distribution and delivery system. Part cable, part satellite receiver, and often part closed-circuit television, SMATV combines the reception of satellite signals that may include the same services offered by cable companies with closed-circuit technology for distribution of prerecorded or live material (when a transmission facility is included in the building) with surveillance capabilities. SMATV most often is found in communities where there are large buildings, particularly if those buildings house inhabitants with similar interests. Senior citizen housing often uses SMATV, as do university and college communities where students live in large dormitories.

The security services offered by SMATV connections often take place through the same cabled system that runs the SMATV operation. Small video monitors in the lobbies of buildings allow residents to switch on a special channel to see who is asking for access to the building.

Only one TVRO antenna is necessary to serve multiple dwellings and no constant contact with a cable company is required, though most SMATV buildings pay cable subscriptions negotiated through zoning and municipal agreements. The TVRO dish usually is placed on top of the building and a small closed-circuit cable operation is run to every apartment or room in the building (see figure 8.1).

Figure 8.1 *Satellite Master Antenna Television.*
The TVRO dish is connected to various apartments in the building while additional connections may be made through closed circuit video channels. From an in-house studio, VCR, or surveillance system, several additional services can be provided to tenants.

In addition to the satellite dish that brings in cable signals, a videocassette recorder located in a strategic location also can play interesting material for the building's residents. Maintenance or hookup fees are usually a part of the residents' monthly assessments or rental costs.

The viability of SMATV to service entire communities suggests a possible scenario for the future. Could SMATV circumvent legal payment to cable companies for the distribution of the same signal? Certainly it could, but the law would be on the side of any cable company that tried to prosecute a community for unauthorized access. Still, communities that currently are not serviced by cable could consider SMATV, or negotiate with cable companies attempting to gain a franchise for lower costs and an even better sense of the audience demographics. SMATV is, then, a combination of services that makes connections between earlier forms of distribution to serve audiences in a different way.

Multichannel Multipoint Distribution Services (MMDS)

Multichannel multipoint distribution services (MMDS) link several channels that use microwaves to transmit information from one point to another. MMDS operates similarly to traditional broadcast television, but the signals transmitted are in the higher ranges of the electromagnetic spectrum. Users require a special transmitter and decoder, but the decoder can be connected to a regular television receiver. MMDS is sometimes called wireless cable.

When the technology became available in the early 1970s, it was referred to as multipoint distribution service (MDS). At the time, only one channel could be transmitted at a time, and as a result, few companies were willing to invest in the special transmitters and decoders. More attention was paid to cable's capability to distribute several channels simultaneously.

When the M representing "multichannel" became viable, thanks to the FCC's allocation of more frequencies to the service, MMDS became more commercially competitive. One of MMDS' most common uses is providing hotels with movies and other pay services. Even though few companies now exploit MMDS as a transmission medium, future services could make this form more popular.

Instructional Television Fixed Service (ITFS)

In recent years many institutions, particularly in the academic area, have investigated the viability of instructional television fixed service (ITFS). ITFS uses a special category of license made available to educational institutions by the FCC.

Each ITFS operation furnishes a certain number of hours of instructional or educational material to its audience every week; the audience usually subscribes to certain services. Since the FCC made ITFS licenses available in 1971, many institutions have attempted to explore how lectures could be transmitted to various locations within an educational system, or how teleconferencing might be used for educational purposes.

The rules for operating an ITFS facility are somewhat flexible depending on the institution, but most ITFS licenses require the programmers to fill at least four hours a day with instructional programming. What they do with the remaining hours is up to them. License holders can sell the remaining hours to syndicators, other program providers, advertisers, or anyone they wish. The ITFS operation has been very popular in areas where instructional programming supplements college or university courses, and the sale of available airtime underwrites the cost of the educational programming.

Telco Distribution

Since the deregulation and divestiture of AT&T, a number of alternative information systems have been considered by the newly constituted Regional Operating Companies (ROCs) and other independent companies. These

203

groups, the telcos, look forward to the opportunity to provide video to homes through traditional telephone cables or the newer optical fibers. While Judge Green's Modified Final Judgment left room for the eventual participation of the telephone companies to compete in video services and other forms of distribution, the terms under which they will be allowed to compete for these services remains a matter of debate.

Since they already have expertise in connecting homes, the telcos could have a tremendous advantage over other video distribution forms. But the terms of the MFJ restrict telcos from controlling other video companies within their own regions. This decision prevents them from becoming too powerful and restricts competition from other companies in the information-providing businesses. Some of the strongest opposition to allowing the telcos to distribute video to homes comes from the cable industry, which has the most to lose if competition for home video distribution is made more competitive.

Possible telco distribution, like ITFS, LPTV, SMATV, and MMDS, offers as an alternative to the traditional distribution systems (UHF and VHF) of broadcasting that service a larger audience. In the future, if their uses expand and their profitability is demonstrated, we can expect to see all of these newer distribution forms become much more popular.

Distant Signal Transfer: Satellites

One of the remarkable features of today's technology is that many ideas proposed in works of fiction have become reality. Frankenstein was an early model of what eventually became high-tech medical operations involving organ transplants; space travel is no longer confined to science fiction; and satellites can transfer information virtually anywhere in the world almost instantly.

Satellite Development

As discussed in Chapter 1, the use of satellites for communication purposes was first proposed in 1945 by Arthur C. Clarke. The first American satellite, Early Bird, was launched in 1956, but much to the disappointment of Americans, the first satellite in space was the Russian Sputnik, launched in 1955.

Satellites have a normal life span of 7 to 10 years. In the early days of satellite development, it was necessary to shoot an inoperable satellite out of its position, after which it would come crashing to earth. Obviously, this wasted any of the potentially salvageable material. Part of the goal of the space shuttle program is to maintain and repair satellites in their fixed positions, and astronauts have been trained to accomplish this mission.

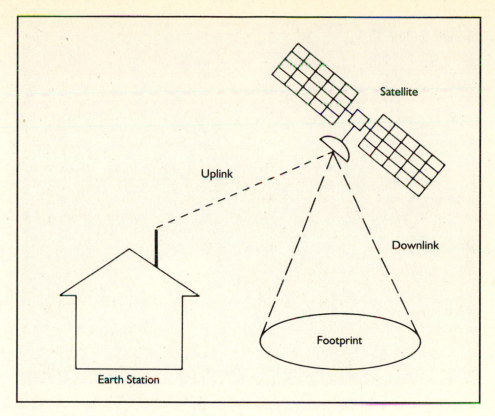

Figure 8.2 *The Path of a Satellite Signal.*

How Satellites Work

The idea behind satellites is very simple (see figure 8.2). Electronic information is transmitted from an earth station via microwave over the uplink. The antenna mounted on the satellite transfers the information to the transponders, or information-processing units of the satellite.

Each transponder is capable of transmitting one high-quality video channel and data in what would be the equivalent of 1500 two-way phone calls. Originally satellites operated with only 12 transponders, then 24, 36, and now, 48. Thus each satellite is capable of a tremendous amount of information processing. As technology is further refined, satellites undoubtedly will be able to process much more information than they do today.

Solar panels extend from the satellite's body to gather energy and to stabilize the satellite's position.

Figure 8.3 *An Artist's Rendition of Satcom C-3.*
Picture Source: GE American Communications

After information is processed in the transponders, it is retransmitted through the downlink. The area of coverage for the satellite information is called the footprint.

Theoretically, one footprint could be large enough to cover all of the continental United States, but for better signal clarity, three to four footprints are better. Receiving dishes, such as TVROs, receive the signal and reprocess it to cable, computer, or any other form necessary for further extension of the message.

Satellites must be positioned 22,300 miles above the equator to be geosynchronous, that is, able to rotate around the earth at the same speed as the land below. When the satellite's orbit is coordinated with the turning of the earth, the satellite can service the footprint 24 hours a day. At this height the satellite is placed in a position equally held by the North and South Poles, as well as by gravity and centrifugal force (see figure 8.3).

To rent a transponder may cost anywhere from $8 million to $11 million per month. Obviously, many companies can't use 24-hour transponder capacity, so they rent only certain hours. One company may only need the transponder for the usual working hours or for part of the workday. Another might need to rent transponder space periodically for teleconference purposes. Some companies also act as brokers for transponder space.

The superstations discussed in previous chapters have found an excellent way to use satellites for signal distribution. By sending their signals to a variety of downlinks, they can multiply the sites of distribution for their products. As more forms of communication use satellite distribution, satellites may be used even more as common carriers.

Direct Broadcast Satellites (DBS)

The direct broadcast satellites (DBS) services were envisioned as a way to deliver messages to highly segmented portions of the audience. In 1979, the Satellite Television Corporation (STC) proposed direct television program broadcasting by means of DBS. Though the FCC initially was interested enough to make some licenses available to companies, the idea was never fully developed in the United States. Some companies proposed that DBS would be a perfect distribution form for teleconferencing; others proposed more direct links to various business sites. But other distributions forms, such as MMDS, LPTV, or SMATV, already existed for these purposes.

DBS has been used effectively outside the United States, and it appears that it is only a matter of time before U.S. businesses again turn their attention to DBS and home entertainment. In Europe, Rupert Murdoch's Sky Channel has experimented with DBS for entertainment distribution. Murdoch's enterprises and other companies are now watching the success of other forms of distribution around the world, and well may consider turning attention to the United States in the near future, particularly if telco distribution of video does not

---

Box 8.1   Satellites and the Space Shuttle

One of the most efficient uses of the space shuttle program has been to deploy, repair, and retrieve satellites. Since the first satellite was deployed by a shuttle in 1962, there have been many satellite missions for shuttles and astronauts.

Often deployment or retrieval of a satellite can be accomplished by mechanical arms that pull the satellite from the shuttle and position it in space by means of computerized controls. But sometimes an astronaut may take a walk in space to make the adjustments.

become profitable, or if it is held up in court by matters of rates or lobbyists from other industries.

Though the cost of DBS is currently too high for most consumers, services may become cost-effective as more TVRO dishes are purchased. Either TVRO dishes or modified television receivers could pick up DBS signals. While costs of receiving dishes are coming down, other alternatives may become more economical.

The Japanese have invented a small rectangular receiving dish called a rectellite, which can be put in any window with a south-facing exposure. A rectellite can receive signals from a broadcast satellite and deliver them directly to your home television set. Eventually satellite distribution of telephony and data to the home could also come through the rectellite.

Cellular Telephone

Cellular telephone companies use a variety of distribution systems that may include satellite, MMDS, or digital transmission in radio frequencies. Also known as mobile telephones, cellular services use a combination of connected technologies to facilitate messages.

The cells of a cellular phone can be thought of as areas of coverage (much like satellite footprints). When in a car a person using a cellular telephone approaches the edge of the cell, a computer switches the call to another cell in which the frequencies are stronger and can support the signal. These calls can be linked to regular wired telephone services through a variety of access points that create the pathway for the call. Personal communication services (PCSs) also use the same distribution format for transmission of signals.

Time/space shifting   As the new distribution services show, each has the capacity to span space and influence a user's perception of time. Obviously, the use of satellites to transmit entertainment does not challenge the audience's sense of the immediacy of the message the way a teleconference or interactive instructional program might. One alternative to traditional use could involve program distribution from countries around the world. Thinking about this type of global interaction suggests a possible connection to how users could think about the world in the age of the satellite.

Audience perceptions   It has been said that satellites eliminate the sense of just how far, or how different other societies and cultures are from the people who see and hear messages from those locations. In this way, satellites do, figuratively, make this a smaller world.

They also influence our perceptions of which world events are important by allowing us to view images sent from distant locations. The real-time sense of the Persian Gulf War gave people around the world an idea of how significant the events were, even though the content of some of the media messages was strictly controlled by the military of both Iraq and the United States. The terror of Bosnians in camps, and the reality of children starving in Somalia become more real to people when the images are transmitted into their homes.

Satellites have become powerful communications technologies, not only for their ability to transmit data and information, but for how viewers have gained access to events around the world. The visual images they transmit into the home are more powerful than any message expressed verbally or in print.

Changes in Reception : Television Receivers

Along with the proliferation of distribution systems, many improvements have been added to traditional home technologies for message reception. In recent years, home television receivers have undergone the greatest change.

While television distribution forms are changing, the receivers now on the market already offer some new features. Many of the selling points include the possibility of using future services.

Enhanced TV

The term enhanced TV is misleading. Some people think the term means HDTV. Contemporary manufacturers, though, already market what they call enhanced TV. These receivers come with the promise of being fully compatible with HDTV when HDTV is available, but they will not accommodate the difference in the size of the picture. The enhanced TV systems marketed today do have better picture quality than regular sets because they use better components to display the image, but they still only use the NTSC system of 525 lines.

Stereo TV

Because television images travel on FM frequencies, the possibility for stereo television has existed since the development of television. The drawback was always the inability or hesitance on the part of broadcasters to send a dual signal from their transmitters. In 1984, the FCC decided to permit stereo sound broadcasts. Immediately broadcasters began to add the necessary technology and soon found that consumers were willing to pay for the feature when purchasing stereo-compatible television sets.

Before television broadcasters began to transmit in stereo, they occasionally would simulcast programs. People at home could hear one channel of sound on the television set, and tune their radio receivers to receive another channel, thereby simulating a stereo broadcast. Concerts (everything from rock to symphony) were the type of programs usually simulcast. Depending upon the location of transmitters, the sound simulcast to radio receivers would be synchronized well with the transmission of the television program, but occasionally a slight lag in time sequence caused by different transmission systems marred the success of simulcasting. Today almost every broadcast facility sends its prime-time programming in stereo. Even many of the syndicators have begun to split the audio that was recorded on one audio channel into two speaker-compatible signals so that they, too, can claim to use stereo sound.

Projection TV

If you've ever seen a big-screen television set that looks as though a film has been projected onto a screen, you've seen projection television. They have been around since the 1970s, but because of size and cost, they most commonly are used in large public places where a number of people watch the screen at the same time. Home projection units have not fared as well but are expected to gain popularity in the near future.

Projection televisions often have a relatively poor picture quality when compared to a regular television image. The reason for this is that the images are more precisely controlled in a regular television receiver. When a projection television projects its image onto a different surface, the result is similar to the projection of film on a screen. But because there is less information contained in a video image compared to a projected film image, the visual quality is poorer.

In 1990 and 1991, sales of projection televisions slowly began to increase. In 1992 the Electronics Industry of America predicted that each year projection televisions would grow by 17 percent in the United States (Joy 1992, C3). In the next few years as the sales are tallied, an increase of that size would be the single highest increase in a new-format TV set since the advent of color television.

Liquid Crystal Display (LCD)

Liquid crystal display (LCD) televisions are the newest form of television marketed today. The picture quality of these screens is superior to even enhanced television sets because the image is reflected by crystals that are activated directly on the screen, rather than projected from behind, as on a regular television receiver. Another advantage is that LCD screens are flat, and the units take up less room than traditional television sets.

Viewer Options

In addition to the current changes in television receivers, consumers will soon be faced with receivers or systems that present unique visual images. The first to be discussed, multi-image TV, already is being marketed. It presents interesting challenges for how much, and what type of information a home consumer can understand or acknowledge within the space of one television screen.

Multi-image TV   One of the most recent phenomena in television manufacturing, multi-image TV enables the viewer to see several images at one time. A multi-image television has the capacity to insert a small box into a corner of the picture screen or, depending on the quality and expense of the technology, to create a split screen. The effect in either case is the potential for viewers to watch two or more channels simultaneously. While these television sets are still extremely costly, their relative popularity shows what has happened to the viewing public's attention span. We have long known that people who use remote controls tend to change channels far more often than people who have to get up to change a channel.

Multi image TV raises the question of how much attention the viewer can give to multiple images. Multi-image receivers are still new, so there has not yet been conclusive research to indicate how much audiences understand or retain while viewing this special form of presentation. Some studies, however, provide information about what types of visuals might attract attention, or become memorable. Levy and Fink (1984) have written that the fleeting quality of messages on television has a negative effect on individuals' comprehension of information. If their research is correct, multiple images will reduce viewers' understanding of what they see. Newhagen and Reeves (1992) have indicated that negative images are most memorable. With more and more competition for the viewer's attention, industries will no doubt have to rethink the number and type of images they use to construct their messages, especially if multi-image receivers become used widely.

Choosing the angle   In 1990, some 150 Continental Cablevision subscribers in Springfield, Massachusetts, became the first television viewers in the United States to use a radically new type of television. This system allowed them to choose and control camera angles during broadcasts of special entertainment. All the viewer had to do was push a button that corresponded with the camera angle desired; the signal would then be transmitted to that viewer's television set. The experiment, called Interactive Television, was a new cable TV technology developed by ACTV Domestic Corporation of New York City. In the experiment, home users could use a special hand-held remote control. The viewers were able to choose different camera angles during the first interactive sporting event broadcast in the United States, a Springfield Indians hockey game. Viewers could push a button and see a closeup of the goalie, a wide-angle shot of the players, or any of several other shots depending on camera position.

In the four-week-long test, Continental Cablevision received praise from consumers who felt that the future of interactive television could be quite intriguing. Most thought that interactive technology would best facilitate children's programming. Others thought that the interactive system might be an interesting way to play video games or to view sports.

Another purpose of the interactive system was to offer home viewers a variety of films to choose from. In many ways, this service is similar to videotex, subscription TV, or pay-per-view. In this case, an on-screen menu was presented and viewers could choose which film they wanted to see over their own system. In the future, this type of interactive system could best facilitate pay-per-view viewing. It could have a significant impact on videocassette distribution and on the movie theater industry.

Any criticism of the audience as passive consumers of television would be laid to rest if viewers become able to actually choose not only television content

Box 8.2   Virtual Reality

Though still in experimental stages for home consumers, virtual reality technology presents a unique combination of image, perceptual manipulation, and audience use. Virtual reality extends the user's senses by allowing them to participate in a three-dimensional visual space. Though it sounds like science fiction, virtual reality creates an artificial environment by combining computers and prosthetic technologies with software to allow users to feel as though they are inside an image. The user wears an eye- or headpiece and glove to give visual and tactile information to the computer, which generates images. The technology worn by the user manipulates two-dimensional images that then appear to the user as three-dimensional.

While virtual reality for home consumers is still costly, software has been designed to simulate a trip to Disneyland, a foreign country, or images from the perspective of other people or animals (Hall 1990). Eventually connections will be possible to link one user of virtual reality to another, for simulated personal interaction (Fisher 1990).

While it sounds absurd, virtual reality has already proven useful in certain venues. It trains surgeons how to use a scalpel, simulates training missions for military personnel, and helps test structural conditions of expensive manufactured goods, such as automobiles and aircraft.

Sources: Trish Hall, "'Virtual Reality' Takes a Place in the Real World" *New York Times*, (July 8, 1990) 1 and 14; Scott S. Fisher, "Telepresence in Dataspace." *Millimeter*, (June 1990) 41; and "Video 'Immersion': Programming Virtual Worlds," *Broadcasting*, (Dec. 9, 1991) 64–67.

but angles from which to view that content. Many new media theories no doubt would evolve, but experiments certainly would render several types of content interesting. Would consumers become more visually literate? It's possible. Or would those who were already visually literate (those who best understood visual complexity), be the ones to take advantage of the technology?

More important questions would be: How much would this technology cost? Who would adapt to it? Who would pay for it? Interactive technology in the home changes our sense of how we use television. Watching television might become a very personal experience, or it could be a communal one, in which people vie for control of the technology that changes the images. Early evidence projects that viewers will understand fewer of the messages that are presented directly to them; but the option to involve themselves more (for example, choosing the camera angle) may involve their perception and perhaps improve their cognition of the message. Newer communication technologies will put some of these assumptions to a greater test (see box 8.2). But because technology is affected by the surrounding social conditions, a technology's purpose shapes the user's perceptions. For this reason, firm predictions are difficult. By the time many of these technologies reach a diverse number of users, the industries, social expectations, and means of distribution may be too different to match any of today's predictions.

Technologies and Content Choice

In addition to the many distribution forms and presentation devices and services, individuals have also used another set of communication technologies to supplement traditional forms. Disc technology, including compact audio discs (CDs) and videodiscs, share some characteristics but have fared differently in the marketplace. Both use digital information processing, which is also the key component to one of the newest distribution forms for audio entertainment, digital audiotape (DAT).

Disc Technology

In the world of music, CDs have revolutionized the recording industry. Videodiscs, which work on the same principle as CDs, competed with videocassettes for the home video market but—largely because they were introduced at about the same time as VCRs—were not as successful in capturing the attention of consumers. The unique characteristics of tape and disc technology have appealed to audiences for different reasons.

Disc technology offers increased capacity for information, better sound and/or picture quality (because of the digital method of coding and reading information), and greater durability. The amount of information stored on discs may vary, but generally, CDs can hold as much as 45 minutes more music than a 33 1/3 rpm record, and videodiscs can store 57,000 frames of information; so much data that if a person were to look at each frame for 3 seconds, it would take 27 hours to review the entire videodisc.

The durable feature of discs has been exploited by manufacturers, but has also led to some misunderstanding about how much handling a disc can take and still function well. Because one cannot record over a disc, the information is considered fixed; that is, theoretically, one could toss a disc around, handle it, and then have no discernible problems in playing it on a disc machine. However, anyone who has used discs knows that while they do provide superior sound and picture quality, they are subject to skipping or distortion.

If a person picks up a disc, the oil from his or her fingers can adhere to its surface. When the laser attempts to read the disc, that oil refracts the light in the same way a glass of water would refract a sunbeam passing through it. This

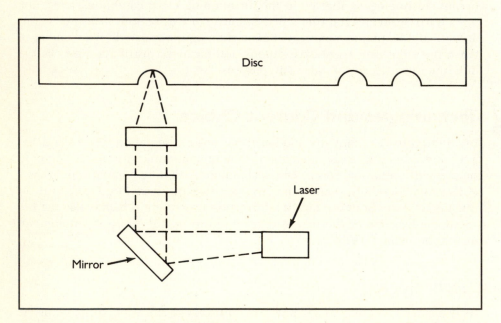

Figure 8.4 *How Disc Technology Works.*
In today's disc technology, all of the material is digitally recorded onto the bottom part of the disc. Precisely etched "grooves" (though they are more square than a record groove) contain both the information (audio, visual, or both) and a numerical message that can be identified by the laser. The laser acts as a record stylus would—except that it never touches the disc. It does, however, locate the numerical code to cue the disc, or find a specific frame of information. The laser then transmits the signal to the audio/visual output units.

causes distortion, skipping, or a popping sound from the CD, or a "glitch," a visual imperfection in a videodisc. Though many people don't realize it, discs can be cleaned with mild dish soap and water to remove the oil or dirt that distorts the message (see figure 8.4).

Compact audio discs (CDs)   Throughout the 1970s, the record industry told Americans that the world soon would face a shortage in polyvinylchloride, the raw material needed to make records. What the record industry did not tell people was that polyvinylchloride is a by-product of petroleum; as long as we have petroleum, there will be no real shortage. The industry's decision to make people think that records could become obsolete was orchestrated specifically to open the new digital compact disc market.

It is true that CDs have far better sound quality than the traditional LPs or 45s, but it is also true that the record industry tends to make far more money through the manufacturing of compact discs than it does through records. CD consumers benefit from getting longer playing times in most cases, but they pay higher prices for the discs.

Videodiscs   Videodisc technology developed during the same era as videotape technology. Some of the earliest experiments were conducted in the late 1960s by Ampex, in the United States, and Sony, in Japan (Nmungwun 1989). But both the Ampex and Sony systems used principles from magnetic tape recording and reproduction, which just didn't work effectively.

In 1972, the Dutch firm of Philips Electronics and the United States' MCA collaborated to introduce "DiscoVision," a laser disc technology that used pre-recorded information on a substance that looked like a shiny 33 1/3 rpm record. What hindered the adoption of videodisc technology was the concurrent development of VCRs, which had more than just a play-only feature. Videodiscs could not be recorded over. While the new disc gave the consumer a high-quality visual image, random access, and improved stereo sound, the discs themselves offered few alternatives. How many times could an interested consumer watch the same disc? By the time videodisc technology was inexpensive enough to try to capture the home consumer market, VCR technology—with its ability to record information from television or cable, and the rerecordable feature of videotape—had gained a clear advantage.

Two competing videodisc formats also added to consumer confusion. In 1981, RCA introduced its SelectaVision mechanical videodisc machine. This model used a stylus that touched the disc to read information in much the same way a phonograph would play a record. At the same time, the optical system, which used a laser to decode the information, was being used by MCA and Philips.

Though the videodisc did not become a common household technology, the optical disc (using a laser) is now used for storage of nonchanging information. This state-of-the-art technology has the ability to rapidly access any specific piece of information in its storage.

Videodiscs have been found useful for a number of interactive purposes. Because the information stored on them cannot be changed, they can be useful tools for providing access maps to people in public places. Malls use them to direct customers to certain stores. Airline terminals provide videodisc information to travelers; libraries use the technology for easy access to research information; and museums use videodiscs to provide more information on exhibits.

Videodiscs also allow supermarkets to expand the number of products they sell. Say, for example, you want to buy a toaster oven. The videodisc technology can present several different types by showing you pictures of each and listing benefits and prices. A computer connected to the disc player can take your credit card number and immediately dispatch the information to the shipping facility. In very short order the toaster oven will be delivered by mail to your home. Supermarkets position the interactive videodisc shopping kiosks in places where customers normally linger (for example, the bakery aisle) and have found that this type of shopping service appeals to customers.

Combiplayers What may make a difference in the home market is the new combiplayer, which plays both compact audio discs and videodiscs. Fourteen different combiplayer systems were introduced in 1991, but the national economy and the saturation of VCRs has relegated videodiscs to lesser importance. Before people are willing to buy yet another home technology that duplicates what is already there, many would like to see what the next big consumer draw will be.

Currently available discs also cannot be rerecorded, though market projections indicate that recordable discs would improve the market tremendously. Some of the new combiplayers have a built-in capacity for rerecording over the discs, which, if software could be developed, would provide a feature that could make the combiplayer and disc technology more competitive with VCRs.

Digital Audio Tape (DAT)

While CD and videodisc technology offers an alternative to records, audiotapes, and VCRs, another development is challenging the recording industry.

Digital Audio Tape (DAT) technology has existed for several years, but the software it uses has been controversial. The quality of the recorded sound on a DAT is so precise that a recorded copy can sound as good as an original. If people were to use DATs to tape radio transmissions or duplicate records or CDs, the sales potential of the recording industry would be cut severely (see box 8.5).

When DATs were introduced to the Japanese market in 1985, they were promoted as a consumer technology that would offer an unprecedented near-

Box 8.5   DAT Problems

". . . what's to stop bootleggers from buying a bunch of records or CDs, copying them on DAT tapes with perfect audio quality and standing outside of Tower Records and as people walk by saying, `Hey Buddy, how about it? What are you going to buy? I have those right here, the exact same quality only I can sell them for half or a third of what they're selling them for in there.' What happens if we get to the point where we can't sell records anymore? All the studios are going to close. The record companies are not going to be able to make any money. Nobody's going to be able to make any music."
—Bob Clearmountain, popular music engineer

Source: By Peter Wilkinson from *Rolling Stone*, September 10, 1987, by Straight Arrow Publishers, Inc. 1987. All Rights Reserved. Reprinted by Permission.

perfect audio quality for home recording.

With the threat of DATs coming into the home recording scene, the Radio Industry Association of America (RIAA) introduced two special types of surcharges for blank tapes. During congressional hearings, the RIAA lobbied the legislature for "A permanent solution to the digital home taping problem before severe incremental damage is caused by the product" (Billboard, 1986 1).

The legislation RIAA recommended would have made a new anti-home-taping weapon available called the CBS Copy Code. This electronic copy protection scheme was designed to prevent music consumers from copying protected music from the radio. It required the installation of a special detection circuit or copy chip into all DAT recorders. The chip would recognize certain encoded music and disable the DAT from recording it. The Copy Code procedure was rejected by manufacturers as being too problematic and too costly for the home consumer, but the controversy involved issues that connect problems of both an industrial and economic nature.

The Japanese had invented a piece of technology that was superior in sound quality even to CD technology. Manufacturers in the United States and recording industry personnel around the world wanted to protect the recording industry and the emerging CD market. For several years the debate centered on whether or not the high cost of DAT technology would prevent consumers from purchasing it and on whether a special tax or anticopying code could be used effectively on the digital audiotapes.

When digital audio technology was released to U.S. consumers in February 1991, manufacturers, record promoters, and the government agreed to resolve the problem by levying a high price on the tapes; a one-hour digital audiotape cost $25. It was assumed that this high purchase cost would prohibit duplication of tapes, since it would still be cheaper to purchase an original record, CD, or audiotape.

The Audio Home Recording Act

On October 7, 1992, Congress passed the Audio Home Recording Act of 1992 that required manufacturers of DAT technology and blank tape to place a surcharge on their goods. Digital audiotape recorders were to collect an additional 2 percent, and blank-tape manufacturers were ordered to charge an additional 3 percent on their sales. These surcharges then would be passed on to performing artists, record companies, songwriters, and publishers to protect them against any unauthorized home recording that might result from digital audio technology (Holland 1992, 1).

The surcharges would be turned over to the Copyright Office of the U.S. Treasury Department for later disbursement by the Copyright Royalty Tribunal, the same organization that oversees payment for other content that is available to the public but does not return funds directly to creative individuals. Videocassette sales or rental and computer software, which is easily copied, are two examples of forms that use the Copyright Royalty Tribunal for the payment of surcharges. The legislation specified that 66 2/3 of the collection would be given to the sound recording fund, which would give 60 percent of its amount to the record companies, and 40 percent to featured performers. The remaining 33 1/3 percent of the total would be divided evenly between publishers and composers (or songwriters) (Nunziata 1992, 88).

The payment plan mandated by Congress is likely to be a model for future technologies and software that are distributed openly and offer audiences duplication opportunities. The actual surcharge is buried in the cost of the technology or the original content distribution form. Consumers contribute to the fund every time they buy or rent new technology or software.

Conclusion

The technologies and services discussed in this chapter illustrate that consumers now have a greater number of options for ways in which they receive certain media messages. These technologies have unique characteristics as tools of communication, but their use of content often suggests a different relationship between traditional communication industries and their audiences.

The impact of many of the new distribution forms is being felt in the home. Certainly the introduction of CDs or DATs to the home is seen as nothing more than an extension of the sound environment provided by a stereo.

The industries that produce these technologies are concerned with providing the audience what it is willing to pay for. But the industries also must figure how best to secure the revenue from future sales or rental of their services.

Each of the technologies discussed in this chapter is similar to other forms. Each has been marketed in different ways with different levels of success. Perhaps the reason for this is that none of the technologies offers consumers anything radically new. Rather, each of the new technologies offers more of the same—replicating information that was available to us in earlier forms. The difference lies more in the quality of the images and sounds we now hear. Each of these new technologies has supplied (to those who can afford them) an improved image or acoustic environment.

SUMMARY

Within a period of 20 years, the number of new technologies available for home and industry use has grown dramatically. Those who can afford to buy are presented with myriad choices for how to spend time interacting with the various technologies. Many of these forms rely less on mass distribution than on individual attention for consumer choice of content. In this chapter, the shift from mass forms of distribution to personal choice technologies has been discussed by examining:

- alternative forms of distribution that target smaller audiences with similar interests
- distribution forms that can be connected to other technologies to make time and space irrelevant concepts for the transmission of images
- new forms of technology that rely on principles of making physical connections to other distribution forms
- how perceptions formed by traditional media may be changed as newer forms become available
- rapid adoption of home technology

DISCUSSION QUESTIONS

1. How have CDs and VCRs changed people's traditional expectations of what audio sound or a moving picture should be like?
2. As satellite transponder space becomes more available, for what purposes could satellite communication be used?

3. Because geosynchronous satellites are located above the equator, many countries have explored the possibility of charging rent for the atmosphere above them. The precedent of international waters has provided a model; a country can claim control only within certain limits—the positioning of geosynchronous satellites exceeds that limit. Are countries with other nations' satellites in close proximity in any particularly vulnerable position? Why?

4. For what purposes might LPTV be used in your community?

5. Does SMATV offer greater options for residents of a building, or can it also be used to invade people's privacy? In your opinion, is there a fine line between the two?

6. Have CDs or DATs changed your own behavior or habits? Do you listen differently? Do you exercise choice more often? If you don't have these technologies, where do you turn for entertainment?

7. What other software or technologies might benefit from having revenues collected and disbursed through the Copyright Royalty Tribunal?

REFERENCES

Abramson, A. 1955. A short history of television recording. *The Journal of the Society of Motion Picture and Television Engineers* 64: 250–51.

Fisher, Scott S. 1990. Telepresence in dataspace. *Millimeter* 41.

Hall, Trish. 1990. 'Virtual reality' takes its place in the real world. *New York Times,* July 8, 1, 14.

Holland, Bill. 1992. Audio home recording act passes. *Billboard,* Oct. 7, 1 and 87.

Joy, Ken. 1992. The top ten hot products at winter CES, *Billboard,* 11 January, C3–C4.

Lardner, James. 1987. *Fast forward: Hollywood, the Japanese and the VCR wars.* New York: W.W. Norton.

Levy, Mark R. and Fink, Edward L. 1984. Home video recorders and the transience of television broadcasts. *Journal of Communication* 34: 56–71.

Newhagen, John E. and Reeves, Byron. 1992. The evening's bad news: Effects of compelling negative television news images on memory. *Journal of Communication* 42: 25–41.

Nmungwun, Aaron Foisi. 1989. *Video recording technology: Its impact on media and home entertainment.* Hillsdale, N.J.: Lawrence Erlbaum Associates.

Nunziata, Susan. 1992. Divvying up the digital royalty pie in the sky. *Billboard,* 26 December, 1, 18.

Ochiva, Dan. 1990. Telepresence in dataspace. *Millimeter* 41.

Video 'immersion': Programming virtual worlds. 1991. *Broadcasting* 120: 64.

Wilkinson, Peter. 1987. What is DAT, and why are the record companies trying to keep it away from you? *Rolling Stone,* 10 September, 72.

Nine

COMPUTERS AND PERIPHERALS

MAKING CONNECTIONS

For a variety of reasons, computers have become a primary communication technology. Large mainframe computers now function as switching systems integrating a host of other technologies and providing system redundancy; smaller mini- and microcomputers extend a number of options for task completion in businesses and homes. While one chapter on computers could never discuss adequately the many ways in which computers are now used, understanding a little of the history and function of computers will illustrate ways in which they influence other forms of communication.

In this chapter the unique communication tool known as the computer will be discussed by addressing:

- the history of the computer's development

- the unique ability of the computer to mediate information

- the computer's ability to change communication processes

- the effect of computers on traditional methods

Chapter

- the computer's connection to social issues such as privacy

In the film *2001: A Space Odyssey,* HAL the computer takes on some personal characteristics that demonstrate how computers potentially could be programmed to "think" like humans. In science fiction and in daily life, the potential power of computers raises questions about the true impact of the technology. Could machines be programmed to perform jobs more efficiently and more reliably than humans? If so, how will people be able to earn a living? If more tasks are completed using computers, will people need human interaction more—or less? Fascination with just how powerful computers could become has been fueled by the many technological advances that have pushed computers from simple machines that manipulate symbols, to today's high-powered supercomputers that process vast amounts of information faster, and with greater precision, than humans.

When computers were in the development stage in the 1940s, the impact of the technology was a matter of speculation. In the 1950s, a prediction was made that someday three or four computers would be enough for the whole world.

Computers are central to making connections among other technologies. Their presence in the world also suggests a point from which we can better understand the connections among social, economic, and technical worlds. Because the computer has become a major component of processing electronic messages and linking other forms of communication technologies, understanding of its development and impact is now as important for students of electronic communication technologies as any other basic tool of information transfer. This chapter will be limited to a description of the way in which computers influence communication and societal values. Four areas will be discussed: (1) a brief history of computers, (2) their use for communication, (3) their impact on the way people perform tasks, and (4) social concerns about their use and abuse.

Within the communication industries, computers handle diverse tasks. They integrate live and prerecorded information from different distribution systems for broadcasting. They control the positioning and operation of satellites for the purpose of connecting networks, sharing information, and transmitting data. They generate codes and functions that operate faster, with more precision than a human could. They generate the intriguing visual images we often take for granted in television and film. As stated in previous chapters, they have had a significant impact in the development of telephony, radio, television, and new distribution technologies.

As computers become smaller, less costly, and more user friendly, their impact can be felt in other areas of communication. From home banking to word processing and from video games to the connection with various technologies in the office or home, computers have become important personal communication technologies. They challenge our everyday assumptions about information processing by speeding up information transfer, changing traditional jobs and work-related activities, and offering a virtually limitless capacity for information storage and retrieval. For many people, their first introduction to computers comes from using a personal computer as a word processor, which can easily become a "work processor." Like many technologies, computers sometimes are feared because they do change the ways in which we perform tasks. But even though they alter the nature of work, elements of traditional tasks are also present. It is the integration of computers and traditional skills that provides an interesting connection between old ways and new. In the transition period, it is possible to see the various speeds at which change occurs.

In his 1991 book, Powershift, Alvin Toffler describes how auto mechanics have become increasingly reliant on computer systems for troubleshooting. In addition to providing access to 100 megabytes of technical drawings and data stored on CD-ROM, computerized systems help mechanics make inferences about how best to complete repairs. Though mechanics still are involved with manual work, reliance on the computer provides a new twist to an old job. Toffler asks the question "When they are interacting with this system are they 'mechanics,' or 'mind-workers'?" (1991). In most cases, the reliance on computers does introduce a new attitude toward necessary knowledge and skill level. Understanding the computer's evolution provides insights into how powerful this technology has become.

How Computers Were Developed

The idea of an information processing machine grew from the integration of intellectual concepts from mathematics, philosophy, mechanics, and the sciences (Haugeland 1987). The first to successfully construct a mechanical model testing these ideas was the 19th-century British mathematician Charles Babbage. His Analytical Engine was designed to perform several mathematical functions, and in retrospect, more clearly resembled a calculator than one of today's computers. Unfortunately, the materials necessary to make his engine work were not yet available. Without vacuum tubes and materials that could transfer information at high speeds, the design could not be translated into a working model. Still, his blueprints and diagrams were complex descriptors of programming logic, symbol manipulation, and machine time, and his work provided the foundation upon which others could improve.

Allen M. Turing was one of the first modern thinkers to apply these theoretical discoveries to the construction of a machine to model human thought. His early treatise, "On Computable Numbers" (1936), contained designs that were far too complex for practical construction, but by the 1950s, Turing had redesigned his plans. Today they provide guidelines for the most sophisticated of computer programs.

Perhaps the most significant discovery was John von Neumann's 1950s development of a computer that had the capacity to go beyond calculator functions. Von Neumann's experimental computer functioned as a logic machine, in that it could perform computations far more complex than Babbage's or Turing's designs. The computer's memory was so large that symbols and numerals could be identified as different from letters. The machine was so sophisticated that it could operate in terms of abstract images such as hieroglyphs. Today von Neumann's early symbol-manipulating computer and logic machine can still be found where it was originally constructed—behind the boiler in the basement of a building at Princeton University.

What made Turing's and von Neumann's ideas possible was Bell Labs' 1949 invention of the transistor. A much smaller, precision semiconductor (conductor of electricity) the transistor could process energy more efficiently than the large, slow vacuum tubes used to convert electrical energy. The transistor provided the conceptual and practical link to the eventual design of the microchip, which uses semiconductors to transfer electrical energy. Surprisingly, the transistor did not revolutionize electronic circuitry overnight. It took some time for the genius of the conceptualization to be translated into something that could be adequately manufactured. Because this design was so complex, tools to manufacture the product had to be developed; before high-

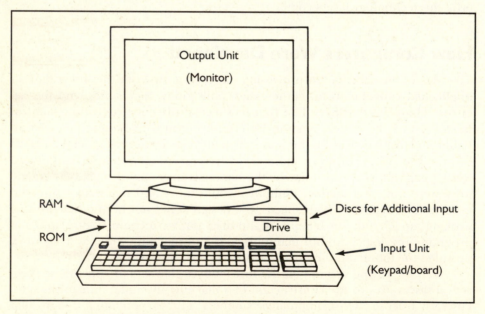

Figure 9.1   How a Microcomputer Works.

quality semiconductors were perfected, high levels of heat generated during electrical processing melted early transistors.

How Computers Work

Babbage, Turing, and von Neumann each contributed to the development of a computer that relies on units specializing in functions that input data, process information with the help of a memory unit, and output data. The more sophisticated these functions are, the more powerful the computer. The micro-computer, or home computer can provide an example (see figure 9.1).

Keyboards are the principle input units for microcomputers. When information is typed on the keyboard, the microprocessors connect the two memory

---

Box 9.1   Early Computers

The first electronic digital computer was built in 1943 at Bletchley Park, Hertfordshire, England. Named Colossus, its purpose was to crack the supposedly uncrackable code of the sophisticated Enigma machine used by the German high command throughout World War II. Enigma generated a code so complex that humans could not think through the system, but the Colossus computer was not subject to human failings, such as fatigue or unsystematic thinking, and it successfully broke the code.

At the same time, Dr. John Mauchly and J. Presper Eckert were working on a machine at the Moore School of Electrical Engineering at the University of Pennsylvania. The Electronic Numerical Integrator and Calculator (ENIAC), which was designed to assess the performance of military hardware, was first switched on in 1946. ENIAC's most notable feature was that it could compute thousands of operations per minute, a feature that allowed it to solve in two hours a problem that would take 100 humans, each working eight hours a day, a year to complete.

Standing 9 feet high and weighing 30 tons, ENIAC filled the space of a small gymnasium. It generated so much heat that industrial cooling fans had to be installed to keep the machinery from melting down. With at least 70,000 resistors and 18,000 vacuum tubes (which failed at the average rate of one every seven minutes), a tremendous amount of electrical energy was required to power the computer. It often was claimed that the lights of Philadelphia dimmed whenever ENIAC was turned on.

Source: Tom Forester, *The high-tech society* (Cambridge, Mass.: MIT Press, 1987) 17.

units—random-access memory (RAM), the temporary storage facility that enables new information to be keying into the computer, and read-only-memory (ROM), which contains the permanent information (for example, the information necessary to match software with keyboard and computer instructions). Disk drives connect to the RAM unit and function as additional program or memory software. Monitors and printers make up the output units.

RAM and ROM chips are parts of integrated circuits that use silicon as the resource for semiconductors. When silicon-based semiconductors are used on integrated circuits, the speed of information transported from chip to chip is measured in billionths of seconds, or nanoseconds.

Babbage's Analytical Engine used an analog mode for information processing. Today's computers operate digitally. This process mathematically codes and decodes information so that the computer can sort quickly. Because digital technology is so precise, it operates more efficiently than analog technology. Using complex mathematical codes, the computer units can coordinate information processing and perform several tasks sequentially—information transferred by high-speed semiconductors routes information through integrated circuits to specific parts of the computer.

Generations of Computers

Technical advances have propelled computer development through different phases called generations. Each generation refers to the level of technical sophistication that influences the amount of information the computer is capable of processing. The newer generations have provided miniaturized computers, which brought down the manufacturing cost.

The first-generation computers used valves and tubes like the von Neumann computer. The second-generation computers used transistors to process information, and the third used integrated circuits. Today most computers operate at the fourth-generation level, meaning that information processing is based on multilayered integrated circuits that allow several functions to operate simultaneously. These computers vary in size and ability. They may be as large as a mainframe or as small as a micro- or minicomputer.

Fifth-generation computers are often called supercomputers. They have extended memories, the capacity for parallel processing (operating multiple functions simultaneously), sophisticated software systems that provide components as diverse as speech or vision recognition (used for security purposes). Some even have the capacity to transform two-dimensional directions into a simulated three-dimensional image. Supercomputers can process more information at greater levels of complexity than ever dreamed of by Babbage, Turing, or von Neumann. The speed of computations is now mind-boggling. In 1987, the fastest supercomputer operated at 250 million computations per second. By the end of that year, the figure was up to 1 billion computations per second (Forester 1987, 42–43). By 1991, speed records were being broken almost weekly, as the figures began to soar to 9.03 billion computations per second and, within months, 12 billion per second.

The ultimate goal, however, is to create sixth-generation computers that not only can simulate thinking processes but can be programmed to think for themselves. The problems involved in developing such computers are so complex that human ingenuity and expertise are not enough to plan for the next

---

Box 9.2   Sixth-Generation Computers and Artificial Intelligence

In 1956, a group of philosophers, physicists, mathematicians, computer engineers, and other learned persons convened at Dartmouth to discuss the possibility of computers that could simulate human thinking processes. These super-expert systems could possibly be used to replicate and reproduce artificial intelligence, the simulation of human intelligence by machines.

Underscoring the development of the intelligent computer is the deeply held view in Western philosophy that thinking is basically the same thing as rationally manipulating mental symbols. Because manipulating symbols is what a computer does, some people are led to believe that a computer could be programmed to think or perhaps have a mind of its own. Cognitive science is the unified field that has been created to study these principles, combining tools and techniques of computer science with methods of experimental psychology.

The work of the Dartmouth group has given impetus to the understanding of neural networks, which eventually will lead to better understanding of the logical inferences of the brain. Neural network research focuses on modeling human brain functions by means of integrated circuits. Artificial intelligence research is not a specific science; rather, it is a special area combining engineering and logic. The possibility for artificial intelligence is not a problem for technology; it is tied to the ability of humans to understand and translate theoretical assumptions into computer language. Research in this area ties together techniques from computer science, experimental psychology, and traditional philosophy.

One of the most intriguing problems for researchers of artificial intelligence has to do with memory. The challenge is to create a computer memory that is vast enough to process all of the humanlike associative meanings possible. To do this, more research on how the human memory works is necessary.

generation. Supercomputers are being used to design the next generation of computers, generally called intelligent computers, because they will be able to program themselves to do certain tasks (see box 9.2).

Unique Characteristics of Computers

While each generation of computers has unique qualities that separate it from the others, all computers share qualities of rapid information processing and expanded memory. These features are central to understanding how computers affect human communication processes.

Presentation of Image

When a personal computer is used for word processing, the amount of information on the screen shows only a portion of the complete text. The computer's memory is more accurate than the user's memory. Because of these differences, the computer user's relationship to the material is different than it would be if he or she were writing thoughts in longhand. Use of computers is very context-oriented. When you use a computer for a video game, your expectation about the outcome of the interaction is fairly clear; you probably will be amused or entertained. Similarly, when you use a computer for word processing, you engage the unique features of the computer. One such feature is the computer screen, which limits the amount of information to the size of the video display terminal (VDT).

In word processing, the presentation of a segment of a longer written piece focuses attention on part of the document rather than on the whole. Those who use computers for extensive word processing have complained that this alters their mental processes by allowing them to think of the written work as a series of "pieces" of information in which the concept of the entire work is easily overlooked. This feature sometimes is blamed for causing thought processes to become more disconnected (Turkle 1984).

Expanded Memory

The other unique quality of the computer is its ability to store and retrieve information at a faster pace than the human mind. In many ways, greater reliance on the computer's memory also affects the user's perceptions. Rather than thinking through processes before committing words to paper, the computer allows users to spontaneously record thought processes; users are limited only by typing speed. Again, the memory function of the computer makes it easier for the user to record and store information. If human memory were being exercised, the desire to rethink and reflect would change the nature of the information. The computer is not subject to human distortion or reflection. Therefore, the user's mental concepts of the information in a computer data base mixes the technological capacity for accuracy with the human process of thinking.

This part of the user's relationship to the computer's storage capacity can be thought of as a dilemma. Computers are capable of storing vast amounts of information, but the logic they use is binary, not human, logic. When an individual uses a computer for data collection, technological and human connections are not always complete.

Infotrack is a popular data base service available in many libraries today. To use Infotrack, you type key words for which the computer will search. If the key word appears in a title of an article, Infotrack counts it as an "information find." If someone were searching for information on high-definition television (HDTV) and keyed in HDTV for the word search, the computer would not read titles such as "Enhanced Television," or "Digital Television" as possible sources. The user would only receive a listing of titles that include the letters "HDTV" and could therefore miss some important information. The concept that computers have "all" the information can be misleading. Belief in the infallibility of computers is dangerous. Computers are only as reliable as their programs and data bases—and the human's ability to use them.

Computers and Communication

Computers increasingly are used as tools to control the operations of business and industry. One computer, performing simultaneous functions, can process more information than thousands of employees. Telephone companies rely on computers to connect calls and generate bills for customer charges. Broadcast operations rely on computers to switch signals from satellite feeds to other automated systems, or to connect live broadcasts with previously recorded information.

The presence of mini- and microcomputers in the home and workplace will be discussed in subsequent chapters, but with regard to the phenomenon of computers and human interaction, it is necessary to address some of the more generic issues.

People Interacting with Computers

Computers, more than any other communication technology, produce a level of anxiety in many potential users. Apprehension about computers often is tied to technological apprehension in general, but for many, computers are powerful tools that challenge contemporary sensibilities. Many individuals have a negative response to how quickly and mysteriously computer functions seem to take place.

Many people reduce their apprehension by learning about computers through nonthreatening systems, such as computer games. When playing such games, the logic behind a computer becomes simplified for the player. Animation and sound effects often contribute to the nonthreatening atmosphere, but the player learns about response time, precision, and control from even the simple act of playing computer games. For this reason, many consumers have purchased personal computers for home use.

Personal Computers

The first computer designed for personal use was the Atari Computer, marketed in 1975 and sold for only $400. In the late 1970s, Apple, Tandy (owned by Radio Shack), and Commodore came along, but it wasn't until 1981, when Hewlett-Packard and IBM developed their home computers, that the personal-computer craze swept the United States.

In 1982, the same year that *Time* magazine featured the personal computer as the "Machine of the Year," only about 2 percent of U.S. households had a computer; by 1992, the number had reached 12 percent.

Because home computers create competition for other home media, their impact can be addressed by investigating the personal habits of home computer users. A 1982 study by Rogers, Daley, and Wu of the Stanford University Institute for Communication Research found that 40 percent of new home computer households had reduced their television viewing by an average of 1.5 hours per day, while only 4 percent reported that television viewing had increased since purchasing a home computer. Respondents cited several benefits of home computers, including the use of the technology for playing games, doing work at home, increasing awareness of the computer world, changing recreational activities, saving time, and, in general, allowing the user to spend more time at home.

Home Computer Software

There currently are more than 200 companies involved in hardware and software manufacture (primarily for use with personal computers), and computer software has become the most profitable of the communications industries (see box 9.3).

Home computers can use commercial systems, like Prodigy, a videotex system that provides access to a wide variety of services, such as banking, airline information and reservations, personal financial accounts management, electronic mail, and newspaper data file access. With the purchase of the software package and a subscription to the on-line service, Prodigy has over 800 features encompassing a variety of information services that can be linked, via modem,

---

Box 9.3   Computer Geniuses

The two most successful entrepreneurs in the personal computer field are Steven Jobs, one of the cofounders of Apple Computer, and William Gates, founder of Microsoft, the most successful software company in the world.

Both Jobs and Gates were college dropouts. Jobs left Reed College to travel to India; upon returning he and a friend created the Apple personal computer. The idea behind Apple was to offer a computer that was easier to use than the market leader, the IBM PC.

Gates left Harvard in 1975 to found Microsoft, the system that made PCs "user friendly." In 1980, IBM asked Gates to provide an operating system for their new personal computer, and the association gave Microsoft the lead in commercial software development. By 1991, William Gates had become the richest man in the world.

---

from IBM- or Macintosh-compatible computers to the information provider.

Other software available for the home includes features like interactive fiction, which allows the user to control the outcome of such stories as Ray Bradbury's *Farenheit 451,* Arthur C. Clarke's *Rendezvous with Rama*, Michael Crichton's *The Andromeda Strain,* and Douglas Adams's *Hitchhiker's Guide to the Galaxy.*

Computers and Social Concerns

The proliferation of computers in today's business and industry operations has brought with it several societal concerns. Among these issues are ethical concerns about (1) right to privacy and (2) legal sanctions for abuses of computer systems.

Ethical Concerns

When computerized information is stored in a data file, some important questions arise. Who has access to the information? How tightly controlled is access to that information? Is the information correct? These and other questions raise a series of problems for companies, individuals, and even nations, because computer data is often transferred by wire or broadcast forms that can be decoded, if one knows the password and the technical system.

Privacy and Security

The computer's potential for breaches of privacy has always been a ticklish legal issue. Supreme Court Justice Lewis Brandeis once stated, "[Privacy] is the right to be left alone, the right most valued by civilized men [sic]."

New Jersey congressman Cornelius Galliger was one of the pioneers in privacy and computer legislation. In the mid-1960s he initiated legislative efforts to preserve the rights of individuals whose privacy had been invaded by information-gathering computers. Even though Galliger attempted to craft legislation, his work did not bear fruit until 1973 and 1974 when specific privacy laws were passed.

The abuse of individual privacy includes such factors as unrestricted personal-data collection, storage of inaccurate or incomplete data, unauthorized disclosure, and inappropriate access to data. Casper Weinberger, former head of the Department of Health, Education, and Welfare, said in 1975 that "Above all, we must recognize that personal freedoms diminish as the welfare state grows. The price of more and more public programs is less and less freedom."

Computerized law-enforcement records pose potential problems, not because arrest records are stored in them, but because often pertinent information does not make its way into those data files. There have been many cases in which individuals have been turned down for employment because of incorrect or improperly updated arrest records.

A study conducted by a professor from the John Jay School of Criminal Justice and commissioned by the U.S. Office of Technology Assessment (OTA) compared a random sampling of criminal history records that had recently been dispatched by three states and the FBI to original files in county court. The study found that in North Carolina only 12.2 percent of the summaries were complete, accurate, and unambiguous. In California, 18.9 percent were accurate; in Minnesota, the number was 49.5 percent. The FBI files fared no better. In a random check of files, the researchers found that only 25.75 percent of the FBI records met the standards set by federal law.

Upon further examination of 400 arrest warrants issued in one day by the FBI, only 10.9 percent had been cleared; 4.1 percent showed no record of a warrant. This led the researcher to surmise that, on the day studied, 17,340 Americans were subject to false arrest based on false or incomplete data.

The more we use computer information for banking, bill paying, record keeping, and basic communication through messaging systems, the more we run the risk of losing our privacy.

Computers could be designed to ensure greater privacy if more concern were given to establishing practices that could be monitored more carefully. On the other hand, this might reduce the computer's user friendliness and so discourage its use.

According to David Burnham (1983) about 50 percent of the population works for a corporation; their employers store a great deal of information about them. Also, the U.S. government collects an average of 17 information items for every person in the country. The largest information gatherers are the FBI and the telephone companies, who have records of every phone call made.

Box 9.4   Connecting with Clifford Stoll

When Cliff Stoll was given the assignment of tracking a 75-cent discrepancy in the computerized accounting records of Lawrence Berkeley Laboratory, he first assumed that there might be a problem in one of the software systems. As he began to trace the 75 cents, he uncovered a case of computer espionage that had eluded even the CIA and the FBI.

After a year of investigating the unauthorized use by a hacker named Marcus Hess, who invaded many computer networks in the United States and abroad, Stoll uncovered a spy ring (based in Hannover, Germany) that sold their stolen computer secrets to the KGB for money and drugs.

This story, recorded in Stoll's book *The Cuckoo's Egg: Tracking a Spy Through the Maze of Computer Espionage*, discusses the ever-present danger of poor security of computerized information. Stoll warns of the potential for unauthorized use of information:

> [It can happen] Whenever someone, tempted by money, power, or simple curiosity, steals a password and prowls the networks. Whenever someone forgets that the networks she loves to play on are fragile, and can only exist when people trust each other. Whenever a fun-loving student breaks into systems as a game (as I might once have done), and forgets that he's invading people's privacy, endangering data that others have sweated over, sowing distrust and paranoia.
>
> Networks aren't made of printed circuits, but of people. Right now, as I type, through my keyboard I can touch countless others: friends, strangers, enemies. I can talk to a physicist in Japan, an astronomer in England, a spy in Washington. I might gossip with a buddy in Silicon Valley or some professor at Berkeley.
>
> My terminal is a door to countless, intricate pathways, leading to untold numbers of neighbors. Thousands of people trust each other enough to tie their systems together. Hundreds of thousands of people use those systems, never realizing the delicate networks that link their separate worlds.

Source: Clifford Stoll. *The Cuckoo's Egg: Tracking a Spy Through the Maze of Computer Espionage* (New York: Doubleday, 1989) 323.

The more we sacrifice personal control over information, the greater the concern for issues of privacy and security. At present in the United States, there are 14 government agencies involved with questions regarding the legislation of privacy. Some have suggested that a bill of information rights should be mandated and enacted.

Computer crime   The fastest-growing crime rate in America is that of "white-collar" crime perpetrated by means of computers. A profile of the typical computer criminal indicates the thief is most often a person 18–30 years old who is not a professional thief.

The government estimates that computer crime costs from $300 million to $5 billion a year, but the most amazing fact is that only about 10 percent of computer crimes are detected; the rest go unnoticed. Most of the computer crime is through bank fraud, especially due to electronic funds transfer. A simple example: an unauthorized person accessing someone else's automatic teller account or credit card number.

The second-largest area of computer crime is found in insurance agencies where phony policies or checks are drafted. The third-largest area is in the theft of computer time, and the fourth, pirating of software.

The material stored in computers is very sensitive. A slight change in electrical energy, such as a surge in electricity or an uneven pulse, can result in a permanent loss of information. A magnet placed near a disk or tape can also erase data, since the base of the software is magnetic and uses magnetic principles for storage and retrieval.

With computer crime on the rise, the cost of goods and services that rely on computers has escalated. But could these crimes be avoided? What type of regulation could control computer crime? What punishment is appropriate? These questions currently are debated in Congress and within various states that are considering creating legislation to protect individuals in our computer-reliant society.

Conclusion

The reduction in cost and the continued efforts toward more high-speed, miniaturized computers have extended their applicability to a variety of settings, for many different purposes. From the initial effort toward simulating human thought processes to today's experimentation with computers that have a far greater capacity to process data and store information, (and possibly to simulate human thought more exactly), computers have grown at a rate that has exceeded earlier dreams.

While many other forms of communication technologies capitalize on content and uses predicted by other forms of media, computers challenge us to think in entirely new ways. The skills necessary for work with computers also change with the purpose and technology used.

Today it is impossible for the industrialized world to think of life without computers. All in all, computers provide a rich opportunity for social scientists to study human adaptation to technology.

SUMMARY

In this chapter the computer's power has been discussed with relation to:
- its central position in controlling information and communication technology
- how the unique features of display presentation and memory influence the user's relationship to content
- increasing reliance on computers to perform time-consuming tasks
- sacrifices in security and privacy brought about by increasing reliance on computers
- the ethical dimensions of massive information stored for a variety of uses

DISCUSSION QUESTIONS

1. Separate the class into two groups, those who use computers and those who do not. With these two groups, debate the merits of computers.
2. Discuss how computers change your relationship to the writing process. Do you feel that you begin to think like the computer?
3. Consider how many transactions you make each day that in some way are reliant on computer technology. What would happen if computers could not complete those tasks?
4. Computers are becoming more user friendly. In the future, what skills do you think will be necessary to operate most computers? Will typing be necessary?
5. How might you integrate computers into your class? Could you interact with others through electronic services? Would you be willing to ask questions of your professor through electronic mail? Would this type of interaction satisfy your educational needs?
6. How secure is your home or school from privacy invasion? How many pieces of junk mail find their way to your home each week? Do you have

237

a clear idea of the number of times your name and address have been sold to telemarketers or direct mail merchants? How do you know?

7. Discuss the ways in which privacy can be violated by increased use of computers connected to other forms of technologies.

REFERENCES

Bolter, J. David. 1984. *Turing's man: Western culture in the computer age.* Chapel Hill, N.C.: University of North Carolina Press.

Burnham, David. 1983. *The rise of the computer state.* New York: Random House.

Forester, Tom. 1987. *High-tech society: The story of the information technology revolution.* Cambridge, Mass.: MIT Press.

Hanson, Dirk. 1982. *The new alchemists.* Boston: Little, Brown and Co.

Haugeland, John. 1987. *Artificial intelligence: The very idea.* Cambridge, Mass.: MIT Press.

Parker, Donn B. 1976. *Crime by computer.* New York: Charles Scribner's Sons.

Rogers, Everett M.; Daley, Hugh M.; and Wu, Thomas D. 1982. *The diffusion of home computers: An exploratory study.* A report for the Institution for Communication Research, Stanford University.

Stoll, Clifford. 1989. *The cuckoo's egg: Tracking a spy through the maze of computer espionage.* New York: Doubleday.

Toffler, Alvin. 1991. *Powershift: Knowledge, wealth, and violence at the edge of the 21st century.* New York: Bantam.

Turing, Allen M. 1936. *On computable numbers, with an application to the Entsheidungsproblem.* Proceedings of the London Mathematical Society, Series 2, vol. 42, 230–265.

Turkle, Sherry. 1984. *The second self: Computers and the human spirit.* New York: Simon and Schuster.

Ten

Technology in the Home
Our Changing Lifestyles

Making Connections

The variety of communication technologies and services available today are creating changes in every facet of our lives. Many of these changes are occurring in the home, where the addition of new technology provides a greater number of options for doing things. Some of the alternatives provided by new technologies and services include activities that have traditionally been done outside, such as working, getting an education, and even shopping! When new ways of doing things become part of the home, people are often less aware of the changes than if they were confronted with change in a different environment. We regard our homes as places of comfort, safety, and relaxation. As a result, we tend to be less critical of changes that occur in the home than of changes that occur in a more stressful environment like work. Nevertheless, technological changes in the home may have a significant impact on personal relationships and the way we think about the home environment.

Home is often considered a haven from the stress and

Chapter

10

activity of work, school, and the "outside" world in general. But as more communication technology makes it possible to work, get an education, and take advantage of entertainment in the home, we need to assess our priorities and how we deal with changing traditional ways of doing things.

This chapter investigates a number of activities we usually take for granted. It also considers the evidence suggesting how and why our lifestyles are changing.

Watch for the following connections:

- "old" technologies like the telephone and television are being used for new and different purposes

- new services are changing the way people traditionally engage in activities

- people are adopting new practices that keep them in the home

- people are making choices about what new technologies and services to purchase

- inequities are created in society when only some can afford new technologies while others are prevented from using them

- traditional values are being challenged, reinforced, or changed by communication options in the home

---

In recent years a number of low-cost communication technologies have presented opportunities for expanded uses in the home. In particular, when telephone, television, and computer technologies are linked together, they can create a variety of options to enhance work, education, and leisure. Additional pieces of hardware, like VCRs, CD players and fax machines, or software, like videotapes and computer programs, can bring environments as diverse as the movie theater, shopping mall, or bank into our homes.

Many of the new technologies and services give us more control of our home environments. Think of how often people use telephone answering machines to screen intrusive phone calls and protect their privacy, or how often people listen to compact discs rather than the radio. The technologies now available for the home give us many more options in choosing our lifestyles, but each exacts a price. There is a monetary price for hardware, software, and electricity, and there is also a sacrifice of interpersonal contact. Think, for a moment, of the number of communication technologies you may have in your home that eliminate the need for face-to-face interaction, or perhaps any contact with other people. Telephone answering machines, electronic security devices, home shopping services, and computerized electronic mail are only a few of today's possible alternatives to engaging in interpersonal communication.

Because each of the new technologies costs us money when we purchase it, subscribe to it, or operate it, home technologies give rise to some ethical questions about technological change. Should only those people who can afford to buy and operate new technologies have them? While the easy answer seems to be "yes," remember the problems raised in the discussion on telephone systems. If only those who can afford the services have access to them, what happens to the poor, those on fixed incomes (like the elderly or disabled), or people who live in areas where services cost more to operate? Is it possible to draw a line between technologies that are necessities and those that are luxuries? Are we increasingly becoming a society of "haves" and "have nots"? What becomes of older communications industries and their employees when new industries force them to declare bankruptcy or restrict services?

The other major issue to consider when thinking about home technologies is how far they will reduce the need for interpersonal activity. The greater the number of entertainment technologies in the home, the less the need to go outside for human interaction. The VCR has eliminated the need to see movies at a public theater. Home video games make it easier to be amused at home than to go to a more social environment like a bowling alley, skating rink, or playing field. Might this lead to greater alienation of individuals from society, or less understanding by individuals of diverse points of view? Could those individuals who opt to study, work, and spend more leisure time at home be losing the ability to interact with a variety of different people, and become intolerant of the cultures or views of others? The film *Being There,* starring Peter Sellers, offers a humorous example of a gardener who never ventured outside the garden walls. His only knowledge of the outside world came from what he saw on television. While he gains a superficial knowledge of the world, he also learns to speak in the phrases and sound-bites that are so common in TV. When he finally leaves his home and garden, ironically (and humorously), the people with whom he interacts think his speech patterns and grasp of world affairs are so impressive, they conclude that he is brilliant, and a prime candidate for political office.

This chapter examines not only some of the new technologies and services that have begun to change the electronic home environment, but also how new practices are changing the world around us. Many of the institutions we take for granted have been forced to respond to the changes brought about by competition in home technologies and services. By considering how changes inside the home have led to change outside the home, it is possible to see how so many technologies have, indeed, forged connections that will change our futures.

Bringing Work to the Home: Telecommuting

The necessity for many households to have two incomes to maintain the standard of living they desire has prompted an increase in numbers of people working at home. Contemporary communication technologies facilitate this type of work arrangement, but it presents certain drawbacks, such as lower wages to workers at home, fewer benefits, and often remuneration based on "piece-work," or the amount of work processed, rather than a salary.

As usual, media images of the future hold a seed of the coming reality. Predictions of a greater emphasis on work in the home began in the 1950s when automation was the wave of the future, but it was the energy crisis of the 1970s that stirred the popular imagination about a more flexible style of work

---

Box 10.1   Who Telecommutes?

When telecommuting began to be considered as an alternative to traditional working arrangements, the beneficiary of the change was thought to be overwhelmingly male, and most often middle-class. According to author Ursula Huws (1991), the futurist literature of the 1970s portrayed the telecommuter as a "creative" worker who possessed greater individualism and was less conventional than an office worker. The telecommuter was almost always presented as wearing blue jeans and phoning in results from a rural location.

With the spread of low-cost personal computers and word processors in the 1980s a different type of telecommuter began to emerge. This one was female and often engaged in clerical work. The profile of today's telecommuter is a woman living in an urban environment who is attempting to balance family responsibilities with some amount of clerical work through telecommuting. She often receives few or no benefits from her employer and a lower rate of pay than a similar worker located at the employer's site.

Sources: Ursula Huws. "Telework: projections," *Futures* 20, 19–31, 1991; United States Bureau of the Census. *Statistical abstract of the United States.* 111th ed. (Washington, D.C., 1991) 394.

and leisure. The term *telecommute* emerged at a time when people began to realize how much energy was expended in getting to and from work by normal means of transportation. Researchers proposing alternative methods produced estimates of the number of millions of barrels of oil that would be saved each year if specified numbers of people worked at home.

At the same time, some Americans became increasingly critical of the power of large corporations and sought alternative ways of using technology. In the process they hoped to change or eliminate bureaucratic structures. Influential books like Ivan Illich's *Tools for Conviviality* (1973), E. F. Schumacher's *Small is Beautiful: Economics as if People Mattered* (1973), and Charles Reich's *The Greening of America* (1970) presented alternative views of the future in which technology would be used to greater advantage. All were optimistic that careful use of technology would not only improve lifestyles, but also sustain the biological environment.

Today the number of Americans working at home at least part-time is estimated to be about 23 million, and that number is expected to increase about 5 percent each year until the year 2000. For many of these workers computers will be the primary tool of work, but additional electronic machines like photocopiers and fax machines will also enhance the home worker's productivity (Dressler and Varven, 1987; Perspectives on office technology, 1987).

Box 10.2   Prime Telecommuting Occupations

Accountants	Lawyers
Architects	Marketing Managers
Bankers	Miscellaneous Managers
Bookkeepers	Personnel/Labor Relations Workers
Clerical Support Workers	Purchasing Agents
Computer Operators	Real Estate Agents
Computer Programmers	Salespersons
Computer Systems Analysts	Secretaries
Counselors	Securities Brokers
Data Entry Clerks	Travel Agents
Editors*	Word Processors
Engineers	Writers
Insurance Agents	

*Added by the editor of this book.
Source: Kelly, Marcia M. "Work-at-home." *The Futurist* 22 (Nov./Dec. 1988), 32.

Services including everything from call waiting to electronic funds transfer may influence the type of work done at home and even how payment is made to workers. With these options, working at home may appear to have greater benefits than drawbacks, but many individuals who have attempted to engage in telework have had mixed reactions. Most telecommuters end up working more than a typical work day (73 percent report working more than an eight-hour day). Most (51 percent) report an increase in productivity, but another 21 percent feel that they actually accomplish less by working at home (Crosson 1990, R10).

Full-time vs. Part-time Telecommuting

While futurist scenarios starting in the 1950s predicted that individuals who worked at home would be able to reduce many daily expenses, such as transportation, business clothing, and child care, these advantages have been offset by drawbacks. Most full-time telecommuters are women who have children at home; these workers must learn how to manage time efficiently so that everything gets done. Elaborate strategies have been suggested, including dressing appropriately for work, creating rigid time schedules, and minimizing coffee breaks. By importing some of the office structure, teleworkers can keep parts of their lives in clearer perspective. Many women's groups in particular have warned that telecommuting could create an electronic sweatshop, in which a woman has to interrupt her work to tend to a child or an aging parent, and ends up doing electronic work in the wee hours of the morning in order to complete tasks (Crosson 1990, R6).

Telecommuting appears to have more benefits in occupations where workers split their time between office and home. In a study of city employees in Fort Collins, Colorado, it was found that many managers enjoyed having the flexibility to do their work at home, and used the option primarily for work on reports and record keeping (Giordano, 1988). Many reported that when part of their time was spent at the workplace, with only some activities done at home, they felt a stronger affiliation with the organization, had a clearer sense of expectations, and benefitted from the interpersonal camaraderie that often enhances a working environment.

Communicating Electronically

Almost any computer with a modem can access some form of **electronic mail (E-mail)**. E-mail is a generic term for any system that transfers information by electronic means. On a large scale, this may encompass things like telegrams and the Post Office's services, such as electronically generated mail (such as the mail you receive with your name inserted within what appears to be a form letter), to the issuance of second class postage for magazine subscriptions and "junk" mail such as advertisements, "special offers," and announcements of new companies in the area. Fax transmissions are also a form of E-mail, as is any type of message on a computer "bulletin board."

Historically, the most inexpensive way to send messages has been to use the services of the U.S. Postal Service (see box 10.3). But customer demand that information be transmitted more rapidly and the availability of electronic information processing have brought new services to consumers. When connections can be made through computers, electronic mail can be cheaper than a stamp. The deregulation of the U.S. Postal Service in the mid-1980s put the Post Office in the position of having to compete with alternative companies for a variety of mail services. At first, the major competition came from large companies like Federal Express and MCI Mail. The Postal Service developed its Express Mail service in an attempt to keep some of that business. At the same time fax machines became more popular, due in part to the deregulation of AT&T, which allowed more information technology to be charged to phone lines, and a greater number of services that were allowed to be transmitted via phone lines. Within a few years, fax technology was able to connect with radio

---

Box 10.3   Competition for Mail Services

Faced with many alternative methods of sending messages available to both home and business customers, the U.S. Postal Service has had to work harder to maintain its customer base and contain costs. Nowadays most first class mail is processed by electronic systems that sort pieces of mail according to zip code, and reduce the number of jobs for mail sorters.

Increasingly, the post office has become the major distributor of second-class mail—magazines and "junk mail." Popular magazines like *Time* and *Newsweek* ship bundles of magazines to regional Post Offices where electronically coded mailing labels are affixed to them, and they are sent to the local level for delivery.

When you receive a piece of mail with your name on both the letter and the envelope, chances are that the post office's electronically generated mail system has been hired to do the printing, folding, stuffing, and delivery.

These services, along with the Post Office's overnight service, Express Mail, were all established to keep the Postal Service competitive as other carriers were allowed to compete for delivery services.

signals for transmission of data, and now portable fax machines enable people to have service in their cars. Unfortunately, some of the portable systems have problems. Extreme heat, such as that generated by the sun on a car, makes the special fax paper turn black.

E-mail for personal messages is rapidly becoming less expensive to operate and use than traditional delivery services. Today both office and home services are available through **local area networks (LANs)** or **videotext** that allow users to send E-mail messages to others who have access to the same system. Not only can E-mail subscribers send letters to other electronic "mailboxes," they can usually find out whether their message has been received or even read. Real time interaction is possible when senders and receivers are both on-line at the same time.

As more work and education takes place in the home, the market for electronic mail services may grow among those who have computers. The services may be hooked up through a direct link by modem to an information provider or through a videotex system. Benefits of using E-mail include direct access to other mailboxes and having a record of transmissions—both important for maintaining consistency and getting quick answers to questions.

Personal Communication Services

The growing number of portable technologies available today has begun to create a revolution in personal communication services (PCSs). These services often use technologies that work on batteries, and some are solar powered, but they all have one thing in common: they bypass traditional wired communication systems. This allows users to operate them in a variety of locations, including cars, offices, airplanes, and even the street.

Cellular telephones are the most common form of PCS in use today, and they illustrate a significant point: when PCS technologies bypass traditional wired systems, they use frequencies in the electromagnetic spectrum to transmit their signals. The FCC has been investigating PCS use and has suggested that new segments of the electromagnetic spectrum be allocated for these purposes. While most of the FCC recommendations are expected to go into the planning stage in 1993 and 1994, it may take some time before available frequencies are reallocated. It is possible that radio and television frequencies could be adjusted up or down to accommodate the growing need for PCS transmission space.

The Smart Home

Perhaps the ultimate electronic home environment is what some people have termed the "smart home." In this setting, many functions required to run a

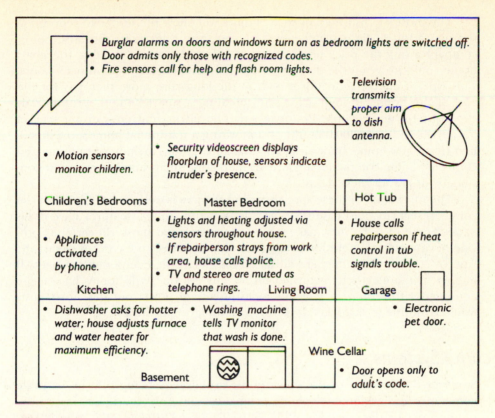

- Burglar alarms on doors and windows turn on as bedroom lights are switched off.
- Door admits only those with recognized codes.
- Fire sensors call for help and flash room lights.

- Television transmits proper aim to dish antenna.

- Motion sensors monitor children.

- Security videoscreen displays floorplan of house, sensors indicate intruder's presence.

Children's Bedrooms **Master Bedroom** **Hot Tub**

- Appliances activated by phone.

- Lights and heating adjusted via sensors throughout house.
- If repairperson strays from work area, house calls police.
- TV and stereo are muted as telephone rings.

- House calls repairperson if heat control in tub signals trouble.

Kitchen **Living Room** **Garage**

- Dishwasher asks for hotter water; house adjusts furnace and water heater for maximum efficiency.

- Washing machine tells TV monitor that wash is done.

- Electronic pet door.

Wine Cellar

Basement

- Door opens only to adult's code.

Figure 10.1 *A Smart Home.*
Source: Matthew L. Wald, "Touch a screen, do a chore," New York Times (Dec. 6, 1990), C1, C12.

home are electronically hooked to a computer and programmed through either a touch sensitive pad (similar to an ATM screen) or a keyboard. While few smart homes actually exist right now, several prototypes have been built for marketing purposes and described as "part Jetson" homes (Wald 1990, C11).

Smart homes may use a computer to control window shades, electric lights, heating and air conditioning, sound systems, and burglar and fire alarms. They may even be able to monitor human activity, such as children playing in the nursery or backyard. This could be done with motion sensors or video screens. Some, with keypads by the doors, can monitor who enters (using a personal code) or exits. When children are left alone at home, a monitor at the parent's workplace can register their activities through a remote device that lets the parent know who has gained access to the house.

The most sophisticated of smart homes will allow the owner to reprogram the operation of light switches, telephones, and televisions. Because power companies vary the price of electricity at different times of the day, the smart home could program the dishwasher or clothes dryer to run at off-peak hours. This type of energy reduction could, in the long run, more than pay for the cost of the house, though at present, building a smart home is prohibitively expensive for most people. Prototype smart homes are currently on the market for anywhere from $300,000 (the cost of wiring a traditional home) to $40 million (for a new home, built with every available option, including computerized controls). Some companies are already marketing smart appliances to test consumers' desire for these items.

The marketing of these appliances and services is designed to highlight the comfort, security, and ease they provide. But the "smart" features have drawbacks. Some of them may make some tasks easier, and most will certainly provide novel entertainment for awhile, but each one raises the costs of electricity. And of course, since they are all based on electronic components, what will happen if the electricity is turned off for any reason? Will homes have to be equipped with redundancy technologies in case of power outages? If so, costs would continue to skyrocket. Is all this technology really necessary?

Security Systems

Some of the features of the smart home are already being offered by cable companies and regional telephone companies that link security services to the phone lines or the television cable. Surveillance technology, like remote sensors, can monitor whether anything or anyone is moving in a house, and immediately activate an alarm at the owner's company or police headquarters. Heat sensors can detect extremes in temperature and notify the fire department.

Additional features include special electronic locks that can be put on some appliances to protect young children. For example, televisions connected to cable can be secured so that children cannot have access to channels showing adult material. Appliances can be secured so that children do not receive electrical shocks.

 Leisure and the Home

Having more technologies in the home may seem to give us greater options for comfort and may also appear to make our lives easier. But evidence indicates that, in reality, technology has done little to change the amount of time spent on household chores. Instead, values have changed to incorporate technology. Standards of cleanliness and mothering, for example, now require more rigor on the part of the woman in the home, and despite microwave ovens, cooking has become more complicated as some items need to be timed for the traditional oven while the microwave is used for other types of food preparation. When we think of what life must have been like before washing machines, telephones, or even television, we feel that lifestyles today must be more leisurely. However, various studies of labor in the home since 1910 and continuing through 1970 show that the amount of time the average homemaker devotes to her work has remained virtually unchanged (Schor 1991, 8).

Today the average American owns and consumes twice as much as the average American did in 1948, but has less free time (Schor, 2; Rybczynski 1991, 35). A traditional myth in America said that life would become progressively easier and more comfortable thanks to scientific progress and the growth of technology. To understand why the promise of the "good life" has not become a reality for everyone, we must again consider how changing patterns in production and the economy have forced people to adapt their behaviors to situations influenced by previous conditions.

Box 10.4   The Changing American Lifestyle: Increased Hours at Work

Total Hours per year
(Market Hours and
Household Hours)

	1969	1987	Change 1969–87
All persons	2426	2473	+47 hours
Men	2442	2514	+72 hours
Women	2412	2436	+24 hours

The figures represent Schor's estimates concerning males and females who are currently participating in the work force (not unemployed), and have been adjusted for the changes in the male/female distribution. From 1968 to 1987 the number of men in the work force actually declined, while the number of women increased. Additionally, Schor notes (37) that men now take on additional household jobs that they performed much less commonly in 1967. It is now estimated that men do about 60 percent as much household work as women, compared with only 40 percent in 1968.

Source: Juliet B. Schor, *The Overworked American* (New York: Basic Books, 1991).

Since the 1930s there have been several shifts in the labor force. The number of women in the work force has increased dramatically, and jobs have changed as new technologies replace some workers. The decline in manufacturing jobs and the increase in service work has also contributed to the changing work environment. But perhaps the biggest impact has been in the number of hours worked in relation to the amount of money considered necessary to support a preferred lifestyle (see box 10.4).

Today, the average person often has to work longer hours and may be evaluated on a different scale than someone in a similar position twenty years ago. Added to this is the economic downturn of the early 1990s which has slowed employment opportunities and reduced wages. People work longer hours for less money. Since the 1950s, when women entered the work force, they have had to learn how to balance their paid jobs outside the home with their unpaid jobs as homemakers. As academics and journalists remind us, the average amount of combined time worked by a mother who also has a full-time job outside of the home, along with the household and parenting duties, is in excess of 70 hours a week (Kessler-Harris 1990). In her book, *The Overworked American* (1991), Juliet B. Schor takes a critical look at how the American appetite for consumer goods has driven us to work longer hours for more pay. It is ironic that our society has so readily accepted the need to work longer in order to buy more goods, with the result that it has less time to enjoy them. Of course, the seduction of many new home technologies has to do with the extent to which they (or their advertising) promise a more comfortable lifestyle. Images throughout the media support the idea that consumption is good, inevitable, and a mark of success.

According to Schor (81), Americans' average hourly wages peaked in 1973, but have declined continually since that time. Individuals now have to work an additional 245 hours—about six weeks—each year just to maintain a standard of living commensurate with 1973 figures (81). These hours are added through overtime, fewer holidays, and shorter vacations. As Schor writes:

> Among the better-paid white-collar employees, large-scale layoffs and cutthroat environment made greater commitment of time and energy necessary to retain one's job. At the low-wage end of the labor market, sweatshops reappeared, with nineteenth-century style conditions (80).

This added pressure has resulted in unmarried men having to accept the greatest increase in hours because corporations often expect younger men to do more to get ahead. Similarly, younger men have entered the job market at a time when there has been a significant decline in earnings, and therefore they have to work longer hours, and occasionally take on a second job, if they wish to improve their material lifestyle.

Some of the products consumed are also those that seem to promise an "easier" life. The number of home technologies purchased throughout the

1980s increased dramatically. Sales of microwave ovens, security systems, air cleaners, and other home appliances rose throughout the 1970s and 1980s, driving people to earn more so they could spend more. As discussed in previous chapters, the number of home communication technologies also increased rapidly throughout the 1980s as VCRs, CDs, and home computers made significant changes in home entertainment options.

The amount of money the average American family spends on entertainment has also increased. According to an industry analysis (Veronis, Suhler 1991, 14), the average American consumer spent $355.98 on entertainment media in 1990. This represented an almost 10 percent increase over expenditures in 1985. The largest spending increases in 1990 were for cable television, books, and home video, which accounted for slightly over 55 percent of the per-person expenses (14).

Leisure Industries

Surprisingly, some of the growth industries today outside the home have to do with meeting the needs of individuals who no longer have the time to do things in what might be termed more "traditional" ways. Physical fitness and interaction with others are two obvious areas of importance, and though the industries discussed below are not directly germane to the home, they have everything to do with leisure and lifestyle.

When people have less leisure time, it becomes more important to spend that time productively. Some of the leisure industries include health spas, aerobics studios, and other types of fitness centers, where routines are often designed to give the maximum benefit in the least amount of time. It could be said that the desire to involve oneself in a leisure industry is a result of believing that technology and machines offer a more "progressive" form of exercise. They also better fit the constricted time schedules of active businesspeople. Ironically, in the days before many home technologies, people exercised muscles through routine activities much more than today, but the contemporary mindset seeks high-tech solutions through improved fitness machines and training procedures.

Technology offers some less-expensive options, however, including how-to videotapes for exercise, golf, skiing, and tennis. The how-to market is one of the largest for home videocassette sales, with celebrity work-out tapes topping the charts.

Media matchmaking   Today technology can even be used to meet people. Electronic dating services have become big business. When computer dating began in the 1960s and 1970s, it was considered a novelty, but some computer dating firms claimed to have created hundreds or even thousands of successful matches. This industry gave birth to several other types of personal connection services.

Video dating is one such service that has grown despite its relatively high cost for participants. In this service, interested individuals pay a fee to see videotapes that have been recorded by other people in which they discuss their interests, what they look for in a companion, and their reasons for seeking friendship. A video dating participant may pay to view tapes, or to create one himself or herself so that others can see their presentation. Surprisingly, the people who take advantage of video dating services are most often professionals because this group has so little leisure time to meet people outside of work.

Telephone "party" lines—discussions among several individuals simultaneously that simulate being at a party (and not to be confused with the traditional party lines that are used to reduce the cost of telephone service by carrying service to more than one home on a circuit), and telephone introduction services are other examples of alternative ways to meet people for personal companionship. Some of these services operate on 900 number telephone lines and introduce people from all over the country who might like to discuss any topic at all, just for the sake of companionship. Many of these calls are legitimate, but some have been known to serve as a method of solicitation.

Figure 10.2   Sample Electronic Dating Ads.

Today many people are wary of casual encounters with others in public places. The prevalence of crime and AIDS, and the desire to maintain control of one's life lead many to consider electronic services as a way to meet compatible individuals.

People seem to use different criteria for deciding who they want to meet when they use electronic dating services than when they meet face-to-face. It is easy to see how "shopping" for companionship by video might rely more on appearance and presentation than it would in face-to-face interpersonal meetings. Might this change expectations for the outcome of the interpersonal interaction?

Traditionally, the best places to meet people were thought to be churches, schools, and workplaces. As attendance has dropped at church services and alternative educational and employment settings change the interpersonal nature of traditional institutions, we may expect to see greater changes in the ways people meet each other. Often these changes are not desired or intentional, but they are a fact of life.

Purchasing and Paying for Consumer Electronic Products and Services

The newer electronic technologies offer a number of alternative services for the home, and as you might expect in a society where consumerism has increased so dramatically, many of these services enable people to consume even more! These services come to us through cable systems, videotex services, direct mail, and even in-store purchasing programs.

Shopping from the home has a long history. The origins may be traced to the street peddler who sold goods from a wagon, but are more clearly found in catalog sales, which date from the turn of the century, and have been very popular for most of that time. But things are changing, as evidenced by the 1992 announcement by Sears, the largest catalog retailer, that it was closing down its catalog sales operation. Clearly, major catalog sales are giving way to other forms of selling goods.

Today, with the success of various merchandising and sales techniques, individuals are bombarded with "opportunities" to shop in many ways. As we discuss some of the more popular forms, keep in mind how the ready accessibility of goods makes it easier for us to make purchases without considering how we will ultimately pay for them.

Television Shopping

Almost everyone today is familiar with some form of home shopping channel. The first and most successful is the Home Shopping Club, which debuted on one cable system in Tampa, Florida, in 1982. By the middle of 1985, the club had a full national network assembled and ready for operation, but what is even more astounding is the number of homes in the Tampa area that claim to have made purchases from the Home Shopping Club that year: 72 percent! (Talarzyk 1989, 135). The number of different shopping channels available on various cable systems varies from year to year, but an overview of how many homes some of them reach will provide an indication of how big a business home shopping services has become (see box 10.6).

Shopping channels generally keep their costs low by carrying discontinued merchandise or only certain selected product lines. Costs are further reduced by eliminating showrooms, sales staff, or other types of commercial overhead. Viewers purchase these items by calling a toll-free number. A computer operator processes the order using the customer's credit card number. After the

Box 10.5   Home Shopping Services

		Homes Reached
Home Shopping Network	24 hours	40 million 40% cable/60% broadcast
QVC Network	24 hours	12 million 85% cable/15% satellite
Shop Television Network	24 hours	17 million cable/broadcast
Television Auction Network	1 prerecorded	68 million cable/broadcast
Telshop	prerecorded	25 million cable/broadcast
Value Television	1 hour syndicated program	9 million cable/broadcast

Source: W. Wayne Talarzyk. "In-Home Shopping: Impact of Television Shopping Programs," in *Cable TV Advertising: In Search of the Right Formula*, ed. R. Batra and R. Glazer. (Westport, Conn.: Quorum Books, 1989) 125–126.

order has been packaged, it is shipped, usually through United Parcel Service, and generally arrives within 7 to 10 days. Returns are handled through the mail and credits are electronically posted through credit card services.

In one report based on a telephone survey of cable television subscribers in New York and Wisconsin, Jones Intercable determined that home shoppers are most likely to be between 35 and 64 years old and have household incomes over $35,000. Sixty-four percent of these shoppers make at least one purchase every month, and 66 percent watch more than one hour of shopping programs per week (Talarzyk 1989, 134).

Telemarketing

The practice of telemarketing, while an effective method of selling goods, has proved to be the most annoying form of home shopping. Telemarketers reach potential customers by phoning their homes. Telemarketers often have some idea of a household's demographics and interests because they purchase lists of households from research companies or other firms that have information about the household consumer habits. These firms can include catalog sales companies, cable television companies, and supermarkets that code purchases electronically while checking against discount or "courtesy" cards.

Telemarketing has been made even more electronic by the use of computers to make the calls and deliver the message. These computerized calls may just give a sales pitch, or they may be sophisticated enough to ask for responses and react with a variety of electronic options. Consider the two following scenarios that are adapted from actual telemarketing calls:

Scenario 1:

"Hello."
"Hi, this is Bob Becker from WQQQ radio. I'm delighted to tell you that you've just won a trip for two to the Bahamas! All you have to do to claim your prize is call our offices during business hours to arrange for one of our customer service representatives to come out to your house and discuss the possibility of having your rugs cleaned with our new "Spot-away" system, . . .

Scenario 2:

"Hello."
"Hi! This is a prerecorded telephone message to tell you about Midtown Mercedes' new financing package for the car of your dreams. Are you interested?

"No."
"Thank you, and have a good day."

Or, if the homeowner answers "yes," the message may continue,

"Fine, we at Midtown Mercedes have come up with an innovative financing plan guaranteed to make it possible for you to drive your dream car tomorrow! . . .

And the message continues.

Videotex Shopping Services

Many of the videotex services now in development share a plan to include at least one shopping service for subscribers. The largest videotex shopping service is Comp-U-Card, which gives subscribers over 250,000 products to choose from when their home computers are linked through telephone lines to the data base. Quite often, the prices for goods in videotex shopping systems are 30-50 percent lower than retail prices, because the service operates with so little overhead and buys goods in bulk quantities.

Many major retailers, like J. C. Penney and Sears, began to study videotex services as early as 1981, and have implemented some trials of their own services to measure the potential market for products and services. More recently, Sears has formed a partnership with IBM to create a videotex service called Trinitex. CBS, an early partner in the Trinitex experiment, dropped out in 1986. If videotex becomes as popular as industry analysts predict, we can expect to see other retailers becoming involved in reaching their target audiences in this way.

Electronic Funds Transfer (EFT)

While there have been several fascinating studies of the relations among consumerism, social practices, and the economy, some of the most compelling research has been in the area of how people think about the goods they purchase (Braverman, 1974; Benson, 1986; Strasser, 1989). **Electronic funds transfer (EFT)** could well provide a case study for understanding how consumer decisions are made when the financial transactions involved are matters of electronic bits regulating balances and accounts, rather than more traditional financial transactions in which money, checks, or credit cards are used by hand to make a purchase.

Every time someone uses an **automatic teller machine (ATM)** to deposit or withdraw money, pay a bill, or check an account balance, a form of EFT is being used. Additionally, credit cards, new technologies such as **point-of-purchase cards** and **debit cards,** and automatic deposit to an account, all use a form of EFT.

Paper currency is a relatively new phenomenon, although the use of coins dates back to ancient Greece. A much more recent introduction to the world of financial transactions was the check, developed in the 1940s, although the practice of issuing company scrip instead of money was in place in the late 1800s. Company scrip was paper that supported purchases by its employees made at approved stores (usually owned or controlled in part by the company) that allowed a line of credit to the consumer in the amount of the value of the scrip. The company then directly reimbursed the store for the goods.

The first credit cards were offered by stores only for use in the same store. Changes in interstate banking in the 1980s and the increased use of computers allowed financial companies to enter the credit market by offering their own credit services, all for a fee and a higher interest rate than that charged by banks. "Mastercard" and "Visa" were trade names for credit cards that were later purchased for use by a variety of sponsoring banks, after the banking industry was deregulated and banks could offer a greater number of financial services.

Electronic funds transfer became possible after the banking industry was deregulated in 1984. Many banks began to offer credit cards, and several cooperated with other institutions to combine the crediting and financing of ser-

---

Box 10.6   ATM and Credit Card Fraud

When ATMs became popular, so did robberies of people coming away from the machines. It was obvious to most robbers that anyone coming away from an ATM was likely to have cash on their person. As the number of robberies increased, so did the efforts of banks to increase security in ATM areas.

A lesser problem involves stolen ATM cards. While passwords prevent easy use of another person's card, surprisingly many passwords are easy to figure out. Often the password is the same as the individual's car license number or house address. If the robber knows the card holder's nickname or pet's name, he or she can easily break the code, and since most machines allow at least one mistake, a robber who makes a mistake the first time can try again later.

Credit card fraud is more prevalent than ATM fraud. Charge slips with carbons enable thieves to find a number and charge a purchase to a card by telephone. Carbonless forms have improved the situation, but as this type of fraud increases, credit customers may switch to point-of-purchase or debit cards, because they are more easily controlled.

vices. Even Sears expanded its retail and credit operations to include H&R Block, Coldwell-Banker Real Estate, and the Discover Card. Still others have entered programs that enable customers to pay utility bills with EFT.

One of the simplest forms of electronic funds transfer is the automatic teller machine (ATM). This service has had unprecedented popularity, primarily because it extends the working operations of banks to 24 hours. Using ATMs allows banks to hire fewer tellers and reduce the costs of processing transactions. When the costs of maintaining a bank teller and an ATM are compared, the bank pays 23 cents for a transaction involving a teller, but only 6 cents for an ATM transaction.

Another form of EFT is direct deposit, which allows an employer or financial agency to automatically deposit a sum of money in an individual's account. The electronic transfer of money eliminates the time needed to send a check in the mail, and is usually far more secure. Not only does the individual benefit from a quick deposit, but the deposit is more likely to clear quickly. The U.S. Treasury is the largest user of this type of EFT, depositing hundreds of thousands of social security and federal employee checks each year. In many companies, direct deposit of paychecks is also becoming more popular.

Point-of-purchase Technologies

Consumers can purchase a specific amount of credit from a store or vendor by buying point-of-purchase cards. Each time the consumer buys something, the amount is charged to the card until the credit is used up. College students may be familiar with these point-of-purchase cards as "copy cards"; you pay for a certain number of photocopies, insert your card, and the charge for each copy is automatically deducted from the card as you make your copies. Point-of-purchase cards have also been used successfully by truck drivers who make frequent stops for large purchases like diesel fuel. The major oil companies have begun to offer point-of-purchase cards to home consumers as well. The cards benefit the companies in that they receive their money up front. For the user, however, there is usually no refund for lost or stolen cards.

Another form of point-of-purchase technology allows your bank to make an electronic funds transfer from your account to a store where you make a purchase. Although you would not handle cash, you would indeed be paying for your purchase immediately and avoiding extra finance charges. Of course, you must be sure the money is actually in your account or the transaction will not be completed, but the constant monitoring of the balance is useful for many people who tend to "overextend" themselves by writing checks or using their credit cards too often.

Debit Cards

Debit cards have the potential to become far more popular than point-of-purchase cards. The technology behind them facilitates many types of information storage and retrieval other than monetary transactions. With a small hologram in one corner, they look like credit cards, but debit cards store vast amounts of information about users, and can be reprogrammed immediately by making a purchase and deducting an amount from the record on the card. Many insurance companies now offer a form of debit card that encodes an individual's insurance information as well as medical information useful in the event of an accident. When Argentina was ruled by its military forces in the 1970s, information cards similar to debit cards were issued to individuals. People were given Digitel cards coded with personal identification information. A card belonging to a person stopped by the police could be read by a computer in the police car for such information as full name, place of birth, and even political affiliation.

France has been using Minitel cards (named for their manufacturer) for several years. Also known as "smart cards," the cards contain holograms automatically updated to reflect additions or subtractions to a customer's bank account. Similar cards have been available in the United States on a limited scale since 1988; they are expected to be as common as credit cards by 1998.

Changes in the banking industry and in consumer behavior make it easier for us to spend money even when we don't have it available at a given time. Overextension with a credit card and overdraft checks occasionally cause problems for even the most conscientious consumers, but debit and point-of-purchase cards will undoubtedly help individuals avoid consumer debt. Still, the important factor to keep in mind is how much easier it is to consume—or want to consume—when products and financing options are easier to obtain. Is there any wonder people find themselves working more to consume more? What would happen if we chose to consume less? Theoretically, we then would need to work less, or perhaps engage in jobs that paid less but were more satisfying.

The relationships between working, purchasing goods and services, and planning a lifestyle that integrates needs and desires in a comfortable, satisfying home environment all reflect contemporary values. Some of those values are suggested by media and other outside sources, while others come to us through our families and friends.

In today's economy, the promise of a better lifestyle through increased technology and services suggests the old question, "which comes first, the chicken or the egg?" Are we driven to consume more technology so we can live a "better" lifestyle, or do we lead a "better" lifestyle because we consume more? At some point the question becomes futile. Instead we can examine relationships among industries, values, and products to arrive at an idea of why we think and behave the way we do. In the case of purchasing goods and paying for them, we need to be realistic about whether the purchases are necessary whether we can pay for them. And of course, how much work are we willing to do to be able to afford the products available?

Entertainment and information technologies for the home take a significant amount of the average family's annual income, and when these technologies are used to increase consumption, the initial costs of the technology or service are only the beginning of the real costs.

Once again, we see that our traditional values and ways of doing things are faced with new options. It is up to us to think critically about how and why we use them, and what consequences they may have.

Changing Values in the Home

As each of these technologies and services becomes available, traditional ways of doing things change. Often these technologies appear to merely provide options for doing things new ways, but they make it easy to ignore what advantages will be left behind if the new ways are chosen. Should we work at home, but join a dating service to meet new friends? Should we invest more money in home communication technologies and forget about going out to movies, theater, or concerts? If we increasingly rely on electricity for our daily survival, should we be surprised when energy rates rise, and are we prepared to function if the electricity is temporarily disconnected? The answers to all these questions depend on our values and lifestyles. But in each case, the situation is far more complex than just making a decision to buy a new piece of technology for the home. And remember, each of the services described in this chapter builds on a form of communication technology that has been used for different purposes in the past.

Privacy

Contemporary architects have begun to accommodate a more electronic lifestyle, even though not all homes of the future will be equipped with smart technologies. More electrical outlets and larger rooms designed to accommodate electronic entertainment centers are features already available to apartment dwellers and owners of condominiums and houses.

Perhaps the single greatest concern to many people is how much privacy they will have when using more home technology. Every time a wire is connected, a service subscribed to, an inquiry about a purchase made, or a credit card or check used, a record of the purchase and information about the consumer is stored in a data base. IRS reports indicate that the U.S. government could come up with at least 14 different pieces of information for every man, woman, and child in the country, based solely on tax returns. Some companies make their profits almost entirely from gathering and disseminating information about people through credit records, health histories, or employment records.

Since this is information that people are generally willing to give, there is a natural assumption that the information will not be used for the wrong reasons. When it became evident that there was a branch of business actively involved in selling names and personal information to other companies, the public outcry motivated Congress to investigate how to secure information about individuals. Data companies are now required to restrict access to infor-

---

Box 10.7   Universal Product Codes

Universal Product Codes (UPCs) were first used in a store in Troy, Ohio, in 1974. Since then, at least half of all U.S. supermarkets have installed UPC scanning systems, and about 90 percent of all goods have been bar coded (Katz, 1990).

The UPC system allows stores to keep computerized records of all purchases, and tells them when shelves need to be restocked as well as how much should be reordered. Even the ordering from suppliers can be electronically processed.

More importantly, the UPC system allows stores to create customer databases consisting of ongoing records of each customer's purchases linked with specific information about the individual or household. "Frequent shopper clubs" attract customers because they guarantee lower prices on some goods from the store. This type of "electronic coupon" reduces the need for paper coupons, which require considerable manual handling in order for the store to obtain reimbursement from manufacturers. In many cases, stores target member households with offers of special discounts and other marketing gimmicks. According to Frank Turek, vice president of sales for a shopping card-marketing firm in New Jersey that reads UPC symbols, "The potential of the cards is almost limitless. If someone goes into a store and spends $63, but doesn't spend a dime in the deli department, that store may want to target him with a promotion for that department."

Source: "Big Database Is Watching," *The Progressive* (April, 1989) 9.

mation about individuals, and must tell consumers what information will be stored about them and for what purposes. But many people never read the fine print on the papers they sign or even realize what information about them is available until something goes wrong. Then they sometimes have a long battle to correct that information.

Information about households and individuals gathered from a variety of sources allows direct marketing firms to target audiences. Specialized companies and services monitor specific information about individuals and their lifestyles. In many locations, the "courtesy card" provided by grocery stores that enables customers to cash checks or pay for goods by check monitors spending habits. Consumers' profiles are matched with a record of their purchases, made by electronically scanning the **universal product code (UPC)** on each item purchased. Then advertising is sent directly to their homes to promote certain products the market profiles indicate will be of interest to the family.

All these marketing efforts increase the rate of return on direct mail efforts and continue to make consumerism attractive to individuals. Decisions to purchase are made easier, as are methods of payment—even though salaries are now lower than in recent years, and people work longer hours to afford these commodities.

Making Choices About Lifestyles

When we are bombarded by media images and ads telling us that consumerism is good, easy, and promises a more comfortable lifestyle, it is easy to avoid thinking about how much we have to work to afford these things. Few of these images show us lifestyles with little or no personal interaction with others.

We are particularly vulnerable to messages we receive in the home, because we are often more relaxed and make decisions more informally and with less concern for their consequences. For these reasons, television shopping channels, telemarketers, and other home service industries direct their efforts toward persuading people to buy things in the comfort of their own homes.

The possibilities of telecommuting or communicating from the home with the use of comfortable, traditional technologies is also seductive, and many people do find the benefits outweigh the drawbacks once they've integrated their home lives with other practices. Still, others find that attempting to introduce technological change to their home lives adds a certain stress to family or interpersonal behaviors.

For many individuals, the changes brought by more technology and the lifestyle images presented in the media are not major problems, but for others, home can become a place where everything but leisure time is available. For people who fill their days with technology at the expense of interpersonal interaction, home can become a prison, and brings with it a prison mentality in which fear of interacting with others becomes greater as time goes on. We need to consider what types of interactions are important and even necessary in order for us to function as completely as possible in today's society. To do so, we must become more aware of the consequences of our technological choices, and maintain our motivation to control communications technology, rather than letting communications technology control us.

CONCLUSION

Many of the new technologies available for the home increase our opportunities to engage in different activities in comfort, but few of them really change the amount of time we spend in daily household routines, and each of them changes our relationship to the home and outside world.

Technology often makes us feel that we're progressive and even successful, but it can also present situations that make it easier for us to be lazy or less contemplative about our actions. As more technology presents greater options to us, we need to be ever-vigilant about the consequences, not only to ourselves but to our families. The need for interaction with other people is a vital factor in the socialization of human beings. If technology becomes a baby-sitter or substitute for learning by exposure to others, can we expect children to grow into well-adjusted adults? How can young children learn about the complex world outside when kept at home and restricted from playing with other children who might have diverse backgrounds and cultures? Will they be able to function in the world of real people and places, rather than the electronic world of television and Nintendo? Will they be able to tell the difference between right and wrong when not confined to conflict that resolves itself in 30 or 60 minutes?

Lifestyles in the electronic age are as complex as they ever were, but survival and success may have more to do with the values we apply and the ways we learn to use technological systems and services. To live a full life, we need to be aware of what happens when we quickly capitulate to the demands of consumerism so that we are able to choose the lifestyle we truly want to live.

SUMMARY

The home is changing as communication technologies offer a greater variety of options for carrying out in the home activities that have traditionally been done outside the home. In this chapter the connections among several technologies, services, and practices have been discussed:

- there is an increase in the number of individuals who work in the home at least part-time, often with the aid of communication technologies
- the number of hours individuals must work to support a consumer lifestyle requires that an alternative work situation in the home be carefully considered
- the home environment is changing as it adapts to more technology, and the smart home represents the ultimate electronically controlled environment
- leisure activities take on a new meaning when home-based technologies offer greater opportunities for entertainment to take place in the comfort of the home
- the ways we shop, play, pay our bills, and communicate with others are all influenced by the number of services and technologies available for the home

DISCUSSION QUESTIONS

1. Think about all the communication technology you encounter in a typical day. How would your life be different if these technologies were not available?
2. Try to imagine how different life was only 20 years ago. What home technologies that are available now were not available then? What home technologies are likely to be available in another 20 years?
3. In one evening, count the number of commercials on television or radio that encourage you to purchase products that only enhance the capabilities that you already have available to you. For example, consider the ads for cellular telephones or television sets with picture inserts, stereo sound, etc. Estimate how much you could spend in a year if you purchased each of these "must-have" products.
4. The average annual income for a family of four in the United States at the end of 1989 was $34,213 (U.S. Census, 1991, 454). Using the costs of products and considering the effectiveness of advertising, what income do you think a family of four would need to live the lifestyle portrayed in most consumer electronics ads?
5. In what ways could personal communication services (PCSs) change your life? How desirable would this be?
6. Discuss what could go wrong with the smart home if there was a power failure. What expenditures would be necessary to make sure the house could still function in a power outage?

7. Discuss how your routines are different when you do have time to stay home. If you had to be more self-motivated to get things done, would home still be the comfortable place it is? Would work and home begin to look more alike?

REFERENCES

Benson, Susan Porter. 1986. *Counter cultures: Saleswomen, managers, and customers in American department stores, 1890–1940.* Urbana, IL: University of Illinois Press.

Big Database is watching. 1989. *The Progressive* 53 (April): 9.

Braverman, Harry. 1974. *Labor and monopoly capital: The degradation of work in the twentieth century.* New York: Monthly Review Press.

Crosson, Cynthia. 1990. Workplace: Where we'll be. *Wall Street Journal* (June 6): R6.

Dressler, Fritz R. S. and Varven, Jean, 1987. Communities in the workplace: How data, voices and facsimile systems are changing the way America works. *Fortune* 116 (October 26): 143–59.

Giordano, Joseph. 1988. Telecommuting and organizational culture: A study of corporate consciousness and identification. Ph.D. diss., University of Massachusetts.

Huws, Ursula. 1991. Telework: projections. *Futures* 20 (January/February): 19–31.

Illich, Ivan D. 1973. *Tools for Conviviality.* London: Calder and Boyars.

Katz, D.R. 1990. Are your groceries spying on you? *Esquire* 116 (March): 87–89.

Kelly, Marcia M. 1988. Work at home. *The Futurist* 22 (November/December): 28–31.

Kessler-Harris, Alice. 1990. *A woman's wage: Historical meaning and social consequences.* Lexington, Ky.: University of Kentucky Press.

Kinsman, Francis. 1989. Telecommuting: An idea whose time has come. *Accountancy* 71 (October): 166–69.

Perspectives on office technology. 1987. *Fortune* 120 (Oct. 26): 143–157.

Reich, Charles. 1970. *The greening of america.* New York: Random House.

Rybezynski, Witold. 1991. Waiting for the weekend. *The Atlantic* 268 (August): 35–52.

Schor, Juliet B. 1991. *The overworked American.* New York: Basic Books.

Schumacher, E. F. 1973. *Small is beautiful: Economics as if people mattered.* London: Blond and Briggs.

Strasser, Susan. 1989. *Satisfaction guaranteed: The making of the American mass market.* New York: Pantheon.

Talarzyk, W. Wayne. 1989. In-home shopping: Impact of television shopping programs, In *Cable and TV advertising: In search of the right formula,* ed. R. Batra and R. Glazer, 123–41. Westport, Conn.: Quorum Books.

United States Bureau of the Census. 1991. *Statistical abstract of the United States.* 111th Ed. Washington, D.C.

Veronis, Suhler & Associates. June 1991. *The Veronis, Suhler & Associates communications industry forecast.* New York: Veronis, Suhler & Associates.

Wald, Matthew L. 1990. Touch a screen, do a chore. *New York Times* (Dec. 6): C1, C12.

Workplace in transition. 1990. *Working Woman* 15 (May): 65–71.

Eleven

Changes in the Workplace

Making Connections

As discussed in earlier chapters, our society is experiencing a shift from creating jobs through manufacturing to relying on information and communication technology to provide new jobs, which are usually in the service sector. At the same time that some work is shifting to alternative settings, like the home, the workplace itself is undergoing change. New technologies and services introduce new ways of doing things. These changes also create a new economic landscape in the United States and elsewhere.

Businesses today need improved communication inside and outside the organization to provide better record keeping and more efficient operations that will help them to become and remain competitive. Computers enable businesses to do all of the above, but tasks dependent upon computers require operators with special skills. Most of the skills necessary will integrate old values and ideas with new ones.

This chapter focuses on how business and the labor force

Chapter

11

are responding to the changes brought by improved technologies and services.

Connections will be made among:

- traditional practices and new technologies and services

- reconciling human needs with a business world where there is greater competition among a number of services and providers

- the goals of corporations and their responsibilities to their employees

- future employment opportunities and the need for education

- changing values necessary for success in the business world

---

Thousands of jobs in the manufacturing and clerical sectors have been made obsolete by **automation.** Technology has changed the entire composition of today's labor force, and has brought about new principles, practices, and opportunities. Perhaps some of the greatest changes are being brought about by new communication technologies and services like the ones that will be discussed in this chapter. Both the government and the private sector have made some effort to respond to shifts in the nature of work, but despite some efforts to deal with employment problems in the United States, the work force is still undergoing a major upheaval.

Someone entering the work force today may not work for the same company for fifty years as did members of the previous generation. Many of the jobs currently available may change significantly within the next ten years. The challenge, then, is to learn what skills and knowledge will be most rewarded and to realize that in the future working will not necessarily provide the same things that it has in the past.

As the issues emerge it will be possible to see the connections among social, economic, and technological forces. By examining the direction of change it becomes possible to consider what type of workplace will exist in the future, and how the world will respond to changes in national and global economies of scale.

Working in America: Social Change and Reindustrialization

The U.S. economy's new dependence on information technology can be seen easily in the composition of the labor force. The public has been aware of the decrease in manufacturing jobs due to plant closings and the growing use of cheaper labor overseas, and the corresponding increase of jobs in service industries such as health care, restaurant management, and retail businesses, since the economic downturn of the 1980s. We are now in a period of **reindustrialization,** which refers to basic changes in types of industries and their practices. Reindustrialization signals a marked change from the types of industries that dominated in earlier years, and it implies that new skills and practices will be necessary. During times of change established ideas of what life "should" be like are confronted by different patterns in employment. Human needs, such as child care, bilingual facilities, and education in how to use new technology must be considered if reindustrialization is to be successful.

During the period 1975–90, the so-called "blue collar" labor force lost over two million jobs. At present, only about 12 percent of the population works in factories, and only l.7 percent works in agricultural production (U.S. Bureau of Labor Statistics, 1990). These changes in traditional fields mark distinct points at which people's assumptions about the nature of work, and about what jobs available, are confronted by a scarcity of familiar jobs (see box 11.1).

Box 11.1   Key Areas of Employment Growth

	New Job Growth 1980–1988	Forecast of Change 1988–2000	
Government jobs	50.6 %	No prediction	
Retail trades	26.9 %	+25 %	
Business Services	16.3 %	+60 %	(computer programmers)
		+65 %	(computer systems analysts)
		+63 %	(securities and financial service sales workers)
Health Services	12.3 %	+74 %	(medical assistants)
		+73 %	(home health aides)
Restaurant Services	11.0 %	No prediction	

Sources: U.S. Bureau of the Census, *Statistical Abstract of the United States,* 109th ed. (Washington, D.C., 1989); U.S. Bureau of Labor Statistics, *Monthly Labor Review,* November 1989 (Washington, D.C., 1989).

While unemployment figures have fluctuated in the early 1990s, generally 5 to 8 percent of the work-eligible population has been unemployed each year since 1988. The remaining 70+ percent are engaged in part-time or full-time work, much of which relies in some way on computers.

Between 1980 and 1988, manufacturing lost 882,000 workers. There were, however, 15.2 million jobs created in the same time period, but the wages paid for these jobs were far less than the average paid in manufacturing industries, and many were dependent upon a different set of worker skills (see box 11.2).

Many of these jobs were part-time jobs, or second jobs held by people who could not make ends meet on one salary; in fact, only 60 percent of the work force at the end of 1991 held full-time jobs. Often, the new jobs lent themselves to at least part-time telecommuting, and most were classified as "service" jobs.

In the 1980s, women made up 63 percent of the work force, marking the first time in history that the number of women in the work force outnumbered the number of men. Most of the women (59 percent) worked in clerical or service occupations. Even though they are a majority, women still tend to earn less than men in comparable jobs. Women in managerial and professional occupations tend to earn 69.9 cents for each dollar earned by a man; women production workers earn 63 cents for every dollar earned by a man, and women police and detectives earn 94 cents for every dollar earned by a man (Ries and Stone 1992, 364–66).

These trends are significant because they indicate that the United States' population and thus its labor pool is changing. Not only will the people who

---

Box 11.2   Earning Power in America

Comparative Average Weekly Wages, 1990:

Construction	$524
Manufacturing	442
Retail	195
Services (including computer, clerical, etc.)	321
Finance/insurance/real estate	358

One-fourth of the work force is temporary, part-time, leased, or contracted workers.

Source: U.S. Bureau of Labor Statistics, *Employment and Earnings*, (Washington, D.C., 1990).

have traditionally controlled business and industry have to acknowledge the interests and needs of minorities and women, but new issues will emerge. Parental leave policies, bilingual requirements, and respect for cultural differences will play a larger role in defining the workplace. The Family Leave Act of 1992, signed into law by President Clinton, was one of the first steps taken by the government to address the problem of parents who must take leave from work for emergency family problems, such as illness. While the leave is taken with no pay, the employer is required to keep the job open for the person's return; as a result of the new law, someone with a sick family member can worry less about losing their job.

One reason social problems such as the one that led to the Family Leave Act are important is that few of the new jobs, particularly in the service industries, are unionized. Therefore, many workers do not receive the level of benefits and salary that unions fought for in previous decades. Most service jobs pay much less than traditional manufacturing jobs. In parts of the country where huge industrial plants have closed, the displaced workers have had few opportunities to find other employment.

The region of the country hit hardest by the change from manufacturing to service jobs is the Rust Belt: Wisconsin, Illinois, Indiana, Michigan, Ohio, and New York. The number of unemployed people in these former areas of heavy industry present problems for communities as well as individuals. Mortgages cannot be paid, bills accrue, and the tax base is weakened, with the result that the entire local economic structure suffers. In areas where there is no possibility for the unemployed to gain work similar to that they lost, some companies have implemented programs to retrain their laid-off employees for different jobs (see box 11.3). On a larger scale, it is difficult to calculate the number of workers now displaced or to predict the number likely to be displaced in the future as a result of automation in the manufacturing sector of the economy. As more products are manufactured and assembled overseas and shipped to the United States for distribution, the number of assembly plants will decline and continue to reduce manufacturing jobs. Some economists predict that by the year 2000 only 9 percent of the U.S. population will be engaged in direct manufacturing activity. Most goods purchased in the United States will be produced in other countries. If this prediction comes true it is reasonable to expect that new jobs created in the United States will continue to be in service areas. Many of these jobs will involve services that benefit a global economy.

Much off-shore production takes place in free trade zones (FTZs) like Singapore, Hong Kong, Taiwan, or Mexico, where multinational companies set up manufacturing plants in which workers are not unionized or guaranteed a minimum wage or benefits. The advantages for companies employing workers in FTZs, which often are located in developing nations, are obvious. In most cases, it is cheaper to manufacture goods outside the United States than inside. By reducing pay, taking advantage of tax incentives, and claiming exemptions on import and export duty arranged by the government in the FTZ, the compa-

---

Box 11.3   Retraining Programs

According to the Department of Labor, by 1987, retraining and assistance programs reached less than 25 percent of displaced workers, almost half of whom were forced to take lower-paying jobs. A Labor Department study titled *Workforce 2000* warned that an aging work force and new jobs requiring special skills will put increasing demands on individuals to continue their educations and upgrade their skills.

At the end of the 1980s, it was assumed that most available jobs required basic skills approaching a 12th-grade level, but by the year 2000, completion of a four-year college education will be the minimum expected of most workers.

Source: United States Department of Labor, *Workforce 2000*. (Washington, D.C., 1989).

---

ny makes a higher profit. The practice of moving jobs overseas has outraged labor leaders and caused concern for government agencies, including the Department of Labor, which keeps track of the number of jobs lost by residents of the United States because of the relocation of manufacturing plants.

Because large corporations have been charged with abandoning their workers during times of reindustrialization, they sometimes provide retraining to improve their public image. Unfortunately, retraining programs are available to only a few displaced workers, and often the new jobs pay less than the old ones.

Corporate Consciousness

Many companies have had to address the ethical problems caused by laying off workers who have no other opportunities for work in their own communities. The pressure on these firms to be responsive to the human needs of workers, and the responsibility they bear to society, have led to a new **corporate consciousness** that was lacking during much of the history of organized labor.

As indicated in previous chapters, demographic patterns and social opportunities have shifted in the United States. With fewer opportunities for interpersonal interaction, many individuals find themselves alienated from their employers, communities, and families. People have a need to feel connected to their environment in some way. Many corporations have attempted to create a sense of community at the workplace, and some have tried to engage workers in activities that do not directly involve their jobs, but serve as a respite from them. Although these actions may appear to be altruistically motivated, consider another possible motivation behind corporate willingness to offer social activities to workers: it is good business to have a happy worker who may enjoy other people at the company so much that he or she is less likely to look for work elsewhere or to do a poor job. In reality, most companies that offer entertainment functions or social gatherings pay their employees less than those that don't, hoping that the interpersonal benefits will be enough to keep workers satisfied. Some companies use incentive programs that reward their salespersons with such items a luxury vacations, or the use of company cars. Some companies give recognition to an "employee of the month." However, these incentives increase competition between workers, and the rewards are received by relatively few.

New Classes of Workers

The monumental shift of business away from manufacturing and toward information processing and service industries is causing an upheaval in traditional social images. American workers have long been called "white collar" workers if they worked in offices and "blue collar" workers if they worked in manufacturing plants. Recently there have been attempts to reclassify workers by recasting the old "collar" metaphor: robotic assembly machines are "steel collar" workers, and people (particularly women) in clerical positions are "pink collar" workers.

These descriptions have been pushed further by journalist Ralph Whitehead (1988), who has suggested two more labor classes: "bright collar" workers, those who work primarily in the world of computerized information, and "new collar" workers, who have been displaced from manufacturing jobs and are now found in service work. While attempts to categorize workers by labeling them according to type of collar are amusing, the important feature of these descriptions is that they signal the change in our society to a greater diversity of jobs. What is significant about this shift is that many of the workers grew up in homes in which family members were either "blue" or "white" collar workers. The new workers' values have been influenced by their families, and their expectations of bettering themselves through education or advancement influence the way in which they make choices about careers. For these people, ideas from their own experiences meet and combine with the values inherent in the new jobs to create a new "breed" of worker. In turn, these workers influence their children's attitudes toward work and education. Throughout the process, changing ideas and values (about work, leisure, and the quality of life) evolve, and these color our outlook on the future.

When people used to one way of doing something confront a new way of doing something, they occasionally come up with creative coping strategies. In the business world many of these strategies involve the accommodation of family needs.

Flextime

Because contemporary workers have so many responsibilities, some companies have allowed employees to choose alternative arrangements in the office. One example is **flextime,** which allows employees to negotiate with their employers to arrange working hours that are more conducive to the nature of their work and their family structures. For example, a couple with children might try to arrange a flextime schedule allowing one person to be home with small children or when older children come home from school. Another reason for flextime might be the need for a worker to return to school or carry out an educational program that will make him or her more efficient in his or her work. Those most likely to have access to flextime hold managerial and professional jobs, and most are members of two-income households (U.S. Bureau of the Census 1991, 394).

One example of flextime would be a single parent engaging in home-based work that allows him or her time to be with children. This might be accomplished through telecommuting or merely working fewer hours than in a traditional job.

Job Sharing

Another strategy for accommodating change in the business world is **job sharing**. In this scenario, two or more people each work part of one job. Of course, they also receive reduced pay and fewer benefits. Job sharing is especially popular today with mothers who do not have the luxury of flextime, but need to have adjustable schedules to allow them to get children off to school or meet them at home when needed. Clerical positions, in particular, can be structured so that more than one employee shares responsibility for the completion of the tasks involved in one job.

College students can also benefit from job sharing. For example, two students could share one job but maintain enough time in their daily schedules to attend classes and study. Perhaps they would work on alternate days, or arrange to be present either mornings or afternoons.

Senior citizens are also prime candidates for job sharing since their expertise is often in demand, even after retirement. A semi-retired person might spend a few hours a day training a new employee or trouble-shooting problems that can be left for others to administer. Through job sharing, the company retains a valued employee, but reduces the demands of, and wages for, his or her work.

Technologies in the Workplace

Technology in the workplace is easy to envision. We carry mental pictures of factories that are fully automated or products that are assembled entirely by machine because we've seen the images so often in the media.

Factory Design and Manufacture

Many manufacturing operations are turning to **computer aided design (CAD)** and **computer aided manufacture (CAM)**. Engineers are using sophisticated computer programs to model new designs and test their stress-tolerance levels and performance—all on a computer screen. Then design specifics are programmed into a computer and automated workers (robots) complete much of the production work. Boeing is one of the U.S. leaders in CAD/CAM: it has designed and tested new jets entirely on a computer screen before moving to a prototype model. Automobile manufacturers, shipbuilders, and satellite and defense industries have all used CAD/CAM to plan and test new models before prototypes are actually built.

In addition to the software systems that lend themselves to this type of design, there are now enhanced computer systems that can be linked to live-action video systems to combine CAD/CAM with live action backgrounds. All these design technologies reduce the time and cost involved when many different models are built and then go through a long, expensive testing period. "Crash tests" that test structural components of automobiles can be simulated by programming a computer to reflect the stress levels of materials and the probability that structural integrity will be maintained upon impact. CAD/CAM lowers the costs of manufacturing while raising profits. The system requires fewer people for design and testing, which reduces labor costs.

CAM is particularly effective at running an entirely automated manufacturing plant. It is possible for one computer to run an automated assembly line, produce reports, indicate problems, and even control for stocking the machines. The robotic devices and computers are silent workers who don't ask for raises, take vacations, call in sick, or come in with hangovers! But they also take jobs away from human workers.

In the Office

It is easy to think of the number of technologies now used in business settings, particularly in an office, where the cost of information handling usually runs the company anywhere from 5 to 30 percent of the organization's total expenses. To cut costs, many firms look to efficient uses of communications technology. The major contemporary office technology is the computer, and in many organizations it takes the form of a number of microcomputers that are linked to a mainframe or to each other. Telephones are also a necessity for businesses, and telephone lines have been linked to fax machines for immediate message transmission. There are a variety of less familiar business technologies, including speech synthesizers that translate text to speech or vice versa, security devices, and video production services that can be used to create everything from training tapes to interactive teleconferencing services from virtually any place in the world. All these technologies must be connected to others to create communication possibilities.

Phone systems and local area networks In order to link either telephones or microcomputers together for internal use, some companies establish **local area networks (LANs)** that serve as internal switching systems for calls and eliminate the necessity for renting common carrier lines for internal communications. LANS have become practical as a result of the deregulation of the telephone industry. Now alternative companies can design and sell entire networking systems (incorporating telephone and computer technology) to businesses that then control their own internal communications systems. The LAN acts as a closed-circuit system that can be connected to outside phone lines through additional interfaces.

There are several types of LANs, but the three most common are called ring, star, and bus networks (see Figure 11.1). Each of these systems makes interconnections between pieces of hardware, creating a conduit for information that does not rely on a common carrier for information processing. Switching systems, like **integrated services digital networks (ISDN),** or the new **Broadband Integrated Services Digital Network (B-ISDN),** will provide a more rapid form of digital information transfer by creating physical links between different technologies. For example, a computer system in an office might be used most often for internal communication, but through ISDN or B-ISDN the system could be connected to any number of additional technologies such as satellites, microwaves, optical fiber, or cable that have the potential to connect with hardware anywhere in the world, without facing the obstacle of incompatible technology.

The concept of a LAN can be understood by investigating how some of the earliest ATMs were connected through ring networks that linked different teller machines associated with the same bank. If a transaction was being processed in one location, the computerized ring would move around from one ATM to another until all ATM branches had been covered. In this way, a person could not move from one ATM branch to another to "fool" the computer by making subsequent withdrawals. Each transaction was fully completed before the ring moved on to the next terminal.

276

Desktop publishing More sophisticated computers and printers have allowed the introduction of desktop publishing (DTP) to the office. This all-in-

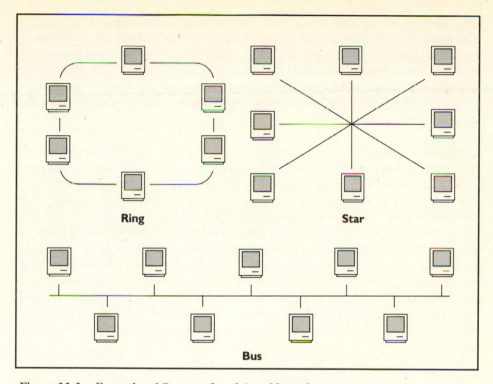

Ring **Star**

Bus

Figure 11.1 *Examples of Common Local Area Networks.*
In each case the computers are linked to others in a certain pattern to facilitate communi-
cation. In the ring network, the messages must pass all units on the ring; in the star net-
work, one unit can be directly connected to another or to several, since the routing can be
switched at the mid-point. On the bus network, each unit must be given signals to by-pass
other units, but all are readily accessible on the LAN.

one publishing system allows businesses to create and revise materials for internal use and for outside clients. In some offices, DTP is a smaller version of
CAD/CAM, allowing a department or company to see what printed materials
will look like before hiring a typesetter and printer.

With high resolution graphics available on computer, and the advent of
digital copiers, desktop publishing allows companies to produce paper materials at a much lower cost than if they hired a designer, typesetter, and printer.
An unintended result of DTP is that the sophisticated technologies create
expectations of very professional presentations, even in internal memos and
everyday business correspondence. The quality of its printed matter influences
how the status of a company is perceived. An investment in technology makes a
company appear more successful.

Desktop publishing is a good example of a new field that will require workers with a variety of skills. A desktop professional needs to have a thorough

knowledge of the software being used, but also needs to be able to write material appropriate for the publication, create basic designs and layouts, and understand the visual power of a printed piece. Desktop publishing often appeals to people who work in such areas as persuasion, public relations, and advertising. It also often appeals to students of communication because it offers the potential for future employment and provides experience in integrating several skills for success in one field.

Corporate video   As more companies produce in-house videotapes and use the variety of video conferencing services available today, they become interested in establishing corporate video centers. One of the first companies to have such a center was Standard Oil, but today most of the major firms throughout the country have their own in-house video operations.

In-house corporate video is expensive to establish, but over time it reduces the costs of having professional companies produce materials specifically for in-house uses. Many corporate video operations develop materials for employee training, new employee orientation, and company updates on new products and procedures. Again, as an up and coming field that lets individuals control most aspects of their work, including writing, producing, shooting, and editing their own video pieces, corporate video is an attractive field for the future.

Teleports

With the increased need for business communication technology to have reliable circuitry and, even more importantly, backup computer files, a new office park concept has been developed called the **teleport.** This type of business complex usually includes a satellite receiving dish, at least two sets of complex computers for information processing and storage, and offices for individuals who process much of the information.

Teleports are a response to traditional business locations that create high real estate costs for a company, transportation problems for its workers, and high costs in maintaining centrally located office operations. Since the businesses most likely to use teleports work in information processing, many of the employees can telecommute from home. At a teleport, the high speed information switching systems can link a variety of services for employees regardless of whether they are at the teleport or working from another location.

A teleport functions very much like a large office with complex switching systems for information processing. If a company does not want to rely on major telephone carriers for most of its communications needs, portions of them might be met through contract companies, LANS, or through a teleport. Employees could access teleport information networks by using their own passwords or codes. Because teleports are new installations, they often take advantage of the most up-to-date transmission systems. Most function with terrestrial cable or optical fiber links, and use ISDN or B-ISDN switching for maximum speed and capacity for linking to other technologies.

One of the first teleports in the United States started as a joint project of the Port Authority of New York and New Jersey, the City of New York, and the financial services firm Merrill Lynch. The Staten Island Teleport was the first high-tech office park and communications center to use optical fiber connections and satellite distribution (see figure 11.2). While the Teleport began functioning in 1985, its construction was coinciding with the breakup of AT&T

Figure 11.2 *The Staten Island Teleport.*

A majority of workers could telecommute and have most of the information processed at the teleport. Computers would back up files, provide instant access to others, and keep an ongoing record of how long, and for what purpose, the employee was linked to certain files or services. In this picture the relaxed, comfortable atmosphere of the Teleport is contrasted with the congested business and residential area (upper picture) typical of a traditional urban environment. In the right corner it is possible to see the satellite dishes; the Teleport complex is the modern building on the left. Note the recreational areas with trees and baseball diamonds (lower picture) for employees and the community.
Picture source: The Teleport - Staten Island

and the interest of several companies that concentrated on exchanging voice and data information via phone lines.

Teleports, which are proving to be major competitors to traditional telephone service, provide business customers with telecommunication capability that relieves crowded urban centers and transportation conduits. They accomplish this by substituting telephone and computer lines that encourage and facilitate telecommuting by workers. Their satellite transmission capability keeps costs low for long distance and international calls. The Staten Island Teleport was constructed to alleviate transportation problems for employees of major businesses who had formerly commuted to offices in the New York and New Jersey area.

The teleport concept has had reasonable success in other locations, especially in the southwest, because of the geographical ease of construction and the growing number of companies locating in that area. In 1989 Japan opened its first large-scale teleport system, Teletopia, which links telecommunications for more than 20 cities and has proved a successful model for other teleports.

Teleconferencing

Teleconferencing is a term that describes the process of using communications technologies for conferencing purposes. It connects various participants through teleports, DBS, or, most commonly, through communication distribution systems such as telephone, satellites, and microwave relays.

The simplest form is audio conferencing, which now has about 90 percent of the teleconferencing business. In most cases audio conferencing needs very little in the way of technology to be successful. The most common approach relies on a speaker phone. Different participants in a room can hear the amplified voice of a person in a distant location and at the same time can talk into the machine. Sound boosters enhance the volume of their voices so that it is not necessary to be close to the phone. Speaker phones can also link multiple sites for conversation.

The second type of teleconferencing is still-motion video conferencing. In this case, still images are transmitted over the telephone wire or satellite signals and full audio conferencing takes place at the same time. At various points during the transmission, the angle of the image can be changed, but it remains immobile. A good use of still-motion videoconferencing would be for the introduction of a new product. A teleconference scheduled to decide the most effective ad to be placed in national print media would be another good example of a still-motion teleconference opportunity.

Full-motion interactive videoconferencing is two-way, and takes place in real time. It is also the most expensive form of teleconferencing available today because it requires a system that sends and receives signals simultaneously.

Some businesses invest in full-motion videoconferencing as an alternative to sending employees to a central location for an in-person meeting, but for many, the costs are too prohibitive to use on a regular basis.

Several television programs use the techniques of full-motion videoconferencing to produce live images for transmission anywhere in the world—when there is a need to have an interactive component to the program. Programs like "Nightline" or the "Academy Awards" use these techniques to pick up images transmitted via satellite from other locations.

A variety of electronic connection technologies could be applied to enhance some features of teleconferencing. Teleconferencing could make use of cable, optical fibers, satellites, or any combination of these forms. Additional fax technologies and telewriting systems such as electronic blackboards can complement some of the systems that use images. The electronic blackboard is useful for illustrating specific examples during a teleconference. If a participant asks for clarification of an issue, the presenter can immediately provide a visual to explain matters. The electronic blackboard is often used in the electronic classroom (a subject discussed in Chapter 14).

The costs of full video teleconferencing include initial installation charges for equipment, which may run about $120,000, and operational costs of about $12,000 per month. International videoconferencing is far more expensive, as different satellites must be accessed for transmitting information from one footprint to another. Because of the expense, many businesses use videoconferencing facilities set up at nearby conference centers or hotels. Holiday Inn, Ramada Inn, Hilton Hotels, Hyatt Hotels, and other hotel chains have installed videoconferencing facilities at some locations.

These new forms of communicating are not without problems, however. Some participants in videoconferences feel apprehensive about presenting views that will be transmitted live to other sites (and perhaps seen by corporate superiors). Others suffer from expectations set up by television, and try to "perform" rather than simply express themselves.

Teleconferencing may require accessing several satellites. If you wanted to organize a two-way interactive teleconference from New York City to Japan, you would have to take several factors into account (see figure 11.3). Because of the curvature of the earth, you would need several relay points. If your call originated from New York City, you would first access a domestic satellite through an uplink with both audio and video capability. To shift to an international satellite to bridge the Pacific, the message would be transferred from the domestic satellite at a point called a gateway.

Because the West Coast of the United States is the best location for overlapping footprints from Japan and New York, that would probably be your chosen gateway. The gateway computer would take your message and transmit it to an international satellite above the Pacific Ocean. That satellite would send the signal down to Japan, where once again it would have to be transmitted to a

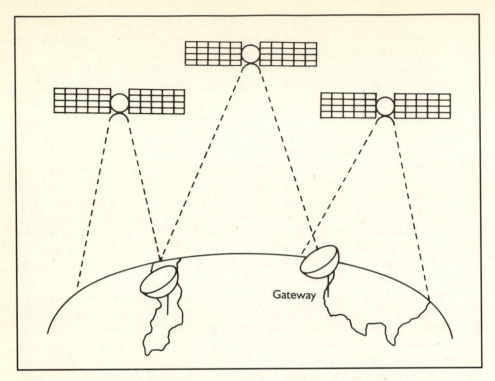

Figure 11.3 *Teleconferencing Between New York and Japan.*
A signal, sent in an uplink from New York, would be routed to a gateway at the other end of the footprint. At the gateway, the signal would be transferred to another point, and before transmission to Japan, the technical standards could be converted so that the signal would be compatible with Japanese equipment.

domestic Japanese satellite. In three satellite jumps, your signal would reach Japan in less than two seconds. There would be a slight time delay of about 1 ¾ seconds in the signal, which would introduce a slight lag in the sense of real-time motion.

Teleconferencing in education   Teleconferencing has become popular as a means of extending education to hard-to-reach locations or for engaging more students in lectures or experiments by particular professors. For these purposes, schools generally transmit live video and audio, but may rely on either phone lines or electronic mail so that students in a distant location may ask questions of the professor (Bellman, 1988).

Education by teleconference has become a major component of many state universities, including those in Alaska, Illinois, Iowa, New Hampshire,

Pennsylvania, Texas, and Wisconsin. The term usually involves some interactive component, such as the students talking with the professor by telephone during a presentation, or the use of electronic mail to answer questions at a later time.

Some full-motion videoconferencing has been used as a means of linking schools in different countries or different schools within a country for interactive dialogue. The Soviet "Space-Bridge" was such an experiment, designed to connect students in Russia with a number of sites in the United States. Similarly, organizations like the *Christian Science Monitor* have funded experimental programs linking various leaders in business and industry to college campuses for interactive dialogues through full-motion videoconferencing.

Though still relatively expensive, videoconferencing has the potential to provide a unique learning environment. As transmission and distribution costs drop, more videoconferencing will undoubtedly be used to engage students in realtime dialogues with people they normally would not have the opportunity to meet. Videoconferencing has exciting implications for education.

Services to Facilitate Work

As new technologies multiply, so does the number of services tailor-made for certain business operations. As we discuss them, you'll realize that many of the services are also available to home consumers, but until they offer features that telecommuters or people at home want to use, most of their profits will come from business.

Videotex and On-Line Services

Many of the features of commercial videotex systems are finding applications in the workplace, where special data services facilitate work. Videotex can both store and retrieve information at a relatively low cost, a feature attractive to a number of businesses. When a company has its own telephone system or LAN, regular access fees charged by common carriers can also be kept lower.

An example of a business that has increased its use of on-line information is the field of journalism. Years ago, a reporter did research on location and used pencil and paper to record the details for stories. Telephones have always been integral to the development of a report or story, but with videotex, today's reporter has several data files to search for information from any number of sources. Among the most commonly used data banks are LEXIS and NEXIS.

Many stories can be written without the reporter ever leaving the office. Data banks with pictures, background stories, and even other newspaper files can be accessed within minutes and the information sent to other departments and editors, and finally to the printing plant. A reporter might write a story and transfer the file to the editor who would change the format or reorganize the story. The editor could then transmit it directly to the printing plant, where it would be set in type electronically and duplicated. These networks, whether part of a videotex service or a LAN, all rely on the most obvious feature of inter-active technology: the ability to send and retrieve information as quickly as the hardware's capability allows.

Electronic Messaging Services

Electronic mail (E-Mail) is a service that can utilize different types of technolo-gies. Most E-Mail services involve some combination of the following technolo-gies: telegraph, telex/TWX services, fax, and computer-assisted messaging ser-vices.

Electronic messaging is not a new phenomenon. It dates in its simplest form from Morse's telegraph in 1844, and it has had a long history. After the telegraph, the typewriter was invented. It didn't take long for a special type of typewriter to be developed that enabled operators to type messages on keys and transmit the message via what became called telex to a receiving telex machine, which also resembled a special typewriter. Telex networks linked various sites through telephone wires for this type of service.

Soon after, the TWX (pronounced twix) machine operated by Western Union was used. This machine allowed operators to punch a tape by typing into the TWX machine, and transmit the message to multiple sites by coding passwords that would route the messages to any number of locations simultane-ously. During the 1950s and 1960s, techniques were developed that allowed telex and TWX messages to be sent to receiving sites electronically, with no human operator present to monitor the receipt. The machine merely printed the incoming message, which was torn off the roll when the operator arrived. We've seen these machines in film and television newsrooms when a fictional "reporter" responds to a bulletin arriving over a wire service. A major benefit of TWX transmissions was that the same message could be sent to numerous sites simultaneously.

Telefacsimile (fax) was soon to follow, but until the late 1980s, the resolu-tion of images transmitted over phone lines was often low. As a result, fax did a poor job in transmitting important documents. Today's fax technology is still not good enough to duplicate originals exactly, but a time will come in the near future when multi-color, high-resolution pictures and graphics will be transmitted by optical fiber.

As microcomputers increased in number throughout the 1980s, their capacity to carry E-mail improved. One of the benefits of using E-mail was acknowledged to be the efficiency of sending a message through electronic means. Approximately one-third of "first time" phone calls never reach their intended recipient because that person doesn't answer or the line is busy. With the average business phone call lasting approximately six to nine minutes, the sending of an electronic message can be far quicker and less costly. (Hiltz, 1984). In addition, there is a record that the message has been sent.

Computer-assisted E-mail may take the form of an "electronic mailbox." Individuals send typed messages into a central computer bank. Recipients access their messages by typing their passwords into another terminal. The number of electronic mailboxes in use has grown impressively in a short time. In 1984, there were approximately 73,000 mailboxes in use in the United States; by 1986, the number had increased to over 1.5 million. Today, there are over 5 million.

The transitory nature of the message is an intriguing feature of electronic mail, but if a hard copy of the message is desired, it may be printed on the individual's printer or accessed from a central printer elsewhere in the system. In most cases, electronic mail reduces the need for paper.

Electronic voice messaging (EVM) is also gaining popularity. Like a telephone answering machine, voiced systems can usually instruct a caller to leave a message, but they also allow other options, including forwarding of the message to an operator or another phone line. By using EVM, many companies have reduced the number of human telephone operators they need to employ and the amount of time spent on routine calls.

Human Interaction with Technology in the Workplace

One area of great concern today is how to adapt current technology so that it may best be used by workers. Shoshanna Zuboff's excellent book *In the Age of the Smart Machine* (1988) discusses how more technology in the workplace calls for new understanding of job tasks and functions. In the many studies she cites, technology is often portrayed as both an enhancement of efficiency and a stumbling block to employee satisfaction.

According to Zuboff, more and more workers believe that advancing technology and new office designs are systems for controlling them. They feel that their privacy is invaded by superiors who key into their on-screen work or through technologies and practices that make their actions more apparent to others.

Citing Jeremy Bentham's architectural innovation called the Panopticon, discussed by Michel Foucault in *Discipline and Punish: The Birth of the Prison* (1979), Zuboff shows how structures and systems can make today's office worker feel imprisoned. In 1787 a factory at Critchef in Russia was built from the design for the Panopticon. The building was later adapted for the purpose of housing convicts and paupers. It consisted of a twelve-sided polygon made of iron and glass, which was intended to create what Bentham called "universal transparency." A tower with windows sat in the center of the structure. Around the walls of the building were rows of narrow cells that housed workers or inmates. Each cell had a window that would allow someone in the main tower to observe its inhabitants, but those inhabitants could not see who was watching them.

Zuboff likens today's information technologies to Panopticons of power. Computers, particularly when linked through LANs or to on-line data bases can automatically and continuously record events, store and process information, provide updates on activity to anyone with a password, and monitor the activities of any workers interacting with them (or not interacting when they should be). The amount of power held by managers in an electronic workplace requires special interpersonal communication skills, so that workers do not feel they are being watched by "Big Brother."

In general, few of the jobs of the past translate easily to the computerized world of today. The result is a need to continually reflect on the job and the role of the worker. Are enough breaks scheduled to allow the worker to stretch and get away from the glare of the VDT? Can telecommuters balance needs of home and work? Is there any encouragement for interpersonal communication outside of interacting with the computer? Will the skills needed by an architect or designer change because of CAD/CAM? Can the job be constructed in such a way as to present a better balance for the worker? It is important for employers to find answers to these questions and many others so that workers can adapt to the changes in the workplace today.

Added to these challenges are those brought about by the stress of working in today's business environment.

Stress in the Workplace

Changes in the work force lead to a certain amount of tension as people readjust their lifestyles. Dual income families and the increasing number of mothers working outside the home have presented new problems for families. Single parents also experience many of the same difficulties as they try to juggle a home, a family, and work at the same time. These issues connect the employee's personal life to the work life in a way that requires some new thinking to handle the problems.

Some companies have become more sensitive to the pressures on their workers. Some labor unions have also attempted to write family-friendly policies into contracts. While progress toward improving worker stress levels has been slow during the recession of the late 1980s and early 1990s, some companies have responded to the need with social programs in the workplace.

According to Ellen Galinsky, co-president of the Families and Work Institute, 33 percent of the major corporations in the country have done almost nothing to help reduce employees' family pressures, and 46 percent are just waking up to the issue. Only 21 percent of the nation's leading companies have aggressive programs that offer benefits like child care assistance, leaves of absence to take care of relatives, referral networks for the care of aging parents, job sharing, and flextime (Lawson 1991, C2).

As the work force continues to undergo change, these important social issues will undoubtedly become a more central focus of concern. They all demonstrate how work, family and personal responsibility, and social responsibility are all connected in a world in which jobs and social relations are changing. These big problems will take time to understand and solve. In the meantime, smaller problems are being examined to better understand the dynamics involved in human/machine interaction in a world where more jobs are reliant on technology.

Ergonomics

The study of the relationship between humans and the technology they work with is called **ergonomics.** The term itself denotes movement, and more specifically, the movement of the human body as it interacts with technology. Specialists in ergonomic design advise video display terminal users about appropriate workstation space, lighting, and other environmental components of the human/technological interface. When assembling workstations, they try to use furniture designed to be comfortable to at least 90 percent of the population.

Since more jobs will rely on computers in the future, making computers more compatible to human needs is fundamental to successfully integrating them into the workplace. Part of ergonomics involves the use of color and graphic displays on the video screen. Although few research studies focus on the semiotic interpretation of color in video usage, we do understand something about physiological perception and the psychological effects of color. New computer screens and software that allow users to change the colors on the screen are efforts to make close work with video display terminals (VDTs) more comfortable, but they also add an element of interest for the user. Lighting, the reduction of noise, fewer distractions, and control over heat and air conditioning is also related to ergonomics and adapting the workplace to using computerized technology. As people learn more about human needs for comfort when working with computers, some of what they learn is not encouraging.

Health Hazards

As we learn more about how the human body responds to working more closely with machinery, we've begun to learn that some jobs can pose health hazards. All video display monitors give off a slight amount of radiation—less than that of a television screen, but the big difference here is that people sit closer to a VDT than to a television set. Some studies have indicated that this radiation may be particularly harmful to certain groups of people, including pregnant women (Carroll 1990, R28). Also, close work with a dirty VDT screen can cause premature wrinkles around the eyes, as the muscles contract to bring a fuzzy image into focus.

The Future of Work in America

The United States government has identified four areas of industrial growth for the next few decades: space exploration, oceanographics, biological and genetic engineering, and communications (Bureau of Labor Statistics, 1988). While this may be good news to students studying the power and future of communication technology, you should realize that the government's use of the term is a generic one encompassing all types of fields, from electrical engineering, computer science, and physics to traditional forms of communication involving mass media or personal, face-to-face interaction. Within the field, however, the Department of Labor predicts modest growth in a number of different industries (see box 11. 4).

But increases in industrial growth may not match the opportunities for new communications workers. As Anderson and Harris (1989) write, even though the amount of communication technology will increase to facilitate greater interaction, employment in these fields, at best, will remain stable (79).

Furthermore, social programs will need to be developed to help workers handle the continued stress of living in a fast-paced, technologically oriented society.

For many of us, this means that as we look to the future we need to acknowledge that change is inevitable. To be prepared, we need to consider possible scenarios. One way to do this is to look at precedents from history. In the field of communication technology, history reveals a continuing convergence of communication formats and services to present new opportunities for the future.

CONCLUSION

As the information technologies used in business and industry continue to develop, we can expect to see new markets open and others close, new oppor-

Box 11.4   Forecast for the Year 2000

Communications industries	Average expected growth 1986-2000
Telephone equipment	4.1 %
Employment	-0.6 %
Communications (except broadcasting)	3.9 %
Employment	-0.9 %
Radio and television broadcasting	3.9 %
Employment	1.7 %
Electronic home entertainment equipment	4.9 %
Employment	-2.1 %
Radio and TV communication equipment	4.2 %
Employment	0.5 %

Source: U.S. Department of Labor, *Economic Trends 1989-2000.* (Washington, D.C., 1989).

tunities emerge and jobs change. The most successful individuals in the future will be those who do not hesitate to continue their education, and who develop a healthy curiosity to understand not only how technology works, but also how it affects individuals, jobs, and society. These people will be best prepared to respond to reindustrialization.

The labor force is experiencing changes related to shifting patterns of production. We no longer rely on the manufacturing of products to supply the greatest number of employment opportunities, but, at the same time, our society hasn't been prepared for jobs that require increasing reliance on communication technology for information processing. As national and global economies respond to these changes, individuals will have to prepare to respond to the new opportunities. The changes in industry and the skills necessary for employment today are different than they were twenty years ago. We can expect to see them change further in future years as there is more competition for services and employment opportunities are developed to respond to the special needs of the work force.

Corporations and individuals will need to develop programs and methods to cope with different social demands. Changing traditional practices adds a level of stress to an already stressful society, but the need for support and a sense of community will remain.

The need for change in the labor force has already created monumental obstacles for the government, the economy, and society to overcome. Only individuals who understand the connections among social principles, values, and the labor force will be in a position to offer intelligent solutions to problems that arise as we move toward a more technologized society.

SUMMARY

Preparation to be part of tomorrow's labor force involves an understanding of how quickly change is affecting economic, social, and political conditions. In this chapter, a number of the changes have been addressed. They include:

- highly paid manufacturing jobs are being replaced by employment that requires different skills and pays significantly less
- the work force is changing as the special needs of women and minorities influence business practices
- Some of today's technologies offer alternatives to traditional ways of doing work: telecommuting, teleconferencing, teleports, on-line services, and a greater reliance on computers
- the changing work force and society need to plan for effectively dealing with the stresses involved by the changes in the labor force and workplace
- the opportunities that are opening are not immediately obvious; they require close consideration and investigation

DISCUSSION QUESTIONS

1. Discuss the future of the communications industries. In what ways will they change in 10 years? In 20 years?
2. Discuss ways in which technologies used for work and leisure are similar. What impact might similarities suggest with regard to quality of life?
3. Consider the changes in a particular industry, for example, telephony. How has the industry responded to increased competition, and in what ways has new technology changed traditional practices?

4. What attitudes do you and your friends have about future employment? Are your goals realistic? What steps might you take to coordinate your goals with a practical plan for achieving them?

5. What do you see as the most significant impediments to job change and mobility in most people's lives?

6. How might offices of the future be designed to accommodate more on-line services? Do you think that flextime or job sharing could account for some design decisions?

7. Discuss how closely the types of jobs available are connected to the national and global economies. Perhaps a good exercise would be to research the promises and the realities of the North American Free Trade Agreement (1992), which includes the United States, Canada, and Mexico. Where have some jobs gone? Does it matter for the national economies in each of those countries?

REFERENCES

Anderson, Joseph M. and Harris, Suzanne. 1989. Communications and future employment trends. *Telematics and Informatics* 62: 71–80.

Bellman, Beryl L. 1988. Interaction of CMC with video telecourses for distance education. *Telematics and Informatics* 5: 389–95.

Bernstein, Aaron; Konrad, Welecia, and Therrien, Lois. 1992. The global economy: Who gets hurt? *Business Week* (August 10): 48–53.

Carroll, Paul B. 1990. Computer confusion. *Wall Street Journal* (June 4): R28.

Christensen, Kathleen E. 1990. Workplace in transition. *Working Woman* (May 15, advertising supplement, n.p.).

Coombs, Linda M. 1990. Impact of computers. *The Bureaucrat* 27 (Summer): 18-20.

Crocker, Olga L. and Guelker, Richard. 1988. The effects of robotics on the worker. *Personnel* (September): 26–36.

Economic Policy Institute 1992. *Wages in America.*

Foucault, Michel. 1979. *Discipline and Punish: The Birth of the Prison.* New York: Vintage Books, 201–02.

Garson, Barbara. 1988. *The Electronic Sweatshop.* New York: Penguin.

Getting a handle on the boom in E-mail use. 1991. *Communications* News 28 (August): 9.

Herrmann, John. 1984. New York's teleport: Going skyward to bring costs back to earth. *Management Technology* 2 (August): 34–38.

Hiltz, Starr Roxanne. 1984. *On-line communities: A case study of the office of the future.* Norwood, N.J.: Ablex.

Johansen, Robert. 1984. *Teleconferencing and beyond.* New York: McGraw-Hill.

Lawson, Carol. 1991. Toward a 'family friendly' workplace. *New York Times* (December 5): C2.

Lee, Patricia. 1983. *The complete guide to job sharing.* New York: Walker and Co.

Lewis, Geoff; Rothfeder, Jeffrey; King, Resa W.; and Peterson, Thane. 1988. The portable executive. *Business Week* (October 10): 102–12.

Magnet, Myron. 1992. The truth about the American worker. *Fortune* 126 (May 4): 48–65.

National Safety Council. 1983. *Video display terminals: The human factor.*

Pearson, George W. 1990. Robotics: A Future view of workplace safety. *Risk management* 37 (October): 42–46.

Ries, Paula and Stone, Anne J., Eds. 1992. *The American Woman 1992–1993.* New York: W.W. Norton and Co., 364–66.

Risman, Barbara J. and Tomaskovic-Devey, Donald. 1989. The social construction of technology: Microcomputers and the organization of work. *Business Horizons* (May-June): 71–74.

Sproull, Lee and Kiesler, Sara. 1991. Computers, networks, and work. *Scientific American* (September): 116–23.

United States Bureau of Agriculture. 1992. *Farm workers in America.*

United States Bureau of the Census. 1989. *Statistical abstract of the United States.* 109th Ed. Washington, D.C.

———. 1991. *Statistical abstract of the United States.* 111th Ed. Washington, D.C.

United States Bureau of Labor Statistics. 1990. *Employment and earnings.* Washington, D.C.

United States Department of Labor. 1989. *Economic trends, 1989–2000.* Washington, D.C.

———. 1989. W*orkforce 2000.* Washington, D.C.

Valeriano, Lourdes Lee. 1991. Executives find they're always on call as computer, fax supersedes time zones. *Wall Street Journal* (August 8): B1.

Volkow, Stuart. 1992. Integration cogitation. *Videography* 17 (5): 44–45.

Whitehead, Ralph Jr. 1988. Will blue-and white-collar concerns be nudged aside by the growing strength of today's new- and bright-collar voters? *Psychology Today* 21 (October): 44, 47–49.

Zuboff, Shoshanna. 1988. *In the age of the smart machine.* New York: Basic Books.

Twelve

Rights, Regulations, and Content

Making Connections

Attempts to control the content of communication technology have always created controversy. In most cases issues of content pit the rights of the sender of a message against the rights of the receiver of a message. Historically, the relationship between the nature of content and the way it is communicated have resulted in different interpretations of the First Amendment to the Constitution of the United States. In this chapter, freedom of speech and freedom of the press are examined with regard to the way in which communication technology poses new questions for them. In each case a connection between the technologies used to distribute content and historically specific social values explains why certain regulations have been created, maintained, or changed.

This chapter explores the precedents that have provided the context for regulation and deregulation of communication technology and content; especially content that may be considered obscene or that introduces difficult moral and ethical questions. In examining the issues, several connections are made, including:

- how First Amendment interpretations vary according to time in history and the type of technology, content, or practice to which they are applied

- how historical precedents are used to guide contemporary interpretations of policy, regulation, and law

- how the control of media content affects or reflects social attitudes, practices, and behaviors

- how economic incentives to control information often favor some interpretations over others

- how legal and historical precedents have influenced issues such as access to information and the control of information

During the 1991 Persian Gulf War journalists and media organizations were criticized for their compliance with military control over access to information. During the same year, Oliver Stone's controversial film *JFK* presented an interpretation of the John F. Kennedy assassination that revived public interest in events that took place almost 30 years earlier. Actress Demi Moore, 7 months pregnant, posed nude for the cover of *Vanity Fair*, provoking many stores in the United States and Canada to ban the magazine. All these events raised questions about freedom of speech and the power of the media to inform, shape public perception, and reflect popular values.

Battles over access to information and expression of ideas have a long history in our society. The First Amendment to the Constitution of the United States guarantees freedom of speech and freedom of the press, but does this mean that anything goes? Do these freedoms also come with a responsibility to protect some members of our society, like children, from material that might be too complex for them to understand? Should there be moral guidelines for media content that is available to a great many people?

This chapter discusses the problems of defining freedom of speech and of the press and presents precedents that have guided contemporary interpretations of law concerning the control of media content. Traditionally, distributors of mass media established procedures that evaluated content with concern for the entire society. Today, the number of distribution outlets and the abundance of media technologies require rethinking content regulations for an audience that is no longer a single mass. Smaller, segmented audiences and the shift from a "trusteeship" model of broadcast regulation toward a deregulated environment give rise to questions about traditional criteria for controlling content, and even the interpretation of the First Amendment.

In previous chapters, regulation of the various media industries was discussed with regard to how it has been applied to each format. This chapter focuses on issues of content. Differences of opinion about what types of content should be regulated or controlled are far greater than differences over regulation of technological innovation or even of entire communication industries. Content is closely tied to social values, which means it will be easier to observe the moral and ethical connections between communication technology and society in this chapter than in any other part of this book.

This chapter has two major themes. First, it considers how new forms of media have required constant negotiation about what constitutes freedom of speech. Second, it explores the efforts of agencies and concerned citizens to influence the regulation of some types of media content. Specific cases are used to illustrate how contemporary attitudes toward regulation and the control of information influence the development, application, and use of communication technology today.

Though most of the technologies discussed in this book are electronic, many of the legal precedents in Constitutional law are based on print media and film. There have been many attempts to apply principles from these areas to other media that have similar characteristics. During the period when the cable industry was being deregulated, cable operators hoped to be considered "electronic journalists" so they would have greater protection by the First Amendment. When the Parents Music Resource Center (PMRC) wanted to control the content of records, they advocated a ratings system similar to the one used for film. Courts constantly battle over the interpretation of the First Amendment, and the body of Constitutional law surrounding questions of content changes constantly as social values change.

The First Amendment

One of the founding principles guiding media content and ultimately, access to information, is the First Amendment. When the Constitution was adopted, many people strongly opposed it because it did not specifically safeguard basic freedoms. To address these concerns, James Madison drafted a series of amendments that became the Bill of Rights. The First Amendment decrees that Congress shall make no law abridging the freedom of speech or of the press. Even though the First Amendment has shaped and molded communication technology regulation, law, and policy since its adoption in 1789, it has also fueled controversies. The way the Amendment is written, it is difficult to deter-

Box 12.1   The First Amendment

The First Amendment of the Constitution of the United States of America:

Congress shall make no law respecting an establishment of religion, or prohibiting the free exercise thereof; or abridging the freedom of speech, or of the press; or of the right of the people peaceably to assemble, and to petition the Government for a redress of grievances.

mine whether "freedom of the press" and "freedom of speech" imply separate types of protection, or whether they are both parts of one freedom (Keane 1991, 128–29).

Over the years, Congress, presidents, the judiciary, the FCC, and the communications industries have all struggled with interpreting the freedom of speech and freedom of the press clauses of the First Amendment. The result has been a hodge-podge of interpretations that often question the real intent behind the writing of the First Amendment. Did the architects of the Amendment mean that "freedom of the press" and "freedom of speech" should be given separate constitutional protection, or are they part of one indivisible freedom? "Freedom of the press" was drafted in the days of print technology. Does this freedom extend to electronic communication technologies like radio, television, and computers (Keane 1991, 128–29)?

In discussions of the First Amendment today, it is possible to see how different legislators and special interest groups have chosen to emphasize some interpretations over others. In Fowler and Brenner's argument for the deregulation of communications industries (1988), the authors state that until 1943, the Supreme Court consistently interpreted the First Amendment as favoring the rights of viewers and listeners over the rights of broadcasters, but that recent changes in the availability of communications technology and in journalistic practices now require an interpretation that the broadcaster's rights take precedence over the viewer's or listener's.

The Communications Act of 1934

Clearly, legislators committed to the philosophy of deregulation interpret the First Amendment differently than do those who advocate the trusteeship model on which communication law for earlier electronic media was based (see box 12.3). Some legislators criticizing deregulation have claimed that the "First

Box 12.2   Court Cases and the First Amendment

Though broadcasters have often invoked the First Amendment, broadcasting has traditionally been given less latitude than the press in exercising constitutionally protected free speech (Teeter and Le Duc 1992, 79). As a result, each case brought before the courts further defines the rights of broadcasters and the public.

In creating their rationale for the elimination of the model for broadcasting, Fowler and Brenner (1988) argue that cases like *Red Lion* (see box 12.10) that view the rights of viewers and listeners as overriding those of broadcasters, no longer are justified.

In fully endorsing the First Amendment and Section 326 of the Communications Act, both of which forbid censorship of broadcasters, Fowler and Brenner review court cases that progressively undermine the effectiveness of the trusteeship model as it had been applied to broadcast media. Citing the example of the need broadcasting has for advertiser sponsorship, courts have traditionally ordered the FCC to "consider the competitive consequences of market entry" (219). This has resulted in "[T]he trusteeship role of the Commission [distorting] competition in the broadcasting marketplace" (219).

In *FCC v. Pacifica Foundation,* the Supreme Court had to rule on whether Pacifica Broadcasting had violated FCC guidelines of decency by airing George Carlin's "Seven Dirty Words" comedy routine. Pacifica claimed that the First Amendment should protect broadcasters too, and that they should have the power to decide what to broadcast. The Court concluded that offensive broadcast signals were similar to indecent phone calls, and that listeners and viewers could not "insulate themselves from offensive program content" (228).

The market approach was endorsed as early as the Supreme Court's 1940 review of *FCC v. Sanders Brothers Radio Station* when the Court upheld the FCC's decision to grant a license to a broadcaster even though Sanders Brothers claimed that another station in the market would create undue economic hardship on their station. The Court endorsed the wording from the Communication Act that stated:

> The Commission is given no supervisory control of the programs, of business management or of policy. In short, the broadcasting field is open to anyone, provided there be an available frequency over which he can broadcast without interference to others. . . (474-75).

Again, in the 1981 *FCC v. WNCN Listeners Guild* decision, the Supreme Court supported the FCC's decision endorsing the view that "the public interest in radio is best served by promoting diversity in entertainment formats through market forces and competition among broadcasters" (235).

These cases represent what Fowler and Brenner call "the Supreme Court's view of the Communications Act," which supports the FCC's endorsement of a "free market model to broadcasting" (235).

Sources: Mark S. Fowler and Daniel L. Brenner, "A marketplace approach to broadcast regulation." *Texas Law Review* 60 (2), 209–57, 1988; Dwight L. Teeter, Jr. and Don R. Le Duc, *Law of mass communications*, 7th ed. (Westbury, New York: The Foundation Press, Inc., 1992).

Amendment is dead." Others have made attempts to revitalize it through changes in our regulatory structures. In any case, the interpretation of the First Amendment remains a hotly debated topic and the results of these discussions have ramifications for new communication technology today.

To put this issue into historical perspective, it will be useful to explore the range of First Amendment interpretations over a number of years. This exercise will shed light on the evolution of and contrasts in its applications. It will let us better understand why regulation and control of content rarely receives unanimous support from constituents. Applications of the First Amendment help us understand the connections among society, law, and changing values because they reflect what ideas may be acceptable at any given time.

The First Amendment in Historical Perspective

If freedom of speech or of the press were absolute, there would be no need to exercise control of information. Attempts to control what we see, hear, and think, are referred to as censorship, propaganda, persuasion, or ideology. Each definition suggests a different political slant, but all relate to how information is protected under the "freedoms" of speech and the press.

The First Amendment is often regarded as both a policy and a law. As a policy, it guides individuals involved in exercising freedom of the press and freedom of speech. When something happens to raise a question about whether a First Amendment right is involved, the situation is examined in a court of law where a judge and jury determine whether what was spoken, written, or recorded is covered by the First Amendment. The records of these decisions become part of the body of First Amendment law and are used as precedents on which to base decisions in other cases with similar characteristics. But because the First Amendment is both a guide (policy) and a guarantee (law), efforts to determine what freedoms it guarantees inevitably lead to ambiguous results.

Box 12.3   Marketplace Rules vs. the Trusteeship Model

The Radio Act of 1912 was the first attempt at broadcast regulation. It led Congress to pass the Radio Act of 1927, which outlined a basic philosophy about how radio should be regulated. Viewing the airwaves as a resource, the Federal Radio Commission (FRC) believed that the public's access to the airwaves should be a matter of trust; that is, the licensing structure should reflect responsibility toward the public's right to hear alternative viewpoints. This "trusteeship" philosophy was in line with social values of the time that strongly supported the First Amendment, but the rationale was not based only on moral grounds. The reason was also an economic one. Freedom of speech and freedom of the press were considered part of the media's responsibility to the public, but the members of the FRC also wanted to encourage more participation in broadcasting for greater competition. From the beginning, the process of licensing broadcast stations was based on the view that there was a scarcity of frequencies available in the electromagnetic spectrum. Licensing broadcasters was considered the best way to ensure a number of different channels (Teeter and Le Duc 1992). This created a precedent for restricting freedom for broadcasters through the licensing procedure, and supported the right of the public to have access to a diversity of content.

In 1969 the Supreme Court reaffirmed that the First Amendment called for broadcasters to air different opinions by stating that: "It is the right of the public to receive suitable access to social, political, esthetic, moral, and other ideas and experience which is crucial here" (Barron 1973, xiv). In 1971, Justice Brennan extended that idea to the print media when he wrote that "Constitutional adjudication must take into account the individual's interest in access to the press."

But with a move to a deregulatory philosophy that emphasized the rights of broadcasters to transmit any messages they wished as overriding the rights of viewers and listeners, the trusteeship model was suppressed. Marketplace philosophy advocates a position that less government intervention (embodied in regulations) encourages business growth.

Advocates of the marketplace model interpret the First Amendment to mean that those who control the media, like newspaper owners, owners of broadcast licenses, or cable companies, also have the protection of free speech. Therefore, what once was an argument for regulations that were intended to provide access to the media for minorities and special interest groups with alternative viewpoints, has now become an argument for owners to transmit only those messages they wish to spread.

Many legislators today fear the loss of First Amendment rights for the public, and discussion about how the First Amendment should be interpreted is still of great concern. In particular, Rep. John Dingell (D., Mich.), chair of the House Commerce Committee, Rep. Edward Markey (D., Mass.), chair of the House Commerce Telecommunications and Finance subcommittee, and Sen. Ernest Hollings (D., S.C.) chair of the Senate Commerce Committee have all gone on record to return to the trusteeship model (Springer 1989, 64).

Sources: Jerome A. Barron, *Freedom of the press for whom?* (Bloomington, Ind.: Indiana University Press, 1973); Dan Springer, Hill showdown: A year of decision, *Channels* 9: 64, 1989; Dwight A. Teeter Jr., and Don R. Le Duc, *Law of mass communications*, 7th ed., (Westbury, New York: The Foundation Press, Inc., 1992).

Censorship   Censorship is "the control of communication between people" (Berger 1982, 1), but the term has always reflected political and social expectations and standards. Surprisingly, truth is not always a defense against censorship, and until a famous 1735 defense in a court of law, truth had *never* proven a successful defense.

Beginning when the first colonists arrived in this country, censorship was used to control the political and moral development of the people. The first public book burning took place in Boston in the 1600s, when the town's executioner burned Thomas Pynchon's *The Meritorious Price of Our Redemption* because it expressed religious ideas that were not approved by the colonists.

In the colonies, printers were required to have licenses to operate, as they were in England. This form of control was used extensively by British governors who attempted to hinder colonial printers who published anything critical of the actions of the British.

The most famous censorship case in colonial America was the John Peter Zenger case in 1735. Zenger, publisher of the *New York Weekly Journal,* was accused of seditious libel because he printed articles critical of the British governor, William Cosby. The charges stated that Zenger had libeled Cosby, or lied about his actions, and that what he printed was seditious, because it criticized the actions of a government official.

Zenger's attorney, Andrew Hamilton, argued that Zenger's accusations that Cosby tampered with election results and that he showed favoritism in appointing his political cronies to office were true, and therefore Zenger was innocent. The jury decided in favor of Zenger. The case marked the first time in history that truth was effectively used as a defense against libel. It established a precedent for juries with the power to determine whether a statement was libelous. Part of this legacy remains with us today. In 1986 the comedian Carol Burnett

Box 12.4   The Roots of Censorship

The word "censor" comes from the Latin and means "to count, assess, or estimate." The first known censors were government officials appointed to conduct a census of Rome in the year 443 B.C. These individuals also had the power to bar from society anyone they deemed had violated accepted social rules of conduct.

Censorship also has roots in ancient Greek culture. Socrates was accused of corrupting the morals of the young by teaching them new scientific ideas. When brought to trial he was found guilty of degrading public morals and sentenced to death by drinking a cup of poison hemlock.

The histories of religious and political movements have been riddled with censorship of ideas that challenged the status quo or incited deviant behavior. Sedition, the act of inciting rebellion against a government, was one of the most common claims of censors.

Though today we often think of censorship as a control of sexual content, most censorship cases before the 1800s focused on issues of politics and religion. It was the introduction of Victorian manners and morals that made sexual matters suspect.

Source: Melvin Berger, *Censorship* (New York: Franklin Watts, 1982).

sued the *National Enquirer* for its report of her alleged alcohol abuse in a public restaurant. The *Enquirer* claimed that she was acting in a loud, drunken manner, and engaging in poor behavior toward another patron, Henry Kissinger. During the five-day court hearing, Burnett's attorney called on restaurant employees who had witnessed the events of the evening. They supported Burnett's claim that the *Enquirer* lied, and Burnett won her case.

Obscenity and the first amendment   Every society has bawdy stories and folk songs, but what constitutes obscenity has been hard to determine. The first law in North America censoring obscenity was passed in 1712 by the Massachusetts colonial legislature. This law made it a crime to publish any song, pamphlet, or mock sermon that might be considered filthy, obscene, or profane. The legislature chose not to define these terms, and lawmakers and courts have wrestled with their definitions ever since. The overriding concern was the belief that questionable material had the potential to corrupt youth and threaten the social order, and therefore it could be banned. Today, groups like the Parents Music Resource Center (PMRC) and Parent Teacher's

Association (PTA) are concerned about questionable content in the recording industry, and occasionally raise the same argument as that mounted in 1712. The basic issues remain the same.

The first attempt at defining obscenity was made in an 1868 English court case, which established a standard that remained in use in England for about one hundred years, and which also influenced American law. An outspoken, anti-Catholic metalworker named Henry Scott had distributed literature implying that priests and young women taking confession had engaged in sexual intimacies. Scott was found guilty, but upon appeal the decision was reversed. Chief Justice Alexander Cockburn provided the definition of obscenity resulting from the case, which said that material was obscene if it had a "tendency to deprave and corrupt those whose minds are open to such immoral influences, and into whose hands a publication of this sort may fall . . .[especially]. . . to the minds of the young of either sex, or even to persons of more advanced years" *(Regina v. Hicklin)*. Known as the "Hicklin Rule," this definition also said that material was obscene if any isolated part of it was offensive to these groups. This interpretation of obscenity placed many earlier forms of literature into a new category of offensive material.

After the Hicklin Rule, even once-respected classical literature became suspect. The Victorian era saw England and the United States conduct a moral crusade that included more book burning and attention to safeguarding the public's morals than ever before. It influenced what could be published and what could be read.

Around the same time that this British test of obscenity was being decided, a New York grocery clerk named Anthony Comstock formed the Society for the Suppression of Vice in the United States. Comstock focused on the use of the post office as the conduit of indecent material. Through his efforts, Congress passed a law in 1865 that made sending obscene materials through the U.S. mail a crime. A second law, the Comstock Law, officially titled the Federal Anti-Obscenity Act of 1873, went beyond the 1865 law by empowering the Post Office to reject any "obscene, lewd, lascivious, or filthy book, pamphlet, picture, paper, letter, writing, print, or other publication of an indecent character" (quoted by Overbeck and Pullen 1985, 257). Comstock became the Post Office's special agent to detect obscenity and banish it from the mails, and throughout his tenure, he boasted that he had "destroyed 160 tons of obscene literature" (quoted by Overbeck and Pullen, 1985, 257).

In the twentieth century, some of the laws set by early precedents slowly began to change, because social attitudes toward printed materials began to reflect a more liberal bias. By 1920 a New York appellate court judge ruled, in *Halsey v. New York Society for the Suppression of Vice,* that a book must be evaluated as a whole rather than being censored for individual passages. Further, the judge said the opinions of qualified critics should be considered before a book is declared obscene. This resulted in the reprinting and circulation of many books that had been previously banned.

In 1933 Federal Judge John Woolsey instituted a practice that would affect all later cases of censorship. He refused to follow the most basic principle of the Hicklin Rule, the idea that a work was to be judged by its effect on the most susceptible members of society. In reviewing James Joyce's great work *Ulysses,* he said a work must be judged by its effect "on a person with average sex instincts" rather than by its influence on the most corruptible members of society, and that the whole work was to be judged—not just the "questionable" parts.

In 1957, the Supreme Court dealt with the question of whether obscenity was protected by the First Amendment, but in the precedent-setting case of *Roth v. U.S.,* the traditions of obscenity and postal laws were reviewed. Samuel Roth had been convicted under federal postal law for mailing circulars, a book, and advertising material that were declared to be obscene. In the determination of the case, Justice Brennan suggested a test for obscenity that addressed whether the material as a whole appealed to prurient interest when the average person applied contemporary community standards to it. Brennan concluded: "We hold that obscenity is not within the area of constitutionally protected speech or press." The decision split the court. Justices Black and Douglas took an absolutist position about the First Amendment, claiming that it protects even obscenity.

The idea that community standards should serve as the model for what was offensive to people within a specific geographic area first arose in 1964 with *Jacobellis v. Ohio.* A theater manager had been convicted of violating an Ohio law by showing an allegedly obscene French film, *Les Amants.* The court found that it was not obscene and that it had been shown in about one hundred cities, including at least two others in Ohio. Once again, the Supreme Court Justices were not in full agreement. Justice Brennan wrote that the Constitution would not permit the concept of obscenity to vary in meaning from county to county or town to town, but Chief Justice Warren dissented, saying that community standards do differ. His opinion has become the prevailing sentiment today.

In 1969 the Supreme Court handed down the last major obscenity decision of the liberal Warren era, *Stanley v. Georgia.* Police had searched Robert Eli Stanley's home for bookmaking materials, and in the process found some films in a dresser drawer in his bedroom. They set up his projector, watched the films, and arrested him for possessing obscene matter in violation of Georgia law. When the case came to court, the determination said that the privacy of one's home is more important than any obscenity considerations. The Court said that the First Amendment protects a person's right to receive information and ideas, regardless of their social worth.

In 1973 the Supreme Court reviewed five obscenity cases and found that in the situations examined, earlier rulings on obscenity and pornography (such as Roth) were superseded and a new standard introduced. Most important of the five cases was *Miller v. California,* involving a man named Marvin Miller who had mailed unsolicited and sexually explicit brochures to a restaurant in Newport Beach, California. The mail was opened by the manager of the restaurant, with his mother present, and both complained to the police that the material was indecent, unwanted, and offensive. The question was whether California could prosecute Miller for sending the material. The Supreme Court found that indeed, the California courts had the right to prosecute, but what emerged from the Supreme Court's review was greater disagreement among judges about what constituted pornography.

The result of *Miller v. California* was the agreement by the justices that there could be no national standard to judge what is obscene or what would appeal to "prurient interest." Justice Brennan, author of the majority opinion in the Roth case, apparently had changed his mind on the issue of obscenity, and now believed that it was protected by the constitution. His reason was that obscenity laws had become too vague with regard to Constitutional protection. However, his change of mind went against the trend of the court. After the 1973 *Miller v. California* ruling, the Supreme Court in general became more conservative about obscenity and pornography, and turned more power over to the states to decide what would be acceptable within their own jurisdictions.

Censorship of ideas   Even though the courts have wrestled with the problems of relating a rationale for censorship and standards for obscenity, there are many forms of censorship that never go as far as the judicial system. Though the Supreme Court's 1969 decision would seem to cover the rights of individuals to have different ideas, some special interest groups, like parents, or religious organizations, advocate forms of censorship for their own reasons (see box 12.5).

Rulings on Film

Because audiences see films in large, dark theaters in the company of strangers, and images are larger than life, the medium of film has always garnered a significant amount of criticism for its potential to impose values on society. Of all the mass media, film has most often been subjected to prior restraint by the government based upon content. Film was not protected by the First Amendment until 1952 because a 1915 Supreme Court ruling had determined that it was a special form of communication unlike any other known at that time. But because film is very popular, many questions about appropriate content have entered the public's consciousness. Many of the precedents for First Amendment applications to other media are drawn from film.

The history of film is a history of social values and censorship. From its earliest days as a sideshow novelty, religious groups, women's groups, and civic organizations have put pressure on municipal and state governments and Hollywood boards to censor films that might potentially encourage people to engage in antisocial or promiscuous activities. Because film was not given First

Box 12.5 Lewd or Literature?

Book burning and censorship have always been powerful measures of the moral values of the group advocating censorship. The first book to be banned for obscenity was *Memoirs of a Woman of Pleasure*, known for its protagonist, Fanny Hill, and written by John Cleland in 1740. The novel focused on the life of a prostitute, and was banned in England. When a bookstore owner in Massachusetts tried to sell it in 1821, he was called a "scandalous and evil disposed person." The judge who tried the case found the book so obscene that he wouldn't let the jury see it. As a result, the bookstore owner was convicted by a jury that hadn't even read the book.

According to Dr. Lee Burress, author of *The Battle of the Books: Library Censorship in the Public Schools, 1950–1985*, the most common books targeted by parents for censorship are:

1. *The Catcher in the Rye*, by J. D. Salinger
2. *The Grapes of Wrath*, by John Steinbeck
3. *Of Mice and Men*, by John Steinbeck
4. *Go Ask Alice*, (anonymous)
5. *Forever . . .* , by Judy Blume
6. *Our Bodies, Ourselves*, by the Boston Women's Health Collective
7. *The Adventures of Huckleberry Finn*, by Mark Twain
8. *The Learning Tree*, by Gordon Parks
9. *My Darling, My Hamburger*, by Paul Zindel
10. *1984*, by George Orwell
11. *Black Boy*, by Richard Wright
12. *The Canterbury Tales*, by Geoffrey Chaucer

Sources: Melvin Berger, *Censorship* (New York: Franklin Watts, 1982); Lee Burgess, *The Battle of the Books: Library Censorship in the Public Schools, 1950-1985* (Metuchen, NJ: Scarecrow Books).

Amendment protection, film industry and government censorship boards attained great power over America's values and its moral climate. Some of the first state censorship boards were established in 1911 (in Pennsylvania) and 1913 (in Ohio and Kansas). By 1915, many states and municipalities had their own censorship boards (Black 1989).

To understand the public's concern about film at the turn of the century it is necessary to remember that stage actors were considered immoral and sometimes indecent. In addition, the values of the American public had been strongly influenced by sexually repressed Victorian England and by religious beliefs that required abstinence from sexual activity outside of marriage, dancing, foul language, and unruly behavior. Film showed images that were larger than life and often portrayed violence, passion, and other strong emotions—all considered inappropriate forms of behavior, especially in a public place.

Adding to negative public perceptions was the widely-held belief that Hollywood was a sinful place. Stories featuring scandal and crime, such as the trial of popular comedian Fatty Arbuckle in 1921 for allegedly murdering an actress, were widely reported. In 1922, Director William Dean Taylor was found murdered in his home with two bullets in his back, and several Hollywood notables were implicated in his death. When popular film stars Douglas Fairbanks and Mary Pickford were married, questions were raised about the legitimacy of her earlier divorce. Eventually Pickford's divorce from her first husband was upheld by the Supreme Court, but the actions of Hollywood's elite continued to be morally suspect.

Attempts at self-censorship   The moral crusades that beleaguered the film industry prodded its leaders to attempt a form of self-censorship before standards were imposed from outside. The first attempt at establishing an industry self-censorship board was presided over by Will H. Hays, who had been Postmaster General of the United States and a chief political strategist during the Harding administration.

Box 12.6   The Moral Climate of the 1920s

The "Roaring Twenties" have often been called the "Age of Jazz" in American history. Jazz music was hot, prohibition was in force but flouted behind closed doors, and new ideas were being expressed publicly by people like Margaret Sanger, who advocated birth control. The Scopes Monkey Trial challenged the belief that creation had occurred literally as it is described in *Genesis*, and substitutes the theory of evolution, which thenceforward would be taught in the public schools.

Many people blamed the movies for introducing sexual permissiveness. Their evidence included the presence on-screen of the sultry Theda Bara and the effective use of movie star sex appeal by Cecil B. De Mille. When talking pictures (talkies) were introduced in 1927, the spoken words of the narrative became possible targets for censorship. When Hays heard the word "damn" used several times in a short film, he said that it did not offend him personally, but that "as a matter of policy we ought to avoid expressions that rub any notable section of the public the wrong way."

Source: Edward De Grazia and Roger K. Newman. *Banned Films* (New York: R.R. Bowker & Co., 1982), 31–32.

Figure 12.1 *Theda Bara.*
In her day the actress Theda Bara was the epitome of sexual suggestion. Her sultry look and skimpy costumes outraged many, and her image of the sex goddess became synonymous with Hollywood's lax moral code.
Picture Source: Museum of Modern Art/Film Stills Archive.

During Hays' tenure in Hollywood, he was often criticized by moralists for not doing enough to enforce morality in films. Some of his earliest attempts included a requirement that studios approve all scripts, and the creation of a list of "Don'ts" and "Be Carefuls" for producers and directors.

In 1934 the Catholic Church and the Legion of Decency put pressure on Hays to sign an agreement to establish a regulatory body called the Production Code Administration (PCA), which would enforce guidelines that had been drawn up in 1930. It would also establish a formula to ensure that all evil actions and immoral behaviors depicted in a film would be punished in the end. During its existence as a self-regulatory body, the PCA influenced the distribution of approximately 20,000 films. As film historian Robert Sklar wrote, the code virtually, "cut the movies off from many of the most important moral and social themes of the contemporary world" (1975).

When television entered the American scene in the 1950s, the moral crusaders of the country turned their attention to it, and some of the controversy about film lessened. More films were being produced in other countries that reflected a broader range of values, and had appeal for different types of audiences. A film by Roberto Rossellini called *The Miracle* (1951), about an Italian peasant girl's encounter with a stranger she believed to be the biblical Joseph, challenged traditional film censorship: in the film, the girl gives birth to a child she believes to be the Christ child.

When the case was brought to the Supreme Court in *Burstyn v. Wilson* (1952), the Court stated that films are "a significant medium for the communication of ideas" and granted them First Amendment protection. This action opened up a range of distribution possibilities for a variety of films, and

---

Box 12.7   Censoring Film Content

Many films have been banned by local or state governments for a variety of reasons.

Some banned films have dealt with topics that seem tame by today's standards. Consider a few of the banned films and the reasons they were censored:

1915, The *Birth of a Nation*, directed by D. W. Griffith: Blacks capture South Carolina and the Ku Klux Klan rescues young women from them and restores order. A subtitle states that the South must be made "safe" for whites.

1955, *The Man with the Golden Arm*, directed by Otto Preminger: Adapted from Nelson Algren's novel. A former narcotics user has a "gift" for controlling card games. A dope peddler coaxes him back to narcotics, his wife leaves him, and he begins life with a girl who helps him kick his habit.

1967, *I Am Curious—Yellow*, directed by Vilgot Sjoman (Sweden): An aspiring actress demonstrates against the Vietnam War outside the American Embassy in Stockholm. She engages in sexual activities with a married automobile salesman in public places.

1967, *Titicut Follies*, directed by Frederick Wiseman: This documentary about conditions in a state prison for the criminally insane shows scenes of a musical show put on by prisoners as well as views of daily life inside the prison. The film was banned in Massachusetts until 1992 on the grounds that it violated the prisoners' rights to privacy. For 25 years the film was not shown publicly in the state.

Source: Edward De Grazia and Roger K. Newman, *Banned Films,* (New York: R.R. Bowker Co., 1982).

allowed the motion picture industry to present a much greater diversity of story lines than before. Film had finally won the right to protection under the law.

Changing the Direction of the First Amendment

With the growing number of forms of communication technology, and a move toward greater deregulation, traditional interpretations of the First Amendment have been eroded. Starting in the 1950s, but gaining momentum in the 1970s, interpretations of "rights," "public interest," and "local standards" have been reconsidered.

While the move toward deregulation began during the Carter administration, the 1980s political era brought market principles as an economic tool to Washington. The economy boomed in the 1980s, and venture capital supported the development and marketing of a number of new communication technologies for the public's consumption. Deregulatory measures opened competition in the telephone, cable, and computer industries, and led to eventual deregulation of the radio and television industries.

At the same time, many First Amendment questions arose. Should cable companies be given the same First Amendment rights as broadcasters? Can a cable company offer uncut, uncensored X-rated movies in prime time because it is not subject to the same standards of obscenity as broadcasters? Should information carried over electronic mail be subject to postal regulations covering censorship, and should there be any special standards if the message may be received by several people?

New distribution forms have challenged the precedents that had been set by print and film. As new situations arise, the desire of distributors to protect their economic interests will undoubtedly influence rulings on the control of information—particularly for questionable content.

The acceptance of deregulation as an economic incentive reduces any control the government or other official bodies might exercise over an industry. Traditional rationales for determining that the rights of listeners and viewers override the rights of broadcasters have already been challenged. How far might deregulation go? Will there be any opportunity to control information in an era of deregulation?

Deregulation as a Philosophy

After World War II, most of the industrialized countries operated their economies under a "supply and demand" model. But during the recession of

1974–79, which was brought about by the oil crisis and by inflation, many countries sought a new form of economic management. In the United States this led to the restriction of social programs. Cuts in public spending became the focus of austerity programs, but the national debt continued to increase.

These economic events were believed to be reversible if government would spend less money on enforcing regulations and would allow "market principles" to dictate business practices. Proponents of deregulation claimed that market-oriented solutions would be more effective and less costly than governmental regulation.

Further, the successful introduction of new technologies and services drained support from the old argument in support of regulation that said that the electromagnetic spectrum offered a limited number of avenues of information. The new technologies and services were seen as solving the problem by offering the public more choices.

Finally, deregulationists claimed that any regulatory structure that requires the federal government to oversee the content of programming would be contrary to the spirit of the First Amendment. These supporters view the "trusteeship" philosophy as a violator of the First Amendment (see box 12.8).

Because cable was receiving a great deal of attention at the time of the deregulation movement in Washington, it became one of the first industries to be deregulated. As a result, it also provided one of the clearest indicators of whether communication industries in fact could be deregulated. Ironically, many legislators later found it necessary to call for a re-regulation of the industry because cable costs for consumers began to skyrocket. The first steps toward re-regulation were taken by the passage of the Cable Television Consumer Protection and Competition Act of 1992.

The Deregulation and Re-Regulation of the Cable Industry

For most of cable's history, starting with its early years in the 1940s, the medium seemed to have no connection with freedom of the press. Because cable was transmitted either by closed circuit or on microwave relays, it was considered a common carrier rather than a communications industry that would eventually program original entertainment and information. The FCC saw cable's function as retransmitting entertainment; it had little understanding of what cable did or what it might be capable of. Also, during the 1970s, the FCC was more concerned with the establishment and licensing of UHF stations as a response to the dominance of the networks over broadcast airwaves.

Between 1969 and 1972 the FCC wrote a set of rules known as the "Consensus Agreement." Broadcasters, cable operators, and the White House Office of Telecommunications Policy (OTP) agreed to cooperate and examine

Box 12.8   Connecting with Mark Fowler

Mark Fowler was Chair of the FCC from 1981 to 1987 under President Reagan. When he left the FCC, he joined the law practice of Latham and Watkins in Washington, D.C. In a telephone interview in December, 1991, he was asked whether, now that some time had passed since his involvement as the chief architect of the deregulation of the media industries, he felt that deregulation had really worked.

Mr. Fowler thought for a moment, then answered with an emphatic *No*. The reasons, he explained, involved changes in Washington that altered the spirit of deregulation from its original intention. Deregulation was distorted by the political activities of bureaucrats and lobbyists. He continued, "If deregulation had been left to develop the way it was meant to, it would have worked."

As Chair of the FCC, Mr. Fowler often stated that deregulation was in the best interest of the public, because it afforded the same First Amendment privilege to broadcasting that print had long enjoyed. In a *Washington Post* article (1984, A27), he stated:

> My insistence on First Amendment rights for broadcasters surprises some who know me as a conservative Republican. Some notable conservatives believe that more, not less, restraint should be imposed on broadcast news organizations, particularly network television, which they view as biased against conservatives.
>
> In this view television cannot be trusted to deal fairly with conservatives and their point of view; tools like the Fairness Doctrine, the argument goes, really protect conservatives by preventing broadcasters from coloring their reporting with a liberal viewpoint to which they are naturally inclined. . . .
>
> I feel that it is correct constitutionally and as a conservative to support less, not more restraint on the press. To my mind, true conservativism means less involvement by the government in the lives and affairs of people. Content regulation of broadcasting is out of place in this scheme.

Source: Mark S. Fowler, "Broadcasting with less restraint." *Washington Post* (July 1, 1984), A27. © *The Washington Post*. Reprinted with Permission.

cable's function. The agreement also allowed cable systems with at least 3500 subscribers to program some of their own material.

By 1973, new pay services like HBO and ESPN still used cable as a subscription-distribution medium. As the number of services offered by cable increased, the FCC had further reason to see cable as a possible answer to the problem of scarcity of channels in the electromagnetic spectrum.

When the Cable Amendment of 1984 was added to the Communications Act of 1934, cable was officially free of the restrictions that had kept broadcasters from engaging in certain activities, like producing programs which they could later syndicate or sell and owning multiple cable operations.

As cable was allowed to grow with no restrictions, conflicts with the broadcasters who were still regulated by traditional means arose. By 1991 the networks had lost a significant number of viewers to cable and claimed that deregulation was being unevenly applied. Broadcasting lobbyists fought energetically to have cable re-regulated, and to create more equitability of business practices between the two industries.

Legislators became the truly concerned over the rise in cable subscription costs after the industry had been deregulated. Between 1987 and 1992 monthly cable rates increased by 60 percent. As they did for the deregulated telephone industry, legislators tried to think of some way to cap high consumer costs while allowing the industry to grow. Many of them began calling for re-regulation to control costs.

The FCC lifted some restrictions on the business practices of the networks in 1992, allowing them to purchase cable companies. The original prohibition had been established by the FCC so that the fledgling cable industry could grow without threat of takeover by the three powerful networks. But even though the FCC ended the 22-year ban on network ownership of cable systems, the networks claimed that the new regulations were still too restrictive to allow them to compete with cable (Arndt 1992, B1–2). The new regulations lifted cross-ownership in the three biggest markets—New York, Los Angeles, and Chicago—but retained restrictions on network ownership (including the Fox network) of cable facilities in smaller markets.

The Impact of Deregulation on Special Types of Media Content

The philosophy of deregulation places the rights of the media owner over the rights of the viewer, listener, or user of the message. This overriding principle has called several past regulation milestones into question, and has led to a concern for the rights of special audiences. In particular, there has been renewed debate concerning the Fairness Doctrine and the control of children's television programming, both of which have experienced many changes.

The Fairness Doctrine   Advocates of diversity in media content have been particularly concerned about the effect of deregulation on the Fairness Doctrine. Added to the Communications Act in 1949, the Fairness Doctrine

Box 12.9   Attempts to Rewrite the Communications Act of 1934

Rep. Lionel VanDeerlin (D., Calif.) made the first attempt to rewrite the Communications Act of 1934. He proposed a rewrite in 1976. VanDeerlin was the newly elected chair of the House Subcommittee on Communications, a committee he knew intimately after serving on it for 14 years. He was well aware of the problems in the communications industries. He had been a news director and anchor in San Diego and a city editor for the *San Diego Journal*. In addition, San Diego was also the site of the largest cable system in the US.

When he became Chair of the committee, VanDeerlin announced a "basement-to-penthouse" revamping of the Communications Act. His fervor worried many people in the industry who thought he might make too many changes. VanDeerlin's goals included repealing the act's Equal Opportunity Statement. He advocated easier access for new entrants to the common carrier industry, which would mean more competition for distribution systems already in place, such as satellite, cable, and optical fiber. He also supported total deregulation of the cable, radio, and television industries. To support the committee's work, the Office of Telecommunication Policy (OTP) began writing a proposal to implement all of the measures Van Deerlin advocated, including a restructuring of the FCC and a reorganization of public broadcasting.

When the proposal was completed, the National Association of Broadcasters (NAB) claimed the plan went too far by because it assumed that a radical restructuring of the Act was necessary. Congress hedged, saying that this was only a review of the Communication Act of 1934.

After significant negotiations and compromises with special interest groups, a press conference was held to unveil HR 13015, a 217-page bill that would replace the FCC with a "Communication Regulatory Commission." The bill stated that government interference in telecommunications would go only "to the extent marketplace forces are deficient."

The rewrite offended everyone. Many communication industries opposed the proposal for a spectrum fee that would require telecommunications companies to pay "rent" on the portions of the broadcasting spectrum they used. Concerned citizens and special interest lobbyists claimed that no provisions were made to guarantee minority access to the media, or to represent opposing viewpoints. The bill met so much opposition on its various points from different interest groups that it failed.

In 1979, the subcommittee unveiled Rewrite II, known as "Son of Rewrite." It too failed, because of opposition from citizens groups and legislators who felt that it contained too much deregulation.

> Some legislators would like to see another attempt at a rewrite, but many of the original complaints have been addressed in piecemeal agreements that have tried to treat the various communications industries more equitably. It appears that targeting specific problems is a more effective means of initiating change than trying to rewrite the Act.
>
> Source: Patrick Parsons. *Cable television and the first amendment*. (Lexington, Mass.: D.C. Heath, 1987).

requires that broadcasters devote a reasonable amount of broadcast time to the discussion of controversial issues so that the public has a reasonable opportunity to hear opposing viewpoints. This doctrine was never codified (enacted into law), but has long served as the statement most central to the responsibilities of broadcasters.

Former FCC Chair Fowler reasoned that the Fairness Doctrine had been well intentioned but suppressive of the goals it sought to secure. Fowler, and other deregulationists since, have claimed that the Fairness Doctrine actually restricts free speech because broadcasters may experience financial losses by airing unpopular public affairs programming (Fowler & Brenner, 1988). In this view, the rights of the broadcasters are paramount to those of the audience

The battle over the Fairness Doctrine has been a lengthy one. The constitutionality of the Doctrine was upheld in 1969 in the Supreme Court's decision in *Red Lion Broadcasting v. FCC* (see box 12.10). The FCC repealed the Doctrine in 1985. In 1987, the FCC reaffirmed its action, claiming that the Doctrine "no longer effectuated the public interest in access to diverse sources of information" (Springer 1989, 66). Still, however, legislators like Sen. Ernest Hollings (D., S.C.) and other advocates of the Doctrine have attempted to introduce legislation that would revive it, and at this writing, the Fairness Doctrine remains a topic of controversy in Congress and the FCC.

Section 315

Changes brought about under deregulation also affect many of the key sections in the Communications Act of 1934. Section 315, the "equal time" provision, requires that broadcasters make time available to all legally qualified candidates for public office, and that their messages may not be censored. The section also sets guidelines for the fees a broadcaster may charge for political advertising. With the number of channels now available for advertising, and the connection of Section 315 to the now defunct Fairness Doctrine in terms of guaranteeing access and the presentation of multiple viewpoints, the "equal time amendment" lacks the power it once had to facilitate the presentation of political information.

Box 12.10   The Red Lion Decision

On November 27, 1964, radio station WGCB, owned by the Red Lion Broadcasting Company of Pennsylvania, carried a 15-minute broadcast by the Reverend Billy James Hargis as part of a "Christian Crusade" series. Hargis discussed a book by Fred Cook titled "Goldwater—Extremist on the Right" that he claimed had been written "to smear and destroy Barry Goldwater." When the author of the book, Fred J. Cook, heard the broadcast, he demanded equal time to refute Hargis' statements, but the station refused. The court determined that Red Lion Broadcasting had failed to meet the provisions of the Fairness Doctrine by not sending a tape, transcript, or summary of the broadcast to Cook or letting him have the right of reply.

Red Lion Broadcasting challenged the Fairness Doctrine on First Amendment grounds, alleging that the rules abridged their freedom of speech and press. When the Supreme Court heard the case in 1969, it determined that the Fairness Doctrine was constitutional, and that it could be applied to a particular broadcast. The Court determined that Red Lion had violated the Doctrine.

Source: Douglas H. Ginsburg, *Regulation of broadcasting: Law and policy towards radio, television, and cable communications.* (St. Paul, Minn.: West Publishing Co., 1979) 499-515.

Children's television   As the media industries were deregulated in the 1980s, steps were taken to lift regulations pertaining to children's television. The changes in this area have frustrated many legislators, lobbyists, and parents, who had been advocating increases in regulation for decades. The history of efforts to regulate children's television programming is lengthy; by contrast, the steps taken to lift existing regulations seemed to happen overnight.

Ever since television was introduced there have been efforts to regulate the content of children's television shows based on theories that children are highly impressionable and unable to make rational decisions about what they watch. As early as the 1950s, a Senate subcommittee was established to investigate juvenile delinquency. Among their findings was the dominance of television viewing by the young. The subcommittee was appalled at the amount of violence portrayed by the medium, and it exposed numerous violations of the industry's attempt at self-regulation—the Television Code of Good Practice, whose guidelines suggested limits of crime and violence permissible for children's television. The subcommittee concluded that a relationship existed between violence seen on television and criminal behavior, though they felt that the available evidence did not adequately explain how violence on television might lead children to behave in an antisocial manner.

The FCC did not become involved in monitoring television licenses and the actions of broadcasters with regard to children's programming until 1960. At that time, the Commission came up with 14 categories for satisfying the public interest, convenience, and necessity (PICN) in order to qualify for renewal of broadcast licenses.

During the 1960s increases in crime and civil unrest led to the appointment of a presidential commission to examine the problem of violence in America. The National Commission on the Causes and Prevention of Violence released its final report in 1969 and an entire volume was devoted to the effects of media violence. It concluded: "Children can and do learn aggressive behavior from what they see in a film or on a TV screen, and they learn it equally as well from real life and fantasy (cartoon) models. . . ."

In 1972 the report of the Surgeon General (funded by the National Institute for Mental Health) concluded that there was a causal relationship between televised violence and subsequent antisocial behavior, and that the evidence was strong enough to require some action on the part of the TV industry, the government, and the citizens.

In 1967 the Carnegie Commission on Educational Television established the Public Broadcasting Service (PBS) to create a network of public and educational television stations as an alternative to commercial broadcasting. At the same time, the Children's Television Workshop (CTW) was created to develop programming specifically for children. This led to the development of "Sesame

---

Box 12.11   Children's Viewing Habits

Children are exposed to extraordinary amounts of media programming each day. Nielsen statistics from 1992 indicate that children aged 2 to 5 watch slightly more than four hours of TV each day. Children aged 6 to 11 watch almost twice as much. Saturday morning television is usually programmed for children, but only a small amount of viewing occurs then by comparison with other times of the week. Most children watch television during weekday early mornings, late afternoons, and early evening hours. By the time they reach elementary school age children's viewing preferences lean toward more adult programming.

Source: A.C. Nielsen, 1992.

Street," a collaborative effort between academic researchers and television producers that established a model for integrating entertainment with educational and pro-social messages for children.

A citizen's lobbying group, Action for Children's Television (ACT), was founded in 1972, initially to investigate violence, but its focus and influence quickly expanded to encompass all dimensions of children's television viewing. Eventually ACT determined that commercialism was a greater villain than violence. Consistent with this new agenda, ACT proposed in 1970 that the FCC require each station to provide programming for children totaling no less than 14 hours per week.

In 1971 the FCC put out its Notice of Proposed Rulemaking to alert the public that it intended to consider ACT's proposals. The result was the 1974 Children's Television Report and Policy Statement, a significant statement for those favoring government regulation that set detailed policies to guide broadcasters in serving the child audience. It went further than the FCC ever had in creating regulation.

The end result was the establishment of departments of children's programming at all networks. Some of ACT's suggestions were adopted, such as the separation of commercials from program content by a five-second slide (called a bumper), and an increase in pro-social themes and plots, with a concurrent decrease in the amount of violence. Advertising was also reduced by several minutes per hour.

In 1975 Congress passed the Family Viewing Act, which required stations to broadcast programs with content appropriate for family viewing (excluding sexual or violent material) for two hours of prime time nightly. The ratings of network shows plummeted, and UHF stations took advantage of the competition's low ratings to broadcast reruns of popular earlier shows. These were tremendously successful!

During Jimmy Carter's administration, the FCC under its chair Charles Ferris once again turned to issues of regulating children's television content. The FCC commissioned several studies examining the amount of children's programming available and comparing it to the programming examined in the 1974 study. When the report was concluded in 1978, the researchers found that no increase in programming with positive values had taken place.

The FCC had to decide whether to return to the 1974 guidelines or to come up with something new. By 1980, it had narrowed the choices to either increasing the number of broadcast outlets in a given market or allowing broadcasters in a market to share responsibility in serving the child audience better.

ACT turned to the Federal Trade Commission (FTC) to put pressure on broadcasters regarding advertising. At the time, the FTC was exercising powerful control over some types of advertising, and it complied with ACT's requests. The most significant regulation proposed by the FTC was to ban all televised advertising for any product which is directed to, or targeting audiences with a significant proportion of children who may not be able to understand the purpose of the advertising. The FTC claimed that much of the advertising was "unfair or deceptive."

Before the FTC had completed its anticipated set of hearings on the proposals, it found itself under political fire. Its Chair, Michael Pertschuk, became the subject of a lawsuit designed to exclude him from the proceedings, charging him with having made public statements supporting a ban on ads prior to hearing all the evidence. Shortly thereafter, the Congress, reacting to intense lobbying, voted to rescind the FTC's power to regulate unfair advertising, and many of the plans to enforce more control over children's advertising were never realized.

The 1980 election of President Reagan, and his appointment of Mark Fowler to the FCC, changed the priorities of government regulation of media. The Reagan/Fowler agenda was significantly different than the previous one. Fowler felt that children's programming was becoming available through alternative means, such as video games, public television, and cable. He also claimed that the growth in new technologies answered the old argument about scarcity.

These actions prodded many media writers to criticize the FCC's actions, asking whether it had gone too far. Some critics said the excessive costs of new technologies would prevent poorer families from using them, and still others wanted to see results before agreeing that multiple channels could increase the diversity of programming.

In 1983 Rep. Tim Wirth (D., Colo.) proposed the establishment of a Children's Television Education Act. Claiming that marketplace rules weren't working, he proposed that each station provide a minimum of one hour of educational programming for children each weekday. His plan collided with other plans to deregulate, and the issue became a political football. Wirth offered to back legislation that would enact deregulation into law if an exception was made for children's programming, but no compromise was reached before the bills died at the end of the 98th Congress (1984). In the 99th Congress (1985), Wirth introduced a modified version of his previous bill, with no effect. The revision would have established minimum hours of children's programming, allowed licenses be revoked for noncompliance, and required strict separation of content and commercials.

Instead, since 1985 the battle for children's television has been won by the FCC and lobbyists on behalf of the television industry, which has benefited from the deregulation of the media.

The Children's Television Act

In 1990, after five years of debate, Congress passed the Children's Television Act, which limited the number of commercial minutes allowed during children's shows to 10.5 minutes per hour on the weekends and 12 minutes per hour during the week. Although President Bush vetoed the bill, Congress overrode him. The Act mandated that stations "serve the educational and informational needs of children," but how those needs were to be determined remained ambiguous.

As a result, stations began to redefine many familiar cartoons and comedies as "educational." Suddenly stations across the country were reporting that "G.I. Joe," "Leave It to Beaver," and "Super Mario Brothers" taught pro-social lessons to children. A report by the Center for Media Education reported that in filings made by 58 stations, programs for children that used news and magazine-style formats were often placed in time slots earlier than 7 A.M., when few children were likely to be watching. After five years of heated debate about the need to

Figure 12.2 *Teenage Mutant Ninja Turtles: The Products Sold with the Film and Television Programs.*
Picture Source: © Mirage Studios

control the commercialism of children's television and the need for positive images, leading to the establishment of the Act, it has already deemed by most legislators and interested individuals to be ineffective.

Today there are few regulations to protect children from opportunistic programming, and few restrictions on sponsorship of programs by products. A 1991 move by the FCC to limit commercial programming—that which featured characters who were also seen in commercials, was challenged by CBS, and by 1992, virtually all restrictions were lifted. The commercial aspects of children's television programming have been allowed to proliferate almost totally uncontrolled, and programs often echo infomercials aimed at adults in their style and attempts to sell products. Judgements about whether characters that represent commercial enterprises, such as Strawberry Shortcake or the Smurfs, and the sale of products that reflect more pro-social values through identification with children, like those from "Sesame Street," make the distinctions between product sales and popular programming even more difficult.

Issues for Today's Communication Technologies

Since many contemporary communication technologies and services have emerged during the deregulatory era, they have been allowed to develop with fewer restrictions on their operation or their content than earlier technologies.

Information technologies, like computers, fax machines, and cellular telephones, as well as information providers, which include directory assistance programs, private companies like newspapers and magazines, and financial enterprises like mortgage, banking, and finance firms, are all allowed to work using their own standards and practices. Many of these, however, are guided by policies or regulations that have been instituted by federal agencies to ensure fairness to consumers. Some of the activities these technologies and institutions encourage have been the focus of First Amendment questions, and questions about other rights, such as the right to privacy.

Ethical Dimensions

Deregulation as an economic philosophy gives power to the already powerful media owners and corporate controllers. If business practices are allowed to dictate what information and ideas may be presented to the public, how "free" is free speech? If no controls are placed on questionable content, what right does the public have to safeguard itself from offensive images?

Two examples illustrate these dilemmas. The first has to do with Hill and Knowlton, the world's largest public relations firm, and its creation of antiabortion ads that were so graphically powerful, they created a public uproar and a controversy that divided employees of the firm. The second issue has to do with the marketing of tobacco products for children.

Hill and Knowlton   In 1990 and 1991 Hill and Knowlton made the headlines. The company was under fire for accepting an account from the League of Catholic Bishops to develop an effective antiabortion campaign. The campaign featured visual images of aborted fetuses and clearly tried to capitalize on the fascination of the grotesque. But before the campaign went into full gear, employees at Hill and Knowlton complained not only about the ads, but also that the firm had sacrificed its standards on behalf of the client. At least two employees resigned, and many refused to work on the campaign (Goodell 1990, 122). Claiming that the firm had been irresponsible in executing offensive advertisements to satisfy the wishes of the client, employees demanded clarification of the firm's objectives from the Chief Operating Officer. Rather than prolong the conflict, Hill and Knowlton canceled the proposed campaign.

Tobacco and children   Though advertising is not the focus of this book, mention has been given to the FTC's responsibility in this area. In recent years the public has become aware that the tobacco industry has aggressively pursued the youth market for cigarettes in several countries.

The average age of American minors who experiment with smoking or who start to smoke is 13. About three million youngsters are already smokers, and every year about two million more join their ranks (Mintz 1991, 592).

In December 1991 The Tobacco Institute announced a 10 million dollar public relations campaign to discourage minors from smoking. However, the Advocacy Institute, which promotes programs for better health, has said that the 10 million dollars is only one-twentieth of what the industry earns from children and teen smokers each year. A large proportion of product giveaways and tie-ins to promote smoking targets young people, because an addicted smoker is a customer for life.

These examples merely suggest some of the ethical questions raised when business is allowed to pursue its own interest without restrictions. They also make a connection between values and business practices that the audience may not immediately recognize.

Reconciling the First Amendment, Regulation, and Values

Our examination of problems associated with interpreting the First Amendment and attempts to regulate or deregulate the communication industries has shown that contemporary values play a large part in determining what is considered "appropriate" content. Obscenity issues have a long tradition of revealing what are socially acceptable forms of content. The protection of ideas under the First Amendment has influenced guidelines for choosing material as new distribution channels open.

But the fact is that deregulation has forced an economic philosophy upon us that seeks to change some of our practices. Ultimately, these new practices lead us toward reinterpreting the First Amendment. Even though many legislators advocate re-regulation of some industries that they believe may have gone "too far" with their new liberties, our society is faced with a major decision: Do the changes we have undergone in recent years require a reassessment of some of our basic freedoms?

Technology has progressed to a point where many of our original laws and regulations are no longer adequate. The number of new services and convergent technologies poses new questions about control and content and challenges some of our old attitudes and laws. We've reached the point where legislators, industries, lobbyists, and concerned citizens all recognize the need for something to be done, but we seem unable to determine the best way to make any changes.

Our personal values today have been shaped by a reflection of the communication industries' approach to more segmented markets. Most people enjoy having access to radio, television, films, magazines, and recordings that reflect the interests of themselves and their peers, and efforts to create regulations that would have the result of limiting diversity have been met with outcries from some factions in society.

The attempts of the Parents Music Resource Center (PMRC) to pressure the recording industry not to produce and sell records with content that is objectionable for children is an example of a consumer concern that turned into an industry issue and then a First Amendment issue. When the PMRC began putting pressure on the Recording Industry of America (RIAA) in 1985 to develop a ratings system for records similar to the one used for films, cries of "censorship" and "violation of First Amendment rights" began to be heard.

Groups like the American Civil Liberties Union (ACLU) lobbied against such legislation. Musician Frank Zappa testified before the Congressional Committee on Commerce, Science and Transportation (1985), which conducted the hearings, claiming that a record ratings system would stifle freedom of expression and have a negative effect on the ability of musicians to earn a living.

The end result was a compromise, with recording companies offering voluntarily to label records "Explicit Lyrics—Parental Advisory" when material might be considered questionable. The RIAA also agreed to print lyric sheets to accompany records, tapes, and discs so that parents could monitor their children's music. The compromise temporarily resolved the dispute, but circumvented the direct First Amendment question and failed to resolve other problems of content, such as the images on record covers.

This type of compromise solution is typical of an attempt by one organization to control the efforts of another. It also demonstrates the diversity of viewpoints being voiced by participants in communications industry controversies. One wonders whether the labeling of records or the printing of lyrics in earlier times would have changed the type of music available. Would songs written in the twenties "pass inspection" today?

Resolution of problems on a case-by-case basis or through compromise is a necessary but problematic means of reaching a decision on important ethical and social issues.

CONCLUSION

The First Amendment has been subjected to many interpretations, but each reflects the attitudes of lawmakers and the values of society of the time. People responsible for judging questionable content in communications media have continued to look to the community for guidance in determining appropriate standards, but the political activities surrounding the resolution of a problem often result in incomplete answers or compromises.

Since embracing the philosophy of deregulation, the U.S. government has abolished many of the regulations that were established in the early days of communications media. But in its haste, the government has created uncertainty for lawmakers, industries, and concerned citizens to resolve. The cry by some legislators today for re-regulation indicates that deregulation may have gone too far.

Deregulation does initially open the field for new players to compete, but establish business in the United States has a long history of protecting itself. Deregulation has also made possible greater vertical integration among communications companies. The end result has been less diversity of information and more redundancy of content. The theory of deregulation is not at fault; the practice is.

SUMMARY

This chapter has reviewed precedents surrounding the control of content in the communications industries. We have seen that:

- there is ambiguity in many definitions of categories used to determine suitability of content; one widely publicized example is obscenity
- controlling information flow through the U.S. Postal Service has been one method used to limit distribution of questionable material

- legal decisions on media content, including print, in which only a part of the material being considered was questionable, have been overturned; now material must be reviewed within its whole context
- "qualified critics" are to be consulted to determine offensiveness
- contemporary community standards are the most important gauge of acceptable material
- the Supreme Court has acknowledged that community standards differ
- the privacy of the home is protected; home is considered a place where an individual may receive any information, regardless of the nature of its content
- attempts by industries to censor themselves have had only moderate success
- movement toward deregulation has placed economic principles ahead of the moral or ethical values of our culture
- as laws reflect the deregulation philosophy, the nature of what we see, hear, and think falls more under the control of the powerful communications companies
- deregulation may be a sound economic theory, but its application has had unfortunate results that have led many to seek re-regulation in the communications industries

DISCUSSION QUESTIONS

1. Based on the material presented in previous chapters and the issues raised in this chapter, do you think deregulation has gone too far, or do you feel that market principles will eventually rectify today's problems in the communications industries?
2. Reflect on the television programs and films you remember best from your childhood. What messages did they give you? Have any of these messages influenced your values today?
3. Make a list of topics you think deserve consideration for censorship. Compare these with lists made by other class members, and consider any differences of opinion.
4. In your opinion, what is the difference between obscenity and pornography?
5. What recently developed media formats have raised questions about the appropriateness of content? On what moral grounds are these situations argued?

6. Discuss how absolute you feel freedom of the press and freedom of speech should be. Consider key issues such as these: Should the names of rape victims be published? Should the infidelities of public figures be publicized? Should the names of individuals arrested for driving under the influence of alcohol or narcotics be published?

7. What role do you think the government should take in regulating the content of broadcasting aimed at children?

REFERENCES

American Press Institute. 1991. Free speech restrictions and the press. J. Montgomery Curtis Memorial Seminar. Preston, VA.

Arndt, Michael. 1992. FCC ends ban on networks owning cable systems. *New York Times* (June 19): B1–B2.

Barron, Jerome A. 1973. *Freedom of the press for whom?* Bloomington, Ind.: Indiana University Press.

Berger, Melvin. 1982. *Censorship.* New York: Franklin Watts.

Black, Gregory D. 1989. Hollywood censored: The production code administration and the Hollywood film industry, 1930-1940. *Film History* 3 (3).

De Grazia, Edward, and Newman, Roger K. 1982. *Banned films.* New York: R.R. Bowker Co.

Demac, Donna A. 1988. *Liberty denied.* New York: PEN American Center.

Fowler, Mark S. 1984. Broadcasting with less restraint. *Washington Post* (July 1): A27.

Fowler, Mark S. and Brenner, Daniel L. 1988. A marketplace approach to broadcast regulation. *Texas Law Review* 60 (2): 209-57.

Ginsburg, Douglas H. 1979. *Regulation of broadcasting: Law and policy towards radio, television, and cable communications.* St. Paul, Minn.: West Publishing Co.

Goodell, Jeffrey. 1990. What Hill & Knowlton can do for you. *New York Times Magazine* 122 (Sept. 9): 44.

Hills, Jill. 1986. *Deregulating telecoms.* Westport, Conn.: Quorum Books.

Keane, John. 1991. *The media and democracy.* Cambridge, Mass.: Polity Press.

Mintz, Morton. 1991. Marketing tobacco to children. *The Nation* 252 (May 6): 577, 591.

Parsons, Patrick. 1987. *Cable television and the first amendment.* Lexington, Mass.: D.C. Heath.

Rothenberg, Randall. 1991. Critics seek F.T.C. action on products as movie stars. *New York Times* (May 31): D1, D5.

Sklar, Robert. 1975. *Movie made America: A cultural history of American movies.* New York: Vintage.

Smith, Robert Ellis. 1979. *Privacy: How to protect what's left of it.* Garden City, New York: Anchor Press/Doubleday.

Springer, Dan. 1989. Hill showdown: A year of decision. *Channels* 9 (Jan.): 64-67.

Teeter, Dwight L., Jr., and Le Duc, Don R. 1992. *Law of mass communications.* 7th ed. Westbury, New York: The Foundation Press, Inc.

U.S. Congress. 1985. Senate Committee on Commerce, Science, and Transportation. *Hearing on Record Labeling,* S. Hrg. 99/529. 99th Congress.

Thirteen

THE INTERNATIONALIZATION OF INFORMATION

AKING CONNECTIONS:

Different cultures interpret the same media content in vastly different ways. But this is just one of the concerns in thinking about the impact of communication technology on a global scale. International communication involves issues as diverse as (*a*) equality of access to technical resources, (*b*) intercultural awareness and understanding of diverse values, (*c*) trans-border business agreements, (*d*) different political philosophies with reference to importing technology and software, and (*e*) the use of communication technology and content to introduce new ideas to a country.

Communication technology makes it possible to link different nations together to increase the exchange of information, but the technical capability to do so brings many other issues to the foreground. The connections made among politics, history, economy, culture, and society all contribute to the impact of communication technology on an international scale. All these concerns are present in the increasingly interlinked world

Chapter

13

that many have called "the information society."

This chapter addresses some of the key issues surrounding the internationalization of information and communication technology. They include:

- the global availability of communication technology

- the political, cultural, and economic elements that contribute to information inequity

- the role of international agencies that work to create a more equitable distribution of technological resources for the people of the world

- traditional business and economic practices that treat the world as a marketplace

- the ethical concerns around the control of global information

- how different countries regard participation in an information society

---

For many years there have been two popular images of the future involving a "linking" of people of the world by communication technology. One image sees the world as being electronically united, much like Morse or McLuhan's predicted "global village," in which people are able to communicate among themselves, and respect each other's cultural autonomy. There has also been a counter-image: a world in which the rich, powerful nations control the technology and content of the media, while the poorer nations have no access to the types of communication systems that could keep their own customs and cultures alive, and allow them to participate in international communication. As is often the case, the real story combines both of these images, leading us to confront the reality that the "information society" is an unequal one that gives benefits and power to some participants while ignoring others.

This chapter explores the promises, threats, and realities of global communications today, and considers how information technology is changing our world. Global communication brings with it the problems of different values, unequal resources, and incompatible social structures. The desires and efforts of international agencies to create communication equity are contrasted with the connections among international legal and economic concerns and business practices, and the desire of nations to control their own destinies.

A Profile of Global Communication

In international communication and information terms, there is no such thing as a "level playing field" because the issues surrounding information equity are often at odds with each other. Economic problems are often created when trade agreements influence where manufacturing is located and where goods are distributed. National resources, such as money, technical know-how, and raw materials, are not always equal.

Political considerations influence who, in any nation, is responsible for policies that influence the acquisition, use, and availability of technology and software. Politics and the economy are often linked when decisions are made about what technologies will be available within a country, or what type of software will be permitted.

Infrastructures are the frameworks necessary for the coordination of various vital systems within a nation. In particular, the energy infrastructure of a nation is a consideration when its policymakers decide to install communication technology. Is electricity available? Do certain technologies (like computers) require air conditioning for maximum effective use?

Social and cultural factors such as religion, education, literacy, and values are also important for understanding how any country responds to the use of communication technology and its content. What might be appropriate in one country could violate religious beliefs in another. The person or institution in any society who guides the moral development of its members is a critical factor in any environment where change is introduced.

When comparing the extent of media resources in various regions and on different continents, there is inconsistency in the types of media available. A brief survey of some of the major forms of media in use throughout the world illustrates some of the inequities in distribution, and also points to the conditions necessary for each form's use. These examples illustrate how the problems mentioned above influence the use of specific forms of communication technology.

Newspapers

When a population is dispersed throughout a region and transportation is limited, even the first step of gaining access to some forms of communication becomes a problem. Geography plays an important role in what forms of communication can be used; 60 percent of the population of the world lives in rural areas. Newspapers and television, in particular, don't reach these people. Illiteracy further complicates matters for newspaper readership in the Less Developed Countries (LDCs), but the way people value the printed word and the diversity of print sources in a country reflect cultural attitudes toward print information. Some cultures place a high value on print as truth; some view print media as propaganda espoused by the dominant political party. Often, the number of sources available to the public is an indication of how highly valued print media are. Also important is the ability of the public to read.

The number of newspapers sold in North America, South Asia, and Europe reflects strong traditions of readers seeking a diverse number of viewpoints as well as levels of literacy that can sustain readership, but newspaper circulation is not always a good indication of how many people actually seek the news. In many countries, newspapers are read by more than one person. For example, in China, newspapers are posted so that many individuals can read one copy. In other countries, like Malaysia or Taiwan, most newspaper readers read several newspapers every day, each of which may have a different political bias.

Print media often reflect the viewpoints of its publishers. Traditions of print in some countries also reflect the bias of a colonial presence that influenced not only the type of news available to people, but even the language in which it was printed. Colonial newspapers often exercised great control over the information, values, and beliefs of the colonized country and served to perpetuate values and ideas that kept the LDC dependent on the colonizing country. In some places the language of the colonists is still the "official" one, such as India and Nigeria, which were British colonies and still use English as the official language. Similarly, French is used as the "official" language in West Africa. In that country French customs, educational systems, and attitudes toward information are still present.

Telephones

Some communication technologies require expensive investments in infrastructure to make them work. When the financial cost of instituting and maintaining an infrastructure strains a country's economy, the inequity of communication resources between the people of a country or region becomes more acute. Telephones are an excellent example. Because they are so prominent in the lives of people in industrialized nations, it is difficult for us to conceive of a place like Ethiopia where there is fewer than one telephone per 100 inhabitants. It may be true that telephone service is useless if you have no one to call, and in many parts of the world where people still live in close communities, a telephone may seem to be an unnecessary luxury. But even in these situations there are times when a telephone is a necessity. There may be times when one telephone could provide a lifeline by allowing village people to reach a doctor, or could allow an agricultural extension service to notify a village of an impending storm or other natural disaster. In these instances, some form of telephone service can mean the difference between survival and catastrophe.

Extending telephone service requires a costly investment in a communications infrastructure. While the cost of the telephone instruments is minimal, the access to other lines and establishing connections are costly, and they are the key features of creating a workable telephone service.

In 1992, the cost to have a telephone installed in Mexico was the equivalent of $300. This expense meant owning a telephone was out of the range of most of the population. In a country like Argentina, where individual telephone installation has cost as much as $1500 (Vizer 1987), new technology has offered a solution to the problem of connecting telephones with expensive cables. Cellular telephone service uses microwaves for satellite distribution, and therefore bypasses the problems of physically connecting a home or business to the larger infrastructure. This also permits greater portability of the phone. As these technologies become more available, some of the inequities in universal telephone service may begin to even out. Until that time, however, the costs of establishing a phone system and creating a payment plan that does not exclude the poor will undoubtedly restrict many of the world's people from having access to a telephone.

Radios

The vast number of radio receivers around the world explains why radio has been called the "massest" of mass media. Radio receivers are usually inexpensive, and broadcasting can reach a number of individuals listening to one receiver. For this reason, radio has been a powerful medium for political, religious, and cultural groups to express their messages to a number of listeners. Even villages or communities in rural areas can be reached by radio when the most effective form of radio broadcasting is chosen for a region: short wave, AM, or FM.

While the number of radio receivers is highest in the industrialized nations, it is also an important medium of information in the LDCs, and has proven to be particularly important in countries that have experienced political instability. There, any information that confirms or denies rumors that spread through a group can become powerful agents of persuasion. Many countries have invested in **external radio** systems that target specific parts of the world with information and entertainment that help shape the image of the originating country. The British Broadcasting Corporation (BBC) has developed a reputation for broadcasting impartial news to the many countries the external service reaches. They broadcast in 36 different languages. Other countries also attempt to reach outside their own borders through external services for other reasons (discussed later in this chapter).

Radio has the power to overcome linguistic problems. Music, whether the listener can understand the lyrics or not, is a powerful influence over emotions and ideas. In many countries, people learn other languages by listening to broadcasts from other parts of the world. New ideas and expressions of other cultures introduce new ways of thinking to people through the low cost means of radio transmission.

Television

Television is, of course, more costly for individuals to use because the receivers are more expensive than radio and require more electricity. Also, the creation and broadcast of television content can be expensive. This has led to a serious question regarding the amount of programming produced in other countries that is made available to foreign markets. When television programs are made in one country and broadcast in another, do they also bring new values and attitudes to the people of the receiving nation? Most scholars agree that they do but are often less in agreement about how significant this issue is for any particular nation.

Some of the major television producers in the United States, Europe, and Latin America have sold previously broadcast television programs and films to countries that cannot afford to fill programming time with original, indigenous material. The United States' third largest export is media content, leading all other countries in exporting media content (and ideas). This has led one researcher, Jeremy Tunstall, to conclude that "the media are American" (1986).

While many nations have their own television broadcast facilities in urban centers, the content may only be seen in the broadcast mode by people in urban areas. Satellite or videocassette distribution may be used to reach the more remote areas.

India is an example of a country that has made efforts to reach its large rural population through a combination of television broadcasting, satellite transmission, microwave relays, and videocassette distribution. Ninety percent of India's population lives in villages where there has traditionally been a low rate of literacy and a high rate of unemployment (Hanson and Narula 1990, 54). Telecommunications, and especially television broadcasting, was determined to be the best way to reach remote villages, and the government established a program of outfitting rural regions with television receivers and power generators so that information could be received.

Since 1982 India has been distributing broadcast messages, created in urban studios and produced in various languages, to regions throughout the country. These transmissions provide information on agriculture, health, nutrition, and education. Occasionally, entertainment programming from other countries is also distributed. In some locations the broadcasts are recorded and played later in schools. In the most remote regions, mobile video vans tour an area, using generators and video equipment so that people in the villages can see the programs.

When people in major urban areas like New Delhi raised questions about how much money was going to the government's rural telecommunication project, the government responded by adding television services in color for urban communities. This action apparently placated some, even though many rural communities remained disadvantaged.

VCRs

The actual number of VCRs available throughout the world is unknown, since in many parts of the world there are few systems in place to monitor sales. In places where consumer electronics are not manufactured inside the country's borders, many products arrive through illegal or unmeasurable means. While VCR manufacturers in most industrialized nations keep relatively reliable statistics on VCR sales and expansion or distribution, LDCs have fewer opportunities to monitor the illegal smuggling or black market exchange of items as small as VCRs.

Many of the VCRs in LDCs are brought in by people who have traveled abroad, like migrant workers, businesspeople, or students who have studied in other countries. Some are disguised and sent through the mail. Most VCRs are either manufactured in industrialized nations or marketed by them, and because goods imported into a country usually bring the government a healthy import tax, many LDCs require that persons bringing VCRs or other consumer electronics into the country pay high duty charges on them. For this reason alone, VCRs are often smuggled into countries illegally.

Computers

Microcomputers are like VCRs in that they are consumer electronics that are often smuggled across international borders to avoid high duty costs. However, many are imported into countries that do not have any indigenously manufactured products for business purposes. IBM has 50 percent of the global market of microcomputers sold for business and personal use (Perspectives 1990). If a country enters into an agreement to purchase microcomputers from any company, compatible software is a part of the package. In this way, the services and systems used, in addition to the hardware, are also influenced by the country that has designed the system, and therefore also act to introduce new protocols (ways of doing things) and ways of thinking.

Controlling the World's Media

In response to and in spite of the inequity in the world's access to communication technology and content, there are many opportunities for extending communication services around the globe. In some cases, there are international agencies with high-minded mandates to extend communication links to other nations. In other cases, the people of the many regions in the world represent potential markets for entrepreneurs to sell products (including media content).

Often the effort to reach new media consumers mixes both altruistic and commercial motives. It is often hard to tell whether extending communication technology and content benefits people or not. In examining the intent and effect of the international agencies discussed in the following section, we will be weighing noble efforts to reach individuals against the real purpose of the agency. While many actions are taken with good intentions, the dynamics of organizational control sometimes restrict international communication, or act as unwitting agents of control of information.

International Agencies

Many administrative bodies have been charged with the responsibility for allocating the world's available resources for broadcasting and telecommunications. Some of them, like the **International Telecommunications Union (ITU)** and its subgroups, were formed to aid manufacturers and governments in standardizing practices and creating a protocol for international cooperation in communication. Others, like the **United Nations Educational, Scientific and Cultural Organization (UNESCO)**, the **Organization for Economic Cooperation and Development (OECD)**, and **International Telecommunications Satellite Consortium (INTELSAT)** were formed for specific purposes by groups with common humanitarian or business goals. Even though some of these groups claim to have an interest in providing communication channels to LDCs, they have not fully answered the needs of many nations.

Each of these groups was created to pursue different aims and goals requiring cooperation in international communication. As we examine them, consider the rationale for each group's existence and the statement that each makes about issues of control, balance of information, and equity in communication.

The International Telecommunications Union (ITU)

The ITU was formed as the International Telegraph Union in 1865, when members convened what was known as the International Telegraph Convention. It is now a specialized agency of the United Nations that coordinates and regulates telecommunication use among all member countries. With 141 member countries, the ITU holds plenipotentiary conferences about once a decade, where an agenda for all the other divisions such as those dealing with the practical issues of global telecommunications—including frequencies, access, and costs—is discussed.

Among the many divisions of the ITU is the International Frequency Registration Board (IFRB). This group of five elected members is responsible for allocating broadcasting frequencies and promoting standardization of equipment and procedures for global telecommunication usage. The IFRB maintains a master registry of all frequencies in use throughout the world and is the agency with primary responsibility for the establishment of frequency equity.

The division of the ITU that usually receives the most press is called the World Administrative Radio Conference (WARC). When this group meets, it has the power to make policy that all nations of the world are supposed to consider when making their own policies about telecommunications, such as satellite placement and technical standards for HDTV.

The most recent WARC took place from February 3 to March 3, 1992, in Spain. At this meeting most of the discussions focused on three issues: adjusting frequency allocations around the world to increase the number of frequencies available for short wave broadcasting, addressing the technical considerations necessary for worldwide digital broadcasting, and examining the compression technologies that will enhance HDTV transmissions and DBS.

UNESCO

The United Nations Educational, Scientific, and Cultural Organization (UNESCO) was established in 1946 to help form partnerships among nations for the enhancement of education, science, and culture in developing nations. Over the years, UNESCO has had several goals for each decade. Among those that involve telecommunications are:

1950–1960:	To serve as a catalyst for the reconstruction of communication facilities and networks destroyed by World War II.
1960–1970:	To develop communication facilities and train personnel in the emerging nations with the aid of UN sources.
1970–1980:	To promote the new communication technologies, particular-ly satellites.
1980–1990:	To help nations and regions develop communication policies and standards and identify long-range goals.
1990–2000:	To stabilize and implement regional and national policies and plans.

INTELSAT

The International Telecommunications Satellite Organization (INTELSAT) was formed in 1964. Its purpose was to regulate and foster international satellite use in the free and nonaligned countries of the world. Today INTELSAT places its emphasis on making satellite transponder space available to countries that cannot pay for its services, and it has a time-sharing procedure with 11 satellites, 224 earth stations, and 125 locations for partial service in 105 countries. Financed by the industrialized nations that contribute to the maintenance of the service, INTELSAT makes time available for voice, telegraph, telex, data, and television transmissions to nations that cannot afford their own satellite services. In this way INTELSAT attempts to create more equity for the poorer nations of the world.

Powerful Manufacturers of Technologies and Systems

While many of the agencies described above provide useful and necessary services for the maintenance and equitable use of communication channels around the world, many other international groups exist with aims and goals that are less altruistic. Many powerful manufacturers have attempted to gain a strong foothold in industrialized nations as well as in the developing world. While it is true that many of these corporations make new technology and services available to developing countries, they exist primarily to earn a profit.

Most of the manufacturing of communication and information technology is done by multinational corporations in industrialized nations, with two of the largest headquartered in the United States. IBM and AT&T have provided the lion's share of communications systems and services to the world, though European and Japanese firms are becoming more aggressive.

In the 1970s, IBM became the largest company in the world, employing more people and generating more profits than any other firm. Not surprisingly, IBM leads the world in the manufacture and sale of computers. The company also maintains a significant share of the market for sales and servicing of other business machines, like copiers and adding machines, and increasingly, services and systems that may include everything from videotex to educational programs for schools.

Since the deregulation of the telephone industry in 1983, AT&T and the seven Regional Operating Companies (ROCs) also began to participate in global communications systems involving telephones, office equipment, and most recently, financial services that include credit and debit cards. AT&T's expertise in creating unified systems of telecommunication that include telephones, fax machines, satellites, minicomputers, and teleconferencing services has given that organization an edge over many others in the wiring of entire telecommunication systems in some countries, like Iran and Saudi Arabia, but the ROCs have been able to compete effectively for smaller markets, like business services or government services.

Other examples of major multinational firms involved in communications and information technology are Siemens (Germany), Thomson Electronics (France), Sony and NHK (Japan), and Philips (Netherlands). The diversity of these organizations is sometimes difficult to comprehend. Many of them manufacture products in other countries, often in **free trade zones (FTZs)** which are areas in LDCs not affected by labor unions, minimum wage laws, and import or export duties. Production costs are lower in FTZs because the multinationals pay less for labor. While there are some companies that operate in good faith with their employees, all too often horror stories about worker exploitation emerge.

In many of the FTZ manufacturing plants workers are treated badly. The maquiladoras, which are foreign-owned assembly plants located in Mexico, mainly in towns along the U.S. border, provide unfortunate examples. Many women working in electronics assembly plants have lost their eyesight because of poor working conditions and the close visual work required by the assembly of tiny electronic components. In connection with other multinational operations, reports of human genetic defects created because workers are forced to use dangerous chemicals with no protection are emerging. The more that is known about the effects of business practices in international operations, the easier it becomes to cast the multinational firm in the role of villain. When all the profits go to industrialized nations, it is easy to see multinationals as organizations that exploit workers in the FTZs.

News Organizations

Since they provide greater knowledge of the events of the world and use satellites to communicate visual information, news organizations that present images from around the globe play an important role in international communications. Though there are roughly 120 news agencies around the world, serving close to 70 nations (Merrill 1983, 15), only a few dominate the flow of news and information to other regions. Most of the world's news is controlled by a few groups that are all based in the industrialized West: Reuters (of Great Britain, but with significant shares owned by Rupert Murdoch), the Associated Press (AP) in the United States, and United Press International (UPI) of the United States, which filed for bankruptcy in 1992. The other major news agency in the world is Agence France-Presse (AFP) of France. Since the Persian Gulf War in 1991, CNN has also risen to the top ranks of the major western news agencies, and Independent Television News (ITN) has provided additional video sources.

In several studies (Adams 1982; Mowlana 1986; Tehranian 1990), researchers have determined that the news gathered and disseminated by these agencies is highly biased in favor of the industrialized nations, and pays very little attention to issues of importance to the LDCs. The LDC frustration with the domination of news that had little relevance to their constituents led to the 1976 creation of the News Agencies Pool of Nonaligned Countries. This group and Interpress, a quasi–public relations firm for Third World development, have been working to develop a different style of journalism more compatible with the aims and goals of the developing nations. The reaction from the West is not surprising. The news from these groups often focuses on the good deals of the leaders of these countries, and on the need for foreign aid. Most editors think of the News Pool and Interpress as tools of the authoritarian regimes they often serve, and therefore carry little if any of the news from these agencies to the industrialized countries. This arguably reflects the low status and nearly invisible image of the LDCs.

International Advertising

Even more controversial than news and telecommunication conglomerates is the presence in LDCs of international advertising agencies from the industrialized nations that seek to cultivate new markets. Because advertising has only one goal—to get people to buy things—advertising in countries where people may be extremely poor, uneducated, and subject to greater pressure from the powerful "mind managers" of advertising raises serious ethical concerns (see box 13.1).

The Media Moguls

Multinationals and advertising companies have been appropriately criticized for their exploitation of people in LDCs because they either pay substandard wages to workers, or encourage people to spend what little money they have on unnecessary items. The "cultivation" of people in LDCs as consumers of foreign products further drains local economies of money that might stay in the country, or be used for more immediate needs, such as improved nutrition, health care, and education. New media markets have also been pursued aggressively by a few media moguls who have taken steps to cultivate potential audiences and sell advertising time.

Murdoch   Rupert Murdoch, the Australian-born media mogul, became an American citizen in 1985 so that he would no longer be subject to restrictions on the number of newspapers and broadcast licenses a foreigner can own in the United States. Murdoch's holdings include print media, such as magazines, books, and newspapers; radio (AM and FM); and television stations (FM, UHF, and cable). He is a shareholder in Reuters, one of the world's largest news services. His controlling ownership in the 20th Century Fox film studio has enabled him to obtain media product for international distribution, and with his ownership of the material produced by the Fox Television network, he has been in the forefront of selling packages of film and television to countries around the world. One of his most ambitious projects has been the European Sky Channel, in which he has a 90 percent interest. The Sky Channel is a satellite service that reaches millions of homes in Britain, Holland, Scandinavia, and Belgium.

Box 13.1   The Top Ten Advertising Agencies in Select Regions of the World

The Top Ten Advertising Agencies in Select Regions of the World
Europe:
1. Publicis FCB
2. Young & Rubicam
3. Saatchi & Saatchi
4. McCann-Erickson Worldwide
5. Backer Spielvogel Bates Worldwide
6. Ogilvy and Mather Worldwide
7. Lintas: Worldwide
8. HDM
9. J. Walter Thompson Co.
10. Grey Advertising

Latin America:
1. McCann-Erickson Worldwide
2. J. Walter Thompson Co.
3. Ogilvy & Mather Worldwide
4. Lintas: Worldwide
5. Duailibi, Petit, Zaragoza
6. Young & Rubicam
7. Leo Burnett Co.
8. Foote, Cone & Belding
9. BBDO Worldwide
10. Saatchi & Saatchi

Asia/Pacific:
1. Dentsu
2. Hakuhodo
3. Dai-Ichi Kikaku
4. Daiko Advertising
5. Asatsu
6. I&S Corp.
7. Backer Spielvogel Bates Worldwide
8. McCann-Erickson Worldwide
9. HDM
10. J. Walter Thompson Co.

Note that many firms operate in several regions.

Source: *Advertising Age.* 11 June 1990, 16.

If there was ever a contemporary individual who fit the character of Citizen Kane, it is Rupert Murdoch. Born in Melbourne, Australia, to a wealthy family, Murdoch inherited his father's business interests in newspapers. The elder Murdoch died in 1952, and Rupert was left to settle his father's debts and manage the remaining newspapers.

Rupert Murdoch then set about building a media empire that extended far beyond newspapers. By 1992 his U.S. holdings included the 20th Century Fox Film Corporation, Fox Broadcasting, the Boston *Herald*, the San Antonio *Express-News*, *New York*, the *Star, New Woman, TV Guide,* major television stations across the country, and book publishers including HarperCollins. In Great Britain, he either owns or has a major interest in the *Times*, the *News of the World*, the *Sun*, Times Books and William & Sons, Amstrad (a satellite dish manufacturer), Reuters, and Pearson P.L.C. He still controls about 60 percent of newspaper circulation and television stations in Australia, and a large share of Ansett, Australia's second largest airline.

Source: Jerome Tuccille, *Rupert Murdoch* (New York: Donald I. Fine, Inc., 1989).

Murdoch's media strategy has been to buy companies or controlling interest in firms that can be **vertically integrated.** This means that one company "feeds" another by producing programs that then can be sold for profit to another firm in the same group that can also make a profit by carrying the program. An example would be his financial interest in 20th Century Fox and Fox Broadcasting, which sell programs to the Sky Channel, which uses satellite dishes made by Amstrad to receive signals.

Murdoch's investment in the Sky Channel was considered by many to be a major attempt to control media distribution for the European Community (EC), but in five years of operation (1983–88), Murdoch lost 102 million dollars (Fisher and Shapiro 1989, J6). The programs distributed included rock videos, a news service (Sky News), talk shows, and serials (with subtitles). But the countries that were in the receiving area of Sky Channel already had programs of this type available through local broadcasts or cable, and were not particularly interested in paying to receive more of the same.

Turner   Ted Turner's involvement in television has been addressed in earlier chapters, but his international activity warrants his inclusion in this chapter. Turner's international interests have taken CNN to 130 different countries around the world. Turner's purchase of 300,000 titles from MGM's film library and the acquisition of half of Hanna Barbera's animated programming have given him a significant amount of entertainment material for international distribution, and his media interests clearly demonstrate the power of vertical integration.

Turner's success in international news has to do with his organization's commitment to using the best technology for international communication, and to hiring individuals with the knowledge to make intelligent contributions to news analysis.

Technologically, the flying satellite link purchased by CNN gave the news organization its first big break by allowing CNN to air the first pictures of the Tiananmen Square conflict in 1989 (Zelizer 1992). The same technology was also used to cover the Persian Gulf War in 1991.

Maxwell   At the time of his death in 1991, Robert Maxwell had already entered the small group of international media moguls with major holdings in print media (primarily newspapers, magazines, and books), and increasing holdings in television, cable, and film.

Maxwell's ownership philosophy was to buy pieces of existing stations in Britain, France, and Spain, which allowed him to control television production and distribution. For a time, he owned the largest interest in MTV-Europe, a

---

Box 13.3   Ted Turner's Media Empire

Though we addressed Ted Turner's business interests in U.S. cable television in a previous chapter, his plans to communicate globally are also an important component of the Turner media empire. Reaching for part of the global market in news and public affairs, Turner's CNN operation now reaches 130 different countries. A second service delivers video news files to news agencies operating in other parts of the world, who then have editors and journalists who are native speakers write the copy and present the images. His news organization also packages news and social issue information for distribution to schools in the United States.

CNN's "World Report" is an international newscast with news and programming from around the world. Participating countries may send any news or information item (on video, if they wish) up to three minutes long for possible inclusion in the program, and CNN agrees to run the stories unedited and uncensored. Contributors then also have the right to use any of the "World Report" material they wish.

Source: Hank Whittemore, *CNN: The inside story* (Boston: Little, Brown & Co., 1990).

Ian Robert Maxwell was born Ludvik Hoch in eastern Czechoslovakia. He once said that one of his earliest ambitions was to own a field and a cow, but at the time of his death in 1991, he was one of the world's major media moguls.

His turbulent youth inspired his quest for power. He joined the Czech underground at the age of 16, and by the end of World War II, he had been commissioned in the field as a British army officer.

Twice he lost everything he owned and rebuilt his empire from the ground up. At the time of his death, Maxwell owned many newspaper, book, and magazine publishing firms, and had major holdings in television, film, cable, and an electronics manufacturer. The Maxwell media empire spanned the globe, but he left an organization that was rife with scandal and intrigue. Upon investigation, it was found that he was heavily in debt, largely due to paying high prices for his acquisitions. His death, ruled by a coroner as "accidental drowning" was investigated and thought by police to have been a murder.

Source: Joe Haines, *Maxwell* (Boston: Houghton Mifflin, 1988).

Box 13.4

Robert

Maxwell

(1923–1991)

movie channel, and magazines that also promoted his holdings, like *Premiere*, which is based in the U.S. and distributed in English-speaking countries worldwide.

Kirch   A mogul less well-known to Americans is Germany's Leo Kirch, who has obtained a large number of German-language media products in print, radio, television, and film for dissemination to German-speaking people around the world.

While Kirch's holdings may seem small by comparison to those of Murdoch, Turner, or Maxwell, his empire is nonetheless significant. His Beta-Taurus Group is a the largest buyer and distributor of German-language programs, and before German unification in 1990, he had control of Germany's largest television network, SAT1. His pay TV channel and a pay-per-view service have been extended to parts of other countries, like Switzerland, where there are also German-speaking people.

Together with Murdoch's and Maxwell's enterprises, and the holdings of Italy's major media mogul, Silvio Berlusconi, Kirch is involved in a consortium to promote European coproductions for the EC and for global distribution.

Box 13.5

Leo Kirch

An independent businessman, Leo Kirch began financing German television programs in the 1970s. His other media interests have involved purchases of German newspapers, magazines, and books. For 20 years he attempted to build a worldwide network of programming in the German language, intended to serve German communities in other nations that might have access to cable or UHF television. Since German unification, Kirch's empire has expanded, and he now controls over 60 percent of Germany's media.

Berlusconi　　In Italy Silvio Berlusconi is known as the powerful mogul behind Italian television. When Italian courts in 1976 overturned the practice of having all television run by the government, Berlusconi established his own stations. They have become so popular that they receive a combined share of 38 percent of the audience, while the government-owned network, RAI, commands 43.5 percent ("Berlesque only" 1989, 80).

Berlusconi has capitalized on his knowledge of and expertise in advertising and he now supports his three Italian stations a full 60 percent through ads. He also controls all the advertising representation for Soviet television in Europe, and commands one-third of the Italian advertising market through his company, Pubitalia.

Berlusconi has become a media mogul to watch because his interests are expanding throughout the European Community. He has purchased shares in television operations in Italy, Spain, France, Germany and the United Kingdom (Carugati 1991). His growing influence is often cited as an example of how power can become concentrated in only a few hands when there are few restrictions on the ownership of media.

While these brief profiles of some of the world's most powerful media barons may give the impression that most of the world's media enterprises are controlled by single individuals, that impression is somewhat misleading. There are a number of major corporations that have rich individuals or families as major stockholders, but there are also powerful corporations with a diverse pool of stockholders that control much of the information flow in the world. In some cases the men we've profiled have some control over the direction of some of these companies, but in general, the major corporations tend to have a large number of stockholders who seem to disappear behind the scenes of daily operation. A few of the most powerful organizations warrant mention.

343

Box 13.6

Silvio

Berlusconi

Silvio Berlusconi's ambition is matched only by his energy. In 1982 he sold his construction business and diversified into areas of media such as television, advertising, and publishing. He quickly became one of the most powerful media moguls in Europe. His acquisition of three television channels in Italy was the result of the Italian government's decision to allow private companies to compete with RAI, the state-run service. But in diversifying his interests so quickly, Berlusconi also raised the ire of Italian politicians, who think he goes too far, too fast.

In 1990 the Italian Senate enacted rules prohibiting the ownership of one television station if the owner has 8 percent or more control of a newspaper publishing enterprise. The Senate also limited the ownership of television stations to two, thereby establishing a rule requiring Berlusconi to divest of some of his publishing interests and one television station.

Berlusconi has effectively managed to circumvent the ruling and has maintained control of all three television stations by selling his newspaper interests. At the same time, the government rulings prevented the Fiat organization from becoming a competitor for Berlusconi's networks. Fiat, with a significant investment in newspapers, found it better to stay in the print media, while Berlusconi's television empire has expanded throughout Europe.

Sources: William Fisher and Mark Shapiro, "Four titans carve up European TV." *The Nation* (Jan. 9–16, 1989): 54; "Berlesque only." *The Economist* (Oct. 14, 1989): 80; and Anna Carugati. "French flop doesn't dim Berlusconi dream." *Advertising Age* (April 27,1991): 118.

Around the world   In other parts of the world, large conglomerates have been established to focus on media product that reflects the cultural values and the major languages of the regions in which they operate. Mexico's Televisa (Spanish) and Brazil's Globo Organization (Portuguese) control most of the distribution of media content in their own languages. Cairo, Egypt is the center for most of the media in the Arabic language. The Hersant organization is the largest publisher of print materials in French, and Springer is the largest publisher of print materials in German.

The control of media content by powerful individuals and organizations reflects how important the business of trading communication content has become. The decisions about what to trade influence what people of the receiving nation know about the producing nation. Exported entertainment and information thus exert subtle influence over the traditional values of the receiving countries. The export of media is synonymous with the export of ways of thinking about the world, and the values exchanged challenge traditional cultures by introducing new viewpoints.

Theories of Development

The many aspects of international communication discussed above, including the power of news agencies to shape what people know, the growing importance of multinational manufacturing firms, and the ethical issues behind the exploitation of markets in LDCs, have been addressed by scholars in the fields of economics, sociology, anthropology, psychology, and of course, communication.

As scholars began to address the possibility of creating programs to change the status of the LDCs, a number of theoretical approaches were investigated. Many of them reflect the values of the eras in which they were articulated.

Before World War II, most LDCs had lost their own identities because the major colonial powers were so firmly entrenched as leaders of government, education, and social life. After World War II, many of the industrial powers found it too expensive to maintain their presence in the LDCs, and they left. Added to this liberation (or abandonment) of the developing nations, improved technologies such as FM radio, television, and the promise of satellite communication attracted attention toward the many parts of the world that had long been forgotten. Transportation technology such as jet planes and improvements in land transport contributed to shrinking the distances between regions. As the industrialized nations sought new markets in which to sell their products, the developing world became more attractive to them. The general attitude was that these nations needed the expertise (and products) of the industrialized world so that they could become industrialized, too. Furthermore, if a nation's capacity to produce goods improved, that nation would then become modernized. This meant that nations would have the resources to begin to deal with their own development issues.

For a long time, the word "development" was synonymous with "modernization." Using technology was considered "progressive," while little concern was given to the importance of maintaining traditions or valuing what people in developing nations already knew.

The developing nations had other concerns besides industrialization. The colonizing countries had set up bureaucracies and social structures in the cities, where they were most likely to profit from the exploitation of the developing country's resources. This exploitation extended to the natives of the urban areas who were often used in subservient roles. In many of the newly freed developing nations, the population was widely distributed throughout the

---

Box 13.7   Defining a Nation's Economic Status

In the 1950s French economists sought a way to describe the exchange of goods among unlike groups of nations. They decided to call the nations that produced goods for their own consumption, but traded them freely on an international basis, the First World. Nations that produced for their own consumption, but kept imports and exports down (such as the former USSR), were classified as the Second World. Countries that had little or nothing to trade and had to rely on other nations for aid were referred to as the Third World.

---

country, and historically they were divided by tribal affiliation, religion, culture, and even language. People in rural areas had no concept of what the "nation" was, or how they belonged to it. In areas like Nigeria, where different tribes, languages, traditions, and values made the concept of one nation impossible for some to accept, a move toward creating a nation was much greater than a political act.

Often, introducing nationalism throughout a region took many years because attitudes had to be changed. The situation was aggravated by the basic problem of getting information out to the people in the farthest districts. The uneven distribution of population in places like Brazil, Somalia, South Africa, and Argentina created obstacles to communication with diverse groups. Even today, there are many parts of the world that have not yet attained status as nations, and others where old antagonisms have made nationhood impossible. Today we even have geographic areas that were arbitrarily declared to be nations, that have since redrawn their political boundaries, like Czechoslovakia and the former Yugoslavia.

As many new nations began to take shape in the 1950s, the dominant theory to explain the pattern of change was called *culture lag*. Originally proposed by William Ogburn in 1927 as an explanation of why societies experience uneven change as new technologies became available, the concept of culture lag became a means of examining how people in urban areas (the elites) of developing nations would always have more, while the people in rural areas (the masses) would have less. Later this theory encompassed the idea of the *diffusion of innovations,* which charted the adaptation and eventual saturation of a technology, practice, or idea in a society by tracking how it moved from elites and "opinion leaders" to the masses.

At one time the United Nations had proposed a program to measure a country's development by counting the number of telephones, movie theaters, radios, and postal facilities that were available to inhabitants. The idea was that a nation's ability to communicate internally would advance the spread of nationalism and support ideas of modernization. It didn't take long for policy-makers to realize that this was a very inefficient means of measuring development, because the number of pieces of technology did not necessarily reflect how (if at all) they were used.

Even attempts to increase literacy in developing nations were once seen as a possible solution to lifting people from their "ignorance." (To those in the Western industrialized nations, if a people did not know about modern technology and the customs that go with it, they were ignorant. Westerners made no allowance for knowledge of one's own culture and society.) Communication scholars Wilbur Schramm and William L. Ruggles (1967) proposed the following chain of development:

1. The literacy rate would begin to rise significantly after 10 percent of a country's population had been urbanized.
2. Thereafter, urbanization and literacy would increase together in a direct relationship until they reached 25 percent.
3. Once societies were about 25% urbanized, literate people would have a higher media consumption than those who were not urban or literate.

Rates of literacy may have no impact on the use of electronic communication technologies available today (with the exception of the computer). The old model of moving from a "first wave" society to a "second wave" society in a linear progression is not always an accurate description of life in today's world, as was discussed in Chapter 1.

The modernization thesis, called for many years "the dominant paradigm," was finally put to rest by Everett Rogers, who wrote "The Passing of the Dominant Paradigm" in 1976. Rogers and his contemporaries articulated a new approach that focused on a developing nation's social structure, the involvement of both indigenous people and people from the industrialized world in its progress, and the complex balance (or imbalance) of the world's natural and technological resources. These factors determine what the nation's most pressing needs are.

Today, instead of looking at the exact amount of technology available in a country, a better measure of development is how programs and technology that are relevant to the people have been introduced. While the inequality of technical resources still indicates communication potential, decisions about aid are often made by considering which technologies and programs help fulfill the basic needs of remote populations. For example, villagers in a remote area of a nation might have significant difficulty reaching a doctor or a nurse in a medical emergency. One reliable telephone that could reach the appropriate personnel could make the difference in a life or death situation.

Other problems in developing nations involve even more basic issues, such as supplying electrical or battery power to run technology, and the expertise to maintain it. When computers are used, air conditioning sometimes has to be made available or the circuits will overheat and melt. These practical problems, along with the cultural and ethical ones discussed later in this chapter, give some idea of the problems involved in creating a true "global village."

The Technologies of International Communication

The most important technologies for international communication are not just the large-scale ones like satellites, broadcast operations, telephony, and computers, though each of these and the switching systems that make them work are necessary. Smaller technologies are even more important and have a greater impact on people within regions. While both large and small technologies have made an impact internationally, three phenomena that are often neglected—ethnotronic technology, clandestine systems, and external radio—are also vital.

Ethnotronics

Small portable communication technologies that are not linked to massive infrastructures, and that can be used by individuals have been called ethnotronic technologies (Joseph and Harkins 1982). These technologies include things like audiocassette recorders, televisions, VCRs, and home computers. Each has the ability to shift time. Ethnotronic technologies, then, can be used at the pleasure of individuals in the privacy of their own homes. They are not forms of mass media, but they are used as forms of informal communication, information, and entertainment. Many ethnotronic technologies are run by batteries and are truly portable. The smallness of the unit means that it can usually be used in private (see also Chapter 1).

Ethnotronic technologies present new options for users, but they also create potential problems in their distribution. Both video- and audiocassettes can be easily duplicated with no payments made to the creators, and the information can change hands many times. This has led to international distribution of pirated cassette material in both audio and video. Singapore and Cairo are two centers that have traditionally led their regions in duplicating illicit tapes and distributing them on the black market. When these are sold, the profit goes to the pirates who made them. In addition to the legal problems posed by the ease of duplication of materials, ethnotronic technologies and their software can also be easily smuggled from one nation to another. It is not difficult to smuggle a portable radio or portable audiocassette player past ordinary border controls. Videocassette recorders, televisions, and home computers are somewhat more difficult to smuggle because they are larger and more obvious. But these too can be smuggled by visitors promising that they are personal materials that will be taken out of the country again or that they are gifts for family members and thus, exempt from the high tariffs that many nations place on these technologies.

Another potential problem is the circulation of audio- and videotapes that are either not approved by mainstream society or not authorized by governments. Whether this would be truly a problem depends on the individual's viewpoint.

The portable feature of ethnotronic technology is critical to understanding the potential impact of these pieces of hardware and software. From 1965 to 1979, the late Ayatollah Khomeini of Iran was in exile, first in Iraq, then in Paris. Throughout his exile he maintained contact with his followers in Iran through telephone calls that were audiotaped and distributed informally. When he was admitted back into his country and assumed power, he did so with a history of involvement with his people, even though he had not been present in the country for many years (Ganley and Ganley 1987).

Once these technologies and software make their way into a country it is very difficult for a government to control the flow of content. For example, in Saudi Arabia any type of pornography is considered a violation of Islamic law. The Saudi definition of pornography is very strict by Western standards. Content that suggests kissing or caressing, shows women in scanty clothing, or involves alcohol or drug use may be considered pornographic. But videocassettes containing this kind of material have been smuggled into Saudi Arabia through entry points in Cairo or through other means. The content violates the primary religious law of Saudi Arabia and brings with it new values and principles. Over a period of time, could this type of content change the fundamental Muslim laws, even though they have been practiced for centuries?

Clandestine Systems

Broadcasting is by its very nature an international form because its signals do not stop at geographical borders. A number of factors influence the range of broadcast signals. Signals sent intentionally, unintentionally, or because of occasional electrical charges from the sun occasionally transmit information outside of the usual broadcast patterns.

Clandestine systems are illegally operated facilities established in violation of government regulation. Radio provides the most economical outlet for clandestine activity, and its source is the hardest to track down. Television has on occasion been operated in a clandestine manner, but the expense and problems of using a portable transmission facility make this harder to accomplish.

Most clandestine radio is operated to send specific messages to a particular audience. The messages are often political or religious. Clandestine radio may be broadcast from ships in international waters; it can be broadcast from a mobile facility, like a van, or even a set location, like a building, although authorities can locate stationary operations and close them more easily than mobile ones.

External Radio

Not all broadcasts of political messages are clandestine. More than 45 countries maintain radio broadcast facilities that send political messages to other parts of the world that act as propaganda (see box 13.8). Often using short wave for the distribution of signals, external systems (intended for transmission of content beyond the borders of the sponsoring country) are usually funded by governments or religious groups.

External radio was created because national governments sometimes want to send news and information to people in a different country. The news and information often has a political or ideological bias, but this is not always the case.

As mentioned earlier, the BBC's external service (called the BBC World Service) provides a fairly neutral version of the news to many countries around the world. The BBC also has an English language teaching service that is broadcast to Europe, Africa, the Commonwealth of Independent States, the Near East, Asia, and South America.

 # Cultural and Ethical Challenges for International Communications

As already shown, the LDCs are at a distinct disadvantage in global communication because they lack technology or money to purchase or develop local production, and sometimes, they lack the ability to use these forms of communication for purposes that are relevant to lives of the inhabitants. The information and even the technology that does make its way to the LDCs is often culturally and ideologically biased in favor of the philosophies, policies, and politics of the industrialized world. At times these philosophies and the practices they entail are at odds with conditions in the receiving country. When this happens, the receiving nation experiences a challenge to maintain its values and exercise its right to autonomy. The issues raised here are often referred to as the North-

Box 13.8   A Sample of External Services

Country	Number of languages	Target Regions
Albania	8	Europe, Middle East, Africa, N. America, and S. America
Austria	5	N. America, S. America, C. America, Europe, Middle East, and Pacific
Belarus (Belorussia)	2	Europe, N. America
Bosnia/Herzegovina	2	Serbia, Croatia
France	11	Africa, Middle East, Europe, S. America, N. America, C. America, Vietnam
Germany	29	Africa, Middle East, Europe, S. America, N. America, C. America, S.E. Europe
Monaco	27	Europe, Russia, E. Europe, N. Africa
Poland	8	Europe, E. Europe, N. America, Russia
Russia	43	Asia, Europe, Middle East, Africa, N., S., & C. America
United Kingdom	36	Europe, E. Europe, Africa, Russia, Asia, SE Asia N., S., & C. America, Middle East
United States	43	Europe, E. Europe, Russia, Cuba, Africa, C. & S. America, Canada, Asia Pacific

Source: *World radio TV handbook, Vol 47* (Amsterdam: Billboard Books, 1983).

South debate, since the industrialized countries are primarily in the northern hemisphere, and LDCs in the south. The clash of philosophy or ideology presents an ethical dilemma too. Whose rights take precedence? Do the rich, powerful countries have the right to force certain technologies or content on their poorer neighbors? The answer from the LDCs is an emphatic "No!"

The Call for a New World Information Order

In 1978, UNESCO adopted a document called the *Declaration on Fundamental Principles Concerning the Contribution of the Mass Media to Strengthening Peace and International Understanding, to the Promotion of Human Rights and to Countering Racialism, Apartheid, and Incitement to War.* As Nordenstreng, (1984, xi–xii) wrote; "Professionally, it was a reminder of the fact that journalism and mass communication, however ideological in nature, has a common ground of universal values on which an international code of ethics can be constructed." What led to the acceptance of the Declaration was a 30-year prelude involving the resistance of the Third World to the media domination of their countries by the industrialized West.[1]

For years, people in the Third World had bemoaned the overwhelming media domination forced on them, particularly in the areas of news and information. Claiming they had the right to **cultural sovereignty,** that is, the right to decide what content they wished to receive in order to protect their own cultures, they called for a **New World Information Order (NWIO)** which would force international media distributors to consider a "balanced flow" of information, rather than what the West, and in particular the United States, called the "free flow." The U.S. position on free flow had to do with its desire to keep channels open for U.S. media product. As a capitalist incentive, "free flow" suggested that reciprocity was welcomed, but the people of the Third World knew that it meant a policy of one-way flow of news and information, particularly from the United States to the Third World.

In summarizing the need for an NWIO, the Tunisian diplomat Mustapha Masmoudi outlined grievances that would need to be redressed:

1. A flagrant quantitative imbalance existed in the flow of information between [the countries of] the North and South.
2. An inequality in information resources existed between the two regions.
3. [The North had created] *de facto* hegemony and a will to dominate.
4. [There was] a lack of information on developing countries.
5. The colonial era was not dead.
6. The North exerted an alienating influence in the economic, social, and cultural spheres of the South.
7. Messages [were] ill-suited to the areas in which they were disseminated. (Masmoudi 1979)

Additionally, the NWIO would include a new legal structure to address several issues. One was the establishment and maintenance of a system that would

---

[1] *The term "Third World" is used in this context because it was the most commonly used descriptor at the time the Declaration was drafted and accepted.*

guarantee the people of the Third World the right to know what information is held about them and the right to quick redress of improper or inaccurate information. Another was the more equitable distribution of communication technologies, especially in the area of satellites. Copyright protection needed to be more equitable. The NWIO also called for more rigorous training and standards for journalists.

As the discussion on a greater presence of information technology in the LDCs indicates, technologies that are developed, manufactured, and controlled by Western industrialized nations clearly conflict with some of the traditions, beliefs, or government desires for people in developing nations.

The *Mass Media Declaration* mentioned at the beginning of this section and the NWIO received a significant amount of attention for several years, primarily between 1976 and the mid-1980s, mainly because the United Nations kept it at the top of its agendas for change. But the two issues caused a tremendous amount of divisiveness, and contributed to the United States' withdrawal from UNESCO in 1988.

There are other countries in the world where "balanced flow" is a far more accepted concept than in the United States, but American journalists have almost forgotten the activities and passion that brought the world's imbalance in news and information to the forefront of the public's consciousness not many years ago.

Today, privatization and other changes in global politics among nations of the First World and Second World seem to embrace the capitalist philosophy and free market principles. While the LDCs still battle for greater visibility and some basic rights agreed to in the *Mass Media Declaration*, many industrialized nations (especially the United States) have abandoned these principles and agreements.

Problems Between Countries of the East and West

While the United States had many reasons for leaving UNESCO, it claimed a right to "free flow" of information was the primary reason for leaving. Political changes in Europe and the former Soviet Union have further changed the nature of news and media flow. The earlier arguments about free or balanced flow have now become nothing more than a prologue to today's information environment.

With the European Community now providing a larger market for media products, and Russia more open to exchange with the West, the issues of cultural sovereignty and propaganda have been reshaped. There is evidence to indicate that the nations of the East and West may indeed be forging a type of global village, with open sharing of information and the presence of news people more readily accepted than in the past.

Problems Between Countries of the North and South

But the problems between the industrialized nations, often referred to as the nations of the North (including Russia) and their interaction with the LDCs, often referred to as the nations of the South, seem to reveal even greater imbalances.

The African nations lag behind the other nations of the South at this point. Policies that have reflected the old "modernization" theory of development and a lack of monetary and technical aid have kept many African nations from resolving the complex problems of development.

In Latin America political instability has exacerbated the difficulty of creating cooperative programs between technology suppliers and the governments that seek to develop their own programs for development, including those that rely on industrial policy.

The region of the world most subject to change at this point is Southeast Asia, represented by the Association for South Eastern Asian Nations (ASEAN). The many countries that make up this region, which includes the Pacific Rim, have focused indigenous production talents not only on manufacturing electronic products but also on marketing through Free Trade Zones (FTZs).

As the experiences of different regions of the world show, many less-developed nations have little control over the influence of industrialized nations and media moguls when it comes to determining what technology and content will be available to them.

Dumping

As information technology becomes more expensive to develop and cheaper to manufacture, multinational firms have consciously or inadvertently forced certain technologies into LDCs, and have been sharply criticized for this practice. Often this occurs as **dumping,** which takes place when obsolete technologies can no longer be marketed in the richer countries, and are then sold inexpensively to LDCs. Since dumping usually brings substandard or discontinued products to the LDCs, the countries find themselves chasing compatible equipment to keep their systems operating. When the United States embraced the VHS videocassette recorder, Japan found a willing market in Mexico and dumped all Beta technology there.

Privacy

One of the greatest problems for a nation today is the threat to its privacy from communication satellites and international computer data bases. To address this issue, the **Organization for Economic Cooperation and Development (OECD),** an organization of 180 countries, has established basic principles and developed the following guidelines for businesses and governmental bodies:

1. Each organization gathering data and each country should limit the collection of personal data about the inhabitants of that nation.
2. Personal data must be accurate and up-to-date.
3. The purpose of collecting personal data should be limited.
4. There should be safeguards against unauthorized access to this data.
5. Nations should be open about their developments, practices, and policies with respect to data about individuals.
6. Individuals should be able to see and challenge information that pertains to them.

Remote sensing   Satellites have the capacity to send vital information back to the country controlling the satellite's transmissions. So-called "spy" satellites are equipped with infrared sensors that can detect the presence of natural resources in LDCs, sometimes before the governments of the LDCs know what they have themselves. The industrialized country may then make some very attractive offers to the LDC for mineral extraction. Before the LDC understands what resources it has, it can be exploited by countries with more thorough information.

Remote sensing also reveals information about the presence of technologies and high-risk or restricted substances. Remote images were used to search for nuclear technologies in Iraq, and have monitored land conditions resulting from the Chernobyl nuclear accident. Remote sensing has been used to measure the amount of pollution in Antarctica resulting from the exploitation of the region's natural resources by a number of countries conducting research there.

Information as a National Resource

Despite the imbalances between rich and poor countries in information technology and content, humanitarian organizations continue to work for ethical guidelines. For more than 40 years, the United Nations' *Declaration of Human Rights* has decreed that all people of the world have the right to privacy, security, and information. This last part means that people have a right to know about events and developments that may affect their lives.

Information is vital to the lives of people in LDCs today, just as it is for those of us who live in the industrialized nations. Information is critical for connection to others, and for providing assistance. It can also be used as a tool for power and political control. The need for principles that work is apparent. We also need leaders who are willing to develop and adhere to the principles! Decisions can no longer support the profit motive at the expense of the individuals involved.

CONCLUSION

Though some international agencies exist to regulate broadcast frequencies and make resources available to countries that can't afford their own communication services, the world remains a place where the technological capacity for communication is unequal. Images of a world in which the integrity of every culture is maintained stand in contrast to market philosophies that seek to develop various regions for the sale of communication technology and content.

While all forms of communication present problems for international understanding, broadcasting presents an inordinate amount because it is global in nature. Broadcast signals have the power to cross political and geographic barriers, and present new ideas. As a result, broadcasting is a powerful means of controlling the extent and the nature of what people know. It is a powerful agent in spreading new ideas.

Sometimes we need to take a break from thinking about large-scale issues of international communication to remember that in many countries there are far more basic needs than the ability to communicate beyond an individual village. Problems of hunger, disease, and pollution are far more important than a controversy over whether or not an African village gets to see reruns of "Laverne and Shirley." The basic needs of individuals must take precedence over the desire of an industrialized nation to sell technologies, systems, and services.

Power, including the power conferred by information, is both beneficent and dangerous, depending on how it is used. Despite the efforts of international agencies to create equity among nations in communication capability, this condition has not been reached. We need to consider how wide the range of information control reaches, and ask basic questions about ethical behavior when communication and politics intersect.

If the world's people are to have a future in which caring for others is part of everyday life, the many issues surrounding international communication must be addressed. As the world becomes an "information society," the nature of these issues must become clear and inspire an agenda for action.

SUMMARY

This chapter has addressed a range of issues concerning the global communication environment. These issues include:

- unequal numbers of technologies and types of technologies exist in regions around the world
- the agencies charged with creating information equality have had mixed success in meeting their objectives
- multinational corporations that operate from a profit motive sometimes violate the rights, needs, and values of other countries
- the ethics behind information equity and control are issues for consideration by nations, businesses, and individuals
- the diversity that characterizes the world is a problem that may be partially overcome by more equitable and conscientious use of communication technologies

DISCUSSION QUESTIONS

1. Discuss the many possible meanings of "global village." How does this powerful metaphor shape the way people think about the future?
2. Discuss whether it is possible today for a country to maintain its sense of history and cultural values in a world where change is constantly being introduced through new communication technology and content.
3. Can international agencies be charged with maintaining the rights of individuals to complete, unbiased information? What political, philosophical, and pragmatic problems must you consider to address this issue?
4. When should the rights of nations or individuals override the interests of business? When should business interests override the rights of nations or individuals?
5. How might a "New World Order" seek to make connections among economic forces, business practices, and cultural values?

6. Pretend you are an alien from another planet planning on coming to the United States. Your only information about the country comes from monitoring radio and television broadcasts. What impressions do you form of the culture? In what ways might people from other countries form their ideas of life in the United States?

7. Under what circumstances do you think a nation should restrict the flow of media content to its population? Can such restrictions be used to protect cultural sovereignty and defend the country against remote sensing and other violations of privacy by advanced communication technologies?

REFERENCES

Adams, William C. ed. 1982. *Television coverage of international affairs*. Norwood, New Jersey: Ablex.

Berlesque only. 1989. *The Economist* (Oct. 14).

Carugati, Anna. 1991. French flop doesn't dim Berlusconi dream. *Advertising Age,* April 27.

Euromonitor Publications Ltd. 1987/88. *International marketing data and statistics*. Oxford: University Printing House.

Fisher, William, and Shapiro, Mark. 1989. Four titans carve up European TV. *The Nation* 248 (Jan. 9–16): 1, 54.

Ganley, Gladys D. and Ganley, Oswald H. 1987. *Global political fallout: The first decade of the VCR, 1976–1985*. Cambridge, Mass.: Harvard Program on Information Resources Policy.

Haines, Joe. 1988. *Maxwell*. Boston: Houghton Mifflin Co.

Hanson, Jarice, and Narula, Uma. 1990. *New communication technologies in developing countries*. Hillsdale, N.J.: Lawrence Erlbaum Associates.

Joseph, Earl C. and Harkins, Arthur M. 1982. The emergence of ethnotronic systems in the 1980s. In *Through the '80s,* ed. F. Feather. Washington, D.C.: World Future Society, 308–11.

Masmoudi, Mustapha. 1979. The new world information order. *Journal of Communication* 29: 172–98.

Merrill, John. 1983. *Global journalism*. New York: Longman, 15.

Miller, Jonathan. 1986. The global picture. *Channels 1986 Field Guide,* 16–17.

Mowlana, Hamid. 1986. *Global information and world communication*. New York: Longman.

Nordenstreng, Kaarle. 1984. *The mass media declaration of UNESCO.* Norwood, N.J.: Ablex.

Perspectives on computing. 1990. IBM Annual Review.

Pouschine, Tatiana. 1988. I, Berlusconi. *Forbes* (January 25): 59–60.

Rogers, Everett M. 1976. The passing of the dominant paradigm. In *Communication and development: Critical perspectives,* ed. E. M. Rogers. Beverly Hills, Calif.: Sage, 121–48.

Schramm, Wilbur and Ruggles, William L. 1967. How mass media systems grow. In *Communication and change in developing countries,* ed. D. Lerner & W. Schramm. Honolulu: East-West Center Press, 57–75.

Tehranian, Majid. 1990. *Technologies of power.* Norwood, N.J.: Ablex.

Tuccille, Jerome. 1989. *Rupert Murdoch.* New York: Donald I. Fine, Inc.

Tunstall, Jeremy. 1986. *The media are American.* New York: Columbia University Press.

UNESCO. 1987. *Statistical yearbook.* Paris.

U.S. Bureau of the Census. 1991. *Statistical abstract of the United States: 1991.* 111th ed. Washington, D.C.

Vizer, Eduardo. Personal conversation with the author. Buenos Aires, Argentina, Sept. 1987.

Whittemore, Hank. 1990. *CNN: The inside story.* Boston: Little, Brown, & Co.

World radio TV handbook, Vol. 47. 1993. Amsterdam: Billboard Books.

Zelizer, Barbie. 1992. CNN, the Gulf War and journalistic practice. *Journal of Communication* 42 (1): 66–81.

Fourteen

THE INFORMATION SOCIETY

Making Connections

The communication technologies discussed throughout this book and the connections they have to social, economic, and political issues present a new world to us: it is often called the information society. In this new social configuration traditional power structures are shaken and different social dynamics begin to shape the way people think about values, ideas, and information.

This chapter summarizes many of the ideas presented throughout the book in order to strengthen the concept that the seemingly disparate parts of our world are connected through both tangible and intangible means. The reality of an information society creates bridges between past practices and new ways of doing things. The connections include:

- past, present, and future visions of what the information society is, and what life in an information society is or will be like

- an understanding of how social and economic changes present new opportunities to some people, but restrict others from access to those opportunities

- how changes within specific contexts lead, reinforce, or sometimes lag behind social change, creating conflicting images of the future

- how the convergence of technologies has blurred the separation of information and entertainment, shaping our expectations of what technology can do and how we use it

- how new communication environments challenge social organization

- a future scenario in which we increasingly rely on information and communication technologies for personal communication as well as for national and international information exchange

---

Understanding what is meant when people say we live in an information age goes beyond simple analyses of the technology, industries, politics, and economics surrounding the phenomenon. Terms like the "information society" describe the social and economic climate of the world in which we live. In a society where the primary economic activity is changing from producing goods to producing information, we are entering a world where most of the results of work are intangible. As we consider what an information society means, we need to be mindful of the fact that as we use more information technology and more information becomes available, our traditional values will also undergo change. New ideas, values, attitudes, and beliefs will begin to take shape.

In creating a vision of the future, we can look to the historical precedents that have led to the development of our present world. We can also make attempts to predict the outcome of social and cultural change based on the examples and the issues raised throughout this book. These connections will help us understand how the past has contributed to the present and to the future. This chapter is the conclusion of this book, but the beginning of future work in the area of understanding the world in which we live.

Defining the Information Society

Although the term "information society" is used extensively in today's world, there are several interpretations of what it means. It would be true to say that every society in history has been based on information. Prehistoric humans needed information for survival. Information about kinship, social groups, and social maintenance contributed to the formation of groups, tribes, and societies. But the term *information* has taken on new meaning today as technology becomes a more important element of communication. As a result, the information society is one in which communication technology plays a very important role, and this fact sometimes leads people to believe that the human's role in information processing is relegated to the background.

The definitions of what constitutes information reflect the biases of the people defining it. One group thinks of information as a commodity to be bought or sold, while another sees information as a term synonymous with *knowledge*. The first interpretation sees the growth in information technologies and their uses as an extension of the industrial revolution, in that processing information is similar to the manufacturing of goods. The latter interpretation sees information as a mental construct. It suggests that information technology is only a tool that extends the human capacity for access to useful information, that when applied, becomes an agent of power.

As these definitions become further refined, we can understand how the two approaches attempt to classify different perceptions of information. A few examples follow, but these are not all-inclusive.

1. <u>Information as a product or commodity.</u> The definition assumes that information is (*a*) *a measurable quantity*. It includes the interpretations of information held by people who work as data processors and electrical engineers. It is also the definition used by telephone companies, which charge for information by the amount of time spent in conversation, using electronic mail, or when on-line data bases or videotex services are accessed. This definition emphasizes the fact that information is something that can be controlled. This definition also assumes that (*b*) *information technology has the capacity to equalize information resources*. Because this definition sees information as measurable, technologies are viewed as tools to measure information exchange. As tools, they act as facilitators of information and are considered politically neutral. In this interpretation, information technology is viewed as a possible equalizer among the people of a society and people of the world. There are many people who feel that the best way to be competitive in today's world is to have the most up-to-date technology. This was the approach taken by the United Nations in the 1950s when more technology was viewed as the path to greater development. It was assumed that the reason LDCs were less "developed" than the industrialized nations was that they had little access to the most up-to-date technologies. The real problem behind the definition of information as a commodity is that the mere availability of technology does not necessarily mean it will be used, used fully, or in ways that are compatible with other practices in a given culture. This definition equates "having" with "using" technology, and

363

disregards problems of technology transfer or interference with an established culture.

2. <u>Information is equal to knowledge.</u> Because this approach sees technological information processing as an extension of the human capacity to process information, there is an assumption that the capacity of the human brain can be "extended" by technologies that have better control over these functions than the human body. For example, the electronic memory of a computer can be seen as an extension of the human brain's capacity to remember. The control of information is less important than the application. This interpretation gives the concept of information a more humane character than the information-as-commodity definition.

It also endows information processing technology with human characteristics, such as **information overload.** This may occur when more information is being processed than can be used. As a result, the system may shut down. We see this happen when telephone circuits become congested by more calls than can be accommodated by the lines. The overload causes the system to break down. This situation is similar to what happens to human beings presented with far too much information for them to grasp. The result is often a shutdown of the mental processes, and the mind goes blank. Information technology defined as "knowledge processors" considers the utility of the action of seeking information.

There is often an assumption that the capacity of any one system to store and retrieve information is infinite. When a person accesses information from any on-line data base or information service, he or she is often provided with brief references from a longer story. Some students believe that on-line services provide listings of all the information available, but in reality, they only give a reference to what has been stored in that data bank. You need to search several files, and even then, you may not get all the references you need if you don't use the right key words. In summary, the amazing capabilities of much information processing technology can easily lead people to think that it is all-powerful and can control what is known about virtually anything. But the reality is that information technology can tell us only what has been programmed into its system, and this depends on the skill of the individual retrieving it.

The Media's Image of the Information Society

Many of our images of the information society come to us through media portrayals that suggest what the future will be like. For years, science fiction stories have predicted a future more reliant on information technology and control. Some of those images have been distinctly utopian, portraying technology as a savior of the future, while others have been dystopian, predicting a future where humans no longer control technology, but technology controls them.

Science fiction often presents technology in a human form, such as the human-like machines in the movies *The Terminator* and *Robocop*.

Part of the appeal of science fiction is its similarity to real advances in science and technology. As we look around our world, we see evidence of authen-

Box 14.1   When Science Fiction Becomes Reality

There have been times when real scientific innovations became known to the public through entertainment media. In the television shows "The Six Million Dollar Man" and "The Bionic Woman," viewers were introduced to bionics, which appeared to be creations of fiction. In reality however, the term *bionics* means the application of biological principles to the design of electrical systems. Real bionic devices have been used for years to replace parts of the human body through prosthesis.

There are two general forms of bionics. The first type is that which was portrayed in the two television programs mentioned above. In each program, the main character has lost some of his or her own physical abilities and has been outfitted with bionic devices that make them superhuman by enhancing senses of sight or touch, or by improving their muscle tissue for greater stamina. Bionics can be used when there is no living muscle or tissue to connect a prosthetic device to the body. A bionic device is a technology (usually controlled electronically or by computer) that can provide accident victims, or those handicapped from birth, with an extra advantage. Some examples of bionics include new hearing devices for the deaf that register vibrations to other senses, motion sensing devices for the blind that transfer vibrations to the hands to signal oncoming traffic or present danger, and electronically controlled walking devices for people who have lost the use of their legs.

More commonly used devices that have also been developed through the efforts of scientists who study bionics are telepresence devices. The term suggests technologies that extend human capacities in a very practical way. Examples of these are pacemakers, artificial hearts, and electronic prosthetics like hands and arms that do connect to the body's nervous system through living muscle, nerve, or tissue.

Sometimes fiction suggests ideas that find their way to reality. The popular television series "Star Trek" introduced a medical application involving a grid with a body superimposed over it. When a crew member was injured, the ship's doctor analyzed what the problem was by isolating the correct section of the grid. When astronauts on the space shuttle venture into outer space, they use medical grids copied from "Star Trek."

Figure 14.1 *Is This Science Fiction or Reality?*
Apollo 11 Commander Neil Armstrong walks on the moon.
Picture Source: Courtesy of NASA

tic scientific achievements that equal or sometimes surpass fictional images of technological breakthroughs. Test tube babies, artificial hearts, satellites, space shuttles, speech synthesizers, robots, and lasers are all real scientific achievements that were predicted in literature, theater, film, or television. But each of the media presentations did more than just introduce new concepts. They packaged these innovations in a narrative structure that expressed the author's interpretation of what the future will be like.

Today, we have many of these fictional images in our minds when we hear about the real advances in technology, and they influence whether we think of technological innovation as good, bad, neutral, or perhaps some of each.

Our real-life images of the information age may not be as exciting as the scenarios put forth by the media, but many of our concepts about the present and future reflect and reinforce interpretations we've seen in fictional forms.

Social and Economic Issues in the Information Society

As we examine increased utilization of technology for communication purposes in diverse contexts, we can see how the capacity for introducing something new to society has the potential to change our habits, traditions, and values. The history of technological innovation provides a background through which we can imagine what our futures hold in each of the cases discussed below. As we look at the use of technology in the following contexts, you will see how communication technology holds the potential for introducing some radically different practices to society.

Teledemocracy

A significant change for the future is the introduction of **teledemocracy**—using electronic media to register votes or opinions. Interactive services that link computers through cable or phone lines are the most common forms of registering people's reactions, but teledemocracy also encompasses formats such as televised call-in programs, mail ballots, interactive services through cable or computer systems, teleconferencing, and electronic mail.

The Qube System was one of the first to explore a primitive form of interactive teledemocracy. As discussed in an earlier chapter, Qube allowed community voters to register their reactions to an issue or cast a vote in a very limited form by pushing a button. Each response was electronically and instantaneously tabulated at a central location.

The topic of teledemocracy has been given more attention in recent years by writers who have both good and bad things to say about the practice of changing our democratic system by more reliance on electronic means of communication. Keane (1991) asks whether new technologies have destroyed, through censorship, traditional values of freedom and the concept of freedom of the press. Arterton (1987) approaches the problem by looking at how the increased number of technologies may increase the number of participants in the democratic process by providing greater access to a variety of people to voice their concerns. Both Jamieson (1988) and Altheide and Snow (1991) have written about how communication technology is changing the democratic tradition through political candidates' manipulation of the media. Perhaps a concern that all of these authors share is one articulated by Toffler (1990), who writes that as our society changes from a manufacturing-based economy to a new "knowledge-based economy . . . we should expect a historic struggle to remake our political institutions, bringing them into congruence with the revolutionary post-mass-production economy (239)."

We actually don't know yet whether teledemocracy could change our traditional democratic procedures, but we can certainly recognize that the potential for change is very great. To better focus on how teledemocracy could institute change, we can draw from an example by Arterton (1987, 82-88).

In the 1970s, Project MINERVA was carried out in New York City. MINERVA was used to explore how groups of citizens too large to attend town meetings could be reached. Two housing complexes, containing 1300, and 2300 apartments respectively, were the focus of the study. In each of the complexes, telephone lines and television were adapted to allow participants to become involved in discussions from their own apartments; radio was also used.

At one complex residents were allowed to hear a panel of individuals speaking over the radio, and at the other, over cable television. If the residents had something to say, they could go to the studio located in their building and air their views. After residents had heard the panel and the opinions of other residents, a system called Telepoller allowed them to "vote" for various options using their telephones.

The results of Project MINERVA indicate that most residents in both complexes preferred the electronic meetings to traditional face-to-face ones. As a result, the project directors were able to assume that MINERVA was successful in showing that people reacted favorably to the new opportunity to voice their

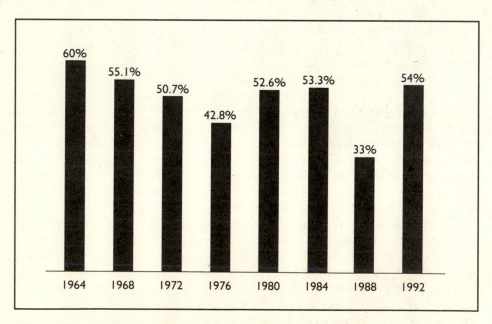

Figure 14.2 *Percentage of Population Voting in Presidential Elections.*
Sources: America Votes *(for 1960–1988); Committee for the Study of the American Electorate (for 1992); Rpt. in "Election Special,"* Time, *Nov. 16, 1992, 18–19.*

opinions, and that they were more likely to take a position when they had greater opportunity to debate the issues among themselves. Other questions were not answered by the study, however, such as how often residents continued to discuss issues among themselves, whether anything was done about the problems discussed, or even whether this system would gain or lose users if used more often over time. As an early experiment, it provided important information on citizen involvement, but lacked continuity.

Could teledemocracy on a broader scale be practical? The number of voters in presidential elections decreased between 1960 and 1988. In the 1992 election, there was a resurgence of voter interest, which political commentators have attributed to both the importance of economic issues to the country in 1992, and the interest generated by the appearance of a serious third candidate, Ross Perot. If teledemocracy were widely implemented, would more people exercise their option to vote?

Figure 14.3 *Bill Clinton on the "Arsenio Hall Show" During the 1992 Presidential Campaign.*
Photo Source: AP/Wide World Photos

There have been many attempts to explore whether teledemocracy would increase the number of people voting, and under what conditions it might be practical. At present there are success stories and reports of failure, but as communication technology becomes more pervasive we may see refinement of many experimental methods and some significant changes to our current practices. It would be interesting to be able to examine who would be most likely to use electronic voting from the home. The ease of electronic voting might increase the number of votes from people who have difficulty getting out of the house such as the elderly and parents of young children. Certainly some of the problems would involve unauthorized access by voters, control of voter eligibility, and monitoring to ensure that each person gets only one vote.

Despite these problems, teledemocracy could alter the way in which people in the United States register their opinions and their votes, but already, electronic communication has changed some of the traditions of political activity. Politicians are well aware of the need to communicate effectively with voters, and campaigns are structured to appeal to audiences comfortable with visual media forms.

During the 1992 Presidential election all three candidates, George Bush, Bill Clinton, and Ross Perot, used television and radio to reach potential voters in new ways. Clinton appeared on entertainment programs such as "The Arsenio Hall Show," and on MTV. Perot sponsored a series of half-hour informational programs shown on television across the country. All three candidates took part in interviews on talk shows and on all the network morning information programs. The image factor of the campaign became a news story in itself (see figure 14.3).

Communication technology has been bringing democratic procedures to other countries through outreach systems (see, for example, Hanson 1991, and Sussman and Lent 1991). One of most notable is occurring in Brazil, where peasants engaged in agricultural reform are sent audiocassettes that describe new policies and procedures. Those people record their responses and questions on audiocassettes and send them back to the agricultural divisions in the regional centers. This type of communication has involved people far more effectively than the traditional system of sending a caseworker out to instruct the workers in the field without allowing them the opportunity to provide feedback to the sponsoring development agency, including questions or comments that could improve the project (Freire 1970).

Media for the Handicapped and Disabled

Those of us who have no difficulty using the forms of communication technology generally available today seldom think of the number of people who cannot use them easily, such as disabled people. More than 43 million Americans have some type of disability (Sikes 1991, 50). More than 26 million Americans have speech or hearing impairments that make it difficult or impossible for them to use a regular telephone (Kisor 1991, 21). Remember that when Alexander Graham Bell invented the telephone, he intended it to be a technology to enhance communication for the hearing-impaired; then compare this original intention to its actual use.

People who are handicapped or disabled have often been excluded from many of the media opportunities most of us enjoy. Until closed captioning was included in broadcast television and on videocassettes, hearing-impaired individuals had few opportunities to follow the complete dialogue of a story. Today, however, thanks to the efforts of the National Captioning Institute, the "Chip Bill" has been passed. This legislation mandates that all television sets manufactured in 1993 and thereafter must contain a device that can read the captions included in television programs. No longer will deaf or hearing-impaired people have to purchase an extra decoder—instead, all televisions will come with the circuitry to make use of messages in the vertical blanking interval (VBI), like teletext.

Additionally, there has been improvement in telecommunications devices for the deaf (TDD). These devices can often connect voice technologies, like telephones, with sight technologies, like computers. A deaf person would be able to read the voiced message from the phone by looking at a TDD. These types of technologies also make communication easier for people with speech disabilities, since they too can use the TDD to transfer messages to other units. They can also make use of voice synthesizers for talking on the telephone.

Blind and visually impaired people can use services such as Reading for the Blind, from an organization in Princeton, New Jersey, that produces books and information on audiotape, and National Public Radio broadcasts of news and information not usually carried by commercial broadcasters. Since 1991 many feature films on videotape and some television broadcasts have included a feature called voiced captioning, which describes non-verbal actions for the blind and visually impaired.

The computer has been a tremendous boon for many disabled people, providing them with equal access to education and information. Virtually all disabled individuals can use special computers in some way. Even quadriplegics who have only the capacity of blowing into a straw use computer technology for various forms of information and entertainment. The number of computers used by the disabled has increased over the years, as evidenced by a report produced by Reading for the Blind (RFP). For its 1991 report, RFP asked its subscribers how many of them had a computer. An astounding 67 percent reported that they did, and another 15 percent said they expected to purchase one in the next year (6).

Computers and software have greatly improved the opportunities for the visually impaired. Computers with enhanced "readers" can magnify the size of visual images from printed matter such as newspapers and magazines. Speech synthesizers can be hooked up to computers to speak to those who are totally blind. People with limited mobility might use a stick held in the mouth to touch computer keys.

For many disabled individuals, computers offer the possibility of working at home by telecommuting. Even more importantly, all these communication devices increase confidence and satisfaction by giving people greater independence.

Medical Facilities

Advances in technology have improved medical care and driven medical costs higher. At the same time, some applications of technology originally developed for communication for purposes other than communication demonstrate different uses, bridging different fields to create connections.

Optical fibers have been used for exploratory surgery and in some cases for the therapeutic surgery itself. An optical fiber inserted into a patient's vein can have several conduits for information. One might be a telescope that sends signals to a monitor, on which the surgical staff can see where the probe is going. A second part of the same optical fiber might be a light, and a third part could be an action component such as a laser, which is sometimes used to treat coronary problems.

Smart cards, based on the same principles as the debit cards discussed in Chapter 10, can be used for storing medical and insurance information. Since the cards can store information on physical condition, blood type, allergies, and previous illnesses, they could provide health care professionals with a profile of the owner when this information is required in an emergency.

Other forms of medical facilities that may rely further on communication technologies have to do with interlinking local area networks with computers and monitors. At Boston's Logan Airport, the infirmary is linked by phone lines to Massachusetts General Hospital. If a traveler were to become ill at Logan, the nurse on call would type the symptoms and any past history into the computer and access a doctor on staff at Mass General. That doctor might interact directly by telephone with the patient or might call on other data bases to develop a picture of the illness. If a smart card is used, the patient's medical history would facilitate the doctor's diagnosis. Computer diagnoses can often be done more quickly and with less human intervention.

Technology and Education

Methods of education are also changing because of social and economic pressures. While the costs of some of the technology necessary for technological instruction are coming down, access to schools where technology is effectively integrated into the curriculum is not assured to everyone. Changes in the kinds of jobs available today and the need to upgrade skills are bringing older students back into the educational setting, but not always in the traditional ways. The changes in our educational structures are coming about through the increasing availability of computers, use of distance learning, and the distribution of educational materials.

Box 14.2   Estimated Use of Computers by All Students in the United States Attending Both Public and Private Schools, 1989.

Percent using computers at school (per 1000)

		Pre-Kinder garten-	Grades 1–8	Grades 9–12	1-4 yrs. college	5+ yrs. college
Sex:	Male	13.9	52.9	38.7	42.1	47.0
	Female	15.6	51.7	39.8	36.8	34.9
Race:	White	17.0	58.4	40.6	40.0	39.5
	Black	7.5	35.7	36.0	35.1	34.4
	Hispanic	8.5	46.9	41.0	43.5	58.0
	Other	9.8	40.3	33.5	33.1	42.1

Percent using computers at home (per 1000)

Sex:	Male	11.0	18.7	23.9	25.4	36.0
	Female	9.3	16.9	17.4	18.1	31.1
Race:	White	12.3	22.3	25.3	23.6	35.4
	Black	3.7	6.8	8.5	9.1	18.2
	Hispanic	9.9	16.6	22.5	23.5	24.7
	Other	2.9	6.6	7.8	11.7	30.2

Source: U.S. National Center for Education Statistics, *Digest of Education Statistics,* 1990.

Computers   Computers in education provide a convenient measure of how long it takes for society to adopt a technology, and they also highlight the very important issue of how affordable technology must be before it diffuses throughout society. We no longer raise eyebrows when college students talk of their reliance on computers—either their own or those that may be available at their schools. We see computers introduced to the curriculum at primary schools in some areas. Not surprisingly, private schools are ahead of public schools in making computers available and teaching computer skills to students, because the cost of hardware and software is passed on through high tuition rates. Until more computers are available to students from all socioeconomic classes, today's computer-reliant jobs will not offer equal opportunity to students. Still, questions need to be answered on what type of instruction different groups of students receive on computers in schools. Are they merely learning rote skills, or are they learning the language of the computer?

On the other hand, one reason the number of computers in homes and schools has soared in recent years is the decline of hardware costs. A look at the use of computers in schools and at home suggests which students are able to learn from computers and use them for information access (see box 14.2).

Educational programming   A change in education that requires a much greater financial input is the use of satellites to distribute information to classrooms in various regions. Whittle Communications' Channel One is a satellite service for distributing daily news programs on current events to schools.

In 1990 Chris Whittle, Chairman of Whittle Communications, founded his controversial project, Channel One, attracting a different type of attention than he had hoped. Whittle, whom *Newsweek* (Hammer 1990, 52) called "The Prince of Targeted Media," had proposed a program of 12-minute newscasts, with two minutes of commercials, that would be sold to high schools around the country. Claiming that his product would address the need for students to become more aware of current events, Whittle's plan quickly raised the ire of parents and legislators who were appalled by the idea of subjecting students to commercials in school.

Channel One uses MTV-like graphics, and presents news of particular interest to teens, such as steroid abuse and AIDS awareness, as well as world events. Whittle offered participating schools up to $50,000 in free equipment, including television monitors, VCRs, and satellite dishes, to entice them to subscribe. While he originally hoped to have 39,000 classrooms subscribing to the service by the end of 1990, he was forced to revise his goal to 8000 classrooms. This total would have given advertisers who paid $150,000 per commercial minute an audience of 6.5 million!

Figure 14.4   *The Electronic Classroom.*

Almost immediately after Whittle announced his plans in 1990, six states enacted legislation to ban Channel One, and more than 6700 schools signed up with Ted Turner's commercial-free "CNN-Newsroom," which distributes information via satellite and cable. By 1992, Channel One had only 2400 subscribing classrooms (Hammer, 1991). Although his plans had not come to fruition, Whittle remained optimistic and continued to search for further possible target audiences for information and advertising.

Distance education   Distance education has used forms of radio, television, video- and audiocassettes for many years, but most of the earlier efforts merely offered supplements to be used in the classroom. In regions of the world where it is difficult to supply villages with teachers, distance learning can be a major tool for development.

Box 14.3   Using the Electronic Classroom

The School of Electrical Engineering at the University of Massachusetts has been using electronic classrooms in the Video Instructional Program (VIP) since 1984. Most of the off-campus students enroll in courses through their work sites, where they are encouraged to keep up with changes in the field and obtain advanced degrees. The classes may be broadcast live, or, in some cases, are videotaped for distribution at a later time.

On-campus students sit in the classroom while the professor delivers the lecture. A specially mounted camera records the professor's notations on the electronic blackboard, and students in the room see the comments on a special video screen.

Usually, the in-class students do slightly better than the off-campus students on tests. While this could lead one to assume that in-class instruction with the professor in attendance is superior to distance learning, other variables could also be factors such as the time available to full-time students to study, or the benefit of having other students, faculty, and the library available.

In the United States, distance learning also presents a possible solution to the need to continually upgrade skills or knowledge when it is difficult or impossible for the student to attend a school in the traditional way. Many colleges and universities have turned to using prerecorded videotapes for instruction. Often videotapes can enhance lectures by showing close-ups of demonstrations on a large screen, or by repeating the demonstrations by rewinding the tape for a second or third showing. Today, however, the connection of videotape and satellite distribution is attracting more attention as schools have adopted or consider using electronic classrooms.

The electronic classroom   Electronic classrooms have electronic blackboards for a professor to write on as she or he presents a lecture. Unlike writing on a traditional blackboard that would be difficult for a video camera to pick up, the electronic blackboard magnifies the images written or drawn by a special electronically sensitive pen. The image that is broadcast or recorded on videotape is not only clearer, but it fits the size and shape of the video display screen to be more readable. Often two-way telephone lines allow students in other locations to contact the professor immediately. If the presentation is live, similar to a teleconference, the participants can engage in dialogue. If viewers in different locations see presentations at a later time, they could send electronic mail to the professor to answer before the next class.

The Convergence of Technological Change and Human Values

Most communication scholars agree that media contribute to a person's socialization and sense of self, but few today would claim that media directly affect all of society, or that media are such an overwhelming phenomenon that every person is controlled by media content. Today, most scholars agree with the position that the media are powerful influences that contribute to a culture's collective memory, and that there is a relationship between popular values and media content. The subtle connections between these observations and the fact that not all classes, ages, genders, regions, or cultures respond to media in the same way make it difficult to point to specific ways in which the media affect values, ethics, and behavior. Searching for simple relationships often yields an incomplete story.

During the 1992 Presidential campaign, Vice President Dan Quayle placed the issue of family values on the political agenda. As discussed in Chapter 5, while commenting on how he thought television was destroying values, he cited the character Murphy Brown's having a child out of wedlock as a bad example for children and an insult to fatherhood. The media had a field day, with headlines screaming "It's Just TV, Dan," and "Quayle Confuses Fact and Fiction." Quayle's remark and the media attention surrounding it prompted journalists and academics to redouble their efforts to address the issue of the relationship between media and society. One communication researcher, Robert Thompson, was prompted to respond to the Vice President's remarks by drawing parallels with popular television shows of the 1950s like "Leave It to Beaver," "The Donna Reed Show," and "Father Knows Best." In all these shows, strong family values permeated the content:

> Yet the baby boomers who were raised on these shows would go on to make divorce a national pastime. By 1969, before a single divorced person appeared as a principle character in a TV series, the number of divorces in this country already had reached an all-time high. If they knew their TV history, students would be more likely to ask themselves whether, if "Murphy Brown's" values are detrimental to families, shouldn't the values conveyed on "Leave It to Beaver" have encouraged families to stay together? (Thompson 1992, B2).

Part of the problem is that values and social reality do not change at the same time. Instead, representations of what might be influence later changes in values. In the days when change was slower, and there was less change with which to cope, individuals had the opportunity to seek a balance between social stability and social change. Today, however, change is introduced so rapidly that many people feel incapable of coping with technological reality and changing values. The stress in today's society has been appropriately described by Wilson P. Dizard, Jr., who has written that:

Technology as a productive force rolls on, while its contribution to social stability grows weaker. And as the distance between technological promise and social effect widens, confidence in technology is eroded" (Dizard 1982, 178).

The strange situation is this: in some ways, our visions of the future are coming true, with increased technology, new ways of doing things, and the capacity for greater communication and access to information. From this point of view, technology is a sign of progress. But at the same time, we see many social problems in spite of advanced technology. Our confidence in the goodness and progressive nature of technology is shaken.

Similarly, there is a blurring of distinctions between the technologies themselves, and between different types of content. One of the realities of the information age is that communication technology that has traditionally been used for entertainment is now also used for information, and vice versa. Toffler (1980) described the convergence of televisions, computers, telephones, and other communication technologies as **infotainment** systems.

We now use that term to describe the blurring of different genres of content. In television production, we can easily see the impact of portable video technology on programming. Programs like "America's Funniest Home Videos" and "America's Funniest People" use home video recordings for the content of their entertainment programs. News style and video production techniques have given us programs like "America's Most Wanted" and "Rescue 911." The most widely watched program in the early 1990s was "Entertainment Tonight," a program that presented feature information on Hollywood and the entertainment industries in a news-format presentation (Network 1993). Half-hour or hour-long commercials (infomercials) that sell such products as diet plans, spot removers, and car polish merge television studio style with advertising style. An important question remains: do people know the difference between information and entertainment, or does this type of convergence in technology and content blur the distinctions in their minds? Do these crossover genres introduce new expectations for entertainment programming, information programming, and even reality? How media literate must we become?

Social Dimensions of Change

Because we call this time in history the "information age," many people make an assumption that the movement to more reliance on information technology is the cause of our social problems. As we've discussed, these connections are not always direct or causal. Instead, we might look at the use of communication technology as an agent of change, and attempt to understand how it contributes to social instability.

The problems of our society are too great to enumerate in one chapter or one book. Therefore, it would be more useful to focus on some of the typical charges against technology and focus on what types of things might help us understand these social dynamics.

Charges Against Technology

In particular, communication and information technology has been blamed for causing individuals to become more alienated from society. Communication technology has been blamed for creating a world in which people tend to stay home rather than socialize with others and thus creating a world of lonely people. The presence of violent images in the media is often blamed for creating a feeling of fear and apathy among many people. In most cases, these social problems are brought about by the complicated intertwining of many factors, rather than communication media alone, but the use of communication media today has the potential to contribute to the feeling that these problems are technologically induced.

Alienation   It is an unfortunate reality that today in the United States we have higher levels of juvenile depression and suicide than ever before. Drug abuse and alcohol dependency are also at all time highs for people in all age groups. Many critics charge that people in our society feel alienated from others because we are experiencing a crisis in values brought about by a segmenting of the American public. As Klein (1992, 21-22) has suggested, it is possible for virtually every ethnic group or race to subscribe to their own newspapers, watch their own television stations, and hear their own radio. The consequences involve less understanding of others, difficulty in sustaining any sense of national community, and problems in understanding common values. Reaching target audiences has been a primary goal for marketers, but accusations about today's alienation go beyond the marketing industry.

As we've discussed, many jobs that are reliant on the computer reduce opportunities for workers to meet with other people, and new practices including telecommuting and distance education replace face-to-face contact with mediated interaction. Also, changes brought to society and the economy by what is often called the electronic cottage challenge us to meet our interpersonal needs despite increasing reliance on technology to facilitate our work. The reference, of course, is to the cottage industries of the industrial revolution, when many people started businesses in their homes.

But when we flip the coin, we also find evidence to show that changes in the availability of technology have been a great benefit to the disabled. Regulations that reduce costs for the elderly, poor, or disabled create communication opportunities that did not exist before these reductions in the costs of technology and services. Public awareness of the potential of these new applications spreads through commercial services, media coverage, and word of mouth. Time and the economy play major roles in determining whether people will avail themselves of new technologies and services, and whether they can develop coping mechanisms to help maintain a sense of balance while experiencing these changes.

Loneliness   Feelings of alienation are closely aligned to loneliness. Once again, when we use communication technology in place of interpersonal communication, we have the potential for feeling the isolation of reduced human contact.

Yet, we still have evidence to indicate that electronic mail, communication opportunities for the handicapped or disabled, and new dating or companion services address problems of loneliness. If loneliness is a social illness, could communication technology be the cure?

There are no clear-cut, easy answers to these questions. Alienation and loneliness are better addressed in terms of the larger social picture. Both occur when society makes major shifts, from the "second wave" to the "third wave" and the "third wave" to the "fourth wave." When society experiences change, people often turn to their traditional behaviors and institutions (like the media industries) to help them overcome the stress of change. Media often become both the instigator and the monitor of change.

The Civil Rights Movement of the 1960s gave us media images of black Americans holding their heads up with dignity, even though they were at times threatened by police or white bigots shouting epithets or engaging in violence. In 1992 in Los Angeles the frustration of people trapped in an economy and social structure that gave unequal treatment to minorities boiled into rage when the media showed a video image of Rodney King, a black man, being beaten by white police. When a jury acquitted the police officers involved, the rage erupted into riots, and much of south-central Los Angeles was burned. In both of these examples, the media were involved, and played a role as catalyst.

Fear   Violence in the media is often blamed for cultivating an attitude that makes people afraid to interact with others and participate in society. Most fear comes from thinking about what might be, not what actually happens.

While there are many theories about the effects of violent programs on viewers' beliefs and behaviors, one of the most striking is explored in the project on *cultivation* conducted by researchers from the Annenberg School for Communications (Gerbner, Gross, Morgan, and Signorelli 1986). In a long-term study, the researchers found that people who watch many hours of television often develop a "mean world syndrome" in which they believe society is more violent than it really is. Citing evidence that crime in prime time is "at least 10 times as rampant as in the real world" and that "old, young, and minority women, and young boys, are more likely to be victims rather than victimizers in violent conflicts" (26), the researchers project that the attitudes and behaviors of heavy television viewers reflect the distortion of reality presented by television.

In another study (1980) the same researchers found that heavy viewers believe that fewer elderly are living longer because the numbers of them presented on television are lower than in reality. For many of these viewers, television images also contribute to their fears about aging and the quality of life for the elderly.

Today, people are living longer, and often in better health, because of technological and scientific advances that have prolonged life and improved the quality of elder care. Still, most of us are raised to believe that we should be self-sufficient, and plan for a future in which we can remain physically and financially independent. Elderly people who cannot care for themselves are often viewed as having failed to retain their independence. Unfortunately, inflation doesn't hold the line for those people who take responsible actions to protect their future, and fate often intervenes with the unexpected.

A popular saying today is that women generally spend about 20 years taking care of children, and 22 years taking care of aging parents. As people live longer, society will necessarily have to consider what can be done to make sure the elderly can live reasonable lifestyles. Fears that the Social Security program in America will be bankrupt by the year 2010 are also preying on the minds of many today.

Apathy   As a result of feeling alienated, lonely, or afraid of what might happen in the world, many people develop a defense mechanism called apathy that causes them to be without concern for anything. A sense of helplessness brought about by the bad news of the world, and technology that is applied "inhumanely," often makes people feel that they have no control over their lives, and therefore they become apathetic.

The reduction of in the number of voters is often attributed to growing apathy toward the democratic system, but, as we've discussed, citizens sometimes can be more inclined to register a vote or belief if the voting structure is made simple and allows them more input.

The Alternatives

All recent changes in society are not necessarily as negative as those discussed above. Some are very positive and give an indication that we may indeed survive the information age and take greater control over our destinies. Through the convergence of telephones, computer services including videotex, and special information files constructed to help people make decisions at times of personal crisis, the number of communications options for people are growing and becoming more readily available, whether through human services agencies or private information providers.

Toffler (1980) calls people who have decided to accept the responsibility for doing more for themselves *prosumers*. Prosumerism is also a way of merging home and work techniques. Prosumers are those who often apply what they learn in "how-to" videos or books to produce something for their own use. Among Toffler's examples are things like automotive or appliance repair, raising fruit and vegetables for home consumption, and diagnosing and treating simple medical problems.

If prosumerism is on the increase, we may see how important it is to be motivated to change what can be changed. As an important value, self-motivation can become one of the most important tools for living in an information society.

Technological Realities

The communication technologies of the information age can no longer be viewed as one-way forms of communication, or neutral pieces of hardware or software. Their continued use presents us with ways of thinking and acting that resonate with our daily experiences. If greater self-motivation is a necessity to survive in an information society, what else might we expect to see in the future? A look at the way these technologies and systems work gives us some ideas of what they demand.

Today's communication technologies:

- have the ability to shift time and space because they are often small and operate quickly because they are electronic; the use of more personal technologies, like CDs, camcorders, and cellular telephones presents us with new ways to control our environments
- often operate faster than the human mind; computer logic is not linear, but associational or intuitive and therefore seems illogical or incomprehensible to many people. Computers have the capacity to produce results faster than humans, and they have memories that are larger and more reliable than human memories. As a result, they change our thinking processes. Product advertising and multi-image media also present images that are more complex than other content or slower media, yet we form images over time in our minds based upon the constructed images presented to us.
- present us with images from any time in history, leading us to be more present oriented, rather than to reflect on historical trends. The "look" of video technologies gives the appearance of reality. It is impossible (unless there is a mistake in production) to tell the difference between live broadcast images or those recorded on videotape. The presence of satellites also has conditioned us to respond to live images from anywhere in the world.

As we look to the future we can expect to see more electronic technologies offering us expanded communication possibilities. To be able to use them effectively while holding on to what makes us human presents a challenge for using them responsibly.

CONCLUSION: BEYOND THE INFORMATION SOCIETY

While vestiges of the agricultural era, industrial revolution, and age of electronics are still present in the world today, we need to consider what will come after the age of information. The information society presents us with a battery of competing images, in which factors such as ownership, regulation, content, and context of use mediate the convergence of technologies. The world we look to in the future will draw from many of these images, and history will show how and why communication technologies contributed to popular principles and values.

These dynamics require us to examine critically the connections that are made in the social use of communications technology. They also ask us to keep asking questions when conditions change, and reflect consciously on the tangential matters that affect our society.

As we think about our future, we have the responsibility to look closely at our present, and analyze how we choose to do what we do. We also need to consider the responsibility we have to those people who come after us by creating a sustainable environment and by creating jobs and educational opportunities that will allow individuals to work effectively despite family obligations. We need to act and make choices that satisfy more than just our own needs.

The inequities in the world are realities that must shape our thinking about the future, and guide us to act in ways that will lead to correcting them. Only if we do these things will we be ready for the future. We cannot be restricted by skills, values, and educations that have prepared us for the past.

Because communication technologies ask us to replace traditional behaviors with new practices, we sometimes are forced to make moral choices about which technologies we use, how we use them, and whether their use is good or bad.

Ethics helps us understand the disposition, character, or attitude of a culture, and often distinguishes our own from other cultures by the beliefs and practices in which we engage. We need to search for a set of ethics that is more responsive to an information society, that addresses the problems of equal access to communication technology at an affordable price, and that will respect the privacy and security of individuals. These are the challenges for all of us who live in an information society.

SUMMARY

In this chapter we examined how the information society has been defined, and what issues are important for living in such a society. Because we live at a time in which there are so many inequities among people, we need to consider whether communication technology can be used responsibly to address some of these problems, or whether it emphasizes certain types of inequality. This chapter has outlined the key issues:

- competing visions of the information society
- a world in which there are inequities in the amount of technology available to different people
- how technology can be used to meet the needs of individuals with special problems, like the handicapped or disabled
- how traditional institutions like the democratic system, schools, and health care providers may benefit from different uses of technology
- how social issues involving individuals' alienation, loneliness, fear, and apathy contribute to instability in the information society
- how principles and values are changing to adapt to a world in which technology plays an increasingly important role

DISCUSSION QUESTIONS

1. Focus on the application of two converging technologies and try to predict what industries will be using them in twenty years. What job skills will be necessary? For what other purposes might these technologies be used?
2. Is there a communication technology you do not have access to? Think about how you might use it if you had it. Then think about a recent communication technology acquisition you may have made. Did it make you as happy as you thought it would to have it? Do you use it as much as you thought you would? Why?
3. How would your day be different if you didn't interact with any communication technology? If you're brave, try it.
4. How would you be able to communicate if you became disabled? In what ways would your life be impeded by a lack of communication technology?

5. Do you think the "information society" is a reality or a convenient title to describe social change? Can you think of a better way to describe the state of the world today?

6. Discuss the need for education in today's world. How many of your classmates intend to go to graduate school? How many will seek additional training? What does this tell you about the need to continue to develop self-motivation and an ability to access and use information?

7. What advantages or disadvantages do people have who do not share a common sense of the history of the society in which they live? For example, in what way might a foreigner in our country have to adapt to the values and ideals presented by this society?

REFERENCES

Altheide, David L., and Snow, Robert P. 1991. *Media worlds in the postjournalism era.* New York: Walter de Gruyter, Inc.

Arterton, F. Christopher. 1987. *Teledemocracy: Can technology protect democracy?* Newbury Park, Calif.: Sage.

Dizard, Wilson P., Jr. 1982. *The coming information age.* 2nd ed. New York: Longman.

Election Special. 1992. *Time,* Nov. 16, 18–19.

Friere, Paulo. 1970. *The pedagogy of the oppressed.* New York: Herder and Herder.

Gerbner, George; Gross, Larry; Morgan, Michael; and Signorelli, Nancy. 1986. Living with television: The dynamics of the cultivation process. In *Perspectives on media effects,* ed. J. Bryant and D. Zillman, 17–40. Hillsdale, N.J.: Lawrence Erlbaum Publishing.

Gerbner, George; Gross, Larry; Signorelli, Nancy; and Morgan, Michael. 1980. Aging with television: Images on television drama and conceptions of social reality. *Journal of Communication* 30 (1): 37–47.

Hammer, Josh. 1990. A golden boy's toughest sell: Chris Whittle struggles to win a $200 million bet on bringing ads into America's schools. *Newsweek,* Feb. 19, 52.

Hanson, Jarice. 1991. Comparative informatics policy in Mexico, Brazil, and Argentina. In *Advances in telematics,* Vol. 1. ed. Singh & Hanson. Norwood, N.J.: Ablex.

Jamieson, Kathleen Hall. 1988. *Eloquence in an electronic age.* New York: Oxford University Press.

Keane, John. 1991. *The media and democracy.* Cambridge: Polity Press.

Kisor, Henry. 1991. What does the Americans with disabilities act of 1990 require? In *Extending telecommunications service to americans with disabilities,* ed. Stuart N. Brotman. Washington, D.C.: The Annenberg Washington Program.

Klein, Joe. 1992. Whose values? *Newsweek,* June 8, 19–22.

Network primetime ranking 1991–92. 1993. *Variety* 349: 38–42.

Recording for the Blind. May 1991. *Survey of borrowers: awareness, usage, satisfaction.* Princeton, N.J.

Sikes, Alfred C. 1991. Statement of the Honorable Alfred C. Sikes, Chairman, Federal Communications Commission Presented at the Annenberg Washington Program's Roundtable Forum on Title IV of the Americans with Disabilities Act of 1990. In *Extending telecommunications service to americans with disabilities,* ed. Stuart N. Brotman. The Annenberg Washington Program.

Sussman, Gerald and Lent, John A., eds. 1991. *Transnational communications.* Newbury Park, Calif.: Sage Publications Inc.

Thompson, Robert. 1992. How to watch a sound bite: students need to study television's effect on politics. *The Chronicle of Higher Education* 38(49): B1–B2.

Toffler, Alvin. 1980. *The third wave.* New York: Bantam.

———. 1990. *Powershift.* New York: Bantam.

United States National Center for Education Statistics. 1990. *Digest of Education Statistics.*

Abbreviations

AM = amplitude modulation
AP = Associated Press
ATM = automated teller machine(s)
B-ISDN = broadband integrated services digital network
CD = compact disc
CD-ROM = compact disc, read-only-memory
CG = character generator
CAD = computer aided design
CAM = computer aided manufacture
CNN = Cable News Network
DAB = digital audio broadcasting
DAT = digital audio tape
DBS = direct broadcast satellite
EFT = electronic funds transfer
EM = electronic mail
ENG = electronic news gathering
EVM = electronic voice messaging
FAX = telefacsimile/facsimile
FM = frequency modulation
FTZ = free trade zones
HDTV = high definition television
HUT = homes using television
IFRB = international frequency registration board
ISDN = integrated services digital network
ITFS = instructional television fixed service
ITN = Independent Television News
ITU = International Telecommunications Union

LAN = local area networks
LDC = less developed country
LPTV = low power television
MMDS = multipoint distribution service
NTSC = National Technical Standards Committee
OECD = Organization for Economic Cooperation and Development
O&O = owned and operated (television and radio stations)
RAM = random access memory
ROM = read-only memory
SEG = special effects generator
SMATV = satellite master antenna television
STV = subscription television
TBC = time base corrector
TVRO = television receive-only
TWX = a Western Union teletype machine (also called telex)
UHF = ultra high frequency
UPC = universal product code
UPI = United Press International
VBI = vertical blanking interval
VDT = video display terminal
VHF = very high frequency
WARC = World Administrative Radio Council

Glossary

3-D TV a television development that will be available in the near future. It uses angles to create a three-dimensional television image in front of the television screen.

access channels cable channels for use by the public.

access points the transitions from one system of telephone distribution to another.

alternator a modulator for continuous radio waves, necessary for voice or music transmission.

amplitude modulation (AM) sending a signal by varying the height of a wave.

analog waves signals that are similar to those used in speech.

archetypes symbols with meanings so basic that people in all cultures understand them.

artificial intelligence a simulation of human thinking processes by a computer.

Associated Press (AP) a wire service for the distribution of news.

audimeter the technology used by the A.C. Nielsen Co. to record television or radio receivership; used for the computation of ratings.

Audion tube booster of electrical energy used in radio and television receivers, invented by Lee DeForest.

augmentation adding additional services, like channels, from other sources.

automatic teller machines (ATMs) electronic banking machines.

automation replacing human labor with technology.

broadband integrated services digital network (B-ISDN) the most sophisticated switching device available today. It includes a conduit that allows for many simultaneous transmissions.

camcorder a portable video camera and recorder in one unit.

carrier signal a continuously produced wave.

Carterfone Decision the result of the 1968 challenge to Western Electric as the only manufacturer of telephones and components legally allowed to connect to the AT&T system. The decision ended Western Electric's monopoly on the manufacturing of telephones.

CD-ROM compact disc with read-only memory; the information on the disc cannot be changed.

cellular telephone a telephone that operates by means of radio waves. Computer and satellite or microwave connections transfer calls as the telephone is moved from one area of coverage (a "cell") to another. Often called mobile telephone.

Chain Broadcasting Investigation the FCC inquiry into the power of the networks to control television broadcasting.

character generator (CG) a technology that creates text materials for video and television production.

chrominance color quality.

clandestine systems unofficial or unauthorized broadcasts usually used for propaganda or political purposes.

coaxial cable typical telephone wire or wired connection for cable TV or between broadcast stations; copper-based distribution wire.

codes systems of signs that are socially structured and culturally learned.

cognition understanding a message within a certain context.

combiplayer term for a technology that plays both CDs and laser discs.

common carrier a service provided to others. It does not provide programming or a specific message of its own.

community access the phrase indicating availability to members of a community of the opportunity to use equipment and share in the creation of programming on local cable channels.

compact discs (CDs) digitally recorded audio discs.

computer aided design (CAD) the use of computer software to develop design systems superior to traditional ones, or, cheaper to test in a simulated (computer) environment.

computer aided manufacture (CAM) the production of goods that are made with the assistance of a computer.

context the situation in which a form of communication technology is used.

cooperative (co-op) advertising sharing the cost of advertising between two or more parties, such as the advertiser, broadcaster, or syndicator.

corporate consciousness the idea that corporations should act in a responsible manner toward employees and society at large.

critical standards ways of criticizing or understanding something.

cultural sovereignty the right of nations or groups to protect their own cultures by deciding what actions best maintain their value systems.

curve of diffusion the pattern of use that emerges when a new technology or service is introduced.

debit card a plastic card that contains circuitry to allow immediate payment for goods along with an instantaneous readjustment of the holder's cash balance.

deregulation the practice of lifting government restrictions to allow for greater competition within an industry.

digital a system in which the message is electronically converted to an even pattern of electrical pulses.

digital audio broadcasting (DAB) sending the radio signal in a digital form.

digital audio tape (DAT) software that uses digitally recorded sound on audio tape.

direct broadcast satellite (DBS) satellites with uplinks and downlinks small enough to direct a footprint to a small area, such as a house.

divestiture the relinquishing of a number of corporate holdings, such as stock, businesses, or interests.

downlink the signal from a satellite to earth antennae.

dumping the term used to describe a concentrated effort of a company or nation to flood a specific market with substandard technology.

duopoly rule the FCC decision limiting any broadcaster from owning more than one station of the same type in one market.

earth station transmission facility for satellite signal distribution.

electrical telegraphy the early description for the telegraph.

electromagnetic spectrum the part of the airwaves that can be effectively used for electronic communication transmissions.

electronic funds transfer (EFT) using computers and electronics for financial transactions, such as ATM use, direct deposit of checks, or for paying bills.

electronic mail (E-mail) messages transmitted by means of computer.

electronic newsgathering (ENG) the process of using portable videotechnology to cover news stories.

electronic voiced messaging (EVM) using electronic technology to leave personal voiced messages, such as an answering machine.

enhanced TV television that uses precision components for a better picture quality.

ergonomics the study of making technology comfortable and useful for humans through improvements in design.

ethnotronics small, portable technologies, such as audiotape recorders or VCRs.

exosomatic memory storage in memory outside of the body; in a computer (for example).

external radio radio programs purposefully targeted to other countries, often for propaganda purposes of the originating country, but also for the purpose of reaching audiences to tell them more about the host country.

fax see telefacsimile.

Federal Communications Commission (FCC) the regulatory body for communications in the United States.

Financial Interest and Syndication rules (fin-syn) FCC rules limiting the ability of networks to own media outlets and produce programs for syndication.

flextime a plan for creating a work schedule that accommodates the lifestyle needs of the worker.

frequency modulation (FM) pattern of waves in the electromagnetic spectrum. FM signals are transmitted in "line of sight."

footprint area of coverage by a satellite downlink.

format the structure of media content.

form as used in this text, the unique characteristics of a medium.

franchise an agreement in which one company is approved for operation in a given area, and allowed to function as a monopoly, such as a cable franchise.

Federal Radio Commission (FRC) forerunner of the FCC.

free sustaining service a programming structure introduced by William S. Palcy that guaranteed affiliates a certain amount of programming and a share of commercial time for regional advertisers.

free trade zones (FTZs) regions in which businesses receive incentives to operate, such as tax breaks or relief from import or export duties.

frequencies the allocations of areas in which signals pass through the electromagnetic spectrum.

gateway a place in which signals are received, changed, boosted, and sent to another relay system.

genres classifications of media content.

geosynchronous description of satellites positioned above the equator and at the same speed as the earth's revolution so that they are operable 24 hours a day.

gigahertz (gH) one trillion hertz.

glitch a visual imperfection caused by a bad edit on videotape.

Golden Age the early days of television when much of the programming was live, and the unique characteristics of the medium were being tested for programming (1947–56).

grandfather clause a statement exempting earlier actions from a new policy or practice.

hertz (Hz) a measurement of cycles per second used for the sound portions of the electromagnetic spectrum.

high definition television (HDTV) an improved television image and the technology necessary to broadcast and receive it.

households using TV (HUTs) the number of households with television on at any given time.

icon in semiotics, the smallest representation of a sign.

iconoscope one of the earliest picture tubes for television.

Independent Television News (ITN) an organization that cooperates with other news organizations for video news exchange.

index in semiotics, a reference to meaning.

information overload too much information for an individual or system to effectively use.

infotainment programming that merges or blurs aspects of traditional information and entertainment genres.

infrastructure organizational system in which related social, economic, and technical systems are mutually supported.

interlacing a pattern of presenting visual information on a picture tube by breaking the image into two fields and presenting the image by scanning each field sequentially.

instructional television fixed services (ITFS) the classification of broadcast licenses that facilitate educational broadcasting.

integrated services digital networks (ISDN) a switching system capable of linking analog and digital technologies.

interactive two-way; the user actively participates in the message exchange.

interactive fiction a computer software program allowing the user to choose from a menu to investigate a variety of alternative actions to participate in creating a piece of literature.

International Frequency Registration Board (IFRB) the division of the ITU charged with allocating available frequencies in the electromagnetic spectrum for broadcast purposes.

International Satellite Consortium (INTELSAT) a group that makes satellite transmission space available to countries at a reduced cost.

International Telecommunications Union (ITU) the agency, responsible for regulating the world's telecommunications.

job sharing a system in which more than one person cooperates for the completion of a job.

kilohertz (kH) one thousand hertz.

kinescope the technique of recording live television off a monitor and onto film for later presentation. Also refers to the film made by this process.

leapfrogging passing from one stage of development to another while by-passing traditional stages.

lesser developed countries (LDCs) the group of countries usually described as making up the third world; also known as developing countries.

liquid crystal display (LCD) presentation of an image on a flat screen.

local area networks (LANs) self-contained wired (cable or fiber) systems for the control of certain forms of information exchange.

low power television (LPTV) broadcast operations that transmit their signals to a small area of coverage; generally 20 to 30 miles in radius.

Luddite a person who fears technology or who is suspicious of the structure of technologies. Named for Ned Ludd, the leader of a group of radicals during the industrial revolution.

luminance brightness.

magnetaphone a device used to record sound on tape.

mainframe large computer capable of processing many functions simultaneously.

market (a) geographic area served by a form of media; (b) classification of audience by demographics.

mass medium technologies and industries that send messages to a large, anonymous audience.

MCI Decision the 1970 challenge to AT&T's Long Lines division resulting in the FCC's permission for communications companies to use means of long distance telephone distribution not owned by AT&T.

medium singular form of media; something that comes between a sender and receiver of a message.

media literacy how people make sense of the messages (visual and auditory) in media forms.

mediation the process of transmitting a message from one form of media to another.

megahertz (mH) one million hertz.

modem a technology that transfers analog signals to digital signals and vice versa; useful for connecting technologies that work with different signal systems.

modified final judgment (MFJ) subsequent rulings resulting from the Consent Decree that specified the deregulation and divestiture of AT&T.

modulation the system in which sound is placed on carrier waves for transmission; also the reverse process in which the carrier signal converts to sound waves.

multichannel multipoint distribution service (MMDS) a terrestrial relay/distribution system that transfers signals from one area to subscribers in many areas.

multi-image TV television receivers that use insert images to display more than one broadcast signal at the same time.

multiple systems operators (MSOs) companies that own and program a number of local or regional cable franchises.

multiplexer a system that processes different signals within the same unit.

nanosecond a billionth of a second.

narcotization the description of what happens to a person when information is no longer stimulating the conscious mind.

narrowcasting targeting specific audiences through distribution means (like cable) that tailor their content to the audience's interests and needs.

neural networks the patterns of neurons in the brain that process information; the study of neural networks provides ways of considering how computers could be programmed for artificial intelligence.

New World Information Order (NWIO)
the request by LDCs for Western media
organizations to present more balanced
information about their countries and
cultures.

NTSC the committee that dealth with standardization of the United States 525 line
scan for television.

optical fiber a distribution system using silicon as the conduit for a variety of communication purposes; fiber optics.

**Organization for Economic Cooperation and
Development (OECD)** a voluntary
organization concerned with promoting
equity among people in areas such as
privacy, opportunity for work, and
advancement.

Owned and Operated Stations (O&Os)
broadcast stations owned by major networks.

pay-per-view a system that allows the audience to request (and pay for) specific
content.

peoplemeters the measurement device currently used by the A.C. Nielsen Co. to
monitor media usage for the establishment of ratings.

perception the act of seeing, hearing, or
otherwise sensing information.

perceptual screen the human being's ability to stop consciously receiving information.

personal computer network (PCN) combinations of personal services in portable
form.

persistence of vision the coordination of
eye and brain to perceive moving
images from incomplete or non-moving
images.

phototelegraphy an early system of sending
visual information over a wired system.

physiological factors biological elements
that affect a person's ability to perceive
a message.

picturephone a contemporary method of
sending visual information over phone
lines.

piggybacking sending more than one signal on a carrier wave.

pixels tiny units of visual information used
in computer graphics.

point-of-purchase a payment system that
allows a buyer to make an EFT purchase
in which the billing for goods is made at
the same time as the purchase.

projection television a television receiver
that displays its image from light sources
in front of the screen.

Qube the early experiment in interactive
cable television sponsored by Warner
Communications.

Radio Group early radio stations associated
with General Electric, Westinghouse,
and RCA.

random access memory (RAM) a description of an input source for computers.

rating a measurement of how many radios
or televisions are tuned in to a certain
channel compared to the potential audience.

Regional Operating Companies (ROCs)
the seven independent telephone companies created from the 22 local companies that were owned and operated by
AT&T prior to the 1984 divestiture.

reindustrialization a fundamental change
in production processes that influence
how an economy operates.

remote sensing the use of satellites or
microwaves to measure the earth's surface to determine temperature, the
presence of natural resources, etc.

retraining programs that help workers
obtain the skills necessary for new jobs.

read-only memory (ROM) discs or units
with fixed information.

saccades the quick movements of the eye
to register sight.

satellite a technologically advanced object
placed in position above the earth to
relay information from one point to
another via microwaves.

satellite master antenna (SMATV) a distribution system that uses a combination of
a satellite receiving dish and cable running throughout specific buildings.

selective attention the process by which
people choose to listen to or view content that they like or agree with.

selective memory the process by which people remember some things and screen out others.

selective retention the process by which people remember images.

semi-automated stations radio and television stations in which some functions are completed by computer programs.

semiconductor devices miniature units that transfer electrical energy.

semiotics the study of signs and the communicative power of images.

share the number of people tuned to a specific radio or television program compared to what others are listening to or watching at the same time.

short wave a directional system of broadcasting in which the signal is bounced from the ionosphere to a location.

signal compression the electronic "squeezing" of a wave so that other signals can piggyback on the same frequencies.

signified in semiotics, the concept expressed in a message.

signifier in semiotics, image suggestive of meaning.

silicon the resource necessary for the manufacturing of semiconductor devices.

simulcast a broadcast over more than one media form at the same time; most commonly, a simultaneous broadcast over television and radio.

smart card a plastic card containing digital information that can easily be read with another compatible technology.

special effects generators technological devices capable of creating visual effects for television.

sponder Lee De Forest's invention that improved telegraph transmission.

stereo TV television with two-channel separation for audio.

strip programming a media schedule that includes several programs.

subscription television (STV) a service that allows audiences to subscribe to a series of programs that appeal to the same target.

supercomputer a fifth or sixth generation computer capable of monitoring its own functions.

superheterodyne Edwin Armstrong's invention that blended two frequencies for improved radio reception.

superstation a powerful independent station that increases audiences through satellite distribution.

sustaining programs programs that have no commercial sponsors.

switching systems devices that convert messages from one system to another.

symbol in semiotics, the concept expressed in a sign.

syndication a distribution system that distributes programming in a sale, lease, or barter system.

syntax the organization of material, such as the elements of a sentence.

technology inventions developed through scientific methods.

technological determinist the position taken by a person who views all social effects of technology as a result of that technology.

technological fallacy a belief in the use or effect of technology that, over time, is found to be untrue.

technological liberal the position taken by individuals who feel technology must be used responsibly.

telco the name used for those regional companies that once were owned and operated by AT&T, and all other independent telephone companies.

telecommunications processes, technologies, and systems used for communicating over distances.

telecommuting system of work in which an employee works at home and communicates with the office by telephone, fax, or computer.

teleconferencing using electronic technologies to connect parties at different locations for conferencing purposes.

teledemocracy using electronic technology to interest people in and enhance the democratic process; often used for informing an electorate or for voting.

telefacsimile (fax) a transmission system for documents that relies on telephone wiring for distribution.

telemarketing using electronic means (like telephones) for sales and marketing purposes.

Telephone Group   the group of early radio stations associated with AT&T and Western Electric.

teleports   informational office complexes using satellites and computers to transfer computer data and telephone traffic.

teletext   a one-way system of text delivery using the VBI in a video signal.

television-receive-only (TVRO)   satellite receiving units; home satellite dishes.

time base corrector (TBC)   a technology that regulates the control track on videotape.

Toll broadcasting   an early term used to describe commercial broadcasting.

transmitter   energy source for the transmission of waves in the electromagnetic spectrum.

transponders   information processing units within a satellite.

trunkline   a bundle of cables that connects the main system to many other systems.

tuner   device that improves reception of radio waves through finding the most efficient area of reception.

turnkey stations   fully automated radio stations.

universal product code (UPC)   an electronic scanning system for sales and inventory purposes.

United Nations Educational, Scientific and Cultural Organization (UNESCO)   a branch of the United Nations focusing an improvements in these areas.

United Press International (UPI)   a news and information wire service.

uplink   the description of the signal sent from an earth station to a satellite.

value added services   additional services not covered through basic use charges, for purchase or rent, to be used with traditional media.

variable resistance   the alternation of an electrical current by a transducer.

vertical blanking interval (VBI)   the spaces between the lines of electrical impulses in a video image.

vertical integration   an ownership pattern in which the same individual or organization has control over a number of different industries that might use or be influenced by content produced by another division within the group.

videocassette recorder (VCR)   a record/playback unit using videotape.

video dial tone   the use of telephone distribution services as common carriers for video programs.

videodisc   a high quality visual and auditory storage system using digital technology.

video display terminal (VDT)   a screen (like a computer screen) that presents video images.

videotape   A form of magnetic tape that records video and audio simultaneously using an electronic method.

videotex   an interactive service using information providers and a combination of video and text services.

visual cortex   the visual information processing area of the brain.

World Administrative Radio Conference (WARC)   the gathering of a group within the ITU to discuss international telecommunications policies.

Index

411